CW00351519

Bahia
The heart of Brazil's northeast

the Bradt Travel Guide

Alex Robinson

edition
1

www.bradtguides.com

Bradt Travel Guides Ltd, UK
The Globe Pequot Press Inc, USA

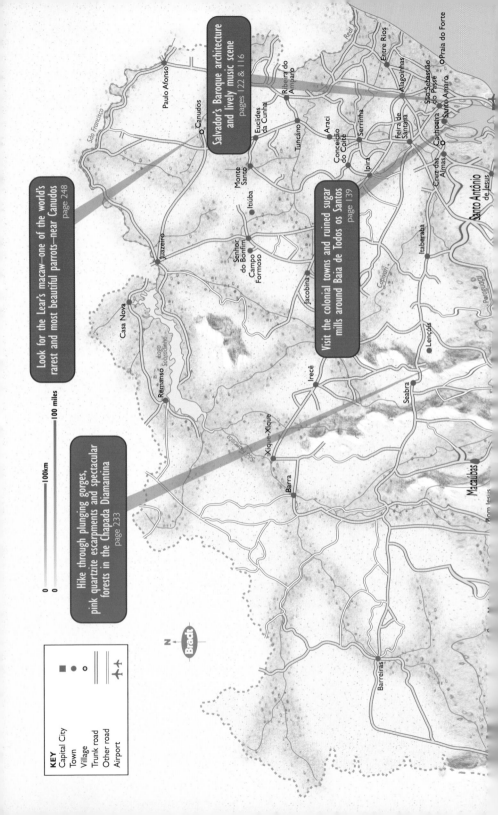

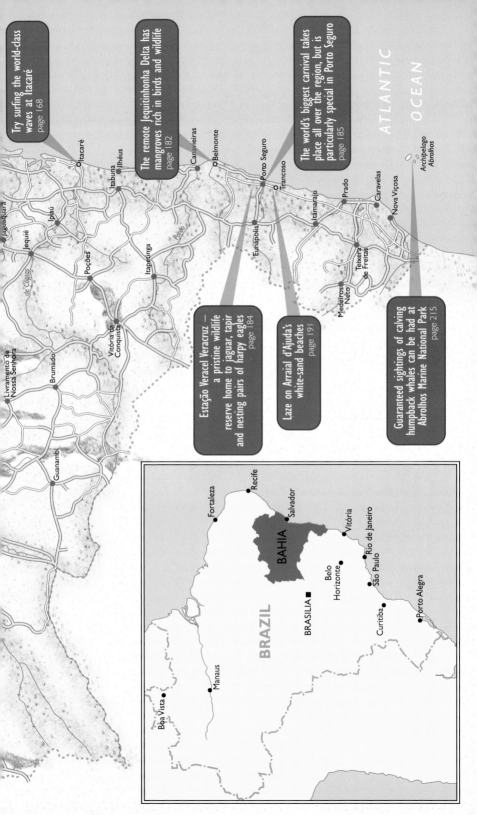

Try surfing the world-class waves at Itacaré
page 168

The remote Jequitinhonha Delta has mangroves rich in birds and wildlife
page 182

The world's biggest carnival takes place all over the region, but is particularly special in Porto Seguro
page 185

Estação Veracel Veracruz — a pristine wildlife reserve home to jaguar, tapir and nesting pairs of harpy eagles
page 184

Laze on Arraial d'Ajuda's white-sand beaches
page 191

Guaranteed sightings of calving humpback whales can be had at Abrolhos Marine National Park
page 215

ATLANTIC OCEAN

Archipélago Abrolhos

Itacaré
Itabuna
Ilhéus
Jaguaquara
Ipiaú
Jequié
Poções
Itapetinga
Canavieiras
Belmonte
Porto Seguro
Trancoso
Eunápolis
Itamaraju
Prado
Caravelas
Nova Viçosa
Teixeira de Freitas
Medeiros Neto
Vitória da Conquista
de Coqus
Pardo
Livramento de Nossa Senhora
Brumado
Guanambi

BRAZIL

BAHIA
Salvador
Recife
Fortaleza
Vitória
Rio de Janeiro
São Paulo
Belo Horizonte
BRASILIA
Curitiba
Porto Alegra
Manaus
Boa Vista

Bahia
Don't
miss...

Salvador's Baroque churches
Nossa Senhora do Rosário dos Pretos church
(AR) page 130

Whale-watching and diving in the Abrolhos Archipelago
The Costa da Baleia is one of the best places in the world for seeing calving humpback whales
(AR) page 216

Stunning white-sand beaches
It's possible to walk along the beaches of the Costa do Cacau for hours without seeing a soul
(AR) page 179

Searching for wildlife in the Costa do Descobrimento rainforests
Brazil is home to almost a fifth of all the world's birds, including the endemic red-breasted toucan (AR) page 13

Hiking in the Chapada Diamantina
The Vale do Capão in the Chapada Diamantina as seen from the summit of the Morro de Pai Inácio (AR) page 233

above left Search for second-hand treasures in Salvador's junkshops (AR) page 121

above right The cobbled streets of Salvador's historic centre bustle with all manner of hawkers and vendors at any time of the day or night (AR) page 122

below Capoeiristas hone their art at one of Metre Railson's classes in Arraial d'Ajuda on the Costa do Descobrimento (AR) page 196

above left Rebeca Mata is one of the most exciting new singers on the Bahian alternative music scene (AR)

above right Master percussionist, composer and African-Brazilian cultural icon, Carlinhos Brown, performs live at the Black Music Centre in Salvador (AR) page 135

below Salvador's queen of traditional samba, Mariene de Castro, has one of the finest voices in Brazilian music and is a spellbinding live act (AR) page 55

Alex Robinson is an award-winning travel writer and photographer who has authored several books on Brazil and the Amazon. He is one of the leading writers in English on Brazil and has written for the *New York Times*, *National Geographic*, *Wanderlust*, *Sunday Times Travel Magazine*, the *Independent on Sunday*, *Condé Nast Traveller*, the *Financial Times*, *Marie Claire* and *Departures* magazine. Alex speaks fluent Portuguese, lived for four years in Brazil, and continues to divide his time between Brazil and the UK.

AUTHOR'S STORY

I remember my Brazilian wife, her family and friends going dewy-eyed over Bahia before I had ever been beyond Rio or São Paulo. Bahia, they said, is where Brazilians dream of when they miss their country – a land of golden tropical beaches, vibrant African-Brazilian culture, great food, spicy music and pretty, timeless colonial towns and cities. The first time I visited it rained solid for three weeks. I was unlucky. But the numerous journeys I've taken there since – for business and pleasure – have made me realise what the fuss is all about. Yet, but for boutique hotels on the beaches and a few Westerners flying in for *Carnaval*, it is still almost unknown to non-Brazilians. So when Bradt gave me the opportunity to set the record straight I was delighted to accept. I spent many months re-visiting a state larger than France for the book, and soon began to realise that I had bitten off more than I could chew. It may only be a small part of Brazil, but there is simply too much in Bahia to set down in any one book. What I offer here is literally a guidebook, a tool which I hope will help visitors discover their own Bahia – whether they are in the craggy mountains of the interior, the wildlife-filled deserts of the *sertão* or those miles and miles of golden beaches…

PUBLISHER'S FOREWORD   *Adrian Phillips, Publishing Director*

When Alex Robinson first visited Bahia, he encountered just ten foreign visitors in a month. In the last couple of years, top travel magazines have shined their spotlights on Bahia's beaches, boutiques and spas, and Leonardo DiCaprio has bought property there. However, it's still a destination off the radars of most tourists, and you won't need to go far to find empty beaches and unspoilt views. But this area's as much about energy and culture as peace and quiet. The samba and bossa nova were born here; it hosts the world's biggest Mardi Gras carnival, and is thick with wonderful colonial architecture. As an expert on Brazilian music, an award-winning travel writer and photographer, and a former long-term resident in the country, Alex is ideally placed to introduce Bahia's rich pickings.

First published October 2010
Bradt Travel Guides Ltd, 23 High Street, Chalfont St Peter, Bucks SL9 9QE, England.
www.bradtguides.com
Published in the USA by The Globe Pequot Press Inc, 246 Goose Lane, PO Box 480,
Guilford, Connecticut 06437-0480

Text copyright © 2010 Alex Robinson
Maps copyright © 2010 Bradt Travel Guides Ltd
Photographs © 2010 See individuals listed below
Illustrations © 2010 Carole Vincer
Project Manager: Emma Thomson

ISBN: 978 1 84162 329 0

British Library Cataloguing in Publication Data
A catalogue record for this book is available from the British Library

Photographer Alex Robinson (AR), Rubens Chaves/Photolibrary (RC/P)
Front cover Carnaval, Salvador (RC/P)
Back cover Beach, Boipeba (AR) ; Church, Sao Felix, Baia de Todos os Santos (AR)
Title page Bahian girl (AR), Abrolhos Archipelago (AR), Tufted-eared marmoset (AR)

Maps David Priestley
Illustrations Carole Vincer

Typeset from the author's disc by D & N Publishing, Baydon, Wiltshire
Production managed by Jellyfish Print Solutions; printed in India

Acknowledgements

With great thanks to Gardênia and Raphael Robinson without whom this book would never have happened. Further thanks to Klauber and Andrea at PortoMondo for their supreme professionalism; Daniel and Daniela at Mata Nativa in Trancoso; William Wisden in Salvador; Vera in Praia do Forte; Carlinhos Brown, Thiago Santana and Mariene de Castro for keeping the music alive; David McLoughlin at BM&A for inspiration, help and guidance; and Adrian and Emma and everyone at Bradt for patience with my hellish schedule.

FEEDBACK REQUEST

For the latest travel news about Bahia, please visit the new interactive Bradt update website: http://updates.bradtguides.com.

This update website is a free service for readers and anybody else who cares to drop by and browse, so if you have any comments, queries, grumbles, insights, news or other feedback, you're invited to post them on the website. Otherwise please write to or phone Bradt Travel Guides Ltd, 23 High Street, Chalfont St Peter, Bucks SL9 9QE, England; 01753 893444; e info@bradtguides.com.

Contents

Introduction

It has long been a mystery to me that whilst the world tramps around Asia, the Caribbean and Australia in search of a great undiscovered exotic location Bahia remains almost completely undiscovered. At least to foreigners. Brazilians have long known it to be one of the world's special places: Bahia is famous throughout the country for its 1,200km of white-pepper-fine palm-shaded sand, for its magnificent Baroque architecture and its rich and vibrant African-Brazilian culture.

I first visited at the beginning of the new millennium, beginning in the capital city, Salvador. I was stunned by the myriad streets of colourful Portuguese mansions and crumbling, gilt-covered Portuguese churches, by the acrobatic martial-arts dance of *capoeira* and by the warmth and beauty of the local people. I travelled north to the sweeping beach dunes at Mangue Seco and watched the moon rise huge over a giant ocean. I trekked through the monkey and parrot-filled rainforests in the south and swam in waterfalls in the rugged highlands of the Chapada Diamantina. In a month I saw fewer than ten foreigners.

Things have changed a little since, but only a little. The world has begun to discover Bahia and this little corner of Brazil now boasts some of Latin America's very best small hotels and restaurants. But they are still visited by a select few; many of whom want to keep Bahia a secret. Even in the resort towns and colonial cities it's easy to find a deserted beach, an unspoilt view or a genuinely friendly local face. These come alongside world-class walking, some of the best wildlife and birdwatching in the Americas and the biggest and liveliest Carnaval celebrations in Latin America.

Part One

GENERAL INFORMATION

Official country name Republica Federativa do Brasil
Location Northeast Brazil
Area 564,273km^2 – a little larger than France
Climate Tropical, sub-tropical and temperate in the south
Status Federal Republic
Population 12,068,764 (2000 census), 14,637,364 (2009 estimate)
Life expectancy 69 years (men), 76 years (women)
Capital Salvador (population 4,080,504) (est 2005)
Other main cities Feira da Santana, Vitória da Conquista, Juazeiro, Camaçari, Ilhéus, Itabuna
Economy Industry, agriculture, mining and service industries
GDP per capita $1,200
Languages Portuguese, indigenous languages
Religion Catholic, Protestant evangelical, African-Brazilian spirit religions
Currency Real (R$)
Exchange rate £1=R$2.79, US$1=R$1.75, €1=R$2.32 (August 2010)
National Airlines, TAM, GOL, Ocean Air
Airports, Salvador, Ilhéus, Porto Seguro
International phone code +55
Time GMT -3
Electrical voltage 110v/220v
Weights and measures Metric
State flag Two white and two red horizontal bands, with a blue square in the top left hand corner bearing a central white triangle
Public holidays 1 January (New Year's Day/Confraternização Universal, Day of Universal Brotherhood); February/March (Carnaval – always 47 days before Easter); March/April (Sexta-feira Santa Paixão, Good Friday); 21 April (Tiradentes); 1 May (Dia do Trabalho, Labour Day); May/June (Corpus Christi –Thurs after Trinity Sun); 28 June (Pilões); 2 July (Independência da Bahia, Bahian Independence Day); 7 September (Independence Day); 12 October (Nossa Senhora Aparecida, Padroeira do Brasil; Our Lady Aparecida, Patron Saint of Brazil); 2 November (Finados, All Souls' Day); 15 November (Proclamação da República, Republic Day); 20 November (Dia da Consciência Negra, Black Consciousness Day); 24 December (Christmas Eve); 25 December (Christmas Day); 31 December (New Year's Eve)

Background Information

GEOGRAPHY

Bahia is a state in the northeast region of Brazil. It sits halfway up the country's coast, some 1,000km north of Rio de Janeiro and 2,000km south of the mouth of the River Amazon. Brazil is huge: it's the largest country in Latin America and the fifth-largest in the world both in area and population. It's big enough to swallow Australia whole and still have room for France and Britain combined. Bahia is far from being the largest Brazilian state, but – at 564,273km^2 – it's nonetheless a little bigger than France and a little smaller than Texas.

Like the rest of northeastern Brazil, most of Bahia is made up of the *sertão* – a vast, flat and arid interior of rocky plains and undulating uplands dominated by xeric *caatinga* scrub forest and *cerrado* (tropical savanna), rising to between 200m and 800m and broken by some of the most ancient, weather-worn mountain ranges on earth. These pre-Cambrian crystalline crags form a spine of rocky *chapadas* – or tabletop mountains – that cut across Brazil in a rough diagonal from the southwest through to the northeast. In Bahia they form the remote Raso da Catarina canyons and reach their greatest elevation in the **Chapada Diamantina (Diamond Hills)**. These hold the highest point in northeastern Brazil, the Serra do Barbado (2,033m), and the second-highest waterfall in the country, the Cachoeira da Fumaça which falls 340m from a cliff top into a deep canyon pool. The Chapada is pocked with caves, cut by underground rivers and divided by deep forested valleys.

West of the Chapada the sertão deserts extend to the deep-blue water of the flooded São Francisco River, the largest river wholly within Brazil, which cuts across Bahia from north to south. The river is one of the largest and longest in the Americas, running a course of almost 3,000km through the heart of the sertão, through the extensive Sobradinho Reservoir, to the twin cities of Juazeiro (in Bahia) and Petrolina (in Pernambuco). In this stretch the river receives its main left-bank tributaries which drain the remote western Bahian sertão – the Paracatu, Urucuia, Corrente and Grande rivers – and its main right-bank tributaries which flow out of the Chapada Diamantina: the Verde Grande, Paramirim and Jacaré. Some 160km south of Juazeiro the São Francisco curves to the northeast, creating the border with neighbouring Pernambuco state and entering a long set of canyons and rapids before disgorging into the sea. The upper rapids are navigable after the rains, but below Juazeiro the river is impassable due to a series of hydro-electric dams, which have also cut the flow of what were once one of the world's most dramatic waterfalls – the Cachoeira de Paulo Afonso. Prior to the damming of the river, 2,800m^3 of fast-flowing blue water plunged 84m over three giant, rugged canyons per second; a sight captured in one of the first and most memorable landscape paintings of Brazil by the Dutch artist, Franz Post.

Eastern Bahia, which runs along the coast, is as wet and fertile as the west is dry and barren. It is divided into two zones: the Zona da Mata and its agricultural hinterland; and the Agreste. Both were swathed in the lush Mata Atlântica or Atlantic coastal rainforest before the arrival of the Portuguese.

In the far north of the state, on the border with Sergipe, the **Costa dos Coqueiros (Coconut Coast)** begins with long, 500–800m-wide beaches backed by 30–40m-high dunes of powder-fine shifting sands which merge into coconut plantations as they run south. Here they meet Salvador, the capital of Bahia state and the third-largest city in Brazil. Salvador sits at the tip of a peninsula which marks the northern head of a bay so large that the first Europeans labelled it as an inland sea. Covering 1,233km^2, the **Baía de Todos os Santos (Bay of All Saints)** is the largest bay in Brazil and one of the biggest navigable bays in the world. It is fed by many rivers which are lined with mangroves where they meet the salt water. These include one of the largest rivers to flow west out of the Bahian sertão, the Paraguaçu (which provided the Portuguese with a navigable route inland), dotted with clusters of islands, the largest of which, Itaparica, seals the bay at its southern end. The area around the Baía de Todos os Santos is called the **Recôncavo Baiano**. Before the arrival of the Portuguese this was a vast semi-wetland of mangrove and Atlantic coastal rainforest. This was felled for sugar cane in the first years of the colony and the Recôncavo is now a fertile agricultural region.

South of the Recôncavo the **Costa do Dendê (Dendê Coast)** begins where a run of large rivers fragment the shoreline into strips of long, broad beaches, mangrove-lined estuaries and low coral-fringed islands. Immediately south of Itaparica island, the Jaguaripe, Taperoá, Guarapuá, Cairu and Inferno rivers meet the Atlantic in a tangle of brackish waterways that have divided whole sections of Bahia from the mainland to form three large islands: the Ilha de Tinharé, whose rocking northern cape is capped with the fortress and now resort town of Morro de São Paulo; the forest-covered, coral-fringed Ilha de Boipeba; and the Ilha de Cairu, which lies east of – and is shielded by – the other two, but doesn't share their Atlantic coast or their beautiful palm-shaded beaches. All the islands and the coast behind them are swathed in secondary growth Atlantic coastal rainforest, patches of which are nominally protected and planted with the introduced (Dendê) palm oil which gives the region its name and Bahian cooking its strong west African flavour.

South of the islands more rivers break the coast up into a large labyrinthine bay – the Baía de Camamu, which is peppered with tiny islands and entirely shielded from the Atlantic breakers by a north-facing mouth. The Serinhaém and Maraú rivers have brackish waters and wild mangroves, and others plunge into the bay over low granite shelves, forming waterfalls at the Cachoeira do Tremembé and the Cachoeira da Pancada Grande. The bay is sealed at its southern end by the finger-shaped Peninsula de Maraú, which is lined with magnificent Atlantic beaches and covered in remnant Atlantic forest and is one of the largest patches of Bahia's extant *restinga* wetlands.

Maraú and the final beaches of the Dendê coast are separated from Itacaré and the **Costa do Cacau (Cacau Coast)** by another of Bahia's great rivers, the Rio de Contas. The fishing village and burgeoning resort of Itacaré sits on its southern bank and a string of sandy coves and magnificent bays – backed by rugged and rainforest-clad coastal hills – runs south from here to Bahia's second-largest port, Ilhéus. South of here the coast is a patchwork of remnant Atlantic coastal forest and cacão plantations, which furnish the world's chocolate-makers with around 4% of their cocoa. Bahia's beaches run long and broad and are backed by coconut palms and a filigree of coastal rivers and wetlands to Belmonte, where another of Brazil's great rivers bursts through to the coast. The **Costa do Descobrimento (Discovery Coast)** begins on Jequitinhonha's southern banks with more long beaches which run south to the historical city of Porto Seguro, the capital of the heavily visited beautiful south. South of here are some of Bahia's most famous beaches. At Arraial de Ajuda and Trancoso they are backed by crumbling sandstone cliffs; these recede into coves at Espelho and long, broad bays around Caraíva and the Ponta do Corumbau where the Bahian coast begins its wildest stretch around Monte Pascoal. This 586m-high, conical granite monolith was the first piece of land sighted by the Portuguese when they arrived at the beginning of the 16th century. It sits in the Parque Nacional do Descobrimento, a large swathe of primary and secondary growth Atlantic coastal rainforest closed to all but scientists.

South of Monte Pascoal the Costa do Descobrimento gives way to the **Costa da Baleia (Whale Coast)** near the uninteresting provincial town of Prado, the first of a series of small provincial settlements in the far south of Bahia. These provide access points to the Abrolhos, a tiny archipelago of rocky islands 30km offshore, set in extensive coral gardens, and whose annually visiting humpback whales give the region its name. Bahia ends in cliffs, beaches and eucalyptus plantations for paper pulp at Mucuri on the borders of Espírito Santo state.

CLIMATE

Bahia's weather is tropical (with dry winters and wet summers) on the coast and in much of the Chapada Diamantina ranging to tropical semi-arid (hot and dry with low annual rainfall) in the sertão. The average temperature in Salvador is 25.1°C (77°F) and the average temperature range is just 3°C. Summer temperatures in Salvador, Ilhéus and Porto Seguro can reach the high 30s, and in the sertão it can get into the 40s, with the hottest months being January, February and March – when anywhere in the state the thermometer rarely drops below 30°C (86°F). The coldest months are July and August, when the monthly average on the coast is 20°C (68°F).

Coastal Bahian weather is influenced by the warm humid trade winds that sweep in across the Atlantic and – the further south you go – by cold frontal systems which move up from Antarctica and bring heavy precipitation often for days on end, and a drop in temperature. Rainfall varies greatly across the state. The coast gets an average of 1,866mm (73.5 inches) of rainfall per year in Salvador and around 1,500mm (59.1 inches) in the south of the state. The driest months are January–February and August–September and the wettest weather is in May and June.

Much of the sertão receives just 800mm (31.5 inches) annually. In the Chapada Diamantina, temperatures are between 25°C and 30°C during the day and around 20°C at night. They can fall below 20°C at night between June and September. The wettest months are between December and March.

The driest seasons are January and February, but this variation is less noticeable in coastal cities like Porto Seguro due to the influence of the sea. Relative humidity is around 80% all through the year. Wind speed is greatest in the spring (September–November).

NATURAL HISTORY

Why does man destroy the natural wealth when he knows that the planet is being depleted and that without it his life in the planet will be impossible?
Why does Brazil allow itself to become a desert when it is one of the richest countries on the planet? For immediate gain in lots, forests are destroyed, resulting in long term destruction, together with utter poverty.
Why give up basic cultivations for the benefit of industrial monoculture? Can the Earth bear this?

Frans Krajcberg – Bahian sculptor based in Nova Viçosa

ECOSYSTEMS Like the majority of Brazil, Bahia falls into the new-world tropical or neotropical biological region. The **neotropics** are one of the most biodiverse regions of the planet. There are more birds, primates, reptiles, amphibians, freshwater fish and plant species here than in any other region in the world and only a fraction of the species have been catalogued. South America was cut off from the rest of the world 100 million years ago when the giant continent which was made up of a union of that continent with Africa broke up (completing the fragmentation of the super-continent of Gondwana which had included South America, Africa, India Antarctica and Australia). It remained isolated until the North American continent collided with what is today Colombia, creating a land bridge at Panama, wiping out many of the larger primitive marsupial mammals, but overall increasing the region's biodiversity.

Unique species developed due to this isolation and because of a complex zoning of ecosystems. In Bahia these are spread across two main habitats: Atlantic coastal rainforest and sertão (the vast hinterland away from the coast). Within the coastal rainforest are reef, mangrove and *restinga* ecosystems, and within sertão *cerrado* and *caatinga* ecosystems.

Atlantic coastal rainforest (Mata Atlântica)

The Atlantic coastal rainforest once ran in a broad 160km-wide swathe along Brazil's east coast, passing through Bahia from Mangue Seco to Mucuri. When the Portuguese arrived in 1502 the forest extended over 2,600,000km^2 within Brazil, but this has now been reduced to less than 5%. Patches remain in Bahia – principally around Itacaré, near Una, on the coast and islands near Tinharé and between Trancoso and Prado in the south.

The Atlantic coastal rainforest ranges in elevation from sea level to over 2,000m (though it doesn't attain these heights in Bahia), giving it a number of distinct zones, including cloud forest (which exists in tiny patches in Bahia in the Chapada Diamantina (see page 235). The forest has been isolated biologically from the other great neotropical forests in the Amazon and Andes, making it one of the most biodiverse regions on Earth. It is one of Conservation International's designated world biodiversity hotspots (*www.biodiversityhotspots.org*) and is the second most threatened biome in the country after the *cerrado*. There are over 20,000 plant species, 40% of which are endemic and over 930 bird species, 144 of which are endemic and 55 of which are threatened.

Figures published by IBAMA (the Brazilian Environmental Protection Institute) in 2003 show that of Brazil's 69 severely endangered mammal species, 38 come from the Atlantic rainforest and 25 of these are endemic. The same is true for amphibians – all 16 of them are endemic to the Atlantic coastal forests, as are 13 of the 20 endangered reptile species. The forests have 21 species and subspecies of monkeys, of which 14 are endangered, 13 are endemic, and several are on the brink of extinction.

Reefs

Much of Bahia's coast is fringed with coral, but it's in a dreadful state, both in terms of coral health and the diversity and density of fish numbers which it supports. Drift-net and long-line fishing in the 1960s destroyed one of the healthiest stocks in the tropical Atlantic, impoverishing fishing villages along the entire Bahian coast and almost completely wiping out dolphin-fish and other larger pelagic species. But there is good news. The Abrolhos Marine Reserve (see page 215) safeguards the largest concentration of coral reefs in the South Atlantic, with many endemic species, including spectacular brain corals, crustaceans and molluscs, as well as marine turtles and mammals threatened by extinction. It is also an important sea bird nesting site, and one of the most important areas in the world for humpback whales – who reproduce and nurse their young in the shallow waters around the islands. In 2002, the Abrolhos region was declared an area of Extreme Biological Importance by the Brazilian Ministry of Environment, based on the Brazilian commitment to the Convention on Biodiversity. Today, the area is well protected and starting to recuperate from the severe overfishing which preceded this legislation.

Mangroves Mangroves (*mangue* in Portuguese) are trees or shrubs which grow in brackish and saltwater in the tropics and subtropics. There are many species adapted to such conditions and not all are related, but the word mangrove is often used as a catch-all. It is more correctly applied to the mangrove family of plants, the *Rhizophoraceae*, many of whose species excrete salt through their leaves. Mangroves support all manner of fauna from *Guiamu* mud crabs and wading plovers and herons to otters, ocelots and larger nursing fish like sharks and bonito. In Bahia there are two principal mangrove species: red and white mangrove, which both occur in abundant numbers on the waterways of Dendê, Cacau, Descobrimento and Baleia coasts. In the quieter patches – around Una and the Ilha de Cairu (see page 161) – they remain good locations for birding and wildlife watching; activities which will need to be self-guided.

Restinga *Restinga* – which is comprised of coastal wetlands, shrub- and small-tree forests and grasslands – forms another of Brazil's unique habitats. Restingas support a relatively high diversity of plants and a moderate level of endemism, including the threatened southern river otter and the endangered restinga and pectoral antwren. Less than 10% of the original vegetation remains and with little protection, the remaining areas are critically threatened. There are restingas on the peninsula de Maraú, between Trancoso and Caraíva and around the mangrove-lined rivers in Prado, where southern river otters remain a relatively common sight.

Sertão
Cerrado The *cerrado* is a mosaic of habitat types which run across central and southern Brazil, northeastern Paraguay, and eastern Bolivia in a tapestry of wet and dry forests, grasslands and savannas, marshes, wetlands, gallery forests and shrublands. It is acutely threatened by the soya and cattle industry and forms the largest ecoregion in the Americas (ahead of the Amazon) and the sixth largest in the world. In Bahia there are extensive areas of cerrado around the Chapada Diamantina and Canudos, at the Morrinhos Reserve, and in the far east of the state beyond the sertão (an area which is remote and very difficult to reach).

The biodiversity of the cerrado is extraordinary. At least 10,400 species of vascular plants and over 780 fish, 180 reptile, 110 amphibian, 830 bird, and 95 mammal species live here. Many are endemic, including some 50% of its 10,000 plant species, 4% of its bird species and a number of mammals, including the maned wolf. This biodiversity is a consequence of the cerrado's myriad habitat types. In places it is dominated by vast stands of spectacular flowering trumpet trees that boast a bloom of iridescent lilacs, yellows and pinks. In others, it is predominantly savanna grassland with *veredas* or buriti palms busy with macaws and large parrots and patrolled by anteaters, and rhea (South American ostriches). An average of 1,270–2,032mm (50–80 inches) rain falls on the cerrado each year, washing over its nutrient-poor but well-drained soils.

Caatinga *Caatinga* is a uniquely Brazilian biome which dominates the sertão – and is often associated with it. It dominates Bahia and the entire Brazilian northeast and although it makes up the largest dry forest region in South America (and one of the richest dry forests in the world) it is little understood. (Indeed, it is little loved by Brazilians who see it as a wasteland and associate it with hardship and deprivation.)

Biologists have recorded that caatinga vegetation is varied and falls into several distinct types – from low shrubs and xeric (drought and fire-resistant) bushes to tall trees that can grow to some 30m high. Beyond this, though, the caatinga's flora and fauna have barely been studied, let alone catalogued, but the little work which has so far been undertaken identifies a diverse and varied cluster of species. Thousands are unique to the region – especially the plants. Scientists have so far counted at least 1,200 species of vascular plants. Of the fauna, three crocodile relatives have been recorded, 80 mammals, some 185 fish species, 44 lizard, 47 snake, four turtle, 49 amphibian and 350 birds. These include some of the world's rarest, such as the Lear's and Spix's macaws – which are among the world's most highly endangered birds and the latter almost certainly extinct in the wild.

Sadly, more than half of Brazil's caatinga has already been completely stripped of its native vegetation or significantly altered through overgrazing, unsustainable timber extraction for firewood, cotton cultivation and damming for hydroelectricity. Much of it is ranked as highly threatened with desertification. Despite these great pressures, less than 1% of Brazil's caatinga is protected and politicians look set to pay little more attention to its conservation. Bahia's handful of reserves are: the **Parque Estadual de Canudos** (which was created to preserve the area's history rather than natural history), the **Estação Ecológica Raso da Catarina**, the **Fazenda Morrinhos** and the **Estação Biológica de Canudos** which is home to Lear's Macaw.

FAUNA Whilst there is no information available on specifically Bahian fauna almost all of Brazil's biomes are represented in Bahia (with the exception of Amazon forest) and it is within this context that we can talk about fauna in Bahia.

Mammals Brazil has more than 500 species of mammals – the greatest number of any country on Earth. These range from big, spectacular animals like tapir to tiny rodents, marsupials and bats, which make up the bulk of the species numbers. Mammals in Bahia are tough to see. The most frequently spotted are primates and rodents like paca, agouti and armadillos.

Primates Brazil is the richest country in the world for primates with some 75 species, many of which are very closely related. Like other New World monkeys they generally have short muzzles, furless faces, short necks, long limbs, and tails which, in many species, are prehensile.

The monkeys can be grouped into two major families: the *Callitrichidae* which is made of up tiny marmosets and tamarins, and the *Cebidae* which constitutes the rest. There are 14 species of marmosets and 17 tamarins in Brazil, including the very rare **golden-headed lion tamarin** (*Leontopithecus chrysomela*) which exists almost exclusively in Bahia where it can be seen in forests near Una. The most commonly spotted is the black-and-white, **ring-tailed tufted-eared marmoset**, which is abundant along the coast.

red howler monkey

Larger monkeys in Bahia are mostly capuchin and howler monkeys, both of which are highly arboreal. **Capuchins** are curious and the larger of the species, the brown capuchin are a fairly common sight in the Chapada Diamantina and Mata Atlântica forests, where they wander through the tree canopy in search of fruit, led by a dominant male scout. **Howler monkeys**, which are also fairly abundant, are heard more often than seen, producing a sonorous, guttural territorial roar at dusk and dawn which can be heard for many kilometres. The critically endangered **woolly spider monkey**, or northern muriqui, with off-white fur, is the largest monkey in Brazil (and Bahia) and is restricted to patches of forest on the southern coast.

Carnivores Most of Bahia's dog species are found in the cerrado and caatinga, with the commonest being the **crab-eating fox** and endemic **hoary fox**. **Maned wolves** – which look like red foxes on stilts – can occasionally be seen in the cerrado including around the Chapada Diamantina, but are rare. Even more elusive is the shy, nocturnal **bush dog**, a dull brown pack-hunting animal with short legs. There are probably fewer than 15,000 of these dogs in the wild.

Bahia's eight species of cat are mostly the same size or a little larger than a domestic cat and all are very difficult to see. **Jaguarundi** is a small, brown, grey or black cat which lives in dense cover – from savanna grasslands to Mata Atlântica rainforest. The very rare **pampas cat** lives in cerrado forest and open grasslands. It looks like a chunky domestic cat, with a broad face, beautiful amber eyes and distinctive pointy ears and is usually buff brown in colour, though it can be mottled. There are usually dark grey tips to the ears. **Oncillas** and **margays** are very handsome spotted cats which live predominantly in closed forest and which hunt at night. Other small spotted Brazilian cats like **Geoffrey's cat** may or may not be present in Bahia – there is no systematic research available. The most spectacular Bahian cats are the

ocelot

nocturnal terrier-sized **spotted ocelot**, the crepuscular (twilight active) and difficult-to-spot **puma**, and the **jaguar**, which can reach up to 200kg in weight and favours forest close to a permanent supply of water.

Marsupials Brazil's non-placental, marsupial mammals are all opossums. There are 43 families, all of which superficially resemble rats and mice with pointed snouts, long and usually hairless prehensile tails, and large, hairless ears. About half the species carry their young in abdominal pouches. The largest, the **common opossum** can often be seen in small towns and city suburbs. Smaller forest opossums are shyer and arboreal. Eleven of Brazil's opossum species are threatened.

Anteaters, sloths and armadillos Despite their very different appearances, these three families of animals all belong to the order *Edentata*, and have similar skeletal structures and circulatory systems. They are highly specialised feeders; anteaters and some armadillos have mouths and digestive systems adapted to feed exclusively on ants and termites, while sloths eat only forest canopy leaves. All are unique to the Americas, and sloths and anteaters are unique to the neotropics. There are three anteater species: the shaggy, Alsatian-sized **giant anteater** can be seen roaming the savanna grasslands of the cerrado and is a relatively common sight in the Chapada Diamantina; the **buff tamandua** is teddy-bear sized and also fairly common; and the fist-sized **pygmy anteater** is a forest-dwelling arboreal species.

Sloths occur in two families – **two and three-toed sloths**. Both are very slow, cumbersome forest dwellers looking like monkeys but with ungainly long arms and bodies and untidy, often algae-stained fur. They are most easily spotted in cecropia trees.

anteater

Armour-plated **armadillos** are most commonly seen foraging in the cerrado. There are 11 species in Brazil, the most spectacular of which is the rare giant armadillo, which can weigh up to 30kg. It is the only diurnal species.

Peccaries, deer and tapir Peccaries and deer are both ungulates – hoofed animals with even numbers of toes on each foot. Peccaries resemble small pigs in appearance, habits and smell. There are two species, the collared and the slightly smaller white-lipped. Both are social animals, moving in large groups, which in the case of the **white-lipped peccary** can number up to 100 individuals. Both species can be aggressive.

white-lipped peccary

There are six species of deer in Brazil, four of which can be seen in Bahia: the **marsh deer** (which has webbed feet), the small, principally forest-dwelling **red brocket deer** and the most commonly seen, the **pampas** and the **white-tailed deer**, both of which favour cerrado forest, particularly the Chapada Diamantina.

Tapir are the largest mammals in Brazil, weighing up to 300kg. They look a little like large, brown pigs with tufty manes, but are related far more closely to horses and rhinos. Tapirs like to live close to water, and their distinctive foot prints (wide and with four toes at the front and three at the back) can often be seen imprinted in the sand on river banks. They are rare in Bahia, but still cling on in the rainforests along the coast and in the Chapada Diamantina.

Rodents and rabbits There are 165 rodents in Brazil, most of which are present in Bahia. They include some of the most fascinating families and species in the world. Most spectacular of all is the Labrador-sized **capybara** – the largest of all rodents – which looks like a huge guinea pig with doe-like eyes and which favours marshy land.

There are several species of porcupines – including a tiny **arboreal porcupine** and related **spiny tree rats** – rarely seen despite being one of the most abundant rainforest species. **Agoutis** and **paca** are large, deer-like rodents with long hind legs. They are the only animals with teeth strong enough to crack a Brazil nut.

Rabbits differ from rodents in having more incisor teeth and longer ears. **Mocó rock cavies** are similar to agoutis, but are dumpier. They are abundant in the Chapada Diamantina. There is only one species in Brazil – which looks identical to the European fluffy-tailed rabbit.

capybara

Bats Among mammals, bats are second in diversity only to rodents and some 40% of all mammalian species in the neotropics are bats. There are at least 140 species in Brazil, many of which are found in Bahia. However, it can be very difficult for anyone but a specialist to identify one species from another. The largest weigh only 200g with a wingspan of 80cm, the smallest only 5g with a 5cm wing span. Almost all are insectivores whilst a few are fructivorous, vampiric or fish and amphibian eaters.

Cetaceans and manatees In January 2009, the Brazilian government designated its entire coastline as a sanctuary for whales and dolphins. Despite this there has been little research into cetacean numbers or varieties in Brazilian waters. Bottlenose and the marine subspecies of Tucuxi dolphin are common along the entire coast and minke, killer (orca) and beaked whales common further out to sea. Southern Bahia around the Abrolhos archipelago (see page 215) is the best place in the Atlantic for observing humpback whales.

REPTILES Brazil has the highest diversity of reptiles in the world. But most are shy, nocturnal, and so well camouflaged that they can be very difficult to see even when close by. This also makes them potentially dangerous – especially snakes. When walking forest trails it is always important never to place hands or feet in places where you cannot see and never to poke around in holes and crevices – especially around tree roots.

Turtles Brazil has both freshwater and marine turtles. They range in size from tiny terrapins found in the streams of the Chapada Diamantina, to giant leatherback turtles – the heaviest of all reptiles and at their largest over two metres long and 3.5 metres wide. Five species of marine turtle nest in Brazil (the loggerhead, hawksbill, green, olive ridley and leatherback turtle), all but the green turtle nest in Bahia, although the leatherback has only been reported as nesting on a few occasions near Prado in the south. The best place to see turtles is through one of the Projeto Tamar (see box on page 226) centres, especially in Praia do Forte.

Whilst abundant in the Amazon River system, freshwater turtles are difficult to see in Bahia and the ecology, status and distribution of Brazilian turtle species in the state has been little studied. They include some ancient *Podocnemidid* river turtle species – a family which has been around since the dinosaurs, like the **Arrau turtle** and **yellow-headed sideneck turtle** – both with pig-like noses and flat shells. They can often be spotted basking on logs or river beaches. The long-necked **Maximilian's snake-necked turtle** is restricted to rainforest streams near Porto Seguro. This tiny species (less than 20cm long) lives in streams with sandy and rocky bottoms and clear water, normally with small waterfalls and is most easily seen in the breeding season between September and January.

Caimans Brazil has no crocodile or alligator species, only caimans. There are six species in Brazil most of which are threatened or endangered – the **black caiman**, **smooth-fronted caiman**, **Yacare caiman**, the **broad-snouted caiman** and the **spectacled caiman**. The largest of these is the black caiman, which can reach over six metres. It is not found in Bahia. The most commonly seen caiman in the state is the two-metre long spectacled caiman, with a distinctive yellow eye patch and olive-brown skin. It is most easily seen at night when its eyes give off a deep-red shine in torchlight.

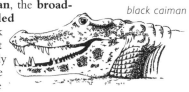

black caiman

Snakes Brazil has the greatest diversity of snake species of any country on Earth. Most snakes are *Colubrids*, a family which includes many of the harmless snakes kept as pets – like the garter snake. Brazilian colubrids include the **striped sharp-nose snake** – a tree-living snake which when stationary looks almost identical to a vine, making it very difficult to see – and false coral snakes. (The North American rhyme –'Red on yellow, kill a fellow; red on black, friend of Jack', does not work in Brazil where the colour patterns of true and false coral snakes are different.)

But as elsewhere, almost none are venomous. Brazilian venomous snakes tend to be nocturnal and hard to find. Brazil's venomous snakes include several fearsome vipers, including the 3.5-metre-long **bushmaster** and the **Gabon viper**, the largest and most powerful (and poisonous) members of their genus in the world. Smaller vipers include the **fer-de-lance** which is abundant in moist forest and cerrado and **rattlesnakes** which are common in the caatinga.

Brazil has some of the largest and heaviest constricting snakes in the world – the **boas** and anacondas. The former are beautifully-patterned and often brightly coloured forest snakes with characteristic heart-shaped heads and which are harmless to humans. **Anacondas** spend much of their time in water and are most easily seen in the Chapada Diamantina. They are the heaviest snakes in the world and only exceeded in length by the Asian reticulated python. Large anacondas strangle and eat livestock and whilst they are rarely dangerous to humans they should be treated with caution.

Lizards The most commonly seen Brazilian lizards are tiny **geckos** – house lizards which can be seen hunting mosquitoes and moths attracted by artificial lights. They make their homes in the eaves of houses, or even in internal rooms. Iguanas, including the spectacular two-metre long, dragon-like **green iguana** are fairly common. And **skinks** can often be seen darting across forest trails in the Mata Atlântica and Chapada Diamantina.

AMPHIBIANS There are three main groups of amphibians in Brazil: frogs and toads, salamanders, and burrowing caecilans – which look like giant blind grey worms and which are seldom seen and little studied. Brazil's colourful **poison dart frogs** are the most iconic of all these. Most are little more than 1.5cm long and many species are restricted to tiny areas of Amazon or Mata Atlântica forest. Amazingly, only three species – out of more than 175 – are used by indigenous people to tip their darts or arrows for hunting.

poison dart frog

FISH Brazil's rainforest biodiversity is well known. Less well known is the biodiversity of its rivers, which is astounding. There are more catfish in the Amazon River system than there are freshwater fish in all the lakes and rivers of North America. Most of Brazil's fish are either chacarins or catfish. Catfish are abundant especially in the Amazon where they reach leviathan proportions – at up to three metres long and 400kg.

Other fish groups include Cichlids – represented by a number of brilliantly coloured popular aquarium fish like discus and flag acara and electric fish called knifefish, the most famous of which is the electric eel – which is found in Bahia. There are also a number of curious freshwater stingrays in the *Potamotrygon* family. These include the beautiful, mottled China and Coly rays. These are most closely related to Pacific Marine rays – evolutes of species isolated from the ocean when the Andes Mountains rose some 15 million years ago, blocking the westward flow of the river and trapping many rays in a vast inland sea. This isolation and the Amazon's tropical climate and seasonal massive changes in water levels created ideal circumstances and great pressure for evolutionary changes, as represented by the huge variety of stingrays found in just the one system. The rays spread from the Amazon River throughout Brazil and are among the most threatened and frequently poached species in Brazil.

ARTHROPODS Many visitors to Brazil worry that there are giant spiders and cockroaches lurking under every bed and clouds of mosquitoes waiting to pounce on every beach and forest trail. Fear not. There are large arthropods throughout

Stings from the bullet ant come in at four on a scale of one to four on the Schmidt Sting Pain Index, and the pain endures for 24 hours. The Satere-Mawe people of Brazil use these ants as part of an initiation rite which marks the passage from adolescence to adulthood. Ants are sedated, knitted into a glove made from leaves with their stings facing inwards. When the ants wake, the initiate boys put the gloves on and wear it for a full ten minutes, after which the hand and part of the arm are temporarily paralysed and the boy remains in a high fever, sometimes shaking uncontrollably for days. To complete the initiation boys must go through the ordeal some 20 times over several months or years.

Bahia, but you will have to look hard to find them, and mosquitoes are seldom the problem they are in countries like Mexico or Thailand. And whilst most visitors to Brazil are far keener to see a jaguar or harpy eagle than they are an insect or spider, it is all too easy to take humble arthropods for granted. Brazil is a country built and maintained by arthropods. Without the pollination, seed dispersal, recycling, farming and decomposition carried out almost exclusively by these creatures the beautiful landscapes of Brazil would be far plainer.

One of the commonest sights in Bahia are leaf-cutter **ants** which can be seen almost everywhere ferrying sail-like bits of plant in serried lines. These are taken to huge community nests where they are pulped and mashed and fed to a unique symbiotic fungus which provide the ants with their day-to-day food.

Cicadas, who provide the soundtrack to forest walks and beach-side candlelit dinners spend more than 90% of their lives as nymphs, living underground before emerging, sometimes for one night only to sing in glorious chorus, mate and die.

Brazil has the greatest number of species of **butterfly** in the world. The most spectacular are the forest-dwelling electric blue morphos, which are as large as an adult hand, and the aurorina clear-winged satyr, whose transparent wings are marked only with a single black spot and a reddish tail-like appendage.

Most notorious of the arthropods are the arachnids. Brazil is home to some of the world's largest tarantula **spiders** and scores of scorpions. Only a few species of either are dangerous to humans. But they include the fast-moving, saucer-sized wandering spiders or Brazilian huntsman, which are highly aggressive.

Other potentially dangerous arthropods include reduvid bugs – which transmit Chagas disease – large centipedes, a few of which are venomous and all of which should be treated with caution, and the solitary *Paraponera* bullet ant – so named because of the long, retractable syringe on its abdomen which injects an incredibly painful neurotoxin (see box above).

BIRDS Brazil is home to almost a fifth of the world's birds. It boasts around 1,750 species, of which 218 are endemic – the highest count of any country in the world, with new species being discovered every year. (Recent additions include the cryptic forest falcon, bare-headed parrot, sulphur-breasted parakeet, pernambuco pygmy owl, sincorá antwren and pink-legged graveteiro). Other famous wildlife destinations like Costa Rica or South Africa pale in comparison. Bahia does not have any Amazon forest but it holds extensive tracts of other unique habitats which are particularly rich in endemics and the region is home to endemics like the Bahia and Diamantina tapaculos and the Sincorá antwren. What is more, Bahia has been little birded and remoter areas – particularly of the *caatinga* and *cerrado* – are pioneer territory.

Sadly, though, Brazil also has the largest number of globally threatened birds: 120 of the 1,212 threatened birds distributed around the world, including two

Background Information **NATURAL HISTORY**

species already extinct in the wild (the Alagoas curassow and the Spix's macaw). Species you are likely to see include:

Cotingas Like the motmots and the trogons (see pages 15 and 17) , the cotingas are Brazil's celebrity birds, with elaborate plumage, glamorous colours and often ostentatious courtship displays. There are some 70 species in total, all but 22 of which can be found in Brazil and most of which live in the high canopy in primary forests, where they search for fruits. In Bahia they include the banded and the **white-winged cotinga** in the Mata Atlântica and the **swallow-tailed cotinga** and **red-ruffed fruit crow** in the Chapada Diamantina.

Cuckoos and anis There are 19 cuckoo and two anis species. Both cuckoos and anis have bizarre breeding habits. Whilst most cuckoos in Brazil are monogamous, a few adopt the parasitic lifestyles of their European cousins; notably the striped and pheasant cuckoos, who lay their eggs in the nests of other species. Immediately after hatching, the baby cuckoos push the rightful nestlings out of the nest. Anis are black, shiny birds commonly seen throughout Bahia who hunt and nest in groups. In some social groups all the individuals contribute to one single community nest.

Flycatchers This huge group of perching birds comprises 220 species in Brazil alone, ranging from some of the world's tiniest birds at 6.5cm to hefty foot-long species. All have broad, flat bills which they use to snatch insects from the air and a dizzying acrobatic flight. Most are fairly dull – with mottled chests and dun backs, but a few, like the blood-red **vermillion flycatcher** (which can be seen in caatinga or cerrado scrubland), are brilliantly coloured. Brazil's most nationally famous bird the lemon-chested, black-and-white-capped ***Bem-te-vi*** (Greater Kiskadee) is a flycatcher. Its song is said to sound like the bird is calling *Bem-te-vi* ('Beng-chi-vee') – 'Good to see you'.

Honeycreepers and cone-bills These small, pretty finch-like birds mostly live high in the forest canopy and are associated with flowering trees, although the most common, the bizarrely named bananaquit – which has a black head, a white eye stripe and a yellow breast, is often seen in parks and gardens.

Hummingbirds Brazil has more than a quarter of all the world's hummingbirds – at 83 species. Many are brilliantly iridescent and they range in size from six to 13cm long. In Bahia the best place to see them is along the Atlantic coast. The smallest weigh less than a large paperclip, all are capable of stunning, acrobatic flight – propelled by rapidly beating wings which flap in a circular motion – a little like helicopter blades. Many have specially adapted bills which allow them to collect their preferred source of nectar. Aside from duller, predominantly green hermits (species of which are widespread in Bahia), male humming birds are usually more brilliantly coloured than females – with distinct gorgets (throat feathers) which change from black to violet, green or electric blue as they turn their heads. Some 30 species of Brazilian hummingbirds are threatened or vulnerable.

Jacamars and puffbirds These (often) brightly coloured, gregarious, insect-eating birds superficially resemble hummingbirds, but are in fact related to kingfishers and largely confined to Brazil (with 38 of the 48 endemic to the country). Both families can usually be seen in busily chattering gaggles next to rainforest streams in the Mata Atlântica forests in the south of the state.

Motmots These elegant, very colourful birds have long, bills and two elongated tail feathers which taper to twin bauble-like conglomerates at the end. They are also related to kingfishers and can be seen anywhere from parkland to open country and rainforest. There are four species in Brazil.

Jays Jays include the crows, ravens and magpies. In Brazil all are jays – there are no crows – and most are forest dwellers. Like their European counterparts they are handsome, exuberant, highly intelligent birds. Most are gregarious, living in groups of five to ten, foraging within a restricted home range and calling raucously to each other from tree to tree.

Manakins These fascinating, brilliantly coloured wren-like birds spend much of their lives in a kind of bird theatre called a lec. This is often a clearing in the forest or a selection of branches in a grove of bamboos or thick vines. Here the iridescent males perform an elaborate courtship display for the dull females, which involves elaborate weaves, dances and flashes of colour from long tails or bright chests and throats. There are 36 species in Brazil, many of which live in Bahia. They include the **white-crowned manakin** in the Mata Atlântica and the spectacularly red-capped **helmeted manakin** in the Chapada Diamantina.

Mockingbirds and thrushes There are only 17 species of this enormous and varied 300-species family in Brazil. In Europe, the thrushes include some of our most familiar garden birds – like song thrushes and nightingales – famous for their beautiful calls. Brazilian thrushes have equally beautiful calls, none more so than the **Lawrence's thrush**, which is found in the swampy land in the Mata Atlântica and possibly the Chapada Diamantina and which can accurately mimic sounds as diverse as an outboard motor and the calls and trills of ovenbirds.

Some mockingbirds which look like thrushes (but which are closely related to starlings) have long tails and short wings and also mimic. There are only three species in Brazil.

Nightjars and potoos Nightjars are nocturnal birds, of which there are 23 species in Brazil, related to owls. They hunt flying insects, so can often be seen basking on dirt roads at night or flying startled across car headlights.

Potoos are far more difficult to spot – with cryptic colouring which perfectly blends with the treebark. During the day they can sometimes be spotted standing completely still at the end of a branch, mimicking a dead stump. At night the **great potoo** gives out a plaintive, mournful rising whistle.

Ovenbirds and antbirds There are more than 100 species of ovenbird in Brazil, most of them small, brown birds which are almost indistinguishable from one another and which have colonised every Bahian habitat from caatinga to rainforest. They are remarkable principally for their nests which vary depending on the habitat they occupy from hard clay mounds in the caaatinga and cerrado to elaborate thatched constructions in the forest.

Antbirds are unrelated, equally dull to look at, smaller still and even more interesting in their habits. They live in the lower parts of the forest canopy and follow troops of marauding soldier ants as they sweep through the forest, killing or consuming everything in their wake. Startled insects who manage to escape are caught by the birds. There are 164 species in Brazil.

Orioles and blackbirds There are 36 species of these diverse and often spectacular jay-sized birds in Brazil. They include the caciques and oropendolas –

which can be easily identified by their pendulous scrotum-like nests which hang from trees in the cerrado and Mata Atlântica. Some, like the cowbirds, are brood parasites – behaving like cuckoos. The **giant cowbird** places its young in the nests of oropendolas. However, unlike cuckoos, the larger cowbird chick is brought up alongside those of the oropendola.

Parrots and macaws These spectacular, raucous birds are forever associated with Latin America and the Caribbean through scores of pirate films and TV commercials. Bahia is home to one and possibly two of the rarest and most beautiful macaws of all: the **indigo blue lear macaw** and **Spix's macaw**. Lear's macaw probably now lives in only one site near Canudos – where it nests in sandstone cliffs. Spix's macaw lives in trumpet tree woodland; exclusively using the trunks of one particular species for nesting. The last male is thought to have died in 2000, almost certainly making the species extinct in the wild. Only 120 birds now exist in the world, eighty of which form the core a captive breeding programmed run by the Brazilian federal government who plan on re-introducing the species to the wilds in inland Bahia.

There are 71 parrot species in Brazil dozens of which live in Bahia. They are divided mainly by size. The sparrow-sized parrotlets are smallest, parakeets are a little larger (at up to 30cm with the tail); parrots range up to 45cm and macaws can reach a metre.

Raptors Brazil's carnivorous birds include five species of vulture, 46 hawks, eagles and kites, 17 owls and 16 falcons. Most spectacular of all these is the rare **king vulture**, with black and white plumage and a red and violet head, and the even rarer **harpy eagle** – at over a metre tall it is the world's largest eagle. The king vulture can be seen along the coast and in the Chapada Diamantina and the harpy eagle in the forests close to Porto Seguro. The commonest raptors are **black vultures** and the wedge-beaked, **crested caracara** (Mexican eagle) which preys on nestlings. Ospreys and **black-collared hawks** (which have a buff back and a distinct black ring around their necks) are commonly seen along river banks. Diurnal **burrowing owls** are frequently seen in the cerrado, often sitting on lampposts or termite nests.

Swifts and swallows These bird families closely resemble each other in appearance and behaviour – with swept back, crescent wings and a fast, swooping flight utilised to catch insects on the wing. However, they are not related. Swifts are more closely connected to hummingbirds than they are to swallows. There are 15 swift species in Brazil and 16 swallows. Most are confined to the Amazon regions but some species can be seen in the interior of Bahia – notably the **bank**, **barn** and **cliff swallows** and the **ashy-tailed swift**.

Tanagers This large, neotropical family of finch-like birds includes some of the most colourful species in Bahia. There are some 80 species in Brazil, some of which are migratory and a few of which are endemic to the Mata Atlântica. These include the beautiful **red-necked**, **seven-colored** and the **opal-rumped tanagers** – all endangered species. The **burnished-buff tanager** is a common sight in the Chapada Diamantina. Tanagers often form mixed-species flocks moving through the forest from fruit tree to fruit tree. A few follow army ants like antbirds and some like the euphonias are highly specialised, feeding principally on mistletoe.

Tinamous, guans and curassows This pheasant-like group of birds are among the first to be hunted out from primary forests and thus serve as indicator species of a habitats health. Tinamous are mottled or dull brown forest floor birds with haunting whoop-like calls. There are 24 species in Brazil. Guans are more turkey-like – often with brightly coloured throat flaps and crests. There are 22 species in Brazil, including the **Alagoas curassow** which lived in Alagoas state just north of Bahia until the 1980s but is now extinct in the wild and the endangered **red-billed curassow** in southern Bahia.

Toucans and barbets With their outsized beaks, distinctive sporadic flight pattern and bright colours, toucans are as iconic of South America as the big macaws. There are 40 species, all of them neotropical. Brazil has just over half, at 23. Big toucans like the **Toco toucan** (which was used for the Guinness adverts) or the **red-breasted toucan** are found principally in primary moist forests throughout Bahia and especially in the Mata Atlântica. Toucans are often mobbed by smaller birds, for whilst they are mainly fruit-eaters, they also raid nests and eat fledglings. Barbets are small, colourful birds with patches of red, orange, yellow and black. And whilst they bear little superficial resemblance to toucans they are relatives. The more brightly coloured males perform courting duets, with one bird singing a note, followed by the other, forming a seamless, lilting melody. There are 75 barbet species, four of which are found in Brazil. Like toucans, they are generally found in moist forests.

Trogons These brilliantly-coloured, chicken-sized rainforest birds are among the most spectacular tropical birds in the world. Brazil has nine species of a total 40 spread between the Americas, Africa and Asia. Trogons are easily recognised – especially the males – which have metallic green, blue or violet heads, back and chests and orange, red or buff breasts. Birds sit erect with their long and squared off tails pointing directly to the ground. Most trogons are forest species and are most easily seen in the Mata Atlântica.

Vireos and wood warblers There are 21 species of agile and elegant forest-living wood warblers in Brazil including seven migrants from North America and 14 vireos. After the house wren the **red-eyed vireo** is the most widespread bird species in the western hemisphere.

Waterbirds Bahia's internal wetlands (particularly around the Chapada Diamantina) and coastal mangroves are home to hundreds of waterbird species. These include the ubiquitous **neotropical cormorant** and the related anhinga which is similar but with a long, thin neck and some 21 species of herons and egrets. Look out for the distinctive little **blue herons** in the mangroves along the coast – you'll often see them with flocks of brilliant white **snowy egrets**, and the rarer **agami herons**, with dark-brown back feathers and a slender, sharp bill, in the swamp land around the Chapada Diamantina. There are some 24 species of duck in Brazil, half of which can be seen in Bahia. They include the South American endemic **Brazilian duck**, which looks like a teal with a brown back and turquoise wings. Terns, sandpipers, frigate birds and skimmers which ply the water with the long bottom bill of their beak are a common sight along the coast, alongside several kingfisher species, largest and commonest of which is the **ringed kingfisher**. A group of shorebirds live and migrate only between Central and South America. They are called endemic neotropical shorebirds, of which there are 27 endemic species, and two endemic families, the seed-snipes and the Magellanic plovers. Some of these can be seen in Bahia – most commonly the **southern lapwing** and the **tawny-throated dotterel**.

Woodpeckers and woodcreepers Almost a quarter of all the world's woodpeckers are Brazilian with some 46 species living throughout the country in an astonishing variety of colours. All the Bahian woodpeckers are forest dwelling and the best places to see them are the Chapada Diamantina and the Mata Atlântica. Almost all have flame-red heads. Woodpeckers use their bills for three things – drilling nest and sleeping holes in trees, digging through bark and wood to catch insects and for drumming against hollow wood to mark territory – with a characteristic rattle which can be heard for hundreds of metres.

Woodcreepers, 35 species of which live in Brazil, are dull brown forest birds perfectly camouflaged against tree trunks. They too use their bills to dig out insects from under tree bark.

Wrens These small, brown birds with characteristically upright, spring tails catch mosquitoes and gnats on the wing. There are 18 species in Brazil, many of which live in the cerrado and moist forests of Bahia. The tiny **house wren** has one of the greatest ranges of any perching bird in the world, nesting in houses and garages from Canada to southern Argentina.

CONSERVATION

NATIONAL PARKS, STATE PARKS AND PROTECTED AREAS
On paper Brazil has stringent environmental legislation and a large system of 299 protected areas covering some 8% of national territory – an area about the size of Texas, or 10% bigger than France. Brazil also claims to have the world's largest forested national park, the Tumucumac Park in Amapa state with 3.8 million hectares (9.39 million acres). On the ground, however, it is somewhat different, with the parks often being sanctuaries for criminals rather than wildlife. Hunting, poaching and deforestation are rife as none of the parks have rangers. Unscrupulous and influential coroneis in the remoter areas are accused of using national parks as their own private game and timber reserves. This situation has only recently begun to change with the exposure of a logging scandal involving the state governments and the federal environmental agency, IBAMA (Instituto Brasileiro do Meio Ambiente e dos Recursos Naturais Renováveis – the Brazilian Institute for the Environment and Renewable Natural Resources, www.ibama.com.br) in Brazil's southern Amazon and Central West in the early years of the millennium.

Brazil's own environment minister, Carlos Minc, has admitted that the country's nature reserves are grossly mismanaged, underfunded, and often ransacked by intruders. An internal study showed 57% have no permanent law enforcement officials, 76% have no management plan, and nearly one-third have no manager. 'We discovered a very serious problem and we called the public to show this ecological striptease', Mr Minc told a news conference in July 2008, adding that 'the current situation is not sustainable' and that in some years the rate of deforestation in protected areas of the Amazon had been higher than in unprotected areas. In the Bom Futuro or 'Good Future' National Park in northwestern Rondonia state, for instance, around 1,600 *garimpeiro* miners, farmers, loggers, and ranchers were plundering the natural resources.

INSTITUTO CHICO MENDES DE CONSERVAÇÃO DA BIODIVERSIDADE (ICMBio,
www.icmbio.gov.br) A division of the Environment Ministry, it administers many of the protected areas, which include the national parks (Parques Nacionais, or PARNA) in Brazil. Many of these are closed to the public and they form part of a complex and, generally, poorly managed system of protected areas which include estações ecológicas (ecological stations), reservas biológicas (biological reserves), reservas ecológicas (ecological reserves), áreas de relevante interesse ecológico

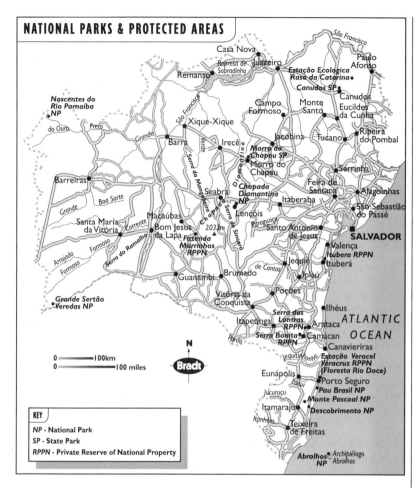

NATIONAL PARKS & PROTECTED AREAS

KEY

NP - National Park
SP - State Park
RPPN - Private Reserve of National Property

(areas of relevant ecological interest), áreas sob proteção especial (areas of special protection), and reservas particulares do patrimônio nacional (private national heritage reserves RPPNs). In all these entities, the exploitation of natural resources is completely forbidden. They are for research, education and recreation only. Three other types of entity are designed to allow the sustainable use of natural resources, while still preserving their biodiversity: Florestas Nacionais (National Forests), Áreas de Proteção Ambiental (Areas of Environmental Protection), Corredores Ecológicos (Ecological Corridors Project).

In addition there are state-protected bodies which include Parques Estaduais (State Parks).Bahia's protected areas are as follows (not all are open to the public):

Parque Nacional dos Abrolhos A marine park in southern Bahia covering 91,300ha protecting unique reef systems, seabird nesting grounds and humpback whale nurseries (see page 215).

Parque Nacional da Chapada Diamantina Covering 152,000ha and preserving caatinga, cerrado, wetlands and coastal rainforest. Fauna includes jaguar, puma, white-tailed deer and anteater (see pages 235–6).

Whilst Bahia is wonderful for birders, guiding at hotels is very rarely available and it is important to plan ahead – both by booking local guides (many of whom can organise an entire package including transport and hotels), to bringing the right equipment and field guides; neither of which are widely available in Brazil.

TOUR GUIDES Both international and domestic birding guides who know Bahia can be difficult to find. **Ciro Albano** (*www.nebrazilbirding.com*) is the best. He is the only uniquely northeast Brazil specialist and one of very few birders and wildlife guides to have grown up in the region and spent a childhood visiting the caatinga (in Ceará state). Ciro offers a Bahian birding tour on his site which includes some incredible private reserves in the Atlantic coastal forests and the western cerrado, offering the chance to see critically endangered species like the Bahia tapaculo. He also has access to harpy eagle nesting sites in the Atlantic coast forest near Porto Seguro. Andy and Nadime Whittaker's **Birding Brazil Tours** (*www.birdingbraziltours.com*) are another good company – though they are based in Manaus. The couple worked with the BBC Natural History Unit on David Attenborough's *Life of Birds* and are ground agents for a number of the major birding tour companies from the US and Europe. **Edson Endrigo** (*www.avesfoto.com.br*) is a São Paulo-based birding guide available for private tours for a minimum of four people. **Mark Andrews** of British-based Wildwings (*www.wildwings.co.uk*) offers excellent Brazil mammal and birding trips and is available for bespoke Bahian tours.

CONSERVATION PROJECTS Save Brasil (*www.savebrasil.org.br*) and **Birdlife International** (*www.birdlife.org*) have important bird-focused conservational projects in Bahia which benefit hugely from private support. They include the Serra das Lontras project (see page 23 and box on page 174). The US-based **Mangrove Action Project** (*www.mangroveactionproject.org*) are working to conserve Bahia's mangrove forests and the Abrolhos buffer zone.

For further reading lists and websites see pages 257–9.

DESTINATIONS AVAILABLE ON GUIDED TRIPS
Estação Biológica de Canudos and Raso da Catarina (see pages 248 and 8). Home to the deep indigo Lear's Macaw – one of the world's rarest parrots. During the winter months it is possible to visit roosting sites at sunrise and see more than 200 macaws leaving their nests. Other spectaculars are the endangered pectoral antwren, scarlet-throated tanager and blue-crowned parakeets.

Chapada Diamantina The Chapada offers a range of different habitats in one easily manageable area and is therefore an excellent birding destination with tracts of tropical, moist and gallery forests, wetland caatinga, cerrado and xeric alpine heathland. There are more than 350 bird species with Atlantic coastal, caatinga and cerrado species and endemics like the hooded visorbearer and the recently catalogued diamantina tapaculo and sincorá antwrens. See also page 236.

Parque Nacional do Descobrimento
Covering 21,129ha in the southern Bahian Atlantic coastal forests and not open to the public at present (though there is no restriction on access), fauna includes ocelot and many smaller primates.

Parque Nacional Grande Sertão Veredas
Straddling the Minas Gerais and Bahia border and protecting 83,363ha of cerrado and caatinga. Fauna includes jaguar.

Baixo-sul This Atlantic coastal montane forest reserve near Valença is administered by Birdlife International and their partner Save Brasil. It protects the critically endangered Bahiatapaculo.

Ituberá Private Reserve This 3,000ha private reserve owned by the Michelin Corporation can only be visited with Ciro Albano (see opposite). It is another of the last strongholds of the critically endangered Bahia tapaculo, which lives here alongside other rarities like Margaretta's hermit, Bahia spinetail and the least-pygmy owl.

Serra Bonita Private Reserve Another large private reserve in southern Bahia with large stands of forest with rarities including pink-legged graveteiro plumbeous antvireo, blue manakin and black-hawk eagle. Visit with Ciro Albano.

The Porto Seguro Atlantic coastal forests The Mata Atlântica forests close to the city are one of the last known nesting sites for harpy eagle in the Atlantic coastal forests. There are also rare banded and white-winged cotingas and red-browed parrot.

Serra das Lontras This 500ha stretch of montane Atlantic coastal forest is administered by Save Brasil and Birdlife International. The reserve is a refuge for nine globally threatened birds including the recently described pink-legged graveteiro, the Bahia tyrannulet which is new to science and two more new species which are currently in the process of being described.

Estação Veracruz and the Rio de Rio Jequitinhonha Delta at Belmonte The wildest major river delta in Bahia is a labyrinth of mangroves, gallery forests and stands of Atlantic coastal terra firma forest. Birdlife International has listed it as an Important Birding Area (IBA) for the Americas. Whilst the area has not been properly studied and there are no lists at present there have been confirmed sightings of very rare species like hook-billed hermit, blue-throated parakeet, golden-tailed parrotlet and band-tailed antwren. Part of the delta falls inside the Estação Veracruz – the largest private Atlantic rainforest reserve in Bahia with 6,069ha of *terra firma* primary forest and restingas. This is said to be the most reliable site in the world for banded and white-winged cotinga. Other birds include black-headed berryeater, ochre-marked parakeet, golden-tailed parrotlet, red-crowned Amazon, hook-billed hermit and golden-spangled piculet. A flock of 37 red-browed Amazon (*Amazona rhodocorytha*) was seen here in the 1990s and the station is the only location so far discovered on the Atlantic coast to have nesting harpy eagles. Visit with Portomondo travel in Porto Seguro, self-guided or with Ciro Albano on request.

Abrolhos Archipelago Whilst it is principally a destination for divers and whale-watchers the Abrolhos islands are also home to the largest colonies of relatively abundant sea birds, including red-billed tropicbird in southern Atlantic, brown noddy, brown and masked booby and sooty terns. Visiting is straightforward.

Parque Nacional de Monte Pascoal
Preserving 22,500ha of Atlantic coastal forest and restinga around the Monte Pascoal monolith with similar fauna to the adjacent Parque Nacional do Descobrimento. Currently disputed as Pataxó indigenous territory (see page 205).

Parque Nacional das Nascentes do Rio Parnaíba
Covering 729,800ha of cerrado forest and straddling the far east of Bahia and sections of Maranhão, Piauí and

In whole or in part, Bahia has five UNESCO-designated areas of global importance. Below is a summary of the reasons for their inclusion on the Heritage List.

DISCOVERY COAST ATLANTIC FOREST RESERVES (*UNESCO World Heritage Site*) The Discovery Coast Atlantic Forest Reserves, which stretch into neighbouring Espírito Santo state, are made up of eight separate protected areas totalling 112,000ha of coastal tropical forest and restinga shrub land. These forests form part of the Brazilian Mata Atlântica rainforests, which are the world's richest in terms of biodiversity. The Discovery Coast Atlantic Forest Reserves have a very high level of endemism – both in terms of flora and fauna and are highly threatened by industrial and agricultural development.

HISTORIC CENTRE OF SALVADOR DE BAHIA (*UNESCO World Heritage Site*) Salvador was Brazil's first capital, and from 1558, the first slave market in the New World. The city retains numerous outstanding Renaissance buildings with many brightly coloured houses decorated with intricate stucco-work.

CAATINGA (*UNESCO World Biosphere Reserve; 03°00' to 16°00'S; 35°30' to 44°00'W*) This Biosphere Reserve is comprised of xeric caatinga vegetation and 'Martius' (Silva aestu aphylla) deciduous forest. It forms an ecological corridor which connects the Mata Atlántica and Cerrado Biosphere Reserve of Central Brazil. Approximately 210,000 people – mostly subsistence farmers – live in the Biosphere Reserve. Many of them harvest caatinga plants which are thought locally to have medicinal properties. The

Tocantins state. Remote and difficult to access and with no infrastructure. Not open to the public (though there is no practical restriction on access).

Parque Nacional Pau Brasil Covering 11,538ha of Atlantic coastal forest and restinga near Arraial d'Ajuda in southern Bahia (see pages 206–7).

Parque Estadual da Serra do Conduru Protecting 9,275ha of Atlantic coastal rainforest on the coast between Itacaré and Ilhéus.

Parque Estadual Morro do Chapéu Covering 46,000ha around the headwaters of the Rio Paraguaçu near the Chapada Diamantina. Difficult to access and no infrastructure.

Parque Estadual de Canudos Protecting some 1,321ha near Canudos principally around the historic sites of the conflict with Antônio Conselheiro (see page 248).

Parque Estadual Sete Passagens Covering 2,821ha of the Chapada Norte near Miguel Calmon town. Difficult access and no infrastructure.

Estação Ecológica Raso da Catarina Covering 105,282ha of caatinga and cerrado near Paulo Afonso. Fauna includes the ultra-rare Lear's macaw, white-tailed deer and puma. The area is contiguous with a private reserve the RPPN Fazenda Flor de Lis, which covers a further 5,000ha.

Estação Biológica de Canudos Protecting some 160ha of caatinga with good birdlife near Canudos (see page 248).

reserve is managed by local and state government and a number of NGOs who are working to promote sustainable usage.

THE ESPINHAÇO RANGE (*UNESCO World Biosphere Reserve; 20° 18'S to 17° 00'S; 43° 40'W to 44° 08'W*) The Espinhaço Mountain Range which stretches from Belo Horizonte in Minas Gerais state, some 1,200km north through Bahia to the border of that state and neighbouring Pernambuco and Piauí. It varies in width from between three or four kilometres to over 100km and acts as a water divider between the São Francisco River basin and the rivers which drain directly into the Atlantic. It rises to 2,017 metres at its highest point and preserves a number of unique biomes, including 'rupestrian fields', which have been barely explored biologically and are thought to have at least 30% endemism. The biosphere reserve covers over three million hectares and in Bahia encompasses the Chapada Diamantina national park.

MATA ATLÂNTICA (ATLANTIC COASTAL RAINFOREST) BIOSPHERE RESERVE (*UNESCO World Biosphere Reserve; 02°50' to 33°45'S; 34°45' to 55°15'W*) The Mata Atlântica Biosphere Reserve, set up in 1992, protects 3,000km of coastal forests in 14 Brazilian states, including Bahia. Associated ecosystems include rainforests, mangroves, restinga, sand spits and upland grasslands which are under pressure from the largest cities in the country, including São Paulo, Salvador and Rio de Janeiro. The aim of the biosphere reserve is to conserve and restore both the forest and ecological corridors as connecting various biomes. The biological diversity of the Mata Atlântica is one of the richest in the world. In Bahia the reserve includes stretches of forest along the entire Bahian coast.

RPPN Fazenda Morrinhos Protecting 210.5ha of caatinga near Queimada in the far north east of the sertão (see page 248).

Serra das Lontras Privately owned and administered by Birdlife International. One of the best birding sites in Bahia (see box on page 174)

Estação Veracruz A Estação Veracruz A 6,000ha private reserve between Santa Cruz Cabrália and Porto Seguro.

See also box *Birdwatching in Bahia* on pages 20–1.

HISTORY

> All down the history of our nation the people have been prevented from having any say in the government of the country.
>
> Miguel Arraes

THE FIRST BRAZILIANS The history of Bahia is the history of Brazil and it is difficult to talk about one without the other. Furthermore, the story of pre-Columbian Brazil is inextricably connected with the history of the Americas, whose mystery only seems to be deepening with time. Indigenous artefacts made from perishable materials – *buriti* palm fronds, reeds and grasses from the caatinga – and a few isolated fragments of spear and arrowheads, charcoal deposits where fires once burned and cave paintings, remain to archaeologists working to transpose the clues of the past into a chronological ancient history.

Up until the 1990s, opinion on the origins of first people in the Americas had changed little since 1949 when Willard Libby invented radiocarbon dating. It seemed that none of the sites found in the Americas contained artefacts that dated further back than 11,200 years. Archaeologists were of the opinion that these were left behind by Siberian nomads who came to be known as the Clovis, after the distinctively bi-facially worked flint spear and arrowheads first found near Clovis, New Mexico. Archaeological remains showed that the Clovis people were hunter-gatherers who followed the migrations of herds of giant woolly mammoths, horses and camels over North America from the Yukon to Panama. The Clovis gradually settled and spread to the Pacific coast and north to the Arctic, becoming the ancestors of North American Indians and the Inuit. They also came to be considered the donor culture for South America.

The Clovis model tied in nicely with evidence from other sciences. Geologists had long known that northern Canada was covered in a great ice sheet 100,000 years ago that began to melt in about 11,000BC, exposing a land bridge at the Bering Straits between the Asian and the American continents. The model was widely accepted until the early 1980s, when new anthropological, genetic and linguistic analyses suggested that the Bering Straits migration had in fact occurred in three stages. The first wave of Siberian migrants, who crossed about 11,200 years ago, entering the Yukon and migrating south through the great plains east of the Rockies, became the Clovis. The second and third waves crossed many thousands of years later: the first group, who migrated southwest of the Rockies and settled on the North American Pacific coast, were ancestors of the Pacific Coast Indians, while the second populated the Arctic, making the Inuit the most recently arrived native Americans.

Controversy about colonisation In the 1990s, Brazilian and North American anthropologists working in the Amazon and in the sertão in Piaui state just north of Bahia began to seriously question the accepted Clovis model. Walter Neves at the University of São Paulo noted that American Indians have far too great a degree of physiological diversity to be descended solely from the Clovis. In 1992, a Brazilian team led by Anna Roosevelt, granddaughter of Teddy, unearthed evidence for a sedentary Amazon civilisation, based in caves at Monte Alegre, near Santarem in Brazil. These 'Pedra Pintada' Indians had been living off the rainforest about 11,000 years ago, making them roughly contemporary with the North American Clovis. However, the Pedra Pintada were very different; even at this early stage they lived more like the Indians who met the first conquistadors, foraging in the forest, making use of a wide variety of plants and animals, manufacturing rock tools and crafting triangular, and distinctly un-Clovis, spear points. Fastidious carbon dating has shown that they were also the first artists in the western hemisphere (the Pedra Pintada caves are so called because of their painted walls). In 1997, the year when Roosevelt's results were published, discoveries at Monte Verde, a peat bog in southern Chile, presented further problems for the Clovis model. The chunks of mammoth flesh, fossilised footprints, charcoal and bits of llama bone found here dated back more than 12,500 years – 1,100 years before the Clovis were meant to have arrived in the New World.

Findings in Ecuador and Peru in 1999 were equally surprising, suggesting that these coastal communities were trading with Central America, cultivating gourds, squash and maize, and living offshore at a time contemporary with Clovis. However, perhaps the most astonishing and controversial discoveries of all came from Brazil's Serra da Capivara – a desert escarpment just 100km north of the Bahian sertão and part of the ancient mountain range that includes the Chapada Diamantina. It was covered in rock art and littered with barely examined archaeological remains. In the late 1980s, Brazilian archaeologist Niéde Guidon began to investigate the Serra da Capivara, discovering a series of hearths, the earliest of which she dated to 46,000BC – by far the most ancient date for human occupation in the Americas. Critics, mainly from North America, pooh-poohed the research, stating that the hearths may in fact be a natural phenomenon, the result of seasonal brushwood fires. But they found it more difficult to dismiss dates obtained from calcite formations, which have covered the rock art from the Toca da Bastianna in the same location. Sampling of this deposit using thermoluminescence (TL dating) revealed a still astonishing date of 34,000BC.

The polite world of paleoarchaeology split into two camps: the traditionalists, who dismissed the dates as the products of poor analysis; and the new guard, who bridled at suggestions that scrupulous research was unscientific. Fierce debate began in Santa Fe in late 1999. The new guard were spurred on by surprise reinforcements: suppressed researchers spoke openly of 40,000-year-old flakes of mammoth bone, of ignored flints from a pre-Clovis age and of articles and requests for research grants rejected by 'the Clovis mafia'. Despite these setbacks, it is now accepted that there were pre-Clovis civilisations in South America before there were Clovis civilisations in the North. Dates for Monte Verde in Chile and Pedra Pintada are now also largely accepted and it is probably only a matter of time before archaeologists agree that the earliest Americans so far documented lived in the Brazilian sertão; perhaps even in Bahia, which has as many (as yet unanalysed) cave sites similar to those just across the state frontier in Piauí.

BAHIA AT THE TIME OF CONQUEST Next to nothing is known about these pre-Clovis inhabitants of the sertão. What is certain is that the painted rock shelters that dot the region were later occupied by a succession of different peoples. By the time the Portuguese arrived in southern Bahia in 1502, Brazil was a vast continent of nations, with indigenous peoples of various genetic and linguistic make-ups engaged in constant skirmishes with each other. Some were probably descendants of those first Brazilians, others of migrants who had entered the continent through Central America. Likewise, Bahia was dominated by a number of different groups. Like the Spanish in Peru and Mexico, the Portuguese arrived in Brazil at a propitious moment. The coast was in the final stages of being conquered by a wave of war-like Tupi-speaking nations, a score of whom occupied almost the entire coast, including Bahia. Only pockets of other, older nations remained, known collectively as Tapuia or 'people of the strange tongue'. In Bahia the Tupi conquerors were principally Tupinambá, and different factions of their tribal groups were engaged in almost constant cycle of vendettas that revolved around kidnapping and cannibalism. The eating of a prisoner from another tribe was an intolerable insult which demanded revenge; involving a retaliatory raid, highly ritualised murder and cannibalism. The inter-tribal wars were to bring downfall to the Tupinambá who readily enlisted Europeans as allies against enemies. Unsurprisingly, their cannibalistic practices also provided the Europeans with 'moral justification' for enslaving them and the vast majority of non-Tupi-speaking indigenous Brazilians who lived in the interior and the sertão.

THE PORTUGUESE It seems incredible today that a tiny nation like Portugal (which had a population of a little over one million at the time) could have dominated so much of the early Renaissance globe. Before Brazil there were Portuguese colonies and trading stations in Japan, Thailand, Macau, all around the African coast and even in Australia. The Portuguese owed much of their success to the Muslims, who they had expelled from their country after a long campaign in the 13th century (more than 200 years before Spain). The defeat of the Muslims was carried to north Africa with the conquest of Ceuta and Tangiers in modern Morocco. This brought a taste for colonisation and new knowledge: maps of the coast of Africa, mathematical skills and navigational techniques unknown to the rest of Europe and designs for ocean-going ships. These were adapted and developed by one of Europe's least-heralded Renaissance men – Prince Henry the Navigator, grandson of England's John of Gaunt, who set up a university for navigation in Sagres on the far southwestern corner of Portugal and Europe. Henry developed the first modern sailing ship, the caravel ('steering nearer to the wind'), which unlike the heavy contemporaneous Mediterranean barges was agile, strong and easy to navigate, with lateen triangular sails allowing luffing and a greater capacity to tack. The caravel was small enough to sail upriver in shallow coastal waters. With the lateen sails attached, it could go fast over shallow water and take deep wind; and with square sails attached it was by far the fastest ship of its time and was strong enough to cross oceans. With caravels the Portuguese discovered the world and with their next ship, the larger nau, they brought spices, tea and silks to Europe from Asia and the Indian Ocean.

It was on an expedition to the Indies around the newly navigated Cape of Good Hope that a minor nobleman Pedro Álvares Cabral and his fleet of 13 ships was blown far off course to the extreme west of the Azores and chanced upon Brazil. The first sight of land was on the 21 April 1500 – a high boulder mountain in southern Bahia which they named Monte Pascoal ('Easter Mountain') and which the Portuguese soon saw was surrounded by lush forest. Cabral ordered one of his captains Nicolau Coelho to make landfall. First contact was made immediately. Chronicler Pero Vaz de Caminha wrote:

> We caught sight of men walking on the beaches ... they were dark and entirely naked, with nothing to cover their private parts, and carried bows and arrows in their hands. Nicolau Coelho made a sign to them to lay down their bows, and they laid them down. He could not speak with them there … because of the breaking of the sea on the shore. He merely threw them a [four-cornered] red hat, and a linen [conical cap] he was wearing on his head and a black hat. One of them gave him a headdress of long feathers with a small tuft of red and grey feathers like those of a parrot. Another gave him a string of very small white beads which looked like seed pearls.

Cabral spent nine days navigating the coast of Brazil – during which time he held the first mass on Brazilian soil and planted a huge wooden cross on the shore, christened the new land Terra da Veracruz (Country of the True Cross) and departed, leaving the locals with flagons of wine and two weeping convicts under sentence of death who had been brought on the voyage with the intention of using them to begin intermarriage and acculturation with any suitable natives the fleet might encounter. Such was the first encounter. And whilst it seemed innocent enough, it was propitious. Religion, miscegenation (inter breeding) and later slavery would be the means by which Portugal would conquer Brazil.

The noble savage Vaz de Caminha's descriptions of Bahia, and the fleet's cargo of dye-wood logs, brought sufficient interest for the Portuguese to send a second fleet to Brazil, commanded by Gonçalo Coelho and including Amerigo Vespucci (who would give his name to the continent) as a chronicler. After navigating some 3,200km of coast, Coelho reported that Veracruz contained nothing of use but trees whose sawdust produced a brilliant red dye of a colour fashionable in contemporary Flanders. Portuguese merchants set up a small trade, with six ships a year sent to the new land. They called the wood Pau-Brasil and such was the unimportance of Veracruz to Europe that it became known in common parlance merely as Brasil, and its people Brasileiros – workers of what the Portuguese had termed brasilwood. By 1503 the trade had become sufficiently lucrative for a small number of French ships to visit Brazil. The trade depended entirely on the indigenous Brazilians who were happy to fell and cut the wood in exchange for axes and other metal tools. For the first three decades of the 16th century the Europeans treated the locals largely with a mix of courtesy and curiosity.

A decade after discovery, the Brazilians had begun to visit Europe – some as slaves brought unwillingly by the Portuguese, but many as free men intrigued by the promise of life in a new land. Tupinikin natives, from southern Bahia, were received at the court of King Manoel I in 1513, and in 1531 William Hawkins of Plymouth brought back a Tupinikin chief to England where he lived for a year and was entertained by Henry VIII at Whitehall. Another chieftan's son, Binot, settled in France and married a Frenchwoman, whilst dozens of Norman men did the opposite in Brazil, some of them purportedly even practising cannibalism.

Early accounts of the Brazilians – especially by non-Portuguese – were highly idealised. Amerigo Vespucci wrote what became a widely circulated letter to Piero Lorenzo de' Medici in 1503 declaring that the Brazilians were beautiful, innocent, free and liberated. Their communities, he said, functioned harmoniously – free of kings, religion, private property and the constraints of sexual morality. His and other, mostly French, accounts almost entirely omitted any mention of cannibalism or the vicious inter-tribal wars between the Tupi groups. They were to inspire Rousseau's musings on the noble savage; and to foster a stereotype of happy-go-lucky, sexually liberated Brazilians which persists to this day.

The first settlements   Despite the brasilwood trade, the new land's lack of obvious mineral wealth or spice meant that the attention it received from Portugal was very much secondary to the spice trade with the Far East. However, as the wood trade grew, the early days of peaceful barter soon degenerated into bloodshed and exploitation, fostered by an increasingly bitter rivalry between the French and Portuguese traders. The Portuguese regarded Brazil as their land, given to them by Pope Alexander VI under the Treaty of Tordesillas of 7 June 1494, which divided the newly discovered lands outside Europe between Spain and Portugal along a meridian 370 leagues west of the Cape Verde islands. The French saw no reason to halt a trade which was earning them money, so the Portuguese began to dispatch warships to sink French trading vessels. The French were furious, Captain Jean Parmentier writing:

> The Portuguese must have drunk the dust of King Alexander to show such
> exaggerated ambition… they… have no right to prevent French merchants from
> landing in lands that they have abrogated, in which they have not planted the
> Christian faith and are neither loved nor obeyed.

The Portuguese clearly accepted his point for in 1530 they sent a fleet of five ships, captained by Martin Afonso de Sousa, to found a colony in Brazil and claim it for Portugal once and for all. Afonso's fleet cruised along the Brazilian coast for two years, ransacking French ships and warehouses. In March 1531 they discovered the Portuguese Diogo Álvares at Itaparica in the Baía de Todos os Santos, a Portuguese sailor who had been shipwrecked at the beginning of the century and who had so impressed the Tupinambá with his arquebus (an early portable gun mounted on a tripod) that he had been given an indigenous name, Caramuru, married the daughter of the chief, Paraguaçu, and been given some 300 warriors to command. Afonso left behind some colonists near Caramuru's land, together with cattle and crops, and their plantation would later become the city of Cachoeira (see pages 150–4). Afonso built his principal settlement at São Vicente, 1,600km to the south, in modern São Paulo state in 1532. And from here, under the instructions of King João III of Portugal, he divided the entire Brazilian coast into 14 captaincies, each spanning from 160–650km of coastline and awarded one to each of a selection of chosen subjects or donatories. Each captain was granted substantial powers, which included the right to wage war and enslave the indigenous people, put to death slaves and colonists and export any product except brasilwood.

The captaincy of Bahia was granted to a veteran soldier and favourite of King João, Francisco Pereira Coutinho, who arrived in the Baía de Todos os Santos in 1535 and began distributing land titles to his crew of brigands and fortune-hunting ex-soldiers. The Tupinambá who were friends or tribal compatriots of Caramuru helped with construction of the buildings including a fortified tower and a settlement fit for over 100 Portuguese colonists. However, as the settlement became more established the rapacious appetite of the Portuguese for land and labour increased and problems began.

Bahia's was a story that was repeated throughout the captaincies. The first generation of Brazilian Indians had been so enchanted by metal tools that they had been happy to fell brasilwood and grant food on a barter system. But their children were less interested. Brasilwood trees were now scarcer along the coast and the labour required to reach and transport them far greater. Besides, by now the Brazilians had enough metal tools and could see little need to accumulate more than they could use. One Jesuit chronicler in Pernambuco observed that the Brazilians 'used to sell a slave for a chisel containing a pound of iron, and also used to sell their sons and daughters and would even sell themselves as slaves'. There should be a ban on any supply of tools to heathen Brazilians he said, because:

> Indians who formerly were nobodies and always dying of hunger through not having enough axes to clear the roças now have as many tools and roças as they want and eat and drink continually.

Coutinho and the other donatories planted sugar cane as a cash crop in their new territories. Sugar cane originated in Bengal but had long been grown by the Iberians. Stands were brought in from Madeira, which was at the time the Western world's largest producer of sugar. *Engenhos* – water-powered mills – were built on the contemporaneous state-of-the-art Madeira model, and all that was lacking was a large manual workforce. However, the Tupinambá refused to work. Producing more than they could consume and working for someone else's profit was as alien to their culture as cannibalism was to the Portuguese; sugar cane was an unknown and therefore valueless food crop to them and agriculture was regarded as demeaning woman's work. When the barter system for labour ran dry the Portuguese began to ransack villages and forcibly enslave the Brazilians, killing all those who resisted.

Brazil is born at Salvador In Tupi eyes, the Europeans had changed from curious aliens with wonderful tools to uncouth barbarians who violated hospitality, attacked local beliefs and used Brazilians as labourers and whores. Widespread fighting broke out throughout Brazil including Bahia. The Tupinambá burnt Pereira Coutinho's crops and mill and forced him to flee from the Baía de Todos os Santos in 1545. Even Portuguese-turned-native Diogo Álvares (Caramuru) and his 300 warriors couldn't prevent it. The donatory of Porto Seguro suffered a similar fate. When Coutinho attempted to return two years later he and all his crew except Caramuru (who fled to France with his Tupinambá wife) were killed and ritually eaten. The death blow to the donatory's skull was delivered by the five-year-old son of a chief who Coutinho had put to death for insubordination a few years previously.

The King of Portugal's response was to declare that a new capital – to govern all the captaincies of Brazil – would be established on the Baía de Todos os Santos. In 1549 he sent another ex-soldier, Tomé de Sousa, as its governor, with a fleet of a thousand mercenaries and colonists, whose number was dominated by 'New Christians' – Jews and Arabs forced to convert to Christianity under the threat of the Dominican-led Catholic Inquisition. They were accompanied by a coterie of clerics, including a band of fierce Jesuits led by the charismatic Manoel de Nobrega. King João gave his governor clear instructions. The Tupinambá should be converted to Christianity: 'Therefore treat all who are peaceful well, favour them always, and do not consent to any oppression or insult being done to them.' He ordered the governor to stop the slaving raids along the Brazilian coast, 'for the heathen rebel [sic] because of this and make war on the Christians, and this has been the main cause of the damage done to us up to now'. Trade would be carried out through weekly markets and colonists would be prohibited from consorting with Brazilians at any other time. Tomé de Sousa was to punish any Tupinambá whom he deemed enemies of the Portuguese, 'destroying their villages and settlements, and killing and enslaving whatever part of them you consider sufficient to act as a punishment and an example'. The remainder should be pardoned on the condition that they accepted voluntary slavery. The king also ordered the construction of large numbers of sugar mills.

Tomé de Sousa arrived in the Baía de Todos os Santos on 29 March 1549. Caramuru, who had now returned from France, chose the location for the new capital of Salvador, on a cliff above a sheltered bay that formed a natural harbour, which the governor cleared of its three Tupinambá villages before beginning construction. The new capital of Portuguese imperial Brazil was formally declared on 1 November 1549 (see page 122).

The Massacres of Mem de Sá The Portuguese king's words would set the course of Brazilian history over the next hundred or so years. They were interpreted entirely in the Portuguese favour. Converted Indians were herded into vast colleges called *reductions*, which were run all over Brazil by Jesuits and which turned the catechised Indians into model Christians, but without the authority to make even simple decisions about their own lives or to ascend the Jesuit ecclesiastical hierarchy when they became priests. However, at least on the reductions they were safe from the plantation owners, who enslaved much of the rest of the population with the collusion of the governor and under the precept that as they didn't accept Christianity they were enemies. The system was of course unacceptable to the Bahian Tupi peoples and to indigenous people throughout Brazil, who became increasingly hostile and bellicose.

It was the third governor – the brilliant administrator and ruthless soldier Mem de Sá – who finally crushed them. Mem de Sá's retaliatory campaigns were brutal. He defeated the Tamoio and their French allies in nascent Rio de Janeiro – destroying the Gallic dream of Le France Antartique – and he conducted a scorched-earth campaign in Bahia. One of his soldiers, Vasconcellos, wrote of one devastating attack on a Tupinikin tribe near Ilhéus. The Indians had avenged the murder of two of their number with the killing of two local Portuguese:

When those savages considered themselves most secure, our men charged in and fell upon them, beheading, wounding and throwing to the ground every living being, men, women and children. Some passed directly from the sleep of night into the sleep of death; others attempted to flee, but ran towards us and fell into our hands .... The forests burned for many leagues and the night was turned into clear day. But when the sun began its day the sad barbarians could see better the magnitude of their slaughter. Parents found their children, and husbands their wives by following trails of blood. For all lay dead beside the paths and the shelter of their hiding-places was turned to ashes.

Fresh slaves for the plantations After the ethnic cleansing of the Tupi people and the ravages of European disease on their population the Portuguese were faced once more with no labour for their sugar mills – which by 1590 numbered 40 or 50 in Bahia alone. So they turned to the interior of Brazil, where expeditions of flag-bearing slave raiders or *bandeirantes* wandered the vast forests and savannas with armies of acculturated Tupi-speaking Indians in search of indigenous villages to ransack and mines to exploit. Indians who had never seen a European were woken in the middle of the night to see their women and children murdered before being themselves shackled and marched through the forests for weeks to a shocking new life cutting sugar cane. Only the Jesuits protected them. The great Bahian preacher, Father Antônio Vieira, travelled throughout Brazil denouncing the *bandeirante* slave trade. He was appalled by what he saw, particularly on the Amazon, and wrote eloquently of the Indians' plight in a series of letters to King João IV:

> ... when people who are not our subjects do not wish to leave their lands this is called rebellion here. And this crime is considered worthy of punishment by war and enslavement.

He preached hellfire sermons from Bahia to Belem and Maranhão, where the *bandeirante* raids were among the worst.

> What is a human soul worth to Satan? There is no market on earth where the devil can get them more cheaply than right here in our own land .... What a cheap market! An Indian for a soul .... Christians, nobles, people of Maranhão, break the chains of injustice and free those whom you hold captive and oppressed!

In 1661 Vieira's work came to an abrupt end when an infuriated mob ransacked the Jesuit college in Belem and succeeded in having the priests expelled from both Pará and Maranhão. It was the beginning of the end for Jesuits. Vieira died in Salvador in disgrace after a piece of vicious calumny (see page 124) and the Society increasingly lost its once formidable power and influence. Less than a hundred years later the governor of Portugal, the Marquis de Pombal, began a campaign that eventually led to the Jesuits being expelled from Portuguese Brazil in 1757, and all the Iberian colonies ten years later. After this, legislation was introduced by Pombal and his half-brother, the Maranhão governor Mendonça Furtado, proclaiming the Indians free and slavery illegal. But the directorate system which replaced the Jesuit reductions was the administrative equivalent of putting a fox in charge of the hen coop. Soon there were so few Indians left to enslave in Brazil that the Portuguese had to find a new continent to terrorise; they began to ship in Africans from Angola and Guinea Bissau.

The Africans The Portuguese had been involved with African slavery since they'd been sailing caravels. (Guanche (from the Canary Islands) and African slaves worked the mills on Madeira and many Africans worked as servants in wealthy houses in Lisbon.) But only when the Brazilian sugar and tobacco plantations ran out of coastal Tupi slaves did they start to trade in large numbers. The increase in shipments of African slaves to Brazil – particularly Bahia, Pernambuco and Rio de Janeiro – began in earnest in the 17th century. By the time slavery was abolished in the late 19th century, Portugal had made some 30,000 slaving voyages transporting more than 4,650,000 Africans, mostly to Brazil. This is more than double the number of voyages undertaken (and almost double the number of Africans enslaved) by the next largest trading country, Britain, and well over ten times the number of slaves brought to the United States.

In Bahia, the transition from a predominantly indigenous slave force to a predominantly African one occurred gradually over the course of around 50 years. The shift can be seen by looking at the changes in slave numbers in individual *engenhos*. At the end of the 16th century, for instance, Engenho Sergipe (which was the biggest mill in Bahia and which was largely owned by the governor's family) had 280 adult slaves, 20 of whom were African. By 1638 the *engenho* had 81 slaves, all of whom were African or Afro-Brazilian (*caboclo*).

Africans were not just more available, they were more resistant to European disease and they were far more productive than the indigenous Brazilians. Africans possessed the skills required to cut and mill cane and they could withstand the back-breaking hard work and intolerably long hours required. Many came from African nations with a long tradition of agriculture, metalworking and skilled artisanship. By the end of the 17th century African slaves had become the engine that ran Bahia, and not just on the plantations. Africans and Afro-Brazilians built the towns and cities, decorated the Baroque churches and were even recruited for the *bandeirante* expeditions. However, they were abominably treated for their labour. 'In the northern provinces,' wrote Thomas Ewbank, an American visitor in the 1850s, 'it is no uncommon thing to tie their hands and feet together; hoist them off the ground and beat them as near to death as possible.' The tortures were carried out even if they did as they were told – just to ensure that they kept doing so. Slaves were often killed in the cruellest fashion if they were insubordinate.

TROUBLE WITH THE DUTCH With the natives quelled and enslaved Africans ensuring huge profit margins on the *engenhos*, Salvador and Bahia and its neighbour to the north, Pernambuco, grew increasingly wealthy in the 17th century. Salvador, Porto Seguro, Ilhéus and the cities of the Recôncavo received handsome European city centres, and as wealthy landowners competed with each other in shows of ostentation, the churches they sponsored became ever more gilt and lavish. Brazil began to attract attention from other European imperial powers, most notably the Dutch.

The Dutch were the middlemen of Europe in the early Renaissance. Dutch merchants had been travelling to Lisbon to buy exotic Asian imports from Portuguese traders since the first caravels had taken their first spice voyages to Indonesia and Thailand, then selling the goods at a healthy profit in northern Europe. The situation changed when the Spanish monarchy became the rulers of Portugal through the accession of Philip II to the throne in 1581 after the death of King Cardinal Henrique the Chaste in 1580. Holland was the enemy of Spain and in 1585 Philip II ordered all Dutch vessels anchored in his ports to be confiscated and their crews imprisoned, an act of aggression he repeated in 1590, 1595 and 1599. Holland's wealth came entirely from trade within Europe. But far from bringing the Dutch to his knees as he had hoped, Philip inadvertently made them far more powerful. Intrepid Dutch shipwrights copied and perfected Spanish and Portuguese boat designs, built a merchant fleet and sailed to buy goods at source in the Far East. In 1602 the Dutch East India Company was founded on a stockholder model which would later be emulated by the British and the Americans and lead to the birth of modern capitalism. By the 1620s the company and the Netherlands itself had become so profitable that the Dutch were the most formidable naval power in northern Europe. Dutch investors began to look beyond Asia and in 1621 formed the Dutch West Indies Company – ostensibly to trade with the Americas from Newfoundland to Tierra del Fuego – and with Africa, but in reality to privateer. The Dutch government authorised the company to build forts in the designated regions, to make treaties with the local peoples and to appoint local administrative officials and clerks. In 1623 the company started to put together an expeditionary force bound for Bahia.

On 9 May 1624 a fleet of 26 ships with 500 cannons and a crew of 1,600 mercenaries arrived in the Baía de Todos os Santos to lay claim to Bahia. The Bahians fled their crumbling fortresses in panic, leaving burning Portuguese cargo ships full of sugar and brazilwood behind them. By dawn on 10 May all the clergy and populace but for the governor and a handful of attendants, had deserted the city. The latter were imprisoned and sent to Holland and a Dutch governor, Johannes van Doorth took over. But the Dutch occupation was short-lived; the invaders were contained within the city by an insurgency during which van Doorth was killed. The following year the Portuguese sent a huge fleet of ships from Pernambuco and Cape Verde to recapture Salvador, together with an army of some 12,000 soldiers. After their failed conquest the Dutch resorted to piracy, sacking ports and wreaking havoc on merchant ships from the Caribbean to Argentina. In 1628, Pieter Heyn captured a huge Spanish flotilla off Cuba and netted more than 14 million florins – twice the Dutch West Indies Company's original capital. The following year the Dutch conquered Pernambuco, renaming the capital Recife Mauristaad after the capable Dutch captain John Maurice of Nassau. He was an enlightened governor by the standards of the Portuguese, encouraging the arts (Dutch painters like Franz Post spent many years in Mauristaad), declaring an amnesty for all 'New Christians' in the city, who were free to practise Judaism and Islam openly once more. Dutch-occupied Pernambuco extended its influence and dominance of the sugar trade throughout northeastern Brazil, including Bahia. The invaders were formally defeated in 1661.

GOLD AND THE RISE OF RIO In 1695 on the Rio das Velhas in the present-day state of Minas Gerais, gold was discovered in significant quantities. There were further discoveries throughout Minas and in neighbouring Goiás – they would have a far-reaching effect on Bahia. Over the next 60 years, the Portuguese gold rush saw Brazil's population more than double, with nearly 600,000 fortune hunters arriving. Almost all of them headed for the country's southeast. Mining overtook sugar to become Portugal's principal source of wealth and political influence, and national identity shifted away from Salvador to another city built on a vast bay – Rio de Janeiro. As the gold rush grew, the *engenhos* increasingly suffered. Enslaved Africans and supplies in general were increasingly expensive, and as Rio became the main port of entry for the entire country, Salvador lost its monopoly and the richest pickings.

Meanwhile Portugal itself was in economic crisis. The Dutch, French and British had long overtaken the Iberians as the principal powers in Europe, with better and faster ships and a larger trade monopoly. Portugal was increasingly left behind. By the mid-18th century it was hugely in debt to its biggest creditor, Britain. Determined to ring every last sovereign out of the mines and regain their former grandeur, the Portuguese ruled over Brazil with ruthless autocracy. Whilst the gold rush brought more integration to Brazil – with the opening up of large tracts in the interior and the establishment of horse trails from Salvador to São Paulo through the sertão and Minas, mining and the passage of goods were tightly controlled. Almost everything of value entered and left Brazil through Rio de Janeiro where it was exorbitantly taxed. In 1763, in an effort to control wealth ever more minutely, the Portuguese shifted the vice-royalty of Brazil from Salvador to Rio. It was a huge blow for Bahia, which slipped into gradual economic decline which has continued to this day.

Portugal runs away from Europe The increasing autocracy of the Portuguese, and the French and American revolutions of the late 18th century, fomented rebellion in Brazil. In the last decade of the century, a group of radical liberals from the mining towns of Minas Gerais, called Inconfidencia Mineira, aimed at full independence from the crown but this ended in the public execution of most of its leaders. There were similar events in Bahia, bitter at its loss of influence to Rio and with an economy in steady decline: sugar from the Dutch Antilles, Guyana and British Caribbean was cheaper and more efficiently produced and cotton, brought in as a replacement, was equally uncompetitive. Like much of the northeast, the state had fallen into poverty and insurrection, with a series of unsuccessful revolutionary movements like the Conjuração dos Alfaiates. This was a grassroots movement akin to the Inconfidencia Mineira, spurred on by a group of Salvador freemasons called the Cavaleiros da Luz (Knights of Light). The cavaleiros held secret meetings where they discussed the overthrow of colonialism and its replacement with a Republican government based on North American liberal principles. They produced pamphlets that were distributed on the streets of Salvador and which earned them widespread support among the working classes, particularly freed slaves. The movement was brutally suppressed by the Portuguese, who imprisoned, tortured and executed the knights and scattered their butchered remains in the streets of Salvador. And then, at the height of discontent, when Brazil was on the verge of rising against the Portuguese, a strange quirk of fate made the two countries literally inseparable, when its monarchy was forced to move to Brazil.

Portugal, tucked away at the far corner of Europe, had been spared the ravages of Napoleon Bonaparte who had taken control of Spain during the first few years of the 19th century. But after his defeat at the Battle of Trafalgar, Napoleon was determined to close Europe to Britain, so he turned his eyes to its trading partner, Portugal, and the British monarchy's oldest allies – the weak and ineffectual house of Bragança. This was headed at the time by the Prince Regent, João – a shy recluse who spent much of his time singing Gregorian chants. João's ministers assured him that resistance to Napoleon was useless, so in November 1807 – with the offer of British protection – the entire Portuguese royal family abandoned their frightened and bemused subjects and left for Brazil, guarded by British warships. It must have been quite a sight. Crowds thronged around the muddy docks whilst the Portuguese court and government boarded some 40 ships, carrying with them the crown jewels, royal library, carriages, horses and full retinue. Mad old Queen Maria, Empress of Portugal and its colonies, was convinced she was being taken to the guillotine and made a hysterical scene on the quayside before being forcibly carried aboard by her courtiers and her grandson Pedro.

So was born imperial Brazil. It was a poor experiment from the start. The British exacted a high price for their help. Under the Treaty of Methuen, signed the following year, all of Portugal's ports were 'opened to friendly nations' – in other words the British. The trade monopoly over Brazil – held until then by the Portuguese crown – was broken and Portugal and its colonies effectually became part of the British Empire. An estimated £200 million in gold left Brazil for England before the end of the 19th century and the imperial Brazilian currency and banking system would be managed by the British for their own advantage, with a systematic spiral of devaluation which made Brazilian goods very cheap for the English market and British goods very expensive for the Brazilians. Further increasing Portugal's economic decline, the imperial government had to borrow money from British banks to buy British goods, which they were required to import.

Nonetheless the Portuguese spared no expense in creating their new imperial capital, which grew in grandeur and opulence until it soon eclipsed what was still Brazil's most ostentatious city until that point, Salvador. New palaces were built to house the royal family and their 15,000 newly arrived nobleman attendants. Neoclassical administrative buildings, libraries and theatres were constructed for their places of work and entertainment. Thousands of slaves were imported to pamper them and a city which had been a relative global backwater was soon thriving. Rio was visited by only 90 ships in 1807, but by some 400 the following year. Whole neighbourhoods built on the European model sprang up to cater for the city's burgeoning merchant class.

King João loved his new homeland, but after Napoleon was defeated at the Battle of Waterloo he became increasingly uneasy about the governance of Portugal itself and, under pressure from Britain who wished to avoid another European revolution, determined to return to Lisbon. He appointed his dashing, Byronic young son Pedro as Regent of Brazil and left him behind with his plain Austrian wife and bevy of adoring mistresses. Pedro was delighted and, realising that weak Portugal was in no position to prevent Brazil's independence, wasted little time in declaring it. In September 1822 on a journey between São Paulo and Rio he uttered his famous Grito de Ipiranga call to arms: 'Independence or Death!' he exclaimed, tearing the Portuguese insignia off his uniform and instructing his soldiers to do the same. 'By the blood that flows in my veins and upon my honour, I swear to God to free Brazil.'

INDEPENDENCE, REBELLION AND THE DEATH OF THE SLAVE TRADE The Grito de Ipiranga spread like a shock wave through Brazil. In Bahia, Cachoeira became the seat of the campaign against the Portuguese, who were ousted from Salvador and Ilhéus. Whilst blood was spilt, Brazil was the only country in Latin America to have a relatively smooth transition to independence, which was recognised by Britain and Portugal in 1825. Pedro and his son Pedro II ruled Brazil from Rio de Janeiro for 67 years, doing little to change the country but much to transform Rio from a port town to a proper capital city on the French model, and into one of the continent's cultural centres. Countless theatres, public parks and spaces and grand neoclassical buildings were constructed, fountains were imported from Vienna, statues commissioned and the city's growing elite enjoyed a charmed life. Wealthy Cariocas imported European furniture and paintings, china and porcelain, employed private French chefs and spent evenings at the opera. But the wealth was for but a few – most of Brazil was poor or enslaved.

The injustice was felt acutely in Bahia, where the revolutionary mood continued. Slaves rebelled in the Recôncavo throughout the imperial period, and in 1835 black Soterpoletanos nearly took over the city during the Revolta dos Malês (Muslim Revolt). General discontent in Salvador had resulted in ever greater polarisation between the now tiny elite and the growing black, poor majority. With increased poverty came even rougher justice for Africans and Afro-Brazilians, both enslaved and freed, who were prohibited from worshipping in *terreiros*, churches or mosques. African Muslims from neighbouring Espírito Santo had seen their mosque razed to the ground in Vitória. Fearing the same in Salvador, a group of black Muslims prohibited from worshipping stood up to the authorities and organised a mutiny on 25 January 1835. They planned to abolish slavery and Africanise Bahia, ethnically cleansing all whites from the state. The Malês were supported by rapidly swelling numbers of Afro-Brazilians and had it been better organised would surely have overthrown Bahia, but precipitous action by a few firebrands alerted the Guarda Nacional – troops set up to keep civic order – who acted swiftly and with the customary mercilessness, crushing the rebellion and killing all the ringleaders and many innocents besides.

The rebellion occurred 28 years after Britain had passed the Abolition of the Slave Trade Act, which outlawed the Atlantic slave trade and led three years later to all slaves in the British Empire being declared free. These events fuelled a burgeoning abolitionist movement in Brazil, which in Bahia was led by intellectuals like the poet Castro Alves (see *Chapter 3*, page 128). Yet even in 1870 there were still slave markets in Brazil and over 1.5 million slaves. Emperor Dom Pedro II introduced the 'lei do ventre livre', by which children born to slaves would be declared free in 1871, and slavery in Brazil was finally outlawed under pressure from the emperor in March 1888. Brazil was the last country in the Western world to abolish slavery. Abolitionism made Dom Pedro deeply unpopular with the coffee and mining aristocracy who were descendants of the first Portuguese and who now controlled the country. Eighteen months after the act was passed, the army deposed Dom Pedro and declared Brazil a republic, complete with a contemporary motto – Ordem e Progresso. Government was based loosely on the US model. The constitution created a republic of 20 states with their own governors and extensive powers of self-government and three elected representatives (*senadores*) in an upper house or senate and a varying number of elected representatives – depending on state population (*deputados*) – in a chamber of deputies; the two together formed the congress. Literate males (who numbered around 3% of the population) had the right to vote. The Church and the state were separated.

THE NEW REPUBLIC Despite its lofty principles, in contrast to the United States or Mexico, independent, republican Brazil was a backward place. Little seemed to have changed since the Portuguese had been ousted. There was no industry – Brazil now earned its money from growing coffee – and the elite who ran the country – whilst nominally republican – were monarchical in attitudes and feudal in practice. Republican Brazil was run by an oligarchy of wealthy coffee-baron families (*patrias*) supported by a network of gangster-like feudal landlords or *coroneis*. The majority of Brazilians were not even seen as chattels; they were ignored altogether. At least in the southeast, where in an act of disgraceful cynicism which sowed the seeds of inequality that plague the country today, the *patrias* chose neither to allow their former slaves to stay in the *senzalas* (their plantation-hut homes) nor to grant them employment (in the jobs they had been performing for generations). Instead they decided to bring in new blood by running state-sponsored advertising campaigns which promised work on prosperous coffee plantations in São Paulo and Rio to Spanish, Portuguese, German and Japanese peasants. Boatloads arrived to a strange shore and a system of debt peonage (bonded labour) that they refused to tolerate. The Afro-Brazilians were left to fend for themselves or fester in Brazil's first slums.

Bahia was too poor to court Europe and like the rest of the northeast and north of Brazil it reverted to medieval feudalism under the *coroneis* who, with their bands of hired thugs or *jagunços*, fought among themselves with the pettiness and bloody ferocity employed by the Tupinambá tribes 400 years previously. The most powerful *coroneis* with the largest private armies wore fine clothes, attended European schools and had the quadruple-barrelled surnames associated with Brazilian descendants of old Portuguese families. The less powerful were former members of the Guarda Nacional. Slaves either found their own plots deep in the sertão where no coronel wanted to live or they became vassals, working on plantations for a wage which was never enough to cover their food and lodging and incurring a debt to the coronel which passed down to their children. For most Bahians the situation has remained the same into the 21st century. However, there were some rebellions; most notably at Canudos where the messianic Antônio Conselheiro (see box on page 247) united brigades of *cangaço* bandits and miscellaneous marginalised groups into a city state which came even closer than the Malês to changing Bahia (and Brazil) radically.

THE 20TH CENTURY At the turn of the 19th century, Brazilian politics was dominated by the *café com leite* (coffee with milk) alliance, which comprised the coffee-growing *patrias* of São Paulo and the cattle ranchers of Minas Gerais. Rio Grande do Sul, where the army was powerful and European ideas dominated, had minor influence, as did Rio as the seat of federal power. The rest of the country provided firebrand senators and congressmen and charismatic presidents, the first of which were Marechal Deodoro da Fonseca (1889–91) and Marechal Floriano Peixoto (1891–94) both from Alagoas, the state to Bahia's north. In the early decades the presidents (who were usually soldiers and backed by the army), mediated between the various groups contending for power, and between Minas and São Paulo. Such interventions were always unconstitutional and therefore gave rise to political instability.

The Prestes Column Tensions between São Paulo and Minas Gerais were fervid. Ranchers from Minas resented the way in which the São Paulo coffee growers used their position to keep the price of coffee artificially high at a time of oversupply. The situation reached a head in the 1920s, when there were a series of coup attempts by the army. Brazil had been economically dependent on Britain at the beginning of the 20th century. This had changed after World War I when the balance of power in the western hemisphere shifted to Washington. Brazil was still exporting its coffee, sugar and raw materials principally to Europe, but manufactured goods now arrived from the United States. A strong dollar and fluctuating Brazilian currency led to increasing debt and even before the Wall Street crash of 1929 the country's export-led economy was in grave trouble, with the government spending a third of its revenue paying off debt. The discontent had led to a growth in nationalism and the emergence of two charismatic leaders, both from the far southern state of Rio Grande do Sul. Left-wingers gathered under Luís Carlos Prestes, a bespectacled, slender intellectual army officer; the oligarchs under Getúlio Vargas, a jovial, avuncular and very wealthy rancher and brilliant opportunist. The populist political jousting between the two and the worlds they represented would define the future of Brazilian politics.

Prestes was the first to move, taking part in a vaguely socialist rebellion in São Paulo in 1924 where he led a column of troops into the heart of the state, linking up with other rebel forces who had been expelled from the capital. Together they formed the Prestes Column (Coluna Prestes), whose aim was to walk through the whole of Brazil meeting the people and fomenting rebellion against the Brazilian aristocracy and the structure of privilege and colonialism they preserved. Their 2½-year, 25,000km odyssey took them from the edge of the Pantanal swampland through the cerrado of Goiás and the arid sertão of Bahia, where they were finally routed by a coronel from Lençóis in the Chapada Diamantina and his *jagunço* army, who drove the Prestes Column into exile in Bolivia (see page 234). The column had garnered little support on the ground, where local peasants were either frightened of the *coroneis* who dominated their lives, or eager to preserve the meagre lots they finally called their own after centuries of slavery. But whilst the Prestes Column failed, the column inches about Prestes were a triumph. He became a hero to the Brazilian press. A left-wing daily championed him as a 'Cavalier of Hope', an epithet which stuck with him until his death. The Communist Party courted and recruited Prestes and dispatched him to Moscow where he worked as an engineer and became a member of the executive committee of the Comintern (the international organisation of communist parties under Soviet control), where he rubbed shoulders with the likes of Mao Zedong.

But whilst Prestes grabbed the limelight, it was Vargas who stole into power. The elections of 1930 saw a win for the São Paulo candidate to rising discontent. The Paulistas were blamed for Brazil's economic woes. They had brought the country to its dire economic straits, proclaimed a clamouring press and intelligentsia by stockpiling coffee instead of selling it, in a vain attempt to manipulate world prices. But prices had fallen and Brazil was broke. The election results were disputed by a coalition of opposition forces. After several months of tension and violence, the army intervened and jocular Getúlio Vargas reluctantly agreed to stand in as interim president whilst the difficulties were being resolved, and stepped nimbly into power. São Paulo naturally resisted and there was a rebellion in 1932, but it was soon put down by federal troops, effectively wiping out the threat to Vargas's authority. In 1934 a constituent assembly drew up a new constitution that reduced the power of the states and gave more power to the president. The assembly then elected Vargas as president for a four-year term.

Vargas and the new state of dependency Vargas was a sharply intelligent populist who understood the mindset of everyday Brazilians as no politician had before him and as every politician has pretended to since, and he manipulated Brazil out of social change brilliantly – preserving the comfort of the elite by steering the country clear of the clamour of Prestes and the pressing problem of European immigrants. The European immigrants courted by the first republicans had proved to be less harmless than the oligarchy had hoped. They arrived in Brazil with strong socialist and Spanish anarchist ideas and revolutionary methods which advocated direct action in the form of strikes and boycotts by workers organised into unions. Their activity was slowly beginning to have some success – with a very gradual shift in power away from the masters to the workers. This was at its most obvious in the nascent industries in the cities where wages were at or below subsistence level and living conditions were appalling.

Vargas recognised that European ideas and ideals would have limited appeal to Brazilian workers if they were offered a more familiar alternative. Brazilians, he thought, even when urban were rural in temperament. They tended to view all relationships, including those with individuals exercising authority, in personal and not ideological terms, which was reflected in rural customs whereby serfs would choose their masters as godparents for their children. Such practices were reflections of the dependency that characterised interactions between people born into slavery and those who owned them. Indeed, slavery had been abolished in Brazil for only half a generation. On assuming the presidency Vargas set about creating a federal state of dependency. He made the states dependent on federal government by replacing all state governors with 'interventors' who reduced the state militias; and he reorganised the system of patronage within the states in favour of his own. Private enterprise too would be dependent on the federal government through a system of labyrinthine bureaucracy. But most importantly he created a state of dependency between government and labour. It was the mirror image of the traditional tie between the masters and the slaves in rural Brazil.

After the Wall Street crash and the collapse of commodities worldwide the Bahia and the poor northeast of Brazil became ever poorer. Even peasants working for the coroneis were forced to migrate to the big cities – some came to Salvador, but most went south to Rio or São Paulo. Here they discovered a social structure very different from the one to which they were accustomed. They had to live in suburban *favela* slums and work in impersonal workplaces with hundreds of strangers from all over the country. Many were disorientated and bewildered. It was the ideal environment for the spread of revolutionary European ideas. Before Vargas, the government had treated labour problems as matters for the police. Unions were crushed. Vargas realised that he could achieve both economic development and the maintenance of the balance of power and wealth in Brazil by adopting a different policy. He presented the government as a warm-hearted authority figure who would take care of Brazilians needs, just as the *coroneis* had back in rural Bahia. He nationalised the union movement, allowing the illusion of freedom of speech with none of the power. The Vargas Ministry of Labour had the exclusive authority to grant legal recognition to the unions, which were organised by the government into state and federal confederations. The government controlled union purse strings and had the absolute authority to hire and fire whoever they liked and they gave the workers a few sweeteners – increasing the minimum wage and setting up a paltry social security system to provide minimum healthcare and retirement benefits – which the president's propaganda apparatus would later exploit to the full, calling him the 'father of the poor' and the 'benefactor of the working classes'. Any independent unions who resisted were crushed.

The return of Prestes: Vargas resigns

During Prestes's sojourn in Moscow the Brazilian Communist Party had been sending reports stating that the country was ripe for revolution. Unaccustomed to the Brazilian hyperbolic temperament the Russians took these at face value and set about preparing Prestes for power. After training he was ordered to return to Brazil to execute a Brazilian Bolshevik uprising. He was assigned an experienced agent to accompany him, Olga Benario, a beautiful young German Jew who was also a crack shot, a pilot, a polyglot and a parachutist. The couple began as comrades but fell in love on the slow boat across the Atlantic and, even though Olga was already married to a Soviet officer, they became lovers.

Brazil's 1935 revolution was planned, financed and directed from Moscow. It was a disaster. The Brazilian Communist Party had wildly exaggerated the country's eagerness for revolutionary change. Federal troops easily vanquished revolts in Natal and Pernambuco and an uprising organised personally by Prestes in Rio suffered the same fate. The rebels killed army officers in the process, which forever alienated the Brazilian armed forces from communism – a fact which the CIA exploited when they manipulated a military coup decades later. Vargas had excellent intelligence and pre-empted every rebel move, and whilst Prestes evaded capture for a short while he and Olga were captured in Rio in 1936. She was pregnant. Prestes was condemned to 47 years imprisonment. Olga was deported to Germany where she gave birth to their baby. She was later captured by the Nazis and died in a concentration-camp gas chamber.

Ever the opportunist, Vargas declared a state of siege against another alleged communist plot in October 1937, suspended the constitution which had prevented him being re-elected and in 1938 proclaimed a new constitution and a new state, which he called the Estado Nôvo. The fascists tried to oust him but failed, leaving him with no effective opposition whatsoever. He silenced the press, emasculated the few independent trade unions which remained and created half a dozen new police forces who were given almost unfettered powers.

During this time, the Vargas regime had seen a transition from a commodities-led export economy to industrialisation with heavy state intervention, with the government involved in mining, oil, steel, electricity, chemicals, motor vehicles and light aircraft. The military were allowed free rein to develop their own armaments industry. So when war came to Europe, Vargas hedged his bets with both Germany and Britain, to see who would provide the greatest assistance for Brazil's industrialisation. Vargas opted to back the Allies after cutting a deal with the North Americans. In return for allowing US military bases to be established in the northeast, he secured loans, technical assistance and other investment for a huge steel plant at Volta Redonda and a string of infrastructure projects. In return, Brazil declared war on Germany in 1944 and sent 25,000 troops to Italy.

The 1943 elections had been postponed because of the war, but Vargas scheduled a vote for December 1945 in an attempt to dispel his fascist image. He allowed the formation of political parties, forming two himself: the Social

Democratic Party (PSD), supported by industrialists and large farmers, and a Labour Party (PTB), supported by pro-Vargas trade unions. There was also the National Democratic Union (UDN), opposed to Vargas, and the newly legalised Communist Party. There were growing fears that Vargas would not relinquish power, and when he appointed his brother as chief of police in Rio de Janeiro, the military intervened. Faced with the prospect of being deposed, Vargas chose to resign in October 1945, allowing the elections to take place as planned in the December. In a bizarre twist of fate Prestes spoke out in favour of Vargas, even appearing on the same platform as the man who had sent his wife to her death. The communists felt that with Vargas in power and committed to free elections they would be better off than under the rule of the military, which remained fervently anti-communist.

They were very nearly right: Prestes became a senator and the party came close to securing office. Instead power was secured by General Eurico Dutra of the PSD, who drafted yet another constitution returning many of the Vargas changes to the liberal principles of the 1891 constitution but keeping his tight control of the unions, his wage and healthcare reforms and the policy of government-funded industrialisation. Foreign-owned railways were nationalised, hydro-electric power was developed and Prestes's Communist Party banned.

The return of Vargas Vargas was keeping busy. He managed to get himself elected as a senator for Rio Grande do Sul and then chosen as candidate for the PSD– PTB alliance in the 1950 residential elections. He campaigned as an avuncular man of the people. Miraculously he won his third presidency; his first by direct elections. From the outset he was beset by the problems of fulfilling populist election promises while grappling with debt and inflation and stern opposition from the increasingly fascistic military. Rapid industrialisation required levels of investment which could only be raised abroad and Vargas was under increasing pressure from the US to open up Brazil to American investors. But protectionists at home were deeply opposed and Vargas found himself in a position that for once he could not control. With inflation spiralling, the economy plummeting and allegations of corruption (after the president's bodyguard was implicated in a plot to kill a journalist which ended up with the death of another man), the army issued him with an ultimatum: resign or face a coup. He did neither, choosing to shoot himself on 24 August 1954, leaving a suicide note denouncing traitors at home and capitalists abroad.

Prestes soldiered on into obscurity: campaigning in elections in the 1960s, fleeing to Moscow with a new wife in the 1970s and returning to Brazil in the 1980s, when his trenchant support of Stalin saw him expelled from a modernised Communist Party. He died virtually penniless in 1990 after spending his final years supported by his long-time friend, the architect Oscar Niemeyer.

Fifty years in five Brazil's next president was an equally colourful character, who seemed determined to out-Vargas Vargas; storming into office in the Bossa Nova era with the promise of taking Brazil 50 years into the future in five years of office. Juscelino Kubitschek, or JK (Jota Ka) as he was known to Brazil, took office in January 1956 and immediately set about building a new space-age capital in the centre of the country – nearly 1,000km northwest of Rio de Janeiro on a flat, dry piece of cerrado inhabited only by armadillos and anteaters. Brasília turned the eyes of the world to Brazil, brought JK immense domestic popularity and a presidential visit from Dwight Eisenhower. But it broke the exchequer and in 1961, the next president, Jânio Quadros, was left to pick up the pieces. The economic problems were so severe that his government collapsed after only seven months and congress unexpectedly accepted his resignation. Power passed to his vice president, João Goulart, a populist and former labour minister under Vargas, who was distrusted by the armed forces after Prestes handed him the poisoned chalice of his political support.

It was a turbulent time in Brazil. The intellectual and university classes were boiling with the excitement of the Cuban revolution. Trotskyist and communist agitators were encouraging land occupation, industrial action from now liberated unions, and a move to secure trade union rights for the armed forces. With the Americans at their most fearful and watchful – after the rise of Fidel Castro – Goulart's powers were curtailed with the appointment of a prime minister and cabinet answerable directly to congress. The nationalist congress then passed legislation cutting foreign companies' annual remittances to 10% of profits, which sparked a massive outflow in foreign capital and a halving of US aid. Goulart had to print money to keep the economy going and the inflation rate soared. When Goulart clashed with congress over approval of an economic adjustment programme and tried to strengthen his position by appealing for popular support outside congress, he alarmed the Americans and the Brazilian elite who feared revolution. In March 1964 the military took over power and Goulart escaped to Uruguay.

The military era With the full support of the US government, who declared the military coup 'the single most decisive victory of freedom in the mid-twentieth century', opposition leaders were arrested, the press censored, labour unions purged of anyone seen as left wing, and the secret police given widespread powers. Political parties were outlawed and replaced by two officially approved parties: the Aliança Renovadora Nacional (ARENA), who were in power, and the official opposition Movimento Democrático Brasileiro (MDB). The puppet congress consisted only of members of these two parties and they approved a succession of military presidents nominated by the armed forces.

Between 1968 and 1973 there was considerable resistance to the military from insurgent groups who carried out a campaign of guerrilla warfare, principally in the cities. The resulting oppression was appalling. Brazilians were forbidden to meet in groups, even to dance the samba, and possession of any book or document deemed suspicious by the numerous secret police was reason enough for arrest and torture. Brazilians disappeared, taken by death squads, and socially conscious singers like Chico Buarque, and the Tropicália founders from Bahia, Gilberto Gil and Caetano Veloso were forced into exile.

However, spurred on by increased aid and investment from their US backer, the military government's economic adjustment programme began to pay dividends. The economy stabilised and grew at over 10% a year between 1968 and 1974, making life easier for the middle classes and cutting support for the guerrillas groups. The period became known as the 'Brazilian economic miracle' but it masked the ever-widening divide between the rich and predominantly white *haves* – descendants of the Portuguese and the Europeans who had been invited as immigrants at the beginning of the century – and the descendants of the slaves and serfs, the predominantly Afro-Brazilian poor. In 1960 after the Vargas regime and JK, the richest 10% of the population received 40% of GDP; by 1980 they were receiving 51%, with the rest of Brazil left with just 13% of GDP.

And like Vargas, the military had focused their industrialisation on the south and southeast. Brazilians from Bahia and, increasingly, the poor marginalised northeast poured out of rural areas into the ever-expanding favela slums which proliferated in the cities, especially in the new industrial centre of São Paulo.

Then just as the military decided to relax their control over the populace, legalise political parties, trade unions and strike action and reduce censorship, the economy collapsed under the burden of pressure-cooker industrialisation and uncontrolled borrowing and lending by a US-controlled World Bank. By 1980 inflation was running at 100% a year and rising, foreign debt was the highest in Latin America at over US$87 billion, and unemployment was soaring. When international interest rates rose sharply in 1982, Brazil was no longer able to pay its creditors and it suspended interest payments. Unwilling to go through another round of authoritarianism and repression, the military relinquished control and Brazil returned to democracy. With a jolt.

Corruption and Collor In 1985 Tancredo Neves was elected as the first civilian president for 21 years. Then a few days before he could take office he suddenly and mysteriously fell ill and died in hospital, to be succeeded by an old patriarch and coronel from the northeast, José Sarney. By this time inflation stood at 300%. Sarney introduced the stringent Cruzado Plan in 1986, freezing prices and wages. It was of little use; as soon as the freeze was lifted inflation exploded again. The government was dissolved after yet another new constitution was drafted by congress and direct presidential elections in November 1989 brought the handsome young populist Fernando Collor de Melo from Alagoas to the presidency, narrowly defeating his firebrand left-wing rival, Luís Inácio (Lula) da Silva. Under direction from the IMF, Collor launched controversial economic reforms – opening the economy to imports, widespread privatisation and a freeze on savings and bank accounts, which saw thousands of Brazilians lose their life savings and Collor stand accused of pocketing billions. By 1991 inflation had reached 1,500% and foreign debt payments were completely suspended. Collor himself was suspended from office after congress voted overwhelmingly to impeach him for corruption, a fate he deftly avoided by resigning on 29 December 1992.

THE *PLANO REAL* AND THE 21ST CENTURY Vice President Itamar Franco assumed power and passed the buck for restructuring the economy to his shy finance minister Fernando Henrique Cardoso. Cardoso was better known as a vaguely left-wing academic sociologist than an economist, but even in the early stages his *plano real* policy proved effective enough to see him voted in as president in the elections of October 1994. Even during the 1997 Asian financial crisis Cardoso avoided an upsurge in inflation and devaluation of the new *real* currency, at the cost of slowing down what was beginning to be respectable economic growth. By the end of his second term of office, inflation was in single figures for the first time in decades. But Cardoso's government had failed to address the country's serious financial inequality which was now so marked that it was having significant social impact – with soaring crime and increasing destitution in the northeast.

In the 2002 elections, the ever persistent left-wing candidate from Pernambuco, Lula da Silva, won the elections against Cardoso's appointed successor in his fourth bid for the presidency. The economy immediately plunged into crisis again – with the *real* losing some 50% of its value against the dollar in less than a year. In August 2002, the IMF came to the rescue with a record US$30 billion loan, subject to tough conditions. But Lula was an experienced politician. He stuck with Cardoso's economic plan, courting rather than alienating the US, whilst investing increasing amounts of money in social projects in the impoverished northeast. The Fome Zero programme and increased rights for the poor saw millions of families lifted above the poverty line in the first decade of the new millennium, and the Brazilian economy has gone from strength to strength. Lula won a resounding second term in 2006, despite running under the shadow of a severe corruption scandal. With Brazil weathering recession better than any country in the western hemisphere and predicted to become the fifth-wealthiest nation on the planet by 2026, he enters 2010 as the most popular elected leader in the world, despite the country's persistent social problems and ever rising urban crime.

GOVERNMENT AND POLITICS

STATE GOVERNMENT Brazil is made up of 26 states (*estados*), of which Bahia is one, and a federal district (*distrito federal*) where the capital Brasília is located. State independence is guaranteed by Brazil's 1988 constitution. Brazil's states maintain a separation between executive and legislature. Each of the 27 governors must achieve more than 50% of the vote to be elected, including a run-off between the top two candidates if necessary. State legislatures have only one chamber. The deputies are elected through an open-list system in which the state serves as one constituency.

Government in Brazil's nearly 5,000 municipalities is also structured with a separation between the executive office of the mayor (*prefeitura*) and a legislative city council (*câmara de vereadores*). Elections for mayor also require the winner to obtain more than 50% of the vote, with the exception of cities with less than 200,000 inhabitants. Local elections are held in the second year between presidential, congressional and state elections.

The states Brazil's 26 states are grouped into regions as follows:

North Acre, Amapa, Amazonas, Pará, Roraima, Rondônia, Tocantins.

Northeast Alagoas, **Bahia**, Ceará, Maranhão, Paraíba, Pernambuco, Piauí, Rio Grande do Norte, Sergipe.

Central West Distrito Federal, Goiás, Mato Grosso, Mato Grosso do Sul.

Southeast Espírito Santo, Minas Gerais, Rio de Janeiro, São Paulo.

South Parana, Rio Grande do Sul, Santa Catarina.

Amazonas is the largest Brazilian state, covering 1,570,847km^2; Sergipe is the smallest, covering 21,962km^2.

Voting Suffrage is voluntary between 16 and 18 years of age and for those over 70, and compulsory over 18 and under 70 years of age. Military conscripts cannot vote.

FEDERAL GOVERNMENT The executive branch is structured with a chief of state and head of government (president), vice president and a cabinet appointed by the president. The president and vice president are elected together by popular vote for a single four-year term. A single individual can serve as president for a maximum of two consecutive terms (there is no maximum number of terms). Elections were last held on 1 October 2006 (with a run-off on 29 October 2006) and are due to be held on 3 October 2010 with a run-off, if necessary, on 31 October 2010.

In the last election, Luís Inácio (Lula) da Silva of the Worker's Party (Partido dos Trabalhadores; PT) was re-elected president with 60.83%, Geraldo Alckmin of the Brazilian Social Democratic Party (Partido da Social Democracia Brasileira; PSDB) was voted vice president with 39.17%.

The legislative branch of government comprises a two-chambered National Congress (Congresso Nacional) with a Federal Senate (Senado Federal) and a Chamber of Deputies (Camara dos Deputados). The Senate has 81 seats made up of three members voted in from each state and the federal district, elected to serve eight-year terms, with one-third of the senators and two-thirds of the senators elected every alternate four years. The Chamber of Deputies has 513 seats, elected by proportional representation to serve four-year terms.

Elections for the Federal Senate were last held on 1 October 2006 for one-third of the Senate and are next due in October 2010 for two-thirds of the Senate. Elections for the Chamber of Deputies were last held on 1 October 2006 and are due again in October 2010.

The judicial branch is run by a Supreme Federal Tribunal with 11 ministers appointed for life by the president and confirmed by the Senate. Under this is a Higher Tribunal of Justice and Regional Federal Tribunals (with judges appointed for life – until 70, when retirement is mandatory).

ECONOMY

Even though millions live in poverty, Brazil has one of the world's fastest-growing economies. Under Lula's first government, from 2003 to 2007, the country ran record trade surpluses and recorded its first current account surpluses since 1992. Productivity gains coupled with high commodity prices contributed to the surge in exports. Brazil improved its debt profile in 2006 and in 2009, during the world slump, it lent money to the World Bank. According to Economist Intelligence Unit predictions given in 2009, Brazil's economy will leapfrog the UK, France and Italy as early as 2011 before becoming the fifth-largest in the world in 2026 with a gross domestic product of US$5.721 trillion in purchasing-power parity terms.

The economy is characterised by large and well-developed agricultural, mining, manufacturing and service sectors. Major exports are coffee, soybeans, wheat, rice, corn, sugar cane, cocoa, citrus and beef, and industries are textiles, shoes, chemicals, cement, lumber, iron ore, tin, steel, aircraft, motor vehicles and parts, other machinery and equipment. Huge oil reserves estimated at five to eight billion barrels have been found off the southeast coast and Brazil has been invited to join OPEC.

The country's GDP (purchasing power parity) was estimated at US$1,998 trillion in 2008 (tenth in the world), with a real GDP growth rate of 5.1% (84th in the world). GDP per capita in 2008 was estimated at US$1,200 (102nd in the world). In 2008 the unemployment rate was 7.9%.

But all is not rosy. The last available data from 2005 show that 31% of the Brazilian population live below the poverty line and divisions between rich and poor are some of the worst in the world, with household income/consumption by percentage share indicating that in 2007 the lowest 10% of the population had just 1.1% of GDP whilst the highest 10% had 43%. Public debt in 2008 was 38.8% of GDP.

BAHIAN ECONOMY Bahia contributed 4.9% of Brazilian GDP in 2004. The largest contributors were cattle ranching and agriculture (10.7%), industry – principally petrochemical (48.5%), services (40.8%). GDP per capita in Bahia in 2004 was US$3,588.

PEOPLE

It is impossible to separate and catalogue all the blood strains of a child born in Bahia. Suddenly a blonde appears among mulattoes or a little Negro baby among whites. That's the way we are, praise be to our God!

Jorge Amado, *Os Pastores da Noite* (Shepherds of the Night)

The very first Portuguese who arrived with Pedro Álvares Cabral in 1500 lusted after the local women and didn't waste any time in procreating with them. The fleet's chronicler was openly prurient about the Tupinambá in his letters to the King of Portugal, saying of one that:

she was so well-built and so well curved, and her privy part (what a one she had!) was so gracious that many women of our country, on seeing such charms, would be ashamed that theirs were not like hers.

And he speaks of how his shipmates 'made merry' with the locals on that first landing. Convicts were left behind to produce children. These *mameluco* (or Portuguese and indigenous) children became the human gristmills that would keep the colony working. They were caught between and rejected by two worlds – neither enslaved Indians nor pure-blood Portuguese; shunned by their father's culture as impure and shunned by the indigenous people who regarded all offspring as the children of their fathers. Women were mere vessels into which the men deposited their seed. They found a middle ground born of these two negatives and this middle ground became Brazil. So much so that the *bandeirantes* who raided the interior in search of slaves from the late 1500s were almost all *mamelucos* or African slaves and the national language was Tupi (the tongue of the Tupinambá and their ethnic cousins who lived along almost the entire Brazilian coast) and not Portuguese.

If Brazilians were not *mamelucos*, they were '*mulatto*' – born of Portuguese and Africans. From the first days of the slave trade, the prettiest African women often fetched prices twice that of the strongest African men. And after purchase they were taken from the *senzala* to work in the master's house, where they were forced to do more than wash dishes. After satisfying master to his fill, the African mistresses were expelled from the house, sometimes with their front teeth removed on order of the cuckolded Portuguese wives and returned to their proper station as slaves engaged in hard labour. If they were lucky, the children sired from these relations were set free or became inheritors of their father's property. But they were often either enslaved by their own fathers (if they were boys) or kept to work in the house if they were girls, and pretty.

Like the *mamelucos* the '*mulattos*' were often spurned by Portuguese and Africans alike, who, as the historian A J R Russell-Wood has noted:

spoke disparagingly of the products of inter-racial alliances, seeing mulattos as the embodiments of the least desirable characteristics of either race.

After five centuries of sex, miscegenation has made race and identity complicated in Bahia. Everyone is an African, an Indian and a European and many Bahians will tell you that in a land as mixed as Bahia there is a racial harmony that exists nowhere else on earth. It certainly looks that way when you see Bahians together, dancing at Carnaval. Yet racism is rife. Turn on the television and you will barely see a black face; the same is true in the Bahian government and the federal government. In 2006, the UN Human Development Index, which measures countries based on health, income and other factors, showed that if measured separately, white Brazilians would be ranked 44th in the world, on a par with oil-rich Kuwait, while its Afro-Brazilians would be ranked 105th, about the same level as El Salvador.

In Salvador city, more than three-quarters of the population is black and Afro-Brazilian culture and religion are the mainstream. Yet merely being black is enough to place a person under suspicion. Ivete Sacramento, who became the country's first black university chancellor in 1998, was quoted in an article in the *Miami Herald* in June 2007 as saying that 'No one has any idea that blacks can be anything more than a maid .... The place of blacks in Brazil is still the place of slaves,' and that except for her family and two other households, every resident in her 64-unit apartment tower was white. Whilst Benedita da Silva, the first black woman to be elected to the federal chamber of deputies, received anonymous letters declaring that black women belong in the kitchen.

Despite the disparities, since the Malê uprisings in Salvador and a few insurrections, black Brazilians have never launched a civil rights movement like those in South Africa or the US and there are almost no black civic groups with the power of US institutions like the National Association for the Advancement of Colored People or financial networks that spur black entrepreneurship. Lula's government has attempted to make a difference, introducing a quota for universities who are required to set aside places for Afro-Brazilian students. But it is an uphill battle against attitudes perpetuated since the influential social historian Gilberto Freyre wrote his *Casa-Grande e Senzala* (The Masters and the Slaves), the first book to define the Brazilian identity, in which he argued that Brazil was freeing itself of racism and even of the concept of race through pervasive miscegenation.

In June 2009, Brazil had an estimated population of 198,739,269 (source: CIA), making it the fifth most populous country in the world.

PEOPLE IN BAHIA In 2006, according to the official census, Bahia had a population of 13,950,146, with a density of 24.7 people/km^2 and an urban population of some 67.6%. Population growth is estimated at 1.1% per year. Only 75% of Bahians have access to drinking water and just 43% to sanitation. Infant mortality was 35.6 per 1,000 in 2005, with 9.7 doctors for every 10,000 inhabitants and two hospital beds for every 1,000 people. Bahia stood at 0.688 on the Human Development Index in 2000, compared to the UK at 0.947 and 0.543 for Bangladesh.

There are no figures for racial mix in Bahia – nor does Brazil systematically measure or record ethnicity, but Bahians' ethnicity is drawn principally from Africans, followed by Europeans (Portuguese and Dutch) and various tribal peoples the largest of which were the Tupi tribal groups, most notably the Tupinambá (see page 25).

LANGUAGE

Bahians speak Brazilian-Portuguese with a sing-song accent and they speak little else. You will find that in the bigger hotels staff speak some English, elsewhere there is only Portuguese. Spanish will get you nowhere. It might look similar on the page, but the sound of Brazilian Portuguese is as different from Spanish as *The Girl from Ipanema* is from *La Bamba*. It is gentler, more feminine and altogether more beautiful. It is a very good idea to have some basic Portuguese under your belt before coming. It's easy to learn and more widely spoken than any other European language except English and Spanish. The BBC (*www.bbc.co.uk/languages/portuguese/talk*) and Sonia Portuguese (*www.sonia-portuguese.com*) offer free online courses.

Relax your mouth when you are in Brazil: consonants are softened here, vowels are lengthened, the mouth is opened more fully. 'R' becomes 'w' seemingly at random: ask a Brazilian which band Mick Jagger sings for, and they'll say, 'De Holeing Sterns'. 'O' becomes 'u': Rio de Janeiro is pronounced 'Hi-u de Janair-u'. 'D' becomes 'j' before a 't' and often before 'e'; 't' becomes 'ch'. This makes Brazilian Portuguese a 'Jifficult' language to pronounce, as you'll be repeatedly told. At the end of a word, 'em' becomes 'eng'; Tudo Bem is pronounced 'Tudo Beng'. The tilde (˜) is most commonly used in *ão,* which should produce a sound like a nasal 'ow' in 'cow', without the final use of the lips that seals the word in English. If it appears at the end of a word, eg: Maracanã, stress this final syllable and push it up your nose. The circumflex (^) opens the vowel: turning 'e' to open 'a' so gardênia is pronounced 'gardaynia'. As in Spanish, the acute accent produces a stress. A cedilla c ('ç') produces an 's'.

For information on where you can learn Portuguese in Bahia see *Chapter 2*, page 46. See also *Appendix 1*, page 249.

STUDYING PORTUGUESE IN BAHIA These language schools offer the chance to learn Brazilian Portuguese in Bahia.

Cactus Language www.cactuslanguage.com. British-based company offering language courses around the world, including Portuguese classes in Salvador.
Casa Do Brasil www.casa-do-brasil.net. Brazilian-German venture offering one-to-one tuition in Barra, Salvador.
Fala-Brasil www.fala-brasil.com. Private tuition in Salvador from Augusto Pondé, who speaks English & some French, & has been teaching Portuguese to foreigners since 1980.

Languages Abroad www.languagesabroad.com. Offers tuition in Salvador, as well as one-to-one homestays with tuition with a Brazilian teacher.
Portuguese in Brazil www.portugueseinbrazil.com. Have good-value group & private classes in Barra, Salvador.
Terra Brasilis www.portuguesecourseinbrasil.com.br. Language school in Barra, Salvador, offering individual & group classes.

RELIGION

There are no separate figures for Bahia but according to the national census of 2000, Brazilians are 73.6% Catholic (nominal), 15.4% Protestant, 1.3% Spiritist, 0.3% Orixá, 1.8% other, 0.2% are unspecified and 7.4% are non-believers.

The situation in daily life is far more complicated. Many Catholics will attend Candomblé ceremonies or call on *mãe* or *pai santo* (spiritual elders) – especially in Bahia. Only evangelical Protestants tend to be exclusive in their worship, and their numbers are growing faster than any other denomination, especially among the lower middle classes.

Candomblé and the other Afro-Brazilian spiritual practices focus on the invocation of a series of archetypal spirits (*orixás*) who possess a chosen devotee whilst he or she is in a trance state during a ritual ceremony in a sacred space called a *terreiro*. Like angelic beings, Hindu gods or Christian saints, these orixás are symbolic of elemental energies connected with human sentiments and the articulations of nature (like the purifying power of flowing water) as expressed through possession in a concentrated archetypal form. The ceremonies are administered by spiritual elders – the *mae* or *pai santo* (holy mother or father). Once present in the ritual, the orixás are propitiated by a sacrifice or an offering and asked to perform a favour on behalf of the devotees.

In symbolic origin, orixás are derived from Yoruba elemental entities or *òrìsàs*. Many are strikingly similar in name and character to those still invoked in Nigeria, Cuba (where the orixá religion is called Santería) or Haiti (where it is called Vudun or voodoo).

Candomblé is said to be the closest to the old west African practices, yet even these incorporate strong indigenous traits. Many of the entities invoked in trance states are indigenous in origin and alien to African traditions – most obviously *o caboclo* who is depicted as an Indian hunter in ritualistic art. Other regional variations – *xangô*, *cavalo-marinho*, *catimbó*, *candomblé caboclo*, and *batuque* – show lesser or greater indigenous Brazilian characteristics, whilst *umbanda* is a 20th-century variation which even more overtly fuses orixá religion with shamanistic techniques.

Candomblé is also deeply Catholic, and not merely superficially so. From the early years of the *irmandades* there was considerable flexibility of worship for Africans. In the 19th century when the Vatican suffered a famous attack of paranoia during the era of Enlightenment, Portuguese priests dispatched to rural areas in Brazil would often express consternation at the level of 'folk belief' practised in church. But the truth is that it had been commonplace for centuries. As long as they didn't interfere with the liturgy and iconography, Africans were left to worship as they chose, and they chose to represent the *orixás* through Catholic saints – just as the Maya chose to with their deities in southern Mexico and

The *Orixás* are not so much gods as guardian spirits or archetypes, often associated with different aspects of the natural world, and each with a distinct personality. There are many Orixás and names and importance varies between the various African-Brazilian spirit religions – of which there are many, the principal being Candomblé and Umbanda. Here are a few of the most commonly encountered Orixás:

Candomblé The lord of the forests and jungles, of medicinal plants and sacred herbs.
Exu The messenger, who makes contact between the Orixás and human beings.
Iansã The spirit of lightning, torrential rain and wind.
Iemanjá (Yemanjá) The queenly spirit of the sea who is petitioned at new year by devotees in white.
Obá The spirit of liberty and freedom fighters.
Nanã the spirit of mud and clay, of estuaries, the force of life and the the Lady of death.
Obaluayê The lord of the Earth, the spirit who brings and cures illness and death.
Ogum (Ogun) The one who shows the way – the spirit of paths and the clearing of paths through the wilderness.
Ossãe The spirit of leaves.
Oxalá The god of peace and faith and in some traditions of power – rather like Zeus.
Oxossí The spirit of hunting, harvest and abundance.
Oxum The Orixá of fresh running water, associated with emotion and purification.
Oxumaré The Orixá of the rainbow and those points which connect Aye (Earth) and *Orun* (Sky); also represents abundance and good health.
Xangô The spirit of justice, associated with fire, thunder and lightning. Linked with Iansã (see above) – a saying in Umbanda states that without Iansã, Xangô makes no fire on Earth.

Guatemala. The Virgin was Yemanjá, *orixá* of the sea (this fitted well as Mary had long been the patron saint of sailors); St George who killed the dragon was Ogun, the spirit of battle; Christ himself was Oxalá – the deity of Being itself, who was also Tupã – the father God of the Tupi people.

Afro-Brazilian religions began to take organised form only in the 19th century after independence from Portugal, when *terreiros* – literally sacred spaces (another indigenous Brazilian concept) – developed in 1830s Salvador. Today there are some 80 million Brazilians who practice some form of orixá religion, often alongside Catholicism and without perceiving any contradiction. See box above.

Atheists in Brazil are generally received with incredulity and pity; lack of belief is perceived as an intellectual and emotional weakness.

EDUCATION

There is free public education in Bahia, but teaching quality is often very poor. According to state government statistics, some 20% of Bahians could neither read nor write in 2004, and above the age of 50 the figure comes closer to 50%. This compares with an estimated 88% literacy rate for the country as a whole.

Brazil has a school-life expectancy (primary to tertiary education) of 14 years and spends 4% of GDP on education (putting it at 105 on the world list), well below Mali but above Argentina. Kiribati leads the list at 17.8%, the UK comes in at number 47 (with 5.6%) and the USA at number 57 (with 5.3%), according to the CIA.

Despite racism and the best attempts of politicians like Antônio Carlos Magalhães, it is African-Brazilian culture that dominates life in Bahia. The story of its survival is remarkable. Africans were brought to Brazil from very different nations. The historian Arthur Ramos divides them into three large groupings: the first of these groups were from Sudanese cultures represented principally by the Yoruba people and by smaller groups from present-day Gambia, Sierra Leone, Ghana and the Ivory Coast; the second were from the Islamic cultures of northern Nigeria – the Peul, the Mandinga and the Hausa – called Malê people in Bahia (see page 34); and the third group were made up of Bantu tribes from the Congo, Angola and present-day Mozambique.

These were peoples captured in small bands, herded together with others as culturally and linguistically alien to them as a 15th-century Frenchman would have been to a Turk and thrown in slaving ships. Here they were shackled neck to neck with others and packed into the reeking holds of ships in a space barely big enough to crouch in and where they had to subsist, eat and excrete for the weeks it took to make the voyage across the Atlantic. Many died on the passage.

In their new land they faced the worst imaginable cruelties. At market they were examined like animals, men assessed by the thickness of their wrists and the quality of their teeth, bought and then marched in a chain-gang convoy to an *engenho* (sugar mill). Here they were expected to work 18 hours a day every day of the year – with Sunday off to cultivate their own minute plots next to the *senzala*. Men and women were separated and without love of family or friends, sex or comfort of any kind they would live until they died of exhaustion, brought on by the work and by the regular 50 lashings they received at the pillory to ensure that they didn't attempt to escape. Depending on the cruelty of the masters, slaves who ran away were lashed to death, roasted alive over a period of days in the mouth of a furnace or forced to live chained to an iron ball.

That African culture survived at all in such conditions is incredible. It did so through the *quilombos*, and the Dutch invasions which disrupted life on the *engenhos* and made escape ever more possible, and through the *irmandades* (lay brotherhoods) formed by free blacks and mulattos in Salvador, Cachoeira and Ilhéus. The *irmandades* offered Africans the chance to consolidate their various racial and linguistic groups and to reinvent a new Brazilian African-ness with Portuguese and Tupi as the common language. However, such exchange was not possible on the isolated, rural *engenhos* and the various regional Afro-Brazilian musical styles and religions developed separately. From the start, the new Bahian African-ness incorporated non-African, and mostly indigenous Brazilian elements.

DANCE Capoeira (see box opposite) was born of a fusion of Tupi and African dance, and is not merely an Angolan foot-fighting technique as is so often claimed. The very word 'capoeira' is Tupi – meaning a cleared patch of ground used to plant manioc and fruits. The capoeira master Gladson de Oliveira Silva claims in his book *Capoeira: do Engenho a Universdade* (*Capoeira: From the Sugar Mill to the University*) that both Father José de Anchieta (the Jesuit founder of São Paulo) and Martin Afonso de Sousa (see page 27), write of the Tupi peoples' fighting dance they called capoeira. Some of the instruments used, however, are clearly African in origin. The bow-shaped, percussive *berimbau* is strikingly similar to the Angolan *umbu*, and the singing style and rhythms are almost certainly African in origin, as are other Brazilian rhythms. The Angolans, for instance, have a rhythm and circular dance called *semba* and the word means 'navel' in their tongue. It became *samba de roda* – probably through *irmandade* gatherings in the Recôncavo.

The spinning, swirling, gymnastic fight-dance of capoeira is the only martial art to have been born in the Americas. Its origin is indigenous – Padre José de Anchieta wrote about the coastal Tupi fighting capoeira in 1595. But it was Brazilian-Africans who perfected the art. They disguised the fight as a dance by setting it to African percussion – the *berimbau, pandeiro*-tambourine, *surdo* – accompanied by choral singing and handclaps. And in the 1700s under Zumbi of Palmares they used it to fight the Portuguese and for a short while maintain an independent African state within Brazil.

You can see capoeira throughout Bahia – including on the beach in **Praia do Forte** (see page 224) and around the Pelourinho in Salvador. For a list of capoeira schools see page 119.

MUSIC There are few countries on earth with a musical heritage as rich and diverse as Brazil. The state of Bahia alone preserves more musical styles than most countries and whilst power-pop may play on most buses and blaring radios – as it does everywhere – a little perusing will make music one of the highlights of your visit. The best website for information on Brazilian music is Brasil Música e Artes (*www.redebma.ning.com*) but here is a brief overview.

Afoxé A distinctive drum-driven music using the Ijexá rhythms taken from the rituals of Candomblé. Huge troupes or *blocos* parade at Carnaval and in the Pelourinho throughout the year and afoxé rhythms have featured on records by Paul Simon and Michael Jackson. The music is best live. Check out Olodum, Ilê Aiyê or the Filhos de Gandhy whilst in Salvador (see page 117). Disc to buy: *Warner 30 Anos* by Olodum or anything by Ilê Aiyê.

Axé High octane, cheap and cheesy Carnaval music played loud and frequently throughout Bahia. Aside from the ubiquitous Carnaval stalwarts, Chiclete com

1 *Millennium* by Dorival Caymmi – featuring many of the composer's most famous songs.
2 *Bicho* by Caetano Veloso – one of Caetano's most enduring albums which includes the classic track 'Um Índio'.
3 *Tropicalia Vol.1: Ou Panis Et Circencis* – the album which began the Tropicalia revolution and which features Gilberto Gil, Caetano and Os Mutantes.
4 *Realce* by Gilberto Gil – one of Gil's best and liveliest post-exile CDs.
5 *Maluco Beleza* by Raul Seixas – from the height of Seixas's Sociedade Alternativa era.
6 *Com Defeito De Fabricacao: Fabrication Defect* by Tom Zé – the album which re-launched Zé's career.
7 *Live from Bahia* by Larry Coryell and Dori Caymmi – wonderful Bahian jazz mixed with Dori Caymmi's sweetly melancholic melodies.
8 *Abre Caminho* by Mariene de Castro – classic rootsy Bahian sambas de roda and samba-tinged melodies.
9 *Alfagamabetizado* by Carlinhos Brown – a captivating fusion of afoxé rhythms and exuberant percussive MPB.
10 *Filhos do Sol* by Olodum – classic Bahian afoxé from the band who played on Paul Simon's *Rhythm of the Saints*.

Background Information CULTURE

Banana, the biggest stars, are skimpily clad muscular women like Ivete Sangalo and Claudia Leite. The music was at its best and most exciting in its early 1980s incarnations. A similar style to axé music called *brega* evolved in the 1980s in the states north of Bahia, particularly Pará. Discs to buy: *Ao Vivo* by Banda Beijo (for quality), *MTV Ao Vivo* by Ivete Sangalo for a taste of the style's biggest star.

Baião A sertão backlands folk music with a percussive two/four beat and a beautiful dance step. It was popularised by an accordion player called Luíz Gonzaga in the middle of the 20th century. The baião rhythm appears in much Brazilian jazz, especially played by the likes of the great Hermeto Pascoal and baiãos have been recorded by international jazz and fusion artists like Chic Corea. Discs to buy: anything by Luíz Gonzaga or, for jazz, Quarteto Novo.

Bossa nova The softly sung, acoustic 1950s musical style which is for ever associated with Brazil through Astrud Gilberto's version of 'The Girl from Ipanema' (see boxes, below and opposite). Discs to buy: *Família Jobim* by Antônio Carlos Jobim, *Chega de Saudade* by João Gilberto.

Brazilian rock and metal Brazilian musicians talk about there being rock from Brazil and Brazilian rock. Some of the biggest hard rock bands in the world are Brazilian – notably Sepultura and Angra. But Brazilian rock is seldom heard outside the country and is listened to mostly by the educated middle class. Lyrics are often thoughtful and musical styles tend to be vocal and band driven rather than focused on the guitar or flashy instrumentals. A definitive Brazilian style of rock emerged in the 1970s after Tropicália, with the Bahians Raul Seixas and the Novos Baianos, both of whom were strongly influenced by northeastern rhythms and English rock. It grew in the 1980s and 1990s under

JOÃO GILBERTO AND THE STORY OF BOSSA NOVA

In the late 1950s, a shy, spectacled, upper middle-class Bahian invented one of the world's great musical styles while mucking about on his guitar. Gilberto had arrived in Rio de Janeiro – the city of samba – and he was toying with the style when he chanced on a new way of playing the samba rhythm, by gently plucking the strings, slowing things down and adding a gentle lilt. João wasn't a great singer so he sang quietly almost in a whisper and when he performed his new style he did so unaccompanied by the usual heavy *surdo* bass and *repenique* snare drums that went along with samba.

João Gilberto was a session musician and his new style caught on with fellow players in Rio de Janeiro's affluent Ipanema neighbourhood, the foremost of whom was the architecture student and pianist, Antônio Carlos (Tom) Jobim. They began to perform and write together. Jobim introduced harmonic complexity and jazzier chord progressions to the João Gilberto sound. These had been inspired by French impressionist composers and by other guitarists like Carlos Lyra who had been experimenting with fourths, sixths and off-key chords after seeing samba players like Custódio Mesquita and Garoto play in Rio in his youth. Jobim started to call the new sound the 'bossa nova' or 'new wave'.

And in 1958 the duo released the Jobim composition, 'Chega de Saudade', performed by João Gilberto and with lyrics written by Jobim's upper middle-class drinking buddy (and a poet, diplomat and graduate of Magdalene College, Oxford) – Vinícius de Moraes. It was a huge hit, so much so that its new wave spread from Brazil to the United States where it became popular with 'cool jazz' musicians like the saxophonist Stan Getz.

In 1962 Getz and his 'cool school' friend Charlie Byrd had released a compilation of bossa renditions gleaned from records Byrd had bought whilst on a diplomatic trip

In 2000, some 40 years after it had had its heyday, bossa nova was reborn through Yugoslavia and New York. An obscure conservatory-trained Serbian electronica producer called Mitar Suboti or Suba set up residence in São Paulo in 1990 after receiving a grant from UNESCO's International Fund for the Promotion of Culture to research African-Brazilian rhythms. His European club tastes and production techniques soon found him working with a string of well-known domestic names. And by 1999 he had helped to set up a record label, Ziriguiboom, to promote Brazilian acts who failed to secure record deals back home.

Then tragedy struck. On 2 November 1999 Suba was working on the post-production of one of the first Ziriguiboom albums – *Tanto Tempo* by João Gilberto's daughter Bebel – when his studio caught fire. He died trying to rescue the tapes. But the album was released posthumously and went on to sell over a million copies worldwide.

Bebel was the daughter of the Bahian inventor of bossa nova, João Gilberto and another singer Miúcha Buarque, and she and Suba had copied her stepmother Astrud's recipe for success: almost all the songs were either old 1950s Brazilian standards (or recalled them), and Bebel's bossa nova was aimed at the music market outside Brazil. It was sung in Portuguese and English with the same wistful, sensual innocence with which Astrud had so captivated 1960s USA. And rather than being set against a background of kit drums and cool sax, it floated over swirling electronica and gentle club beats.

Since its release *Tanto Tempo* has made bossa nova the sound of Brazil the world over. Brazilians are puzzled. Bossa is as old hat in Salvador as skiffle is in London and remains firmly on the fringes of the music scene. If you hear it at all in Bahia it'll be in a Western bar or a hotel lobby.

to Brazil in 1961. It was called *Jazz Samba*. It was the best-selling jazz album of the year and earned Getz a Grammy (for a version of Tom Jobim and Newton Mendonça's 'Desafinado'). Eager to repeat the success, Getz decided to record a second bossa nova album, this time using Brazilian musicians. He contacted Jobim and João Gilberto to ask if they'd participate. Both were delighted. But as neither of them spoke English they brought along an interpreter for the studio sessions – João's wife Astrud Gilberto.

All but two of the songs on the album were Tom Jobim compositions, sung by Gilberto in his trademark soft, almost spoken vocals backed by his guitar and a light Brazilian rhythm section, with Getz adding cool, breathy sax. The album opened with 'A Garota de Ipanema'. During the practice in the studio, João suggested that his wife should sing a chorus in English after his Portuguese verse. Her wistful, dreamy Portuguese-tinted English met with such approval from Stan Getz that the following day they recorded a complete English version sung by Astrud.

'I'll never forget,' she said in a later interview, 'that while we were listening back to the just-recorded song at the studio's control room, Stan said to me, with a very dramatic expression: "This song is going to make you famous".'

Getz was right, so much so that Astrud Gilberto would never return home. 'A Garota de Ipanema', released as 'The Girl from Ipanema' (with English lyrics vastly inferior to Vinícius de Moraes's), was an enormous hit and it produced a bossa nova craze in the United States. The song rocketed into the Billboard chart and Astrud and bossa nova were propelled to stardom. *Continued above* strong influence from the British new wave, with names like Os Paralamas do Sucesso, Skank, Titãs, Jota Quest, and Legião Urbana fronted by the charismatic chronicler of end of the mood of post-dictatorship Brazil, Renato Russo. It has since spread into as many diverse forms and style as rock in the US and the UK with a strong representation by metal bands like Madame Saatan – a power trio fronted by a wispy, angel-voiced female vocalist. Discs to buy: *Novo Aeon* by Raul Seixas, *O Descobrimento do Brasil* by Legião Urbana, *Madame Saatan* by Madame Saatan.

Choro Brazil's counterpart to ragtime mixes traditional Portuguese musical styles with late 19th- and early 20th-century European dance-hall music and early Afro-Brazilian jazz. Initially popular in the belle époque through virtuoso instrumentalists like the master flautist and saxophonist Pixinguinha it has undergone a resurgence since the beginning of the new millennium and can often be heard played in smaller bars and restaurants. Discs to buy: *Pixinguinha* by Pixinguinha or, for modern virtuoso guitar choro, *Mafua* by Yamandu Costa.

Clube da Esquina In the mid-1970s a group of musicians from Bahia's neighbouring state of Minas Gerais, led by the golden-voiced Milton Nascimento,

BAHIAN CULTURAL ICONS: GILBERTO GIL

When he's on form and in the mood Gilberto Gil and his band are one of the hottest live acts in the world. I remember seeing him on a good night in the Barbican in London over ten years ago. After the first song even the iciest and most British of the audience were up and dancing on the seats or in the aisles.

Gilberto Gil was born and brought up in an intellectual middle-class family in Bahia. From the age of three he knew that he wanted to be a musician – initially he became an accordion player, and then after hearing João Gilberto playing bossa nova on the radio, a guitarist. By the time he reached his teens he was regularly performing in Salvador and composing jingles for Bahian radio. By his early 20s he had moved to the south, first to São Paulo where he met Chico Buarque amongst others, and then to Rio. Here he became a well-known television personality, with his own show *Ensaio Geral* and a popular album *Louvação* to his name. After Elis Regina and Sergio Mendes had hits with his songs, Gil seemed well on his way to becoming a mainstream Brazilian recording artist.

But this was not to be. In 1967 Gil separated from his first wife and began a relationship with Nana Caymmi, the daughter of the famous Bahian composer, Dorival. This relationship and his previous meetings with Chico Buarque were to forge his political consciousness and change the course of both his life and Brazilian music. At the now legendary third Festival da Record music competition in 1967 Gil performed together with Os Mutantes, Nana and an old friend from Bahia, Caetano Veloso. The atmosphere of political protest that surrounded the festival, the undermining of commercial pop in favour of artistic expression, marked the performances as the first manifestation of a new style of socially aware, electric Brazilian music. It came to be known as tropicália and Gil, Caetano, Gal Costa and Tom Zé emerged as its exciting new stars. Tropicália took much of its inspiration from the Brazilian artistic movement of the 1920s known as antropophagia – cannibalism – where European and international artistic and philosophical influences were 'consumed' and allowed organically to regrow as Brazilian. And so tropicália consumed psychedelia, reggae, Fela Kuti and rock and produced a new completely Brazilian sound, strong on rhythm and jazz harmonies and free from the constraints of traditionalism and Western imitation-rock that had caused the 1960s released a CD which changed the face of Latin American music. *Clube da Esquina* was a hauntingly beautiful selection of songs rich with harmonies and jaw-dropping singing reflecting on daily life for the Brazil's poor majority. In lyrical sentiment it had much in common with the politicised Nueva Canción movement spearheaded by Mercedes Sosa in Argentina, but the music of *Clube da Esquina* was far more sophisticated. So much so that Nascimento was courted by American jazz musicians from Herbie Hancock to Pat Metheny. Discs to buy: *Clube da Esquina* and *Minas* by Milton Nascimento.

Forró You'll hear this accordion and triangle-driven barn dance two-step jig all over Bahia's smaller beach resorts. It's accompanied by a very close, staccato dance whose basic steps are one of the easiest of all Brazilian dances to master. Discs to buy: forró is best danced to live but *O Flor da Paraíba* by ex-Trancoso resident Elba Ramalho has some great tracks.

Mangue beat This musical and artistic movement burst out of Recife in Brazil's northeast like a musical explosion in the 1990s. The movement was led by Chico Science, one of Brazil's greatest ever live performers and his band Nação Zumbi who fused powerful hip-hop rock with Pernambuco African rhythms like

musical scene in Brazil to become stagnant. Unfortunately tropicália wasn't received well by the military government and Gil and Caetano were arrested, imprisoned and then exiled in London. They were lucky; their fame was immortalised. Other musicians had their tongues cut out.

On his return to Brazil in 1972 Gil exploded back into the Brazilian music consciousness with a huge hit album, *Expresso 2222*, and two big hit singles, *Back in Bahia* and *Oriente*. He has never left the national consciousness since, either as a singer or increasingly as a politician. He was elected a city councillor in Salvador in the 1980s and when Lula came to power in 2003, with Gil's Green Party support, Gil was appointed minister for culture. In his inauguration speech Gil set out his agenda – to promote the Brazilian culture which has always been strongest – that of poor and predominantly black Brazil:

> The way I understand the term 'culture' goes far beyond the restricted and restrictive domain of academic concepts and the rites and liturgy of a supposed creative and intellectual class. No one will ever hear me pronounce the word 'folklore' …. 'Folklore' is everything not included, because it lacks currency, in the panorama of mass culture. It's produced by uneducated people, by 'modern primitives', in a kind of symbolic ghetto of the present day set aside for all that is of merely historical interest …. There is no 'folklore'. Everything is culture.

One of the first projects he initiated was a culture programme in the world's largest slum city, Roçinha in Rio de Janeiro. Some of Rio's most exciting concerts are now held here; in the midst of a cubist sea of little breeze-block shacks and antennae jutting out high above the plush apartments and white-sand beaches of São Conrado.

When musicians make political statements or lead political lives in Brazil they are not treated with the scorn that they are in the UK and US. Gilberto Gil is living proof of this. In the early days he could so easily have become another anodyne pop artist, but instead he chose to create a new artistic movement, tropicialia, and he has emerged as one of Brazil's foremost proponents of the use of art for social and environmental change.

Maracatu. Mangue beat was the Tropicália of the 1990s, reinventing and revitalising Brazilian popular culture, as punk had done in 1970s England, and paving the way for films like *City of God* and artists like Seu Jorge and Rappin' Hood (see *Rap Brasileiro* opposite). Disc to buy: *Afrociberdelia* by Chico Science and Nação Zumbi.

Musica Popular Brasileira Brazilian popular music (MPB) is a fusion of Brazilian musical forms and international influences and covers a vast spectrum of artists and bands. Key names include Chico Buarque, the Bob Dylan of Brazil, whose beautifully crafted politically motivated lyrics saw him exiled during the dictatorship; Jorge Ben, whose archetypically Rio de Janeiro samba funk tracks include the famous 'Mas Que Nada'; Tim Maia, whose samba soul paved the way for the funk of the likes of Seu Jorge; and Brazil's current international musical favourite and honey-voiced Marisa Monte. There are too many albums to recommend even a handful, but most Bahian record shops allow customers to sample.

TROPICÁLIA

In the late 1960s Salvador had a San Francisco moment. Cool mingled with creativity when a florescence of film-makers, artists and above all musicians came together to smoke copious amounts of cannabis and create a new artistic movement. Names like Caetano Veloso, Gilberto Gil, Tom Zé, Glauber Rocha and Gal Costa wanted to change artistic life in Brazil, and they had Andy Warhol's iconoclasm and capacity to seize the public imagination. The movement they created became known as *tropicália* or *tropicalismo* after a work by the avant-garde artist Helio Oiticica.

It's difficult to define tropicália; like many things Brazilian it is as much a feeling as an intellectual statement. And the mood was of insurrection. Caetano Veloso, one of the first founders once said: '*Tropicália* is the opposite of bossa nova.' Bossa Nova (the music forever associated with Brazil through 'The Girl from Ipanema') had been middle class, white and genteel. In the beginning of 1967, when the music began, the tropicalistas had felt suffocated by the Brazilian cultural elite. They were staid, snobbish and racist. Tropicália would be young, noisy and irreverent. Acoustic instruments were abandoned in favour of electric – something as revolutionary in Brazilian music as Bob Dylan's use of the electric guitar had been to contemporaneous US folk. Themes and rhythms were drawn from the roots of African and indigenous Brazil and not the European heritage. Caetano turned set satirical poems by Gregório de Mattos (see *Literature*, page 58) to music. Gilberto Gil openly alluded to African-Brazilian religions like Candomblé. And the first tropicália album was released with a psychedelic cover and a title which was a satirical swipe at the elite's use of entertainment to control the masses in Brazil – *Panis e Circenses* (Bread and Circuses).

Mariene De Castro (*www.marienedecastro.com.br*) is Bahia's finest samba singer. Her first album *Abre Caminho*, released in 2006, won a Prêmio da Música Brasileira, Brazil's most prestigious music award. She's exhilarating live and often plays in Salvador at the Forte de Santo Antônio Alem do Carmo (shows are advertised on her My Space page and website). Here are her tips for what to do in Bahia:

> Be sure to try and see a samba de roda; traditional Bahian samba. This is some of the best and most exciting music in Bahia. You can hear some of the best artists from the Santo de Casa cultural movement in the Praça Pedro Arcanjo near the Pelourinho on Saturday evenings and they often play in Rio Vermelho.

Rap Brasileiro Brazilian rap and hip-hop has one of the largest audiences in the world and more than any other music in the country it is the sound of the *favelas*. Apart from the crudest 'baile-fink' styles, lyrics are usually highly political and bands and artists are engaged in work with favela communities. The music itself often owes as much to samba artists like Bezerra da Silva and Mangue Beat standard-bearer Chico Science as it does to US styles. Discs to buy: *Em Sujeito Homem 2* by Rappin' Hood, *Sobrevivendo no Inferno* by Racionais MCs, *Rough Guide to Brazilian Hip Hop*.

Samba Brazil's most famous musical style – which in its most famous form is the soundtrack of Rio Carnaval – was born in Rio de Janeiro of Bahian origins at the turn of the 20th century. As well as Rio Carnaval samba, samba takes many other forms. Its rootsiest is Bahian samba de roda – adapted from the Angolan *semba* rhythm by Bahian slaves in the Recôncavo, and performed by a ring of drummers and singers and two central dancers (who interchange with others

Tropicália swept out of Salvador through Brazil just as the Beatles had swept out of Liverpool, picking up acolytes like São Paulo band Os Mutantes, along the way. Its mix of drug-soaked cool, hippy clothes and avant-garde intelligence contrasted markedly with the clean-cut, clean-living conservative norms promoted by the military dictatorship and appealed to the burgeoning educated middle classes throughout the country.

The military began to take offence. In October 1968 Caetano Veloso, Gilberto Gil and the Mutantes played a series of shows at the Rio de Janeiro nightclub Sucata, where they brandished a flag emblazoned with the moniker 'Be an outcast, be a hero' and allegedly inserted offensive verses into the national anthem. The shows were stopped.

The following month a jury at a big competitive music festival awarded first prize to Tom Zé for the song *São Paulo*, third prize to Caetano and Gil for *Divino, Maravilhoso* and fourth prize to Tom Zé and Rita Lee from Os Mutantes for *2001*. The Federal Censorship Department began to edit or ban tropicália songs. In December Gil and Caetano were arrested and were subsequently exiled to London.

Tropicália had had a little more than a year of official life. Yet it continued to influence Brazilian music for generations, finally reaching the rest of the world through David Byrne in the late 1980s.

Caetano and Gilberto Gil would return to become members of Brazil's artistic establishment. And Gil would become minister for culture in Lula's government. They are still releasing great music in the second decade of the new millennium. (See box *Ten Essential Bahian CDs*, page 49).

Tropicália is most often associated with Gilberto Gil and Caetano Veloso but when the movement began in the late 1960s it was Tom Zé who was considered its great intellectual. In an interview with Brazil's *Época* magazine Zé complained of having being 'buried' deliberately by his fellow Tropicalistas and by the press. 'I was the Trotsky of the movement,' he stated. By the mid-1970s he had been pushed into exile and forgotten.

Then in 1986 David Byrne chanced upon Zé's classic CD *Estudando O Samba* in a São Paulo music store and fell in love with the album. He asked his friend – the self-confessed father of Tropicália – Caetano Veloso, 'Who is Tom Zé?' Caetano either deliberately or accidentally confused him with another singer, Tuzé de Abreu. But Byrne tracked Zé down, nonetheless, recording him and resurrecting his career. Since then Zé has gone from strength to strength, playing to sell-out audiences in New York and Europe and gradually getting the recognition he deserves in Brazil. He's still recording well into his seventies and in 2006 released his strongest album since the 1970s, a companion to *Estudando O Samba* – *Estudando Pagode*.

According to Brazil's Academy of Folklore pagode is house party music of the kind played at home around the barbecue. It lies at the heart of Brazilian society and is as popular nationwide as axé music is in Bahia. Zé exploits this and cuts a pagode cross-section through macho attitudes towards women in Brazilian popular culture, society and by extrapolation the world at large. On the CD, Zé plays with pagode rhythms from their earliest incarnations – as associated with artists like Bezerra da Silva – to the more modern, as typified by popular bands like Harmonia do Samba. He intertwines these with jilting Zappa-esque rock complexity, classical chorus, sound-effect interludes, soliloquies and lyrical bossa nova reflections.

The result is a magnificent avant-garde tour de force as profound and experimental as Carla Bley's *Escalator Over the Hill* or Beefheart's *Safe As Milk*, yet resolutely neo-Tropicália. It's a wonderful recording that deepens on every listen.

from the circle like *capoeiristas*). It is magical seen live and is sometimes performed in Rio Vermelho or the Recôncavo towns. Samba canção, or sung samba, gave rise to bossa nova (see box on pages 50–1) and is more guitar-driven. Pagode is a modern, popular form of samba associated with family dance parties and beach barbecues. All sambas are dances as well as rhythms, involving stationary waists and hips and very fast leg and feet movements. They are tricky to master. Discs to buy: for samba de roda and Bahia roots samba look for discs by Roberto Mendes, Riachao, Raimundo Sodré or Mariene de Castro; for samba canção search out Vinícius de Moraes and Baden Powell, João Bosco, Paulinho de Viola and Martinho da Vila; for pagode and popular samba there is no better than Bezerra da Silva.

Tropicália Brazil's counterpart to the musical revolution that began in San Francisco and the underground clubs of London in the late 1960s and produced some of Latin America's most exciting music, film and art. See box on pages 54–5 for the story. Discs to buy: *Bicho* by Caetano Veloso, *Realce*, *Luar* or *Refazenda* by Gilberto Gil, *Estudando o Pagode* by Tom Zé, *Tropicália Panis et Circenses* by vaious artistes.

FILM Brazilian cinema has been more strongly influenced by cinematic movements in Europe than in the United States, and Bahia has played an integral part in its development.

Brazilian cinema really began in earnest in the 1940s with *Rio 40 Graus* (Rio 40 Degrees) directed by Nelson Pereira dos Santos, which introduced the film techniques and ideas of the Italian Neorealists to the country, beginning what came to be known as the *Cinema Novo*. This influenced a new generation of film makers and in 1962 São Paulo director Anselmo Duarte became the first Brazilian director to win the Palme d'Or at Cannes and be nominated for an Oscar with his film *O Pagador de Promessas* (The Keeper of Promises), which is set in the sertão of Bahia and Salvador (see page 130). The film was critical of Brazil's social divide – a trend which continued with another Nelson Pereira dos Santos film, again set in the sertão, *Vidas Secas* (which is listed by the British Film Institute as one of the 360 greatest films in World Cinema) and with the films of Bahian director Glauber Rocha (see box below). The Tropicália movement of the 1960s saw films heavy with allegory like Joaquim Pedro de Andrade's *Macunaíma* based on the novel by Mário de Andrade.

Brazilian cinema went into steep decline with the censorship and repression of the military dictatorship, only really to recover in 1993 when a federal law created financial incentives to encourage Brazilian film production. *Central do Brasil* (Central Station), directed by Walter Salles and set partly in the backlands of Bahia – and which won the Golden Bear Grand Prix at the Berlin International Film Festival in 1998 and the Golden Globe's Best Foreign Film in 1999 – was a product of this initiative. This was followed in by Fernando Meirelles' Academy Award-nominated *Cidade de Deus* (City of God). Recent releases inlcude Fábio Barreto's *O Quatrilho* in 1995, which became the first Brazilian film to be nominated for the Academy Award for Best Foreign Language since *O Pagador de Promessas*, 2007's gritty social realist study of corruption in the police force, *Tropa de Elite* (Elite Force) and in 2010 the biopic *Lula, o filho do Brasil*, telling the story of President Luis Inácio Lula da Silva, and cost 17 million reals, reputedly making it the most expensive film in Brazilian history.

BAHIAN CULTURAL ICONS: GLAUBER ROCHA (1939–81)

In the early 1960s, Glauber Rocha brought the ideas of Italian neorealism and France's *nouvelle vague* to Latin America as *cinema novo* and reinvented Brazilian cinema. His motto was that 'a camera in the hand and an idea in the head' is enough to make a film, born from experiments with low-budget films during his days as a law student at the University of Bahia.

This became the motto of a movement which was integrally connected with tropicália in its rejection of the intellectual and commercial establishment and the production of small-scale, self-financed films which were socio-realistic rather than romantic and escapist as was the norm for Brazilian cinema of that time. Rocha and his fellow film-makers focused on Bahia's poverty, violence and social contrasts.

In his first feature film *Barravento* (Storm), made in 1962, is set in a Bahian fishing village and mixes Candomblé magic with social commentary, deliberately blurring the lines between the two. *Deus e o diabo na terra do sol* (God and the Devil in the Land of the Sun) which is set in **backland** Bahia similarly mixes mythological and allegorical imagery with an exposé of the dire poverty of the **sertão**. It won the international film critics award in Cannes in 1964 and established Rocha as a leading Brazilian film-maker.

Terra em transe (Land in Trance), made in 1967, is a thinly disguised attack on Brazil's military dictatorship, through an allegory set in the fictional state of Eldorado, governed by white intellectuals and soldiers. Like the tropicálistas, Glauber Rocha was censored by the dictatorship and in November 1965 was imprisoned for demonstrating with other intellectuals in front of a hotel in Rio de Janeiro.

LITERATURE Brazilian literature in English suffers from standing in the long shadow of Latin American Spanish writers and a consequent lack of interest (or lack of investment) from English-language publishing houses. Translations when they exist tend to be poor, even of magnificent and important novels like *Grande Sertão: Veredas* (The Devil to Pay in the Backlands), published in 1956 (see below).

There was no printing press in Brazil until the arrival of the Portuguese court in Rio de Janeiro in 1808 (after which cultural institutions were established in the French model), so Brazilian literature got off to a late start. There was plenty written about Brazil prior to this, but even Brazilian-born writers like the great rhetorician **Antônio Vieira** and the satirical poet **Gregório de Matos** were published in and associated with Portugal and written for a European audience. As such they were also influenced strongly by European trends, which from the outset were given a national twist to render them Brazilian. Thus Romanticism in Brazil was rendered Indianism in the mid-1800s by the part-indigenous **Antônio Gonçalves Dias** and **Jose de Alencar**, whose poems and plays idealised the noble savage with all the European fervour of a Rousseau and utilising the plot lines of Walter Scott's novels. Gonçalves Dias pines after a lost paradise in *Canção do Exilio*, while Alencar's *Iracema* tells the story of a love affair between an indigenous woman and a Portuguese man, which as an allegory of the conquest is almost offensive considering the brutality of real events.

TEN BAHIAN WRITERS

ANTÔNIO VIEIRA This great Jesuit scholar, writer and preacher was born in Lisbon in 1608 but was brought up and educated in great part in Bahia and spent most of his life in Brazil. Vieira is regarded by the Portuguese as the greatest and most eloquent pre-20th-century stylist in the language after Camões. His great eloquence averted wars in Spain, secured rights for Christian Jews and saved thousands of indigenous lives on the Amazon. Whilst his attitudes towards the indigenous peoples seems paternalistic to modern eyes, for his time he was a great campaigner for human dignity.

(ANTÔNIO FREDERICO DE) CASTRO ALVES This young abolitionist poet died at only 24 after devoting much of his short life to campaigning through lyric poetry and public speeches against slavery in 1870s Bahia and Brazil. He was a strong influence on Ruy Barbosa.

RUY BARBOSA DE OLIVEIRA One of the early Republic's few intellectuals, Ruy Barbosa was an fervent abolitionist famous for his fiery oratory and for his sharp journalism in the *Diário da Bahia* newspaper. Barbosa spent time in London in the 1890s, from where he wrote a fascinating series of travel letters, 'Cartas da Inglaterra' for the *Jornal do Comércio*.

GREGÓRIO DE MATTOS The most famous Brazilian Baroque poet was born in Salvador in 1636 and was known as the Boca do Inferno (mouth of hell) for his biting satires of his native city. *Que falta nesta cidade? Verdade* (What is missing in this city? Truth), *Que mais por sua desonra? Honra* (What more can make you dishonourable? Honour), *Falta mais que se lhe ponha? Vergonha* (Is there anything else left to add to this? Shame), he wrote of Salvador.

JORGE AMADO Bahia's most famous novelist (and Brazil's most widely translated) started life as a communist championing the poor and ended it as a popular novelist, writing rosy caricatures and novelistic chronicles of Bahian folk traditions. These often feature highly sexualised depictions of black women which have had him accused of racism and sexism. But he is much loved in Bahia.

Alencar was the foremost writer of his day, but was overtaken by Rio de Janeiro-born, Afro-Brazilian **Joaquim Maria Machado de Assis** after his death. Machado de Assis was in another league, and was the first truly Brazilian voice in Latin American literature. Like other Brazilian writers he paid stylistic and thematic homage to European trends – with attacks on societal mores in the tradition of Dickens and how they shaped human character in the naturalistic tradition of Zola. However, Machado de Assis's voice was altogether different – closer to Dostoyevsky than the French in his use of psychologically flawed and unreliable narrators which undermined the authorial role and anticipated modernism. His novels include as *Memórias Póstumas de Brás Cubas* and *Dom Casmurro*, both of which suffer from dreadful translations in English. Machado de Assis founded the foremost literary institution, the Brazilian Academy of Letters.

The republican era began with the elite Brazilian families turning their back on their own people after their hands were forced over the abolition of slavery, by inviting Europeans to work on the coffee plantations in place of the freed slaves. The consequences of this resonate through Brazilian society to this day. **Euclides da Cunha's** *Os Sertões*, the greatest literary work of the republican era is a brilliant if prolix analysis of the dichotomy and division which existed (and continues to exist) between Brazil's haves and have-nots. The book follows the brutal Bahian Canudos campaign, with many meditations and asides on the injustices which

CAETANO VELOSO One of the creators of the tropicália movement, celebrated for his poetic lyrics. His memoir, *Tropical Truth*, is a poignant – if egocentric – chronicle of one of the most interesting and formative moments in modern Brazilian history – the start of the military dictatorship. There are some fascinating descriptions of 1960s Salvador.

JOÃO UBALDO RIBEIRO A writer of contemporary fiction whose *Viva o Povo Brasileiro* (translated An Invincible Memory) set on an *engenho* in Bahia is an epic historical novel following two families – one of aristocrats, the other of slaves – through many generations and changes. It's a fascinating portrait of the growth of Bahia and a satire of the endless search by Brazilians for a sense of identity, which, Ribeiro seems to conclude, does not exist.

ZÉLIA GATTAI AMADO An important Brazilian memoir writer born in São Paulo but married to Jorge Amado and who adopted Bahia as her home. Her *Anarquistas, Graças a Deus*, recounts her youth growing up as a child of Italian immigrants, and the impact of European political ideas on Brazil during the time of the Vargas government. *Um Baiano Romântico e Sensual* profiles her life with Amado.

(ALFREDO DE FREITAS) DIAS GOMES One of 20th-century Brazil's most influential playwrights, principally through the adaptation of his play *O Pagador de Promessas* – the first Brazilian film to win a Palme d'Or, as well as the Special Jury Prize at the 1962 Cannes Film Festival and a nomination for the academy award for Best Foreign Language Film.

JOSÉ OLÍVIO PARANHOS LIMA One of the foremost Brazilian *cordel* writers. *Cordeis* are traditional popular poems written in simple rhymes and distributed as pamphlets, often with xilograph illustrations. *Cordeis* are the direct descendants of popular medieval poems from Spain and Portugal and influenced the uniquely Brazilian spontaneous *emboldada* and *repentista* sung poetry. They can be picked up for free all over Bahia.

brought such a situation about. It has been translated as *A Rebellion in the Backlands*. **Alfonso Lima Barretto** (another Afro-Brazilian Carioca) was also deeply critical of the republican elite's bombastic and arrogant mediocrity, as seen through a bookish, working class Brazilian intellectual in *O Triste Fim de Policarpo Quaresma* (Sad End of Policarpo Quaresma).

Modernism arrived in Brazil with two Paulistanos, **Oswald** and **Mário de Andrade**. Whilst it was influenced by the French it was, in reality, not much more than an attempt to discover a Brazilian literary (and generally artistic) identity. Both writers journeyed in search of this after colonialism, imperialism and the end of slavery. Mário's journey was literal (he travelled throughout the country in search of myths and legends and a sense of Brazilian-ness amongst the people which he expressed in his attempted national epic *Macunaíma*). Oswald's was literary – he launched the Antropofagismo Movement, which attempted to consume foreign influences (as the Tupinambá had consumed the Portuguese – the word means cannibalism), and reincorporate them into Brazilian literature, then express them in a national context. Two other important poets emerged at this time: Pernambucano **Manuel Bandeira** and Mineiro **Carlos Drummond de Andrade**. Both were more genuinely modernist, free of concerns about Brazilian-ness and free to express the more personal and introspective concerns of late modernism – in the spirit of W H Auden.

It was only in the 1930s that Brazilian writers seriously began to notice or idealise the majority of Brazilians. **Gilberto Freyre**'s *Casa Grande e Senzala* was a sociological analysis of the relationship between the Portuguese masters and the African slaves and how it shaped contemporary Brazil. Whilst suffering from romanticism it was the first book to show that (let alone how) Africans had shaped Brazilian identity. It inspired a series of social realist novels set on *engenhos*

FOUR CONTEMPORARY SALVADOR ARTISTS

SÉRGIO RABINOVITZ Bahia's most important painter studied at the Cooper Union School of Art in New York City and has paintings in the Davison print collection. He depicts New York and Salvador through abstract impressions with strong lines and colour. See work at Rua do Balneario 6-E, Amaralina, Salvador (71 3248 1071; www.sergiorabinovitz.com; by appointment).

CHRISTIAN CRAVO A recipient of a Guggenheim fellowship, who produces haunting images of backland Bahia in the tradition of Sebastião Salgado. At Foundation Pierre Verger Photography Gallery (2a Travessa da Ladeira da Vila América 6, Engenho Velho de Brotas, Salvador; 71 3261 7453; www.pierreverger.org, www.christiancravo.com; 08.00–12.00 daily (to the public) & 14.00–18.00 (by appointment)).

DEOSCOREDES MAXIMILIANO DOS SANTOS (MESTRE DIDI) One of Brazil's most important African-Brazilian artists whose work is strongly rooted in Candombeé and who has shown at the Pompidou Centre in Paris. At Rua Bartolomeu de Gusmão, Rio Vermelho, Salvador (71 3331 6247; denisson@atarde.com.br; by appointment).

MARIO CRAVO NETO Produces iconic studio images influenced by Candomblé and which explore the connection between the spirit and the body through an integration of nude figures and natural objects. Represented by the Yancey Richardson Gallery, New York. At Galeria Paulo Darzé (Rua Dr Chrysippo de Aguiar 8, Corredor da Vitória, Salvador; 71 3267 0930; www.paulodarzegaleria.com.br; by appointment).

in the northeast by **José Lins do Rego**. **Graciliano Ramos** was concerned with similar themes in his biting, Marxist-inspired novel *Vida Seca* set in the impoverished sertão. Modern Brazil's greatest writer, **João Guimarães Rosa,** was also inspired by the sertão. He invented a new Brazilian language infused by the idioms of the backland people for his dreamy, metaphysical masterpiece, *Grande Sertão: Veredas.* The post-war period saw Brazilian literature examine the family – especially in **Clarice Lispector**'s fervid domestic dramas set in middle-class Rio like *Laços da família*.

It also saw the emergence of realism – in the gloriously epic, bombastic fictionalised history of Rio Grande do Sul, *O Tempo e O Vento* by **Erico Verissimo** and in the bawdy, romanticised Bahian romps of **Jorge Amado** (see *The Pelourinho*, page 128) – one of Brazil's best-selling novelists abroad.

Literature suffered in the 1960s and 1970s under the censorship and oppression of the military dictatorship. But in recent years a series of stimulating new novelists have emerged, many of them published in decent translations by Bloomsbury. **Milton Hatoum**'s stories, like *The Brothers,* examine the post-abolition immigrant experience at the beginning of the 20th century through the eyes of a Lebanese in Manaus. **Patricia Mello**'s powerful novels, like *Inferno* set in the favelas of Rio, have inspired films like *Cidade de Deus* (City of God) and **Ivan Angelo**'s novels such as *Tower of Glass* are lurid and sharply satirical accounts of contemporary middle-class mores.

ARCHITECTURE Brazilian architecture began with Portuguese colonial building in the fledgling settlements in São Vicente, Salvador and Olinda. Styles were basically Portuguese, with adaptations for the tropical climate. Bahia – and especially Salvador preserves some of the best and most enduring examples of the zenith of this style – the Portuguese Baroque and Rococo. Baroque evolved during the Counter-Reformation in 17th- and 18th-century Europe – beginning in Italy with the sculptures of artists like Gian Lorenzo Bernini. In the spirit of the Counter-Reformation, these transposed the hierarchical ideas of the Gothic into a more personal and emotional style – exemplified by Bernini's statue of Saint Theresa in Ecstasy. This new expressiveness was transferred into architecture. By the time the style had reached its most exuberant in the Rococo, it had become a visible statement of the wealth and power of the establishment. In Bahia this was comprised of the wealthy Portuguese sugar-mill owners, who competed to bestow Salvador and the cities of the Recôncavo with ever more ornate churches. These were often paid for through lay brotherhoods – made up of the wealthy elite and affiliated with a particular monastic order. Salvador is home to some of the most lavish Baroque and Rococo churches in Brazil, most notably the Convento de São Francisco and the Church of the Ordem Terceira do São Francisco.

From the second half of the 19th century Brazilian architecture became strongly influenced by the French. This French influence began with King João VI who invited the French government to seed Brazil with European culture under the French Artistic Mission of 1816. This influence continued in the 20th century when in 1936 Le Corbusier supervised the design of the first major modernist building in the Americas, the Ministry of Education Building (Palácio Capnema) in Rio de Janeiro. The team that worked with him comprised, amongst others, urban planner Lucio Costa, the landscape designer Roberto Burle Marx and most importantly the architect Oscar Niemeyer. These three went on to shape – as a team or individuals – the course of Brazilian architecture from the 1940s into the 21st century. They built countless modernist buildings throughout the country, including the wave-shaped Church of Pampulha in Belo Horizonte (designed by Niemeyer) and the new capital city of Brasilia, which was inaugurated in 1960. The style forged by Costa, Burle Marx and Niemeyer is characterised by a preponderance of concrete, which is often used in a daring curvilinear fashion – to produce monumental buildings. Niemeyer's buildings were described by Brazilian writer Regina Rheda as being 'great to photograph and lousy to live in'. Niemeyer influenced countless Brazilian architects including Luis Filgueiras Lima – whose Sarah Kubitschek Hospital in Salvador is one of Bahia's most celebrated modernist buildings.

Brazil's other internationally celebrated architect is 2006 Pritzker prize-winning Paulo Mendes da Rocha, born in Bahia's neighbouring state of Espírito Santo. Rocha's work is more understated than that of Niemeyer and is informed by the ideals of the Escola Paulista da Arquitetura Brasileira (the São Paulo School of Brazilian Architecture), of which Rocha can be considered a founder. This school grew up largely in the Faculdade de Arquitetura e Urbanismo of the University of São Paulo (FAU-USP) and can be loosely summed up by the axiom that architecture should be raw, clean, clear and socially responsible – or in other words that it should be cheap to build and simple in design. Like Niemeyer Rocha predominantly works in concrete and has no buildings in Bahia.

The World's Green Portal
Sustainable Tourism & Communities Outreach
www.pozoni.com
/sustainabletourism.php

2

Practical Information

WHEN TO VISIT

The best times to visit Bahia are late July–December and mid-February–April (though in 2011, as Carnaval is late, it will be the second week of March–April), when the weather is warm, dry and the crowds not too oppressive.

Bahia's humid tropical climate makes it warm all year round. The wettest months along the coast are April to July, when it can pour on and off for days and the sky is a damp grey blanket. August has sporadic wet weather and it is drier from September to the end of February, making these the best months for good weather.

Bahia gets busy during the school and university holidays (times vary from school to school), when it has its high season. In general this runs from the third week of December to the end of February and during the entire month of July. Within this is 'ultra-high' season of New Year's Eve and the four days on either side and Carnaval week which begins on the Friday preceding Shrove Tuesday (Terça Feira Gorda) in any given year. Shrove Tuesday dates for the next few years are as follows: 8 March 2011, 21 February 2012, 12 Febuary 2013, 4 March 2014, 17 February 2015. During the ultra-high season prices often double.

HIGHLIGHTS

Bahia is larger than any country in western Europe and it offers a country's worth of attractions – from glorious tropical beaches, dramatic craggy mountains and rainforest wilderness to some of the finest Baroque architecture in the New World, distinctive Afro-Brazilian and indigenous American cultural life, and vibrant, energetic music. The following highlights list is of course not exhaustive.

SALVADOR'S BAROQUE ARCHITECTURE In its historic city centre around the Pelourinho, Bahia's capital preserves one of the largest collections of Baroque buildings in the Americas. Rows of brightly painted 17th- and 18th-century mansion houses climb up steep cobbled streets. Stately squares are faced with spectacular Portuguese churches. These include the Igreja e Convento de São Francisco whose Rococo interior is covered with lavish decorations in gold leaf, the Igreja da Ordem Terceira de São Francisco and a cluster of beautiful Carmelite churches. Wandering around the historical centre for a day or two is one of Salvador's many delights. See pages 122–32.

SALVADOR'S MUSIC SCENE There is music on every street corner in Salvador, from pounding Bahian power-pop called axé to roots Afro-Brazilian drum choruses playing afoxé, Brazilian reggae, the twang of *berimbau* bowed percussion instruments playing the rhythms of capoeira and the 1970s rhythms of Caetano Veloso and Gilbert Gil's tropicália. And now, with the inauguration of Carlinhos Brown's new International Center for Black Music and Museu Du Ritmo there is a first-class venue to hear the best of the city's music, right in the city centre. See page 132.

CAPOEIRA Seeing this martial-art dance performed well is unforgettable. To a chorus of African-Brazilian singing and percussion, fighters spin around each other in mock combat, never touching but performing a series of lunges, kicks and punches with dizzying speed and precision. Salvador is the capoeira centre of Brazil. And the art cannot only be seen here it can be learnt at one of the many capoeira schools in the Forte de Santo Antônio Alem do Carmo. There is capoeira throughout the state, with an excellent and popular school in Arraial d'Ajuda on the Costa do Descobrimento. See page 196.

CARNAVAL Brazil and the world's biggest, brashest and most bacchanalian Carnaval takes place in Salvador with huge parades in the streets including the *blocos afro* comprising troupes of hundreds of Afro-Brazilian drummers. There are also other exciting carnivals throughout Bahia – with big crowds in the party city of Porto Seguro and smaller gatherings on the beaches in Morro de São Paulo and Itacaré. See pages 92–3.

BAÍA DE TODOS OS SANTOS In their chronicles, the Portuguese conquerors who first saw this vast wine-glass bay said that it was large enough to harbour all the fleets of Europe. Its calm waters are dotted with little islands fringed with beaches and the fertile soils of its hinterlands known as the Recôncavo are home to colonial towns and ruined sugar mills which were responsible for Bahia's early wealth and many of the worst cruelties of the age – slavery. See pages 139–55.

MORRO DE SÃO PAULO This tiny island town surrounded by pearly beaches backed by shady palm trees has attracted travellers on the Brazilian beach trail for decades. Time here is a mix of up-tempo nightlife and balmy beach days. See page 173.

ITACARÉ'S SURF BEACHES Bahia's finest surf pounds the beaches around this little town on the Costa do Cacau which has frequently hosted ASP World and Billabong Girls Pro surf championship events. See page 182.

JEQUITINHONHA DELTA IN BELMONTE Bahia's largest river after the São Francisco meets the Atlantic in a series of waterways lined with mangroves and gallery forests, rich with bird and wildlife. It's possible to cross between the Costa do Descobrimento and Costa do Cacau here via the towns of Belmonte and Canavieiras on one of Bahia's remotest and most beautiful backwater trips. See page 182.

ESTAÇÃO VERACEL VERACRUZ One of Brazil's most spectacular private wildlife reserves sits within an hour's drive of Porto Seguro. The forests here are pristine and home to jaguar, tapir and nesting pairs of harpy eagles – the largest eagle in the world. See page 184.

COSTA DO DESCOBRIMENTO RAINFORESTS The double UNESCO-listed Atlantic coastal rainforests of southern Bahia swathe the highlands and mountains behind the coast and have one of the highest biodiversities of any location on the planet. They are particularly rich in birds and primates. Three national parks protect the forests: Pau Brasil and Descobrimento, which cannot be visited without special permission; and Monte Pascoal, which is open to the public (see page 206). There are a number of private reserves like Estação Veracel Veracruz.

BEACHES OF THE COSTA DO DESCOBRIMENTO Bahia's famous powder-fine brilliant white sand is at its most delectable in the south around Arraial d'Ajuda, Trancoso and the towns of the southern Costa do Descobrimento (Discovery Coast). The state's best appointed and most romantic hotels are also found here. See *Chapter 6*.

TRANCOSO'S CHIC BEACH SCENE In a few decades Trancoso has gone from sleepy cliff-top fishing village to small luxury resort, visited by the Brazilian and increasingly the international jet set. And whilst it has some of the finest hotels and restaurants in the country it remains low key, low rise and low profile. See page 196.

ABROLHOS NATIONAL PARK Bahia's only marine national park is one of the best locations in the southern Atlantic for diving and snorkelling with a rich biodiversity including huge endemic brain corals. Humpback whales calve in the waters nearby and sightings are almost guaranteed between June and November. See page 215.

MUSEU ECOLÓGICO KRAJCBERG These two beachside museums are filled with artworks from the world's foremost ecological sculptor – the Polish Holocaust survivor and artistic polemicist Frans Krajcberg. His engraved reliefs of leaves and sand furrows, and wooden assemblage sculptures of tortured mangrove roots and torn rainforest wood both champion nature and declaim the violence perpetrated against it. It's worth coming to Nova Viçosa just to see the work. See page 218.

ILHA DA CASSUMBA The wild beaches, forests and mangroves of this beautiful river and ocean island sit between the Costa da Baleia and the Costa Dourada in the far south of Bahia. See page 218.

HIKING IN THE CHAPADA DIAMANTINA These rugged table mountains in the heart of Bahia's arid region offer some of Brazil's most spectacular hiking and walking scenery, with plunging gorges and waterfalls, forests, wetlands and pink-tinted quartzite escarpments offering splendid wilderness views. See page 242.

CANUDOS AND THE LEAR'S MACAW SANCTUARY This tiny village in the sertão interior was the site of one of Brazil's most tragic historical events when the Brazilian army crushed a rebellion from a messianic leader and his ragtag army. The caatinga wilds nearby are home to the deep indigo Lear's macaw, one of the world's rarest, largest and most beautiful parrots. See page 248.

SUGGESTED ITINERARIES

Set on the map of Brazil, Bahia looks tiny. But don't be fooled, Bahia is bigger than France. Roads are poor and attractions spread out, so even those considering flying should plan a journey carefully. Here are a few ideas:

SEVEN DAYS: ROMANTIC GETAWAY
Day 1 Arrive Salvador, transfer to Convento do Carmo, Villa Bahia or Pousada Boqueirão. Dinner in Amado, Trapiche Adelaide or Soho
Day 2 Sightseeing Salvador
Day 3 Transfer to Txai in Itacaré via Ilhéus
Day 4 Txai spa
Day 5 Transfer to Espelho d'Agua or Villas de Trancoso in Trancoso; dine in Cacau
Day 6 Trancoso beaches; dine in Capim Santo
Day 7 Transfer to Salvador for return home

For **ten days** in style add Vila Sereia in Boipeba (and ask for a duplex cabin closest to the beach); dine in the Santa Clara.

How to do it Through Tatur Turismo (see page 68).

SEVEN DAYS: BAROQUE AND AFRICAN BAHIA
Day 1 Arrive Salvador. Check into a hotel or hostel in Barra or the Pelourinho
Day 2 The Pelourinho and Baroque churches
Day 3 Bonfim church and a *candomblé* terreiro
Day 4 Visit the Museu do Ritmo and Ilê Aiyê or Olodum to see afoxé drumming
Day 5 Transfer to Cachoeira
Day 6 Return to Salvador to visit the Museu Afro-Brasileiro. Go to see some live music
Day 7 Return home

How to do it Through Tatur (see page 68).

TEN TO 14 DAYS: BIRDWATCHERS AND WILDLIFE PHOTOGRAPHERS
Day 1 Arrive Salvador, immediate connection to Valença
Day 2 Visit the Ituberá Private Reserve
Day 3 Transfer to Porto Seguro
Day 4 Visit Estação Veracruz and the rainforests around Porto Seguro
Day 5 Porto Seguro–Monte Pascoal National Park
Day 6 Visit the Serra Bonita Private Reserve
Day 7 Transfer to Salvador and to Canudos
Day 8 Visit the Lear's macaw nesting site in the Estação Biológica de Canudos
Day 9 Visit the Raso da Catarina Sanctuary, transfer Salvador
Day 10 Return home
For **fourteen days** add the Chapada Diamantina.

How to do it Through Birding Brazil Tours or Ciro Albano (see page 68).

II DAYS: HIKING AND BEACH
Day 1 Arrive Salvador. Check into a hotel or hostel in Barra or the Pelourinho
Day 2 Sightseeing Salvador
Day 3 Transfer to the Chapada Diamantina
Day 4 Chapada Diamantina Travessia Diamantina long hike
Day 5–8 Chapada Diamantina
Day 9 Return Salvador, catamaran to Morro de São Paulo
Day 10 Relax on Morro de São Paulo
Day 11 Return Salvador and flight home

How to do it Through Tatur (see page 68).

14 DAYS: BEACHES, REEFS AND RAINFORESTS OF THE COSTA DO DESCOBRIMENTO
Day 1 Arrive Salvador, transfer to hotel in Santo Antônio or the Pelourinho
Day 2 Salvador sightseeing, afternoon flight (or overnight bus) to Porto Seguro
Day 3 Check in to hotel in Porto Seguro, Arraial d'Ajuda or environs
Day 4 Full day visit to the Estação Veracel Wildlife Reserve
Day 5 Transfer to Caraíva. Afternoon river trip
Day 6 Transfer to the Mata Nativa pousada in Trancoso
Day 7 Day tour with Mata Nativa. Relax in Trancoso
Day 8 Visit to Espelho beach. Overnight in Trancoso

Day 9 Visit to Monte Pascoal National Park and overnight in Prado
Day 10 Morning river trip in Prado, transfer to Caravelas
Day 11 Visit to the Abrolhos islands for whale watching and snorkelling or diving
Day 12 Transfer to Nova Viçosa and visit to the Ilha da Cassumba
Day 13 Visit the Kracjberg museum
Day 14 Return to Porto Seguro for the transfer to Salvador and flight home

How to do it Through Portomondo Tours (see page 68).

14 DAYS: BACKPACKER BEACH
Day 1 Arrive Salvador. Check into a hotel or hostel in Barra or the Pelourinho
Day 2 Sightseeing Salvador
Day 3 Catamaran to Morro de São Paulo
Day 4 Morro de São Paulo
Day 5 Transfer to Barra Grande via Valença and Camamu (or short flight)
Day 6 Barra Grande and the Peninsula de Maraú
Day 7 Barra Grande and the Peninsula de Maraú
Day 8 Transfer to Itacaré
Day 9 Itacaré surf beaches
Day 10 Itacaré surf beaches, night bus to Port Seguro for Arraial d'Ajuda
Day 11 Arraial d'Ajuda, visit to Jaqueira Pataxó village
Day 12 Arraial d'Ajuda
Day 13 Transfer Porto Seguro for bus to Salvador
Day 14 Return home

How to do it Through Orbita or Portomondo tours (see page 68).

TOUR OPERATORS

Local tour operators are listed in the various chapters. The operators below offer either trips around Bahia (and Brazil as a whole) or one or several regions in the state.

UK
Audley New Mill, New Mill Lane, Witney, Oxon OX29 9SX; ✎ 01993 838 610; www.audley.co.uk. Salvador is included on this company's colonial Brazil tour with the option of bespoke extensions to other parts of Bahia.
Journey Latin America ✎ 020 8747 8315; www.journeylatinamerica.co.uk. A broad range of options in Bahia including a 12-day tailor-made trip visiting 'the best of Bahia' (Salvador, Lençóis, Cahoeira, Morro de Sao Paulo & the Maraú Peninsula) for a very reasonable price.
Songlines Music Travel ✎ 020 8505 2582; www.songlines.co.uk/musictravel. Specialist Carnaval packages in Salvador with a break on the beach afterwards. Tour guides offer the chance to meet many of the musicians & to hear the best live music as well as attend the key Carnaval shows.
Sunvil Sunvil Hse, Upper Sq, Old Isleworth, Middlesex TW7 7BJ; ✎ 020 8758 4774; www.sunvil.co.uk. Tours to Salvador & the Chapada Diamantina.
Tell Tale Travel 1st Flr, 25a Kensington Church St, London W8 4LL; ✎ 0800 011 2571; www.telltaletravel.co.uk. Painstakingly researched sustainable holidays in Bahia & throughout Brazil, with homestays & light adventure trips aiming to integrate locals & visitors & show Bahia from a Bahian perspective. Good value.

Specialist
Naturetrek Cheriton Mill, Cheriton, Alresford, Hants SO24 0NG; ✎ 01962 733051; www.naturetrek.co.uk. Wildlife tours throughout Brazil with bespoke options available for parts of Bahia.
Reef and Rainforest ✎ 01803 866965; www.reefandrainforest.co.uk. Tours throughout Brazil including one which visits the Pousada Lagoa do Cassange on the Peninsula de Maraú & Salvador

(coupled with whale watching for southern right whales in Santa Catarina state & a visit to São Paulo). Accommodation in Corumbau & bespoke Bahia-only options are also available.

US

Brazil Nuts 1610 Trade Center Way, Unit 4, Naples, FL 34109; ☎ 239 593 0266; f +1 239 593 0267; www.brazilnuts.com. Tours & hotel booking throughout Bahia.
Discover Brazil ☎ 888 457 3266; www.discoverbrazil.com. Trips throughout Bahia in all areas except the Costa da Baleia.
Ela Brasil Tours 14 Burlington Dr, Norwalk, CT 06851; ☎ 203 840 9010; www.elabrasil.com. Former ballet dancer Cynthia Izoldi's company offer wonderful small group tours around Bahia & Brazil in general. Trips

Specialist

Birding Brazil ☎ +55 92 638 4540; e rrabybrasil@yahoo.com; www.birdingbrazil.com. Richard Raby is one of the only US operators taking wildlife & birdwatchers to Bahia (most go to Rio & São Paulo state, Mato Gross & Minas Gerais). Destinations in Bahia are limited to Monte Pascoal & Estação Veracruz.

BAHIA

Orbitá R Marquês de Paranaguá 270, Ilhéus; ☎ 073 3234 3250, 073 9983 6655; www.orbitaexpedicoes.com.br. Trips around the Costa do Cacau & Dendê, including the Peninsula de Maraú, Baía de Camamu & the Reserva Biológica de Una. Transfers to the Costa do Descobrimento through the Rio de Jequitinhonha estuary.
Portomondo Ponta do Apaga Fogo 1,Marina Quinta do Porto Hotel; ☎ 73 3575 3686;

Wildwings 577–9 Fishponds Rd, Fishponds, Bristol BS16 3AF; ☎ 0117 9658 333; www.wildwings.co.uk. Brazil jaguar tour in the centre of the country with an optional Bahia extension.

make the most of her extensive insider knowledge & support local communities.
Santours 6575 Shattuck Av, Oakland, CA 94609; ☎ 510 652 8600; f 510 652 8601; toll free: 1 800 769 9669; www.santours.com. Packages throughout Brazil including Bahia & with some light nature tours.
Tell Tale Travel ☎ 0800 011 2571; www.telltaletravel.com. Carefully researched sustainable holidays in Bahia & throughout Brazil, with homestays & light adventure trips aiming to integrate locals & visitors & show Bahia from a Bahian perspective.

Focus Tours PO Box 22276, Santa Fe, NM 87502; ☎ 505 216 7780; www.focustours.com. Environmentally responsible travel throughout Brazil with some tour options including parts of Bahia.

www.portomondo.com. Tours & transfers all around the Costa do Descobrimento & Baleia, hotel & private house booking in Trancoso & beyond, trips to the Abrolhos & Monte Pascoal & excellent north to south journeys via beaches & national parks.
Tatur Turismo Av Tancredo Neves, Salvador; ☎ 71 3114 7900; f 71 3114 7901; www.tatur.com.br. Tours throughout Salvador, Bahia (& Brazil), flight bookings & general help & advice. Irish-run & long established.

Specialist (also see box, _Birdwatching in Bahia_ on pages 20–1)
Birding Brazil Tours www.birdingbraziltours.com. Bespoke options only.
Ciro Albano www.nebrazilbirding.com. The best operator for the northeast of Brazil offering the broadest

spread of Bahian birding & wildlife sites, including Estação Veracruz, Canudos & the Chapada Diamantina.
Edson Endrigo www.avesfoto.com.br. Bespoke options only.

_i_ TOURIST INFORMATION

There is no Bahian tourist information service outside of Bahia. Information about the state is supplied by the international tourist offices run by Embratur (_www.embratur.gov.br_). Contact details are listed below. The state tourism office is Bahiatursa (_www.bahiatursa.ba.gov.br_), based in Salvador (see page 109)

France ☎ +33 1 5353 6962; f +33 1 5353 6700; e ebt.fr@embratur.gov.br, assistant.ebt.fr@embratur.gov.br, info.fr@embratur.gov.br.

Germany ☎ +49 69 2197 1276; f +49 69 9623 8733; e ebt.de@embratur.gov.br, assistant.ebt.de@embratur.gov.br, info.de@embratur.gov.br.

Italy ☏ +39 02 8633 7791; **f** +39 02 8633 7400; **e** ebt.it@embratur.gov.br, assistant.ebt.it@embratur.gov.br, info.it@embratur.gov.br.

Japan ☏ +81 3 5565 7591; **f** +81 3 5565 7593; **e** ebt.jp@embratur.gov.br, assistant.ebt.jp@embratur.gov.br, info.jp@embratur.gov.br.

Portugal ☏ +351 21 340 4668; **f** +351 21 340 4575; **e** ebt.pt@embratur.gov.br, assistant.ebt.pt@embratur.gov.br, info.pt@embratur.gov.br.

Spain ☏ +34 91 503 0687; **f** +34 91 503 0099; **e** ebt.es@embratur.gov.br, assistant.ebt.es@embratur.gov.br, info.es@embratur.gov.br.

UK ☏ +44 20 7396 5551; **f** +44 20 7396 5599; **e** ebt.uk@embratur.gov.br, assistant.ebt.uk@embratur.gov.br, info.uk@embratur.gov.br.

US *East Coast:* ☏ +1 646 378 2126, **f** +1 646 378 2034, **e** ebt.us@embratur.gov.br, assistant.ebt.us@embratur.gov.br, info.us@embratur.gov.br; *West Coast:* ☏ +1 310 341 8394, **e** ebt.us2@embratur.gov.br, assistant.ebt.us2@embratur.gov.br, info.us2@embratur.gov.br.

RED TAPE

Citizens of the European Union and Switzerland, Mercosul countries, some Caribbean and Central American countries, Malaysia, Thailand, Israel and some African countries do not require visas to visit Brazil. US, Australian, Indian, Canadian, Chinese and New Zealand citizens require visas. The situation can change at any time so check with the Brazilian consulate for the latest information. On arrival visitors are issued with a form which must be filled out in black ink and subsequently a 90-day entry pass which can be extended to up to 180 days at any Polícia Federal station in the country. The form must be kept with the passport for the duration of the stay and presented on leaving. Loss will incur long delays and a fine. Passports must be produced on police demand. A photocopy will often do. Brazilian nationals must enter and leave Brazil with their Brazilian passport only.

Those requiring a visa are prohibited from engaging in business, work or academic activities in Brazil, and first arrival in Brazil must take place within 90 days from the date the visa was issued. A visa is good for multiple entries within the visa's duration.

Visas must be completed online on the Brazilian Consulate website (Brazilian Consulate in Washington: *www.consbrasdc.org*) before being printed out. Passports need a six-month validity and should have at least two adjacent blank visa pages available for the visa stamp (excluding the pages reserved for amendments and endorsements). Applicants need to submit one recent 2x2-inch passport-type photograph, front view, and showing entire face, on a white background. Snapshots, computer pictures and picture photocopies are not accepted. In addition there needs to be a presentation of an itinerary printout, or a photocopy of round-trip ticket or e-ticket, or a letter signed by the travel agency, addressed to the Brazilian Consulate, attesting to the acquisition of the ticket and informing of confirmed round-trip bookings. The notarisation of documents issued in the US must be done by a notary public within the jurisdiction of this consulate.

Visitors need a yellow fever vaccination certificate if they have travelled within the last 90 days to any of the following countries: Angola, Benin, Bolivia, Burkina Faso, Cameroon, Colombia, Democratic Republic of Congo, Ecuador, French Guiana, Gabon, Gambia, Ghana, Republic of Guinea, Liberia, Nigeria, Peru, Sierra Leone, Sudan or Venezuela. A yellow fever vaccination is also advisable if traveller destinations in Brazil include any of the following states: Acre, Amapá, Amazonas, Goiás, Maranhão, Mato Grosso, Mato Grosso do Sul, Pará, Rondônia, Roraima, Tocantins or the Federal District (Brasília).

Visas for US citizens cost US$130 in January 2010.

Practical Information **RED TAPE**

2

IN BRAZIL

Canada *Embassy:* Av das Nações Quadra 803, Lote 16, 70410-900 Brasilia DF, ☎ 61 3424 5400; *Consulate:* Av Atlântica 1130 5th Flr, Atlântica Business Center, Copacabana, Rio de Janiero.

Ireland *Embassy:* SHIS QL Conjunto, 05 Casa, 09 Lago Sul, Brasília, CEP 71630 255, ☎ 061 3248 8800; *Consulate in Rio:* Rua 24 de Maio 347, Riachuelo, Rio de Janeiro, CEP 20950-090; ☎ 021 2501 8455, ✉ rioconsulate@ireland.com; *Consulate in São Paulo:* Av Paulista 2006, Conjunto 514, São Paulo, CEP 01310 200, ☎ 011 2387 6362.

UK *Embassy:* Setor de Embaixadas Sul, Quadra 801, Lote 8, CEP 70408-900, Brasília, ☎ 61 3329 2300, http://ukinbrazil.fco.gov.uk/en; *Consulate-General in Rio de Janeiro:* Praia do Flamengo 284/2 andar, 22210-030, Rio de Janeiro RJ, ☎ 21 2555 9600, ✉ britishconsulaterio@terra.com.br; *Consulate-*

General in São Paulo: Rua Ferreira de Araujo 741 – 2 Andar, Pinheiros 05428-002, São Paulo, ☎ 11 3094 2700, ✉ saopaulo@gra-bretanha.org.br; *Honorary Consulate in Salvador:* Av Estados Unidos 18-B, 8° Andar-Comércio, Edificio Estados Unidos, Salvador, Bahia CEP 40010 020, ☎ 71 3243 7399; ✉ adcos@allways.com.br.

US *Embassy:* SES – Av das Nações, Quadra 801 Lote 03, CEP 70403-900, Brasilia, DF, ☎ 61 3312 7000, http://brasilia.usembassy.gov/; *Consulate in Rio de Janeiro:* Av Presidente Wilson 147, Castelo, 20030-020, Rio de Janeiro, ☎ 21 3823 2000; *Consulate General in São Paulo:* Rua Henri Dunant 500, Chácara Santo Antônio, São Paulo; *Consulate in Recife:* Rua Gonçalves Maia 163, Boa Vista, CEP 50070-060, Recife, Pernambuco, ☎ 81 3416 3050.

ABROAD

Angola Av Presidente Houari Bouedienne 132, CP 5428 Miramar, Luanda; ☎ +2442 44 1307/2010/2871/4759; ✆ +2442 44 4913; ✉ emb.bras@ebonet.net

Argentina Cerrito 1350, CP (C1010ABB), Buenos Aires; ☎ +5411 4515 2400, 4515 2500; ✆ +5411 4515 2401; ✉ embras@embrasil.org.ar; www.brasil.org.ar/

Australia 19 Forster Cres, Yarralumla, ACT 2600, Canberra; ☎ 61 2+62732372/62732373/62732374; ✆ 61 2+62732375; ✉ brazil@connect.net.au; www.brazil.org.au/; ⏲ 09.00–17.00 Mon–Fri.

Austria Pestalozzigasse 4/1,1010 Vienna, Austria; ☎ +431 512 0631/512 0623; ✆ +431 513 8374; ✉ mail@brasilemb.at/konsular@brasilemb.at/secom@brasilemb.at

Belgium 350 AvLouise 6eme Etage, Boite 5, B-1050 Bruxelles, Belgium; ☎ 322 640 2015; ✆ 322 640 8134; ✉ brasbruxelas@beon.be; www.brasbruxelas.be

Bolivia Av Arce, s/n esq Rosendo Gutierrez, Edificio Multicentro, Mezanino, Caixa Postal 429, La Paz, Bolivia; ☎ +5912 216 6400; ✆ +5912 244 0043/212 8808; ✉ brasil@brasil.org.bo; www.brasil.org.bo.

Canada 450 Wilbrod St, Ottawa, Ontario K1N 6M8, Canada; ☎ +1613 237 1090; ✆ +1613 237 6144; ✉ mailbox@brasembottawa.org.

Czech Republic PANSKÁ 5, 11000, PRAHA 1,Prague, Czech Republic; ☎ +420 224 321 910; ✆ +420 224 312 901; ✉ brazil@brazil.cz/embaixador@brazil.cz

Denmark Kastelsvej 19, 30 Andar,2100 Copenhagen, Denmark; ☎ 45 3920 6478/45 3555 5020; ✆ 45 3927 3607; ✉ embaixada@brazil.dk/konsulat@brazil.dk.

Ecuador Av Amazonas, 1429 y Colon, Edificio Espana, Piso 10, Caixa Postal 17 01 231, Quito, Ecuador; ☎ 2563 141/142; ✆ 2504 468; ✉ ibec-ecu@transtelco.net; www.embajadadelbrasil.org.ec.

Finland Itainen Puistotie 4 B 1, 00140 Suomi, Helsinki; ☎ +358 (0)9 684 1500; Fax: +358 (0)9 650 084; ✉ brasemb.helsinki@kolumbus.fi; http://brazil.fi

France 34 Cours Albert 1er 75008, Paris; ☎ 0145616300; ✆ 0142890345; ✉ ambassadeur@bresil.org; www.bresil.org.

Germany Wallstrasse 57, 10179, Berlin; ☎ 030 726 28 0; ✆ 030 726 28 320; ✉ brasil@brasemberlim.de; www.brasilianische-botschaft.de/

Guyana 308 Church St, Queenstown, Georgetown, PO Box 10.489, Guyana; ☎ +592 225 7970/1/2/3; ✆ +592 226 9063; ✉ brasemb@networksgy.com

India 8 Aurangzeb Rd,110011, New Delhi; ☎ 9111 2301 7301; ✆ +9111 2379 3684; ✉ brasindi@vsnl.com

Ireland Penthouse 6th Flr Block 8, Harcourt Centre, Charlotte Way, Dublin 2, Dublin; ☎ +3531 475 6000; ✆ +3531 475 1341; ✉ info@brazil.ie; www.brazil.ie

Israel 23 Yehuda Halevi St, 30th Flr, Tel Aviv 65136, Israel; ☎ 9723 691 9292; ✆ 9723 691 6060; ✉ embrazil@netvision.net.il; www.brazilianembassy.org.il

Italy Piazza Navona, 14 00186, Rome; ☎ 06 683981; ✆ 06 6867858; ✉ info@ambrasile.it; www.ambasciatadelbrasile.it

Japan 2 11 12 Kita Aoyama, Minato-ku, 107 8633, Tokyo; ✆ 03 3404 5211; f 03 3405 5846; e brasemb@brasemb.or.jp/administracao@brasemb.or.jp; www.brasemb.or.jp/

New Zealand Level 9, Deloitte Hse, 10 Brandon St, 6011, PO Box 5432, Wellington 6145; f 64 4 473 3517; e brasemb@brazil.org.nz; www.brazil.org.nz

Norway Sigurd Syrs Gate 4 – 0244, Oslo, Norway; ✆ 22 54 07 30; f 22 44 39 64; e consular@brasil.no; www.brasil.no

Paraguay Calle Coronel IrrazÃ¡bal c/ Elygio Ayala, Casilla de Correo 22, Asuncion; ✆ +595 21 248 4000; f +595 21 212 693; e parbrem@embajadabrasil.org.py; www.embajadabrasil.org.py

Peru Av Jose Pardo 850, Lima 18, Apartado Postal 2405, Peru; ✆ 511 421 6763/241 4066; f 511 445 2421; e embajada@embajadabrasil.org.pe/gabemb@embajadabrasil.org.pe

Portugal Estrada Das Laranjeiras 144, Lisboa 1649-021; ✆ 35121 724 8510/35121 724 8700/8521/8522; f 35121 726 7623/35121 726 9607; e geral@embaixadadobrasil.pt

Spain Calle Fernando El Santo 6, Codigo Postal 28010, Madrid, Spain; ✆ 34 91 702 0635/677 547 005; f 34 91 700 4660; e consular@embajadadebrasil.es; www.brasil.es/

Switzerland Monbijoustrasse 68, 3007 Berne, ✆ 4131 371 8515/4131 370 2911/12/4131 370 2929; f 4131 371 0525; e info@brasbern.ch

UK 32 Green St, London W1K 7AT; ✆ 020 7399 9000; f 020 7399 9100; e info@brazil.org.uk; www.brazil.org.uk

US: New York 1185 Av of the Americas (6th Av), 21st Flr, New York, NY 10036; ✆ 917 777 7777; f 212 827 0225; e consulado@brazilny.org; www.brazilny.org

US: Washington 1025 Thomas Jefferson St, NW, Suite 300W, Washington DC, 20007; ✆ 202 238 2700/202 238 2712; f 202 238 2725/26; e consular@brasilemb.org; www.brasilemb.org

Uruguay Boulevard Artigas 1328, Apartado Postal 16.022, Montevideo, Uruguay; ✆ 5982 707 2003/2119/2036; f 5982 707 2086; e evideu@brasemb.org.uy

Venezuela Calle Los Chaguaramos Con Avenida Mohedano, Centro Gerencial Mohedano – Piso 6, Apartado Postal 3977 Carmelitas 1010, La Castellana 1060, Caracas, Venezuela; ✆ 58212 261 7553/5505/6529/2433/3457; f 58212 261 9601; e brasembcaracas@cantv.net

GETTING THERE AND AWAY

✈ **BY AIR** Approximately 20 airlines (see list below) fly to Salvador – Bahia's main city – from Europe, North America and Latin America. These include American Airlines (who fly direct weekly from Miami), Air Europa (who fly via Madrid three times weekly), Condor (who fly via Frankfurt), TAP (who fly daily via Lisbon), TAM (who fly daily from London or New York via São Paulo), Air Italy (who fly via Milan).

Brazil is itself well served by international carriers, most of whom fly to São Paulo. Domestic connections between that city, other Brazilian state capitals and Salvador are frequent and usually inexpensive. For domestic airlines see page 86.

International tickets are least expensive in October, November and a week or so after Carnaval and at their priciest between June and September and in the Brazilian high seasons (generally 15 December–15 January, the Thursday before Carnaval to the Saturday after Carnaval, and 15 June–15 August).

INTERNATIONAL AIRLINES SERVING BRAZIL

Aerolineas www.aerolineas.com. For Buenos Aires from São Paulo & Rio de Janeiro.

Aeroméxico www.aeromexico.com. For Mexico City from São Paulo.

Aerosur www.aerosur.com. For cities in Bolivia from São Paulo.

Air Canada www.aircanada.com. For Toronto from São Paulo.

Air Caraibes www.aircaraibes.com. For Haiti, Martinique & Paris from Belém.

Air China www.airchina.com. For China via Beijing from São Paulo.

Air Europa www.aireuropa.com. For Madrid from Salvador.

Air France www.airfrance.com. For Paris from São Paulo & Rio de Janeiro.

Air Italy www.airitaly.it. For various Italian airports from Fortaleza.

Alitalia www.alitalia.com. Milan from São Paulo.

American Airlines www.aa.com. Major US cities from São Paulo, Rio de Janeiro, Salvador, Recife & Belo Horizonte.

2

Avianca www.avianca.com. Bogotá from Rio de Janeiro & São Paulo.
British Airways www.britishairways.com. London from São Paulo.
Condor www.condor.com. Frankfurt from Recife & Salvador.
Continental www.continental.com. Newark from São Paulo & Rio.
Copa www.copaair.com. Panama City & Havana from Manaus & São Paulo.
Delta www.delta.com. Atlanta from São Paulo & Rio.
Emirates www.emirates.com. Dubai from São Paulo.
GOL www.voegol.com.br. Montevideo, Cordoba & Lima from São Paulo.
Iberia www.iberia.com. Madrid from São Paulo.
KLM www.klm.com. From Europe via Amsterdam from São Paulo.
Korean Air www.koreanair.com. Seoul via LA from São Paulo.
LAN www.lan.com. Lima, Santiago from São Paulo & Rio.
Lufthansa www.lufthansa.com. Frankfurt & Munich from São Paulo.
META www.voemeta.com. Guianas from Belém & Boa Vista.

South African Airlines www.flysaa.com. Johannesburg from São Paulo.
StarPerub www.starperu.com. Lima & Cusco from Rio Branco
TAAG www.taag.aero. Luanda from São Paulo.
TACA www.taca.com. Lima from São Paulo.
TAF www.voetaf.com. Cayenne from Fortaleza, Macapá & Belém.
TAM www.tam.com.br. Asunción, Ciudad del Este, Cordoba, Frankfurt, London, Madrid, Miami, Milan, Montevideo, New York, Paris to São Paulo & Rio.
TAP www.tap.pt. Lisbon & Porto to Aracaju, Belo Horizonte, Brasília, Cuiabá, Curitiba, Fortaleza, Foz de Iguaçu, Goiânia, João Pessoa, Londrina, Natal, Porto Alegre, Porto Seguro, Porto Velho, Recife, Rio Branco, Rio de Janeiro, São Luís, São Paulo Congonhas & Guarulhos., Teresina & Vitória — some on a code share basis.
United www.united.com. Chicago, Los Angeles, New York, Miami & Washington to São Paulo & Rio.
Varig www.varig.com. Bogotá, Buenos Aires & Caracas to São Paulo & Rio.
Verde Airlines www.flytacv.com. From Lisbon & Boston to Fortaleza via Cape Verde.
VistaPluna www.pluna.aero. Montevideo to São Paulo & Rio de Janeiro.

Salvador's Luís Eduardo Magalhães Airport

(*Praça Gago Coutinho, São Cristóvão; 71 3204 1010; www.infraero.com.br*) Also known as Dois de Julho, Salvador's airport lies 32km east of the city centre. There are ATM machines, a 24-hour tourist information counter, a post office, car rental agencies, giftshops and cafés.

Airport transfers An executivo bus connects the airport with the historic centre every 30 minutes, between 06.00 and 22.00, costing R$5. Tickets for fixed-rate taxis (R$60 for Barra or the Pelourinho), are available from the desk next to the tourist information counter.

OVERLAND There are no trains connecting Bahia to the rest of Brazil or South America. But Brazil has overland connections to the following countries. All are by road unless otherwise stated. From the Brazilian border cities there are onward bus services to larger cities and from there to Salvador and other Bahian cities.

AIRPASSES

TAM (*www.tam.com.br*) and Gol (*www.voegol.com.br*) offer a 21-day Brazil Airpass that can only be bought outside Brazil. Prices vary according to the number of destination airport stops (starting with a maximum of four). Tickets must be used within 30 days of the first departure date. The same segment may not be flown more than once in the same direction, except for connections. The same city may not be used as an origin and/or destination more than once, except for connections.

Argentina Via Porto Alegre in the South with flights to Salvador.

Bolivia Via Rio Branco – for flights to Salvador via other Brazilian cities, Guajará-Mirim for Porto Velho and flights to Salvador via other Brazilian cities or Corumbá for Campo Grande and flights to Salvador.

Colombia Via Tabatinga for flights to Salvador via other Brazilian cities.

Guyana Via Boa Vista for flights to Salvador via other Brazilian cities.

Guyane Via Macapá for flights to Salvador via other Brazilian cities.

Paraguay Via Ponta Pora – for connections to Campo Grande and flights to Salvador and Ciudad del Este for Foz de Iguaçu and flights to Salvador.

Peru Via Rio Branco for flights to Salvador via other Brazilian cities or via the Amazon River at Tabatinga for flights to Salvador via other Brazilian cities.

Uruguay Via Porto Alegre in the South with flights to Salvador.

Venezuela Via Boa Vista for flights to Salvador via other Brazilian cities.

BY BUS Buses are Brazil's principal form of inter-city transport and Brazil has a very extensive network. However distances are often enormous and journey times should be factored in to any travel itinerary well ahead. There are frequent buses from Salvador to most Brazilian state capitals and large cities – including the major international hub cities of São Paulo and Rio (24 hours plus and 18 hours from Salvador by bus or 14–16 or ten hours from Porto Seguro). Inter-city buses are generally of a higher standard than their equivalent in Europe or the USA.

BY CAR Cars can be hired for driving between Brazilian states, but again distances are huge and surcharges hefty. It is better value to fly between other state capitals and Bahia and rent locally.

HEALTH *with Dr Felicity Nicholson*

Private healthcare in Brazil is very good in Bahia's university cities, especially Salvador, with modern facilities and well-trained doctors. Doctors tend to over-prescribe by UK standards, using antibiotics and pain killers liberally. Private dentistry is excellent and cheaper than its equivalent in Europe or the U.S. There is a public system too but it is severely overstretched and under-funded.

If you are taking regular medication, make sure you have plentiful supplies even though an equivalent may be available over the counter, it is not always possible to be sure of the quality of the medicines especially in more remote parts. Dengue fever is the principal serious viral disease in Bahia. Bacterial diseases include traveller's diarrhoea and bacillic dysentery and tuberculosis (TB). Parasitic diseases include Chagas disease (trypanosomiasis) and minor infections like cutaneous larva migrans (bicho geografico) and chiggers (bicho do pé).

People new to exotic travel often worry about tropical diseases, but it is accidents that are most likely to carry you off. Road accidents are common in many parts of Brazil so be aware and do what you can to reduce risks: try to travel during daylight hours, always wear a seatbelt and refuse to be driven by anyone who has been drinking. Listen to local advice about areas where violent crime is rife too.

IMMUNISATIONS Preparations to ensure a healthy trip to Bahia require checks on your immunisation status: it is wise to be up to date on tetanus, polio and diphtheria (now given as an all-in-one vaccine, Revaxis, that lasts for ten years), and hepatitis A. Immunisations against hepatitis B and rabies may also be recommended. Proof of vaccination against yellow fever is not needed for entry into Brazil, but the World Health Organisation (WHO) recommends that this vaccine should be taken by those over nine months of age, for health reasons if you are visiting endemic regions within the country. This includes northern and western Bahia. Your GP or travel clinic expert will tell you if you are not able to take the vaccine. If that is the case then you should ensure that you use cover up clothing and an insect repellents containing 50–55% DEET during the daytime in particular, if you are in the relevant areas of Bahia.

Hepatitis A vaccine (Havrix Monodose or Avaxim) comprises two injections given about a year apart. The course costs about £100, but may be available on the NHS; protects for 25 years and can be administered even close to the time of departure. Hepatitis B vaccination should be considered for longer trips (two months or more) or for those working with children or in situations where contact with blood is likely. Three injections are needed for the best protection and can be given over a three-week period if time is short for those aged 16 or over. Longer schedules give more sustained protection and are therefore preferred if time allows. Hepatitis A vaccine can also be given as a combination with hepatitis B as 'Twinrix', though two doses are needed at least seven days apart to be effective for the hepatitis A component, and three doses are needed for the hepatitis B. Again this schedule is only suitable for those aged 16 or over.

The newer injectable typhoid vaccines (eg: Typhim Vi) last for three years and are about 85% effective. Oral capsules (Vivotif) may also be available for those aged 6 and over. Three capsules over five days lasts for approximately three years but may be less effective than the injectable forms. They should be encouraged unless the traveller is leaving within a few days for a trip of a week or less, when the vaccine would not be effective in time.

Vaccinations for rabies are ideally advised for everyone, but are especially important for travellers visiting more remote areas, especially if you are more than 24 hours from medical help and definitely if you will be working with animals (see *Rabies* page 80).

Experts differ over whether a BCG vaccination against tuberculosis (TB) is useful in adults: discuss this with your travel clinic.

Visit a GP or travel clinic at least six weeks before leaving for Bahia to find out up to the minute information on vaccinations and general health risks for Bahia. It is a good idea to take out travel insurance, know your own blood group and if you suffer a long-term condition such as diabetes or epilepsy make sure someone knows or that you have a Medic Alert bracelet/necklace with this information on it.

TRAVEL CLINICS AND HEALTH INFORMATION A full list of current travel clinic websites worldwide is available on www.istm.org/. For other journey preparation information, consult www.nathnac.org/ds/map_world.aspx. Information about various medications may be found on www.netdoctor.co.uk/travel.

UK

Berkeley Travel Clinic 32 Berkeley St, London W1J 8EL (near Green Park tube station); ☎ 020 7629 6233; ⊕ 10.00–18.00 Mon–Fri; 10.00–15.00 Sat.
The Travel Clinic Ltd Cambridge 41 Hills Rd, Cambridge CB2 1NT; ☎ 01223 367362; e enquiries@ travelclinic.ltd.uk; www.travelcliniccambridge.co.uk;

⊕ 10.00–16.00 Mon, Tue & Sat, 12.00–19.00 Wed & Thu, 11.00–18.00 Fri.
The Travel Clinic Ltd,Ipswich Gilmour Piper, 10 Fonnereau Rd, Ipswich IP1 3JP; ☎ 01223 367362; ⊕ 09.00–19.00 Wed, 09.00–13.00 Sat.

Edinburgh Travel Health Clinic 14 East Preston St, Newington, Edinburgh EH8 9QA; 0131 667 1030; www.edinburghtravelhealthclinic.co.uk; 09.00–19.00 Mon–Wed, 9.00–18.00 Thu & Fri. Travel vaccinations & advice on all aspects of malaria prevention. All current UK prescribed anti-malaria tablets in stock.

Fleet Street Travel Clinic 29 Fleet St, London EC4Y 1AA; 020 7353 5678; e info@fleetstreetclinic.com; info@fleetstreetclinic.com; www.fleetstreetclinic.com; 08.45–17.30 Mon–Fri. Injections, travel products & latest advice.

Hospital for Tropical Diseases Travel Clinic Mortimer Market Centre, Capper St (off Tottenham Ct Rd), London WC1E 6JB; 020 7388 9600; www.thehtd.org; 09.00–16.30 Mon, Tue, Wed & Fri, 10.00 –16.30 Wed. Offers consultations & advice, & is able to provide all necessary drugs & vaccines for travellers. Runs a Travellers Healthline Advisory Service (020 7950 7799) for country-specific information & health hazards. Also stocks nets, water purification equipment & personal protection measures. Travellers who have returned from the tropics & are unwell, with fever or bloody diarrhoea, can attend the walk-in emergency clinic at the Hospital without an appointment.

InterHealth Travel Clinic 111 Westminster Bridge Road, London, SE1 7HR, 020 7902 9000; e info@ interhealth.org.uk www.interhealth.org.uk; 08.30–17.30 Mon–Fri. Competitively priced, one-stop travel health service by appointment only.

MASTA (Medical Advisory Service for Travellers Abroad) London School of Hygiene & Tropical Medicine, Keppel St, London WC1E 7HT; 09068 224100; e enquiries@masta.org; www.masta-travel-health.com. This is a premium-line

number, charged at 60p per minute. For a fee, they will provide an individually tailored health brief, with up-to-date information on how to stay healthy, inoculations & what to take.

MASTA pre-travel clinics 01276 685040. Call or check www.masta-travel-health.com/travel-clinic.aspx for the nearest; there are currently 50 in Britain. They also sell malaria prophylaxis, memory cards, treatment kits, bednets, net treatment kits, etc.

NHS travel websites www.fitfortravel.nhs.uk; www.fitfortravel.nhs.uk or www. fitfortravel.scot.nhs.uk; www.fitfortravel.scot.nhs.uk. Provide country-by-country advice on immunisation & malaria prevention, plus details of recent developments, & a list of relevant health organisations.

Nomad Travel Clinics Flapship store: 3–4 Wellington Terrace, Turnpike Lane, London N8 0PX; 020 8889 7014; e turnpike@nomadtravel.co.uk; www.nomadtravel.co.uk; walk in or appointments 09.15–17.00 every day with late night Thu. Also has clinics in west & central London, Bristol, Southampton & Manchester – see website for further information. As well as dispensing health advice, Nomad stocks mosquito nets & other anti-bug devices, & an excellent range of adventure travel gear. Runs a Travel Health Advice line on 0906 863 3414.

Trailfinders Immunisation Centre 194 Kensington High St, London W8 7RG; 020 7938 3999 www.trailfinders.com/travelessentials/travelclinic.htm; 09.00–17.00 Mon, Tue, Wed & Fri, 09.00–18.00 Thu, 10.00–17.15 Sat. No appointment necessary.

Travelpharm The Travelpharm website www.travelpharm.com. Offers up-to-date guidance on travel-related health & has a range of medications available through their online mini-pharmacy.

Irish Republic

Tropical Medical Bureau 54 Grafton St, Dublin 2; +353 1 2715200; e graftonstreet@tmb.ie; www.tmb.ie; Mon–Fri to 20.00 & Sat mornings.

For other clinic locations, & useful information specific to tropical destinations, check their website.

USA

Centers for Disease Control 1600 Clifton Rd, Atlanta, GA 30333; (800) 232 4636 or (800) 232 6348; e cdcinfo@cdc.gov; www.cdc.gov/travel. The central source of travel information in the USA. Each summer they publish the invaluable Health Information for International Travel.

IAMAT (International Association for Medical Assistance to Travelers): 1623 Military Rd, #279 Niagara Falls, NY 14304-1745; 716 754 4883; e info@iamat.org; www.iamat.org. A non-profit organisation with free membership that provides lists of English-speaking doctors abroad.

Canada

IAMAT (International Association for Medical Assistance to Travellers) Suite 10, 1287 St Clair St

West, Toronto, Ontario M6E 1B8; 416 652 0137; www.iamat.org

TMVC Suite 314, 1030 W Georgia Street, Vancouver, BC V6E 2Y3; ☎ 604 681 5656; e vancouver@ tmvc.com; www.tmvc.com. One-stop medical clinic for all your international travel health & vaccination needs.

Australia and New Zealand

TMVC (Travel Doctors Group) ☎ 1300 65 88 44; www.tmvc.com.au. 30 clinics in Australia & New Zealand, including: Auckland Canterbury Arcade, 174 Queen St, Auckland 1010, New Zealand; ☎ 64 9 373 3531; e auckland@traveldoctor.co.nz; Brisbane 75a Astor Terrace, Spring Hill, Brisbane, QLD 4000, Australia; 07 3815 6900; e brisbane@ traveldoctor.com.au; Melbourne 393 Little Bourke St, Melbourne, Vic 3000, Australia; ☎ 03 9935 8100; e melbourne@traveldoctor.com.au; Sydney 428 George St, Sydney, NSW 2000, Australia; ☎ 2 9221 7133; e sydney@traveldoctor.com.au.

IAMAT 206 Papanui Rd, Christchurch 5, New Zealand; www.iamat.org

South Africa

SAA-Netcare Travel Clinics ☎ 011 802 0059; e travelinfo@netcare.co.za; www.travelclinic.co.za. Eleven clinics throughout South Africa.

TMVC NHC Health Centre, Cnr Beyers Naude & Waugh Northcliff; ☎ 0861 300 911; e info@ traveldoctor.co.za; www.traveldoctor.co.za. Consult the website for clinic locations.

AILMENTS

Diarrhoea and intestinal upset Around half of people new to exotic travel are likely to get an episode of travellers diarrhoea. That said the better restaurants in Bahia have good sanitation and diarrhoea is usually no more than an occasional nuisance born of unfamiliar diet. The best remedy is rest and plenty of fluids taken with rehydration sachets (Dioralyte, Electrolade or in Brazil Hidrafix or Solução Sal Açúcar). However, there are simple measures you can take to avoid getting travellers' diarrhoea in the first place and you will also avoid typhoid, paratyphoid, cholera, hepatitis, dysentery, worms, etc. Travellers' diarrhoea and the other faecal-oral diseases come from getting other peoples' faeces in your mouth. This most often happens from cooks not washing their hands after a trip to the toilet, but even if the restaurant cook does not understand basic hygiene you will be safe if your food has been properly cooked and arrives piping hot. The most important prevention strategy is to wash your hands before eating anything. You can pick up salmonella and shigella from toilet door handles and possibly bank notes. The maxim to remind you what you can safely eat is:

PEEL IT, BOIL IT, COOK IT OR FORGET IT

This means that fruit you have washed and peeled yourself, and hot foods, should be safe but raw foods, cold cooked foods, salads, fruit salads which have been prepared by others, ice cream and ice are all risky, and foods kept lukewarm in hotel buffets are often dangerous. That said, plenty of travellers and expatriates enjoy fruit and vegetables, so do keep a sense of perspective: food served in a fairly decent hotel in a large town or a place regularly frequented by expatriates is likely to be safe.

If symptoms persist beyond five days or if there is blood and/or slime and/or a fever with the diarrhoea then you should see a doctor as soon as possible. A stopping agent such as loperamide (Imodium) can be used when you are unable to let the diarrhoea just happen. It is not suitable for children under nine years of age. If the diarrhoea persists for more than three days then you should seek medical advice and always if there are other symptoms present.

Bacterial travellers' diarrhoea can be treated with Ciproxin (Ciprofloxacin) – a useful antibiotic. You need to take one 500 mg tablet when the diarrhoea starts and if necessary a further tablet 10–12 hours later. If there are no signs of improvement after 24 hours the diarrhoea is likely to be viral and not bacterial. However, it could be that the bacteria are resistant to the antibiotic so you should seek medical advice if symptoms persist. If it is due to other organisms such as those causing giardia or amoebic dysentery then the best treatment is tinidazole or failing that metronidazole. Seek medical advice.

Chagas disease Or American Trypanosomiasis is a potentially serious disease caused by the protozoan *Trypanosoma cruzi* and is spread by the biting or Reduviid 'kissing' bug (*Panstrongylus megistus*) which is endemic in Central and South America. The disease is most prevalent in rural areas where the bugs live in mud walls and only come out at night. Avoidance is the best method so when travelling through an endemic region try not to sleep in adobe huts where the locals sleep, keep away from walls when sleeping and use mosquito nets. Spraying the insides of rooms with an insecticide is also a good idea.

Symptoms include swelling around the site of the bite followed by enlargement of the lymph glands and fever. Long term symptoms include damage to the heart causing sudden death and paralysis of the gut causing difficulty in swallowing and severe constipation.

LONG-HAUL FLIGHTS, CLOTS AND DVT

Any prolonged immobility including travel by land or air can result in deep vein thrombosis (DVT) with the risk of embolus to the lungs. Certain factors can increase the risk and these include:

- Previous clot or close relative with a history
- People over 40 but > risk over 80 years
- Recent major operation or varicose veins surgery
- Cancer
- Stroke
- Heart disease
- Obesity
- Pregnancy
- Hormone therapy
- Heavy smokers
- Severe varicose veins
- People who are very tall (over 6ft/1.8m) or short (under 5ft/1.5m)

A deep vein thrombosis (DVT) causes painful swelling and redness of the calf or sometimes the thigh. It is only dangerous if a clot travels to the lungs (pulmonary embolus). Symptoms of a pulmonary embolus (PE) include chest pain, shortness of breath, and sometimes coughing up small amounts of blood and commonly start three to ten days after a long flight. Anyone who thinks that they might have a DVT needs to see a doctor immediately.

PREVENTION OF DVT
- Keep mobile before and during the flight; move around every couple of hours
- Drink plenty of fluids during the flight
- Avoid taking sleeping pills and excessive tea, coffee and alcohol
- Consider wearing flight socks or support stockings (see www.legshealth.com)

If you think you are at increased risk of a clot, ask your doctor if it is safe to travel.

There is no preventative vaccine or medication for Chagas disease and treatment is difficult as agents toxic to the trypanosomes are also toxic to humans.

Malaria The risk of malaria in Bahia is low enough not to take malaria tablets but it is still important to do everything you can not to get bitten by mosquitoes both during the day (see *Dengue fever* below) and at night. Use an insect repellent that contains around 50–55% of a chemical called DEET. This needs to be reapplied to exposed skin every 4–6 hours and again after being in water. If you cannot tolerate these and prefer to use natural repellents, ensure that they contain both citronella and eucalyptus oil and use every one–two hours. Wearing long sleeves and trousers after sunset is a good extra precaution and ensure that you sleep under permethrin impregnated bed nets if you are not in air-conditioned accommodation. You can never be too careful about being bitten by mosquitoes as there are several mosquito borne diseases for which there is no prevention or treatment.

Dengue fever This is an infection transmitted by a group of viruses called flaviviruses which are spread by *Aedes aegypti* mosquitoes. These are fast-flying dark black and white mosquitoes which bite during the day. Dengue is widespread in coastal Bahia, in both rural and suburban environments. Dengue has flu-like symptoms – high fever, weakness, headaches and nausea. It usually occurs in two phases. The first is characterised by a fever and a skin rash. This generally clears up after a few days to return in a milder form a few days later and then finally disappear altogether.

In some cases dengue can be more severe. It can cause strong pain in the bones and muscles. And in a very small number of cases it can develop into Dengue Shock Syndrome (DSS). This stage usually affects children under ten but can occur in adults and has a high mortality rate – especially with infants. It is characterised by abdominal pain, sudden collapse, cool clammy extremities, weak pulse, and blueness around the mouth. There is easy bruising and the fever becomes haemorrhagic, with, blood spots in the skin, spitting up blood, blood in the faeces, bleeding gums and nosebleeds.

There's a much greater risk of DSS when a person has immunity to one of the other types of dengue virus as a result of previous infection.

There is no specific treatment for dengue beyond drinking plenty and resting. Painkillers based on paracetamol (tylenol in Brazil) should be used as aspirin, ibuprofen and dorflex can increase the risk of haemorrhage. Those who are severely affected should be taken to hospital. Although it may take a number of weeks, most people recover fully without further problems.

WATER PURIFICATION

There are at least three ways to treat water: boiling, filtering or adding chlorine dioxide. If water is contaminated (from floods, streams or lakes), boiling is the best method. Turbid water should be filtered before boiling or adding chlorine. If you haven't got a water filter then you may have to improvise by using coffee filters, paper towels or a cotton tee shirt in a funnel.

When boiling: bring the water to a bubbling boil for a full minute. Cover and allow to cool. If boiling is not possible, treat water by adding commercial chlorine dioxide tablets or drops. Mix thoroughly and allow to stand for at least ten minutes before using (60 minutes if the water is cloudy or cold).

There are various commercial products available which are chlorine in tablet form or liquid form and various filter systems. Ensure that the water filter is of a reputable make (eg: Aquapur) which will remove bacteria, viruses, cryptospiridia and giardia.

The best way to prevent getting dengue fever in the first place is to use insect repellents containing around 50–55% DEET on exposed skin during the daytime.

Leishmaniasis This skin infection caused by a protozoal parasite transmitted by forest midges (phlebotomine sandflies) is not common in Bahia. Symptoms are a raised lump, which leads to a purplish discolouration and a possible ulcer.

Bilharzia or schistosomiasis Bilharzia or schistosomiasis is a disease that commonly afflicts the rural poor of the tropics. There is one form in South America – Schistosoma mansoni. It is an unpleasant problem that is worth avoiding, though can be treated if you do get it. It is easier to understand how to diagnose it, treat it and prevent it if you know a little about the life cycle. Contaminated faeces are washed into the lake, the eggs hatch and the larva infects certain species of snail. The snails then produce about 10,000 cercariae a day for the rest of their lives. The parasites can digest their way through your skin when you wade, or bathe in infested fresh water. Winds disperse the snails and cercariae. The snails in particular can drift a long way, especially on windblown weed, so nowhere is really safe. However, deep water and running water are safer, while shallow water presents the greatest risk. The cercariae penetrate intact skin, and find their way to the liver. There male and female meet and spend the rest of their lives in permanent copulation. No wonder you feel tired! Most finish up in the wall of the lower bowel, but others can get lost and can cause damage to many different organs.

Although the adults do not cause any harm in themselves, after about 4–6 weeks they start to lay eggs, which cause an intense but usually ineffective immune reaction, including fever, cough, abdominal pain, and a fleeting, itching rash called 'safari itch'. The absence of early symptoms does not necessarily mean there is no infection. Later symptoms can be more localised and more severe, but the general symptoms settle down fairly quickly and eventually you are just tired.

Although bilharzia is difficult to diagnose, it can be tested at specialist travel clinics or hospitals. Ideally tests need to be done at least six weeks after likely exposure and will determine whether you need treatment. Fortunately it is easy to treat at present.

Avoiding bilharzia If you are bathing, swimming, paddling or wading in fresh water which you think may carry a bilharzia risk, try to get out of the water within ten minutes.

Avoid bathing or paddling on shores within 200m of villages or places where people use the water a great deal, especially reedy shores or where there is lots of water weed.

Dry off thoroughly with a towel; rub vigorously.

If your bathing water comes from a risky source try to ensure that the water is taken from the lake in the early morning and stored snail-free, otherwise it should be filtered or Dettol or Cresol added.

Bathing early in the morning is safer than bathing in the last half of the day.

Cover yourself with DEET insect repellent before swimming: it may offer some protection.

HIV/AIDS The risks of sexually transmitted infection are moderate to high in Brazil, whether you sleep with fellow travellers or locals. About 80% of HIV infections in British heterosexuals are acquired abroad although predominantly from Africa and India. If you must indulge, use condoms or femidoms, which help reduce the risk of transmission. If you notice any genital ulcers or discharge, get treatment promptly since these increase the risk of acquiring HIV. If you do have unprotected sex, visit a clinic as soon as possible; this should be within 24 hours, or no later than 72 hours, for post-exposure prophylaxis.

Rabies (*Raiva*) Rabies is carried by all mammals including bats and is passed on to man through a bite, scratch or a lick of an open wound. You must always assume any animal is rabid, and seek medical help as soon as possible. Meanwhile scrub the wound with soap under a running tap or while pouring water from a jug. Find a reasonably clear-looking source of water (but at this stage the quality of the water is not important), then pour on a strong iodine or alcohol solution of gin, whisky or rum. This helps stop the rabies virus entering the body and will guard against wound infections, including tetanus.

Pre-exposure vaccinations for rabies is ideally advised for everyone, but is particularly important if you intend to have contact with animals and/or are likely to be more than 24 hours away from medical help. Ideally three doses should be taken over a minimum of 21 days. Incomplete courses can course confusion amongst treating doctors who then don't know what to do. Contrary to popular belief these vaccinations are relatively painless.

If you are bitten, scratched or licked over an open wound by a sick animal, then post-exposure prophylaxis should be given as soon as possible, though it is never too late to seek help, as the incubation period for rabies can be very long. Those who have not been immunised will need a full course of injections. In order to prevent rabies effectively you need to have human rabies immunoglobulin injected into the wound and the balance intramuscularly in a different limb. This product is hard to come by and very expensive. If this product is not available and you have not been vaccinated prior to exposure then you will need to evacuate to a city or even another country to get it. If you are offered equine (horse) immunoglobulin then this is better than nothing at all and may be more appropriate than spending time travelling. Equine immunoglobulin carries a

TICKBORNE TYPHUS FEVER

This disease is most prevalent in the US but also occurs in western and central Mexico, Panama, Costa Rica, Colombia and Brazil. It is a rickettsial disease transmitted by ticks which is characterised by a sudden onset of a moderate to high fever typically around 3–14 days after a tick bite. This is accompanied by chills and reddening of the eyes. About three days later a rash appears on the extremities of the body including the palms and soles then spreads over the body. Without treatment it can be fatal in up to 25% of cases. The disease cannot be spread from person to person and the tick needs to stay on the body for four–six hours before spreading the disease.

Ticks should ideally be removed as soon as possible as leaving them on the body increases the chance of infection. They should be removed with special tick tweezers that can be bought in good travel shops. Failing that you can use your finger nails: grasp the tick as close to your body as possible and pull steadily and firmly away at right angles to your skin. The tick will then come away complete, as long as you do not jerk or twist. If possible douse the wound with alcohol (any spirit will do) or iodine. Irritants (eg: Olbas oil) or lit cigarettes are to be discouraged since they can cause the ticks to regurgitate and therefore increase the risk of disease. It is best to get a travelling companion to check you for ticks; if you are travelling with small children, remember to check their heads, and particularly behind the ears.

Spreading redness around the bite and/or fever and/or aching joints after a tick bite imply that you have an infection that requires antibiotic treatment, so seek advice.

slightly higher risk of side effects but the risk of rabies is far higher. It is also important to check the type of vaccine on offer. Often brain-derived vaccine is all that is available and this should not be accepted. Ensure that you have good insurance to evacuate you to a city or other country that has either HDCV, PCEC or vero cell derived vaccine.

Tell the doctor if you have had pre-exposure vaccine, as this should change the treatment you receive. And remember that, if you do contract rabies, mortality is 100% and death from rabies is probably one of the worst ways to go.

Sun exposure Even when there's a cooling sea breeze or cloud cover Bahia's sun is formidable. Cover up well and bring plenty of suncream. It's widely available in Brazil but the higher protection factors (30 or above) are exorbitantly expensive. For light skin it is important to use a high factor sunscreen (30-50) with UVA and UVB. But even the darkest skin will burn in Bahia.

Other tropical infections Cutaneous larva migrans (*bicho geográfico*) is a skin infection by a nematodal worm whose larvae are found in animal faeces. It is characterised by an itchy moving spot which leaves a red trail. It is easily treated with Thiabendazole cream or Albendazole tablets (both available in pharmacies in Brazil). Jiggers/chiggers/chigoe fleas (*Bicho do pé*) are burrowing fleas (*Tunga penetrans*) which enter the skin – usually of the feet under the nails where they lay eggs which form cysts with a little black head, before hatching into hundreds of little babies. They are easily treated, by covering the cyst with Vaseline for a day and then gouging it out with a sterile needle. There are also small (harvest) mites called chiggers which bite humans – these are harmless and unrelated.

Venomous animals Australians may champion their funnel web spider, but Brazil can boast the world's deadliest spider: the Brazilian wandering spider also known as the Brazilian huntsmen (*Phoneutria bahiensis spp*). *Aranhas armadeiras*, as the huntsmen is known in Portuguese, is responsible for more human deaths than any other. These side-plate-sized fast-moving nocturnal hunters like to roost in dead leaves, sheds and wood piles and are extremely aggressive when disturbed. However, the risk they pose is negligible: a study paper published by the São Paulo Institute of Tropical Medicine in January 2000 concluded that only 0.5% of all bites involve serious envenomation, and that only ten deaths had ever been recorded since records began.

The story for snakes is similar. Bahia has some nasty forest vipers – the bushmaster (Portuguese: *Surucucu*) which is the largest and most powerful venomous snake in the new world, and the fer-de-lance (Portuguese: *Jararaca*) is also aggressive and highly venomous. Both species rarely bite and even then not all bites result in venom being administered.

Those who are unfortunate enough to be bitten by a venomous animal should try to photograph the culprit and then seek medical attention as quickly as possible. Many so-called first-aid techniques do more harm than good: cutting into the wound is harmful; tourniquets are dangerous; suction and electrical inactivation devices do not work. The only treatment is anti-venom. In case of a bite that you fear may have been from a venomous snake:

- Try to keep calm – it is likely that no venom has been dispensed.
- Prevent movement of the bitten limb by applying a splint.
- Keep the bitten limb BELOW heart height to slow the spread of any venom.
- If you have a crêpe bandage, wrap it around the whole limb (eg: all the way from the toes to the thigh), as tight as you would for a sprained ankle or a muscle pull.
- Evacuate to a hospital that has anti-venom.

And remember:

- NEVER give aspirin; you may take paracetamol, which is safe.
- NEVER cut or suck the wound.
- DO NOT apply ice packs.
- DO NOT apply potassium permanganate.

If the offending snake can be captured without risk of someone else being bitten, take this to show the doctor – but beware since even a decapitated head is able to bite.

SAFETY

Brazil in general has a bad reputation for robbery and violence, but the latest statistics available as this book went to press showed that some 180,000 British nationals visit Brazil annually and yet only 241 have required consular assistance, with by far the largest group needing help with missing passports and the second largest for arrests. However, robberies and assaults do occur. And when they do the assailants are almost always armed. Whilst visitors to Bahia should be more vigilant than they would be back home, it is unlikely they'll encounter any problems if a few golden rules are adhered to:

- Be discreet. Dress down and bling-free. It's a good idea to wear Brazilian-brand T-shirts and flip-flops/thongs, to keep cameras and valuables out of sight in a modest bag when they aren't being used and to carry only what you will need for the day with you.
- Keep some notes in a pocket or a purse and larger amounts in a money belt.
- Avoid beaches and back streets after dark.
- Keep an eye out for anyone following you.
- Use taxis from taxi ranks.
- Be very wary of accepting invitations to visit someone's home.
- Drug possession – even of cannabis – incurs severe penalties.
- Never argue with a police officer or official. Treat them with deferent suspicion.
- Ask your hotel to contact the tourist police if you have any problems.
- Never enter a *favela* (slum community) without an organised specific invitation from a tour company or organisation. Most violence in Bahia takes place in Salvador's *favelas*.
- Credit card fraud is common. Use a debit card wherever possible and keep a spare card for emergencies in your hotel safe, if there is one, in a sealed envelope (for extra security – to indicate fraudulent access to the safe). Try to keep sight of your card at all times and use a credit card (as opposed to debit) only when really necessary.
- Mobile-phone cloning occurs. Take care of your handset.
- Email yourself a .txt or scanned .jpg attachment of your documents: passport, credit cards, travel insurance, etc.

WOMEN TRAVELLERS Brazil is less safe than Europe or North America and just as all travellers, solo women travellers should be cautious in Bahia; especially off the beaten track and in Salvador. It is a good idea to book ahead and book tours through agencies. You will rarely be on your own unless you choose to be. It is nearly always possible to meet people in hostels, hotels or on group tours – especially in the more touristy locations like Morro de São Paulo, Arraial d'Ajuda, the Chapada Diamantina

There have been increased cases of the use of a cocktail of drugs called *Boa Noite Cinderela* (Good Night Cinderella) in robberies and sexual assaults in Brazil. The cocktail is added to drinks bought by a 'friend' – usually on the beach, at Carnaval or other such parties or even in the hotel room from an invited or solicited guest. The boa noite cocktails comprise one or several of Flunitrazepam (Rohypnol), ketamine and gamma-hydroxybutryate (GHB). All are colourless (although official Roche Rohypnol had a blue dye added post-1998). Symptoms begin with drowsiness, a distant sound to one's own voice and other noises, slurring of speech and general muscular grogginess. It's easy to mistake the initial signs for drunkenness. The eventual sleep can last up to 24 hours. To avoid being drugged you should purchase your own drinks or accept only sealed bottles and keep them within sight to avoid them being drugged. And remember, not all the perpetrators are Brazilians.

and Salvador. Unwarranted attention is common around the Pelourinho, especially at Carnaval time when men seem to think it their right to grope and kiss in the tight, thronging crowds.

Be wary of walking in city streets unaccompanied at night, especially Salvador. Where you have to get around on your own after dark, taxis (from a taxi rank) are always worth the extra expense; women are the easiest targets for muggings. When travelling intercity try to avoid arriving after dark if possible and as ever be suspicious of over-friendly strangers.

If you think you are being dogged and followed, walk into the nearest smart hotel or restaurant – even if it is just to order a coffee or to express your concerns to the staff at reception. Security is an issue in Brazil and staff will always be sympathetic and protective. They will also order you a cab and make sure you get into the vehicle safely.

Rape and sexual assault The incident of rape and other sexual offences in Bahia is statistically low. However, single and small groups of women should be extra vigilant during Carnaval. Rape itself is rare. But there have been reports of attacks against both men and women, and some have involved a cocktail of 'date rape' drugs called *Boa Noite Cinderela* 'Good Night Cinderella' (see box above).

TRAVELLING WITH CHILDREN Travel with children is straightforward in Bahia. Brazilians adore children, and kids are generally more welcome and better attended to than back home. Children are never expected to be seen but not heard, and always allowed to run around pretty much everywhere. Even expensive restaurants provide children's seats and most have children's' menus, crayons and paper to keep them happy. Many hotels offer a discount family rate, don't charge for children under five and can provide an extra camp bed for a double room. A handful of the more exclusive beach resorts do not accept children. If planning to stay in such a hotel it is best to enquire ahead. Children under three generally travel for 10% on internal flights and for 70% until 12 years old. On tours children under six usually go free or it is possible to bargain a discount rate. Prices on buses depend on whether the child will occupy a seat or a lap. Laps are free and if there are spare seats after the bus has departed the child can sit there for free.

Transport can involve long waits in *rodoviárias* (bus stations) – but there are generally restaurants and plenty of places to sit down. Whilst it is best to bring Kwells from Europe or the US for motion sickness, Dramin – which comes in dropper bottles – is available in Bahia. Two glasses of strong *maracujá* (passion fruit) juice act as a weaker natural substitute.

Practical Information SAFETY

2

DISABLED TRAVELLERS Facilities for disabled travellers in Bahia – and in Brazil as a whole – are very poor. It is very rare even for hotels or public buildings to have disable toilets, access ramps are rare and public transport and taxis are almost entirely devoid of disabled facilities. Pavements are often in a poor state of repair or crowded with street vendors requiring passers-by to brave the passing traffic. However, despite these obstacles, Brazilians are always very eager to help and disabled travellers are seldom left to fend for themselves. Most shopping centres and public car parks have disabled spaces and drivers should bring a disabled sticker.

Organisations and sources of information Disability Travel (*www.disabilitytravel.com*) is a comprehensive US site compiled by travellers in wheelchairs who have been researching disabled travel full-time since 1985. There are many tips and useful contacts (including lists of travel agents on request) and articles, including pieces on disabled travelling worldwide. The company also organises group tours. Global Access News (*www.globalaccessnews.com*) provides general travel information, reviews and tips for disabled travellers. The Society for Accessible Travel and Hospitality (*www.sath.org*) provides some general information – though very little on Brazil.

Brazilian organisations include the Sociedade Amigos do Deficiente Físico (*www.aibr.com.br/sadef*) and the Centro da Vida Independente (*www.cvi-rio.org.br*).

There are a number of specialist and general operators offering holidays specifically aimed at those with disabilities. These include Responsible Travel (*www.responsibletravel.com*), CanbeDone (*www.canbedone.co.uk*) and Access Travel (*www.access-travel.co.uk*) – though Bahia was not listed as of 2010. For more personal advice, it's certainly worth contacting Rosangela Berman Bieler (**e** *rbbieler@aol.com*), a Brazilian disability rights activist who is involved with the Tourism for All Network (*www.iidi.org/en/rede-de-turismo-para-todos.htm*).

GAY AND LESBIAN TRAVELLERS In general Bahia is tolerant of gay and lesbian travellers, with fairly liberal attitudes in the larger urban centres and the tourist towns. Opinions in the sertão and rural areas are far more conservative and it is wise to adapt to this. There is a well-established scene in Salvador. Local information can be obtained from Cultura (*Rua do Sodre 45*) near the Museu de Arte Sacra da Bahia, which publishes a guide to the gay scene in the city for R$10. There is further information on the Grupo Gay da Bahia website (*www.ggb.org.br*).

WHAT TO TAKE

Here is a basic packing list for travel in Bahia beyond Salvador, including wilder areas. Light (in colour and material) trousers, shorts, one long-sleeve shirt, skirts and underwear. Thin cotton or modern wicking fabrics (that move sweat away from the skin to the outer surface of the fabric, where it evaporates) are best. Bahians dress very casually. It's best to do likewise.

- A shawl or light waterproof jacket for evenings
- Mosquito net embedded with insect repellent. The bell-shaped models are best.
- Sun protection (high factor)
- Mercurochrome or similar antiseptic
- Earplugs for surfing and cockerels
- Athlete's foot powder
- Tea tree oil
- Antibiotic ointment
- Penknife

- Inelegant daypack/bag – to attract minimal attention
- Camera case to attract minimal attention to the camera
- Sun hat
- Sunglasses (with UV filter)
- Light Gore-tex walking shoes or boots if you intend to trek. Buy from a serious, designated outdoor brand like Brasher or Berghaus, not a fashion house. Wear them in before you come. Nothing gives a tourist away more than new shoes.
- Money belt
- Torch (flashlight)
- Birdwatching field guide and small binoculars
- Snorkel and mask
- UK, US or European socket adapter (other Europeans or North Americans will find their own plugs will fit Brazilian sockets).

WHAT YOU CAN BUY THERE

- T-shirts – local brands make you less conspicuous and they are sold everywhere.
- Insect repellent (Johnson's Off! aerosol is best)
- Beachwear
- Flip-flops/thongs
- Painkillers
- Shampoos and soaps
- Beach shawl (kanga)
- Vitamins etc

$ MONEY

The Brazilian unit of currency is the *real* (R$; pl *reais*) divided into 100 centavos. In August 2010 the rate was US$1 = R$1.75, £1 = R$2.79, €1 = R$2.32. Notes in circulation are 100, 50, 10, 5, 2 and 1 (the last of which is becoming increasingly rare). Coins are 1 real and 50, 25, 10, 5 and 1 centavos.

CASH Cash sums over US$10,000 must be declared on entering Brazil. Residents may only take out the equivalent of US$4,000.

Bring cash US dollars to Brazil and two debit cards – ideally one MasterCard/Amex, and one Visa. It's also worth having a credit card as back-up.

CREDIT CARDS Credit cards are widely used. Diners Club, MasterCard, Visa and American Express are widely accepted. Cash is easy to exchange in banks or larger hotels, though rates can be poor. They are far worse for travellers' cheques with up to US$20 commission per transaction. Many banks change a minimum of US$300 cash or US$500 travellers' cheques. Be sure to advise your bank that you are travelling, as cards are often automatically blocked on unadvised withdrawals from Brazil.

ATMS Automatic teller machines (ATMs) or cashpoints are widespread in Bahia. They offer the cheapest and most convenient way of withdrawing money and usually the best rates of exchange. They are usually closed after 21.30 in large cities. The best banks for international cards are Bradesco, HSBC and Banco 24 horas. A handful of Banco do Brasil branches accept international cards.

MONEY TRANSFERS Money sent to Brazil through transfers is normally paid out in Brazilian currency, so do not have more money sent out than you need for your stay. It can take up to four weeks to clear the bureaucracy.

BUDGETING

As a very rough guide, prices in Bahia are about the same as in the US, and two-thirds that of the UK. Allow R$60–80 per person per day for travelling cheaply in Bahia, ie: staying in hostels, eating cheap and travelling on buses rather than planes.

The cheapest accommodation is nearly always a bed in a hostel dormitory. Hostel rooms tend to be pricier than the cheaper hotels and hotel breakfasts are also more generous and almost always included in the price. A late breakfast can usually serve as a replacement lunch. Buy fruit, bottle water, bread rolls and snacks in markets rather than supermarkets and eat set meals (*prato feito/almoço*) or buffets (*Bufê livre*) in padaria bakeries or simple wayside restaurants. Night buses can often be the cheapest way to travel as they save on overnight accommodation.

SAMPLE PRICES IN BAHIA

Dorm bed	from R$30
1½ litre bottled water from a supermarket	R$2
Main meal	from R$8
Sandwich in a bakery	R$6
Cup of coffee in decent café	R$3

GETTING AROUND

✈ **BY AIR** Because of Bahia's size and rough roads, flying is often the most practical way to cover long distances, such as Salvador to Porto Seguro. Internal air services within Brazil are well developed with airports in Salvador, Ilhéus, Porto Seguro and smaller airports in Barra Grande, Lençóis and Morro de São Paulo. Deregulation of the airlines at the turn of the millennium greatly reduced prices between Salvador and Porto Seguro. When booked through the internet, low-cost airlines offer fares that can often be as cheap as travelling by bus. Paying with an international credit card is not always possible online, but it is usually possible to buy an online ticket through a hotel, agency or willing friend without surcharge. Many of the smaller airlines go in and out of business sporadically.

Airlines operating in Bahia

Abaeté Aeroporto Internacional Deputado Luís Eduardo Magalhães, Salvador; ☎ 071 3377 2555; www.voeabaete.com.br. Operate from Bom Jesus da Lapa, Guanambi & Salvador.

Addey Táxi Aéreo Aeroporto Internacional Deputado Luís Eduardo Magalhães, Salvador; ☎ 071 3377 1993; www.addey.com.br. Operate between Morro de São Paulo, Barra Grande & Salvador.

Aero Star Aeroporto Internacional Deputado Luís Eduardo Magalhães, Salvador; ☎ 071 3377 2555; www.aerostar.com.br. Operate from Barra Grande, Morro de São Paulo & Salvador.

Azul ☎ 0800 702 1053; www.voeazul.com.br. Operate from Salvador & throughout Brazil.

GOL ☎ 0300 789 2121; www.voegol.com.br. Operate from Ilhéus, Juazeiro do Norte, Porto Seguro, Salvador & cities throughout Brazil.

Oceanair ☎ 0300 789 8160; www.oceanair.com.br. Operate from Salvador & cities throughout Brazil.

Passaredo ☎ 016 3514 7111; www.voepassaredo.com.br. Operate from Vitória da Conquista & codeshares with TAM in Porto Alegre & Salvador. Services throughout Brazil.

TAM ☎ 011 5582 8811; www.tam.com.br. Operate from Ilhéus, Porto Seguro, Salvador, with services throughout Brazil & connections to North America & Europe.

Webjet ☎ 021 4009 0000; www.webjet.com.br. Operate from Ilhéus, Salvador & throughout Brazil.

🚗 **BY CAR** Bahia has an extensive system of roads both federal and state. Roads close to the main cities are well maintained. Others, including the federal BR-101 coastal highway can be badly pocked with holes in places. Driving long distances can be trying on axles and patience.

Car hire To hire a car in Bahia you will need a photo driving licence, a credit card and proof of identity. Rates can be very high if you hire within Bahia itself. It is cheapest to rent from abroad online through a large company. Companies working in Brazil include Europcar (*www.europcar.com*), Holiday Autos (*www.holidayautos.co.uk*), Sixt (*www.sixt.com*), Hertz (*www.hertz.co.uk*) and Brazil Car Rental (*www.brazilcar.com*).

Cars run on three different forms of fuel in Brazil – petrol (gasoline), natural gas and alcohol. Through the 'powerflex' system many cars will take two or even three forms of fuel into the same engine. Alcohol is cheaper but less efficient – you need about 50% more alcohol than regular petrol for the same distance. Natural gas is more widely available than in any other country in the world and can be found at most large petrol stations. Fuel prices vary from week to week. Note that petrol is often contaminated with acetone or methanol in order for petrol stations to make the largest possible profit and engines often run inefficiently.

Driving security Avoid driving at night if possible – especially in remote areas. Bring a mobile phone with you in case you break down. It can be risky to ask for help from other motorists. When parking leave no valuables visible and park as close as possible to your destination. Adult minders or street children will generally protect your car fiercely in exchange for a tip.

◀ BY BUS Travel by bus is easy and comfortable. Brazil has some of the finest bus services in Latin America. There are three standards of bus: *comum* (aka *convencional*) can be slow, not very comfortable and fill up quickly; *executivo* are more expensive, comfortable (many have reclining seats), and don't stop *en route* to pick up passengers, so are safer; *leito* (literally berth) operate at night between the larger cities. *Leito* are the most comfortable and most expensive services, with reclining seats, toilets and sometimes refreshments. Air conditioning can make buses cold at night, so take a jacket. Buses stop every two to four hours for meals and toilet breaks.

Bus stations are called *rodoviárias*. They are frequently outside the city centres and have restaurants, lavatories and often left-luggage stores or guarda volumes. Bus tickets are cheapest at *rodoviárias*. Travel agents often add a surcharge of around 10%. Buses usually arrive and depart in very good time. Many town buses have turnstiles that can be inconvenient if you are carrying a large pack. Urban buses normally serve local airports.

↪ ACCOMMODATION

Bahia offers plenty of accommodation choice: from camping and hostels at the lower end, through to mid-range guesthouses and small hotels, to five-star business hotels and luxurious boutique beach resorts. Usually accommodation prices include a breakfast (*café de manha*) of rolls, ham, cheese, cakes and fruit – with coffee and juice; there is no price discount if you don't eat it.

Most of Bahia's larger hotels can be booked through tour operators (or their own websites) and at a fraction of the rack rate. Whilst its reviews are often penned by resort staff or their rivals, Tripadvisor offers a one-click price listing for a number of the larger tour operators, including Expedia (*www.expedia.com*), LateRooms (*www.laterooms.com*), Hotels (*www.hotels.com*), Venere (*www.venere.com*) and Splendia (*www.splendia.com*). It is also possible to search through those company's sites.

At the budget end of the market Hostelbookers (*www.hostelbookers.com*), Hostels (*www.hostels.com*) and Hostelworld (*www.hostelworld.com*) offer a similar service. Many Bahian hostels are part of the International Youth Hostel Association (*www.iyha.org*) chain. But again be circumspect about the reviews. A similar service for campsites is offered by Camp in Go (*www.campingo.com*) – although their Brazil options were limited in 2010. The Brazilian Camping Club (*www.campingclube.com.br*) has more comprehensive listings but no booking service.

Couchsurfing (*www.couchsurfing.org*) and Servas (*http://joomla.servas.org*) offer the latest alternative to hostelling or camping, with a homeshare exchange service whereby members offer their homes to other members visiting their city.

HOTELS Bahian hotels operate according to the international star system, although five-star hotels are not price controlled and hotels in any category are not always of the standard of their star equivalent in US, Canada or Europe. Many of the older hotels offer double rooms which are cheaper than those in hostels. Rooms come in different categories. Normally an *apartamento* is an apartment room with a separate living and sleeping area and sometimes cooking facilities. A *quarto* is a standard room, *com banheiro* is en suite and *sem banheiro* is with shared bathroom.

Boutique hotels Bahia has some of South America's finest small luxury hotels, the majority of which are clustered around Itacaré and Trancoso.

Pensões These simple hotels often fall outside Brazil's hotel star system. Yet they can offer comfort at a two- or three-star level, if not the business services required to earn them a star. Rooms are usually small by US standards but generous by European and usually come with en-suite bathrooms, fans, a writing table, wardrobe and little else. Some have fridges and air conditioning. A few hotels have only offer shared bathrooms.

APARTMENT AND BEACH HOUSE RENTAL A number of companies offer private home beach rentals and apartments in Salvador for Carnaval. These include Paradise Properties (*www.pp-bahia.com*), who have apartments in Salvador and Portomondo (*www.portomondo.com*), and Casas Charmosas (*www.casascharmosas.com.br*), Matueté

BAHIA'S TEN BEST HOTELS

1 **CONVENTO DO CARMO, SALVADOR** Colonial splendour, with a Baroque chapel and cloisters (see page 109).
2 **BOQUEIRÃO, SAVADOR** Colonial boho in distressed wood and ochre, with beautiful bay views (see page 110).
3 **TXAI SPA, ITACARÉ** Beachside pampering; still intimate, though the cabins are proliferating (see page 169).
4 **SAGE POINT, ITACARÉ** Marine bric-a-brac, ocean spray. For surfers there is no other choice (see page 169).
5 **POUSADA LAGOA DO CASSANGE, MARAÚ PENINSULA** Remote beaches and responsible tourism (see page 167).
6 **FAZENDA DA LAGOA, UNA** Beach luxe in virgin wild. Shame they are clueless about wildlife (see page 178).
7 **ETNIA, TRANCOSO** Rustic beach chic in a tropical garden with a spectacular reflection pool (see page 197).
8 **ESPELHO D'AGUA, TRANCOSO** Nascent responsible tourism and fabulous beachside cabins (see page 197).
9 **MATA NATIVA, TRANCOSO** In a garden of flowering trees and with eco-trips (see pages 197–9).
10 **TAUÁNA, CORUMBÁU** Bahia's most beautifully designed hotel on a remote strand of sand (see pages 204–5).

(*www.matuete.com*) and Brazilian Beach House company (*www.brazilianbeach.com*) who rent villas and beach houses in Trancoso.

POUSADAS *Pousada* is a catch-all term for a range of accommodations, from a family-run bed and breakfast to a small hotel. Pousadas often present better value and more charm than the blander hotels.

ALBERGUES The Brazilian equivalents of the backpacker hostel offer the cheapest accommodation for travellers prepared to share a dormitory room (*dormitório*) with a group or strangers. Many also have double rooms. These are often more expensive than double rooms in guesthouses. Almost all the hostels listed have internet, lockers, tour information and luggage storage.

CAMPING Those with an international campers' card pay only half the rate of a non-member at Camping Clube do Brasil (*www.campingclube.com.br*) sites. The Clube has sites throughout Bahia which can be found on their website. It can be difficult to get into some Camping Clube campsites between January and February. Private campsites charge about US$8–15 per person. For those on a very low budget and in isolated areas where there is no campsite, service stations can be used as camping sites. They have shower facilities, watchmen and food; some have dormitories. There are also various municipal sites. Campsites often tend to be some distance from public transport routes and are better suited to those with their own transport. Be sure to use campsites with security guards. Never camp wild or by roadsides, as armed robbery is a real risk.

✖ EATING AND DRINKING

Bahia has some of the best food in Brazil, African-infused, rich with sauces and seafood and a welcome break from the national cuisine of meat and rice and beans. And unlike most Brazilians, Bahians have discovered the chilli pepper; though in far smaller doses than those to which most British curry lovers will be accustomed. Afro-Bahian cooking is a syncretism of west African, indigenous Brazilian and Portuguese styles. *Feijoada*, the national dish, was born of the leftovers scrounged by the slaves – offcuts and offal from all manner of meats, thrown in a pot and left to its own devices during work and served with that indigenous Brazilian staple, manioc flour. The most famous Bahian dish is *moqueca*, almost certainly a Tupinambá dish: fresh fish, prawns or crab cooked slowly in dendê palm oil and coconut milk with garlic, tomatoes and optional cilantro and chilli. *Vatapá* and *caruru* are pastes made from prawns, nuts, bread, coconut milk and dendê oil. They are

2

often served stuffed into a ball of *acarajé* (squashed black-eyed peas or beans deep fried in dendê oil and served split in half) which probably originates from west Africa where there is a similar ritual dish called *àkàrà*. *Xinxim de Galinha* is a rich, spicy chicken stew cooked with dendê oil and fragrantly spicy.

MEALS AND MEALTIMES There are no set mealtimes in Bahia and timing is extremely informal. Breakfast (*café de manhã*) is usually served between 07.00 and 10.00. It usually consists of bread rolls, ham and cheese, fruit, very sweet cereals, fruit juice, tea and coffee. Coffee often comes with sugar and milk already added – usually in large amounts. If you don't want milk, ask for a *café sem leite*, and without sugar *sem açucar*. Lunch (*almoço*) is the main meal of the day and is generally served between 12.00 and 15.00 and supper from 20.00. Restaurants serve a full menu in the evenings, but for Bahians, supper (*janta*) is generally a light meal – perhaps a cooked sandwich (*lanche*) or a soup (*sopa*) or some *acarajé*.

WHERE TO EAT *Restaurantes* (restaurants) are either á la carte, buffet or *rodizio*. Buffet restaurants offer the best value and many sell plates by weight (per kilo). Rodizio restaurants (which are often *churrascarias* – spit-roast meat restaurants)

INGREDIENTS (serves 4)

2kg chicken thighs
300g peeled jumbo shrimp
Salt and ground black pepper to taste
Juice of 2 limes
1 tbsp cooking oil
1 chopped onion
1 garlic crushed clove
½ green pepper, cored, seeded and diced
2 tomatoes, seeded and chopped
1 cup chicken stock
3 chilli peppers
1 egg cup ground cashews
1 egg cup ground peanuts
¼ cup ground shrimp
⅓ tsp fresh grated ginger
¼ cup cilantro (coriander), chopped
⅓ cup coconut milk
Vegetable oil

METHOD Wash and dry the chicken and shrimp and season with salt and pepper. Place the chicken pieces in a bowl, add the juice of 1 lime; mix and marinate for 30 minutes. Put shrimp in another bowl, add the juice of half a lime and marinate for 15 minutes.

Heat one tablespoon of vegetable oil in a large pot over high heat, add the shrimp and sauté for a few minutes. Remove from the heat and set aside. Heat one more tablespoon of vegetable oil and slowly brown the chicken pieces on both sides. Then remove from the heat and set aside.

Drain the pot, add the cooking oil and warm over medium heat. Add onions and garlic and sauté until soft. Add the green pepper and sauté for five minutes more. Add the tomatoes and stock and bring to a boil. Add the chicken, reduce heat and simmer covered for half an hour, or until the chicken is tender. Remove the chicken from the pot and set aside.

Add the chilli peppers, cashews, peanuts, ground shrimp, ginger and salt and pepper to the simmering liquid and stir. After a few minutes add the chicken, shrimp and the cilantro (coriander) and simmer for about five minutes. Add the juice of half a lime and the coconut milk. Cook for three minutes, remove from heat and serve.

Practical Information **EATING AND DRINKING**

2

charge a set price for an eat-all-you-can buffet salad and plates brought hot from the kitchen by waiters. They are usually *churrascarias* but they can be pizzerias, pasta or Japanese restaurants. The best restaurants are in Salvador and are of international quality.

Padarias (bakeries) and *Lanchonetes* (diners) serve set meals (*pratos feitos*), tapas (*petiscos*) snacks (*lanches*) or savouries (*salgados*) as well as coffee, juices and desserts. Cafés serve coffee and snacks.

DRINKS Brazilians are not big wine drinkers and many restaurants do not have a wine list. Beer is the alcoholic drink of choice for most Bahians. Brazilian beer is light, bottled and similar to lager. It is served ice-cold and usually in bottles (*garrafas*). Small bottles are often called *longee neckee* (from the English 'long neck'). Draught beer is called *chope* or *chopp* (after the German Schoppen, and pronounced 'shoppi'). It comes with a big, foamy head, whose creaminess determines the *chope*'s quality for most Baianos. There are various national brands, which include Bohemia, Brahma, Skol and Antartica. The best beer is from the German breweries in Rio Grande do Sul. The national liquor is sugar cane rum (cachaça, also known as *pinga*). When mixed with pulped limes (or other fruits), sugar and crushed ice the result is a caipirinha, and when weaker, a batida.

Fruit juices or *sucos* are made from an extraordinary array of tropical fruits and frozen tropical fruit pulps. Many are unknown outside South America and a number are unique to Brazil. Bahian specialties include, light, refreshing *mangaba* and *umbu* and tart *seriguela*. Other delicious juices are *açaí* – a palm berry from the Amazon – *caju* (cashew fruit), pungent, sweet *cupuaçu* and *cacau* (cocoa fruit).

CARNAVAL IN BAHIA

Nowhere celebrates Mardi Gras like Brazil. *Carnaval* in Brazil is a unique experience. It's *the* big holiday of the year – a time where the entire country, from wealthy oligarchs to favela kids, let go, let rip and relax over a long weekend of hedonism and revelry. Salvador confidently claims to have the biggest and best carnaval in Brazil. Rio and Recife disagree. Over the Mardi Gras weekend there are *carnavais* in every city and town from Porto Seguro to the depths of the sertão. Wherever you are in Bahia expect not to sleep.

THE STORY OF CARNAVAL Brazil may do it best, but Carnaval is not unique to Brazil. It's a Catholic celebration, a bacchanalia of indulgence that traditionally takes place on Shrove Tuesday (but often the weekend preceding it), immediately before the beginning of the feast of Lent – a time of privation and penance that remembers Christ's 40-day sojourn in the desert and his crucifixion.

Brazilian Carnaval mixes the Portuguese Catholic celebration with a remembrance of Africa through an adaptation of traditional African rhythm and ritual. In Rio the rhythm is samba, a fusion of Angolan drum patterns and European polka. In Bahia you won't hear samba. Here the streets throb to afoxé – pounded out by giant African-Brazilian drum troupes – or axé, its more commercialised, gaudy counterpart. The costumed Carnaval troupes or *blocos* that march to these rhythms, either in the streets or designated arenas, are derived from traditional parades conducted by African tribal nations in the Portuguese colonial era. The parades were an effort to preserve various cultural identities in the face of the forced homogenisation of slavery.

Brazil's and the world's largest and most raucous Carnaval takes place in Salvador (*www.carnaval.salvador.ba.gov.br*). Unlike Rio's, this is a street festival and until the 1990s it was dominated by the powerful percussive street parades of the *blocos afro*, troupes of some 200 drummers accompanied by singers atop mobile sound trucks. Their pounding, visceral rhythm is powered by enormous surdo drums that beat out a deep, booming 'bumbum bumbum bum' anchor, overlaid by a sharp, crackling tattoo from *repique* hand drums. The overall effect is astonishing. The most famous of the *blocos afro* – **Ilê Aiyê** – whose members are all exclusively black and Bahian, take to the streets outside their headquarters at Ladeira do Curuzu on Carnaval Saturday night. And **Filhos de Gandhi**, the original *bloco afro* – founded in 1949 – parade on the Sunday and Tuesday. The sound and sight of their 6,000 members dancing through the streets, a river of white and blue in an ocean of multi-coloured Carnaval revellers, is one of the highlights of Salvador's Carnaval.

But the *blocos afro* are becoming increasingly marginalised by cheap and cheesy high-octane Bahian power-pop or axé – performed at ear-drum-splitting volume by scantily

PUBLIC HOLIDAYS

1 January	New Year's Day/Confraternização Universal (Day of Universal Brotherhood)
February/March	Carnaval (always 47 days before Easter)
April	Sexta-Feira Santa Paixão (Good Friday)
21 April	Tiradentes
1 May	Dia do Trabalho (Labour Day)
May/June	Corpus Christi (Thursday after Trinity Sunday)
28 June	Pilões
2 July	Independência da Bahia (Bahian Independence Day)
7 September	Independence Day (Brazil)
12 October	Nossa Senhora Aparecida, Padroeira do Brasil (Our Lady Aparecida, Patron Saint of Brazil)

dressed, dynamically dancing divas (like **Ivete Sangalo** or the star of the moment, **Claudia Leite**) and power-pop combos like **Chiclete com Banana**. They and their backing bands wiggle on the roofs of vast trucks or *trio electricos*, which plough a furrow through the multitudes, dragging a cordoned-off few in their wake, protected by a rope and security personnel and dressed in expensive *trio electrico* T-shirts. The best night for the *trios electicos* is Shrove Tuesday itself, when the trucks meet in Praça Castro Alves for the **Encontro dos Trios**, playing in rotation until dawn. The event can be watched from the street or vast grandstands erected on scaffolding. And it is not uncommon for major stars from the Brazilian and international music scene to make surprise appearances. In the past they have included Bono. The other major centre for Salvador is the beach suburb of Barra, frequented by the *blocos alternativos* and including **Timbalada**, a drumming group formed by renowned percussionist Carlinhos Brown (see box on page 134). It's possible to pay to join most of the parades and buy tickets for the grandstands, either through a UK tour operator or through the *blocos* themselves. For more information see the official Carnaval site.

CARNAVAL ON THE BEACH Bahia's beaches offer an alternative Carnaval closer to nature but with equally frenetic, axê-powered partying. The biggest celebrations are in Porto Seguro and Arraial d'Ajuda – the Carnaporto (*www.carnaporto-axemoi.com.br*) – which rival Salvador's in scale, Morro de São Paulo (*www.morrodesaopaulo.com.br*) and, for something chic and cheerful, Trancoso or Itacaré. There are more traditional, local Carnavals in the sertão.

SAFETY AT CARNAVAL With so many tourists and such big crowds, Carnaval has a bad reputation for crime. Here are a few golden rules:

- Dress cheaply like a local – in flip-flops/thongs, board shorts and a (Brazilian) T-shirt
- Keep your camera hidden when not in use
- When away from the crowds at night never walk with purpose and never along empty streets or the beach.
- Ask your hotel for news on areas where thieves tend to operate.
- Take taxis from designated stands or your hotel
- Have a little ready cash in your pocket, some in a belt and the bulk in the hotel
- Never resist a robbery

See box *Carnaval Glossary* on page 94 for an explanation of terms.

Practical Information **PUBLIC HOLIDAYS**

2

2 November	Finados (All Souls' Day)
15 November	Proclamação da República (Republic Day)
20 November	Dia da Consciência Negra (Black Consciousness Day)
24 December	Christmas Eve
25 December	Christmas Day
31 December	New Year's Eve

FESTIVALS

JANUARY

Nosso Senhor dos Navegantes, Salvador This huge dawn procession on New Year's Day is a key event of the Candomblé calendar. It begins with the arrival of a boat called *Gratidão do Povo* (Gratitude of the People) bearing an effigy of Senhor Bom Jesus dos Navegantes (Good Jesus of the Sailors) in the Baía de Todos os Santos next to the Igreja da Boa Viagem in Bonfim. It is followed by a flotilla of other vessels and accompanied by processions of Bahians.

Lavagem do Bonfim, Salvador Salvador's second-biggest festival falls on the first or second Thursday after Epiphany in January (this varies – ask the tourist office for forthcoming dates). Bahians bearing flowers lead processions of tens of thousands of pilgrims and drummers from the Church of Nossa Senhora da Conceição in the *cidade baixo*, to the Igreja do Bonfim (a Catholic church). On arrival they wash the steps of the church in honour of Christ (who is also the *orixá*). Parties around the Igreja do Bonfim last until almost dawn.

Festa da Ribeira, Salvador This takes place on the Monday immediately following the Lavagem do Bonfim in the beachside neighbourhood of Ribeira, with live music, dancing and general revelry.

Lavagem de Santo Amaro, Santo Amaro This festival is celebrated in the Recôncavo town of Santo Amaro, usually on the last weekend of January when

---

A CARNAVAL GLOSSARY

AFRO BLOCOS These are troupes of up to 200 drummers who parade through the streets accompanied by singers on mobile sound trucks. The most famous are Filhos de Gandhi, Olodum, Timbalada and Ilê Aiyê.

BLOCO These are the individual themed Carnaval parades fronted by a drum troupe or a trio electrico. It's possible to join one, if you buy their costume and pay between US$180–450.

CAMAROTES These grandstands that line the street in Campo Grande allow you to see the show at leisure without being squashed and tussled by the crowd.

REI MOMO At 20.00 on the Thursday before Shrove Tuesday, the keys to the city are handed to this Carnaval King and the party officially begins.

TRIOS ELECTRICOS These 15-yard-long trucks are walled with deafening sound systems pumping out frenetic axé music. Above them are scantily clad, gyrating dancers and Salvador's most popular performers, like Ivete Sangalo, Daniela Mercury and Chiclete com Banana.

thousands gather in the centre of the town to dance samba de roda and process through the streets.

FEBRUARY
Festa de Yemanjá, Salvador This takes place on 2 February in the Rio Vermelho neighbourhood and is one of the most important Candomblé celebrations in Bahia, dedicated to the *orixá* of the sea. After dawn fireworks, offerings are left in the Casa do Peso (the weighing house used by the local fishermen); here they are loaded into boats and taken 10km out to sea and floated on the waves. Those that don't return are said to have been accepted by Yemanjá (Virgin Mary). The evening sees traditional music played by the likes of Mariene de Castro.

Carnaval Starts on the Friday preceding Shrove Tuesday every year. Shrove Tuesday dates for the next few years are as follows: 8 March 2011, 21 February 2012, 12 February 2013, 4 March 2014, 17 February 2015. See also box on pages 92–3.

JUNE
Festas Juninas (Festas do São João) See box above.

AUGUST
Festa da Boa Morte, Cachoeira One of the most important festivals in Cachoeira takes place on 13, 14 and 15 August, when the Irmandade da Boa Morte (Sisterhood of the Good Death) parade through the streets. Parties involve samba da roda, capoeira and Candomblé devotion.

Festa da Nossa Senhora d'Ajuda, Arraial d'Ajuda Lots of parties and processions celebrating the town's patron saint. Usually on 14 or 15 August.

DECEMBER
Reveillon (New Year's Eve) Celebrated all over Bahia and with the biggest parties in Porto Seguro, Morro de São Paulo and Salvador where Barra hosts a huge stage with some of the state's biggest musical names playing. After midnight Candomblé devotees in white robes light votive candles set into depressions in the sand on the beach, and toss flowers into the sea for Yemanjá. On Itapagipe beach next to the Igreja do Bonfim in Boa Viagem another party lasts until dawn when the Nosso Senhor dos Navegantes parade takes place.

SHOPPING

Unlike its South American neighbours, Brazil does not have a strong and varied arts and crafts tradition. Shopping habits in Bahia are closer to Europe or North America than they are Bolivia or Peru. Bahians like to shop in malls. Carefully crafted traditional souvenirs are thin on the ground.

Brazil has by far the largest, most vibrant and creative **fashion** industry in South America. São Paulo and Rio host the continent's most important fashion shows and Brazilian boutique labels are stocked in the world's finest department stores, including: Osklen (for smart casual men's surf-ad beach wear), M Officer, Forum and MOB (for well-cut casual women's clothing), Salinas, Vivere, Rosa Cha and Lenny (for swimwear), Havaianas (the world's most fashionable flip-flop).

The cities also have world-class **jewellers** like H Stern, indeed almost two thirds of the world's coloured gemstones are from Brazil. Shops in the Mercado Municipal in Salvador, Lençóis and the beach towns like Itacaré sell **bead jewellery** made from seeds and stones from the Amazon and cerrado.

Shops in Salvador sell uniquely Brazilian **percussion instruments** like the *berimbau* (bow-shaped and with a gourd sound bell), the *cuíca* and *onças* (friction drums which sound like a fox crying and which are used in *samba da roda*), tambours and *tambourins* (hand drums) and *pandeiros* (tambourines) and *atabaque* (sharp, ratatat street drums). Brazil has a large record industry and hundreds of home-grown artists, many of whom like Caetano Veloso, Gilberto Gil and Thiago Santana are Bahian. Shops like Cana Brava records (see page 96) sell a broad choice of quality **CDs**. The Rede BMA (*http://redebma.ning.com*) website is a great place to hear music selections before purchasing them.

Northeastern Brazil, particularly Pernambuco is famous for its naïve **clay figurines** made by traditional artists like Zé Caboclo and Mestre Vitalino. Many are available in Bahia – especially in the Mercado Modelo in Salvador and small shops in towns like Lençóis and Itacaré.

OPENING HOURS Small shops tend to open at 10.00 and close at 18.00. Big shops and malls tend to open from 10.00 to 22.00. In the larger cities they stay open far later. Larger shops and boutiques tend to open from 09.00 to 18.00.

PAYMENT Prices in Brazil are almost invariably fixed. Personal cheques are not accepted without two forms of Brazilian identification, a social security number (CPF) and an ID card (RG/RNE). Credit cards are widely accepted, but purchases may also require presentation of ID.

MARKETS Larger towns have a mercado municipal. These generally sell fruit, meat and other foodstuffs. In Salvador, the mercado also sell musical instruments, leather, lace, clothing and some arts and crafts. Look out for the eye-catching bags and purses made from can ring-pulls.

SHOPPING MALLS Shopping malls are called *Shoppings* (pronounced *Shoor-paings*) and in Bahia are restricted to the largest towns. The best by far are in Salvador. They stock local (and a handful of international) brand fashion, cosmetics, electronics, music, books and so on. Most have tour agencies, hairdressers, banks and cinemas and a large food area with chain restaurants. All are air-conditioned.

ARTS AND ENTERTAINMENT

Theatre is popular in Brazil and there are plenty showcasing classical and contemporary drama in Bahia, especially in Salvador. However, all performances are in Portuguese so I haven't listed theatres in the text. Those that do speak Portuguese will find a full list of shows on www.guiadasemana.com.br. The site also lists classical music, dance and cinema showings. International films (including blockbusters) are usually dubbed (*dublado*); showings in English are marked LEG (*legendas* – subtitles). For *Music* see page 49 and for *Capoeira* see also page 49.

PHOTOGRAPHY

Bahia is a great place for pictures, but be careful with your camera; they are a favourite target for thieves. Always carry your equipment in an unobtrusive bag. Brazilians are not precious about having their pictures taken, but can get angry if you do so without permission. Photography is prohibited in many public buildings (notably churches in Salvador) and you should never take pictures of the police, the military or in *favelas* without permission from locals.

MEDIA AND COMMUNICATIONS

INTERNET Brazil is seventh in the world in terms of domestic internet usage and there are internet cafés in even the smallest towns. They usually have a sign outside inscribed 'LAN house'. Rates are usually around R$5 per hour. Most hotels and hostels at least have internet in reception and increasing numbers have WiFi. This can be at exorbitant cost.

TELEPHONES Brazil loves the mobile phone and coverage is excellent and very widespread. However, prices are very high; the steepest in the world when this book went to press and you will need a Brazilian social security number (CPF) to buy a SIM card. Hotel staff are usually willing to help out by buying one for you. They are available at most news stands for between R$5 and R$10. Fibreglass, half-shell phone booths called *orelhões* (literally 'big ears') can be found all over Bahia. They take pre-paid phone cards (*cartões telefônicos*), available from newsstands, post offices, supermarkets and pharmacies. They cost around R$7 for 40 units and around R$12 for 90 units. International phone cards (*cartões telefônicos internacionais*) are increasingly available in tourist areas and are often sold at hostels.

To make a call it is necessary to dial an operator code in front of the area code and phone number. A call to Salvador, for example, from any other municipality begins with the code of the phone company chosen (eg: 31 for Telemar) followed by, 71 for the city of Salvador, and the 8-digit number of the business or individual. The same is true for international calls where 00 is followed by the operator code and then the country code and number. The most common operator codes are Embratel (021), Telefônica, (015) and Telemar (031).

POST (CORREIOS) Airmail from Bahia to Europe takes around seven days from larger cities and longer from small towns. Letters take around five days to the US. Post offices can by recognised by a distinctive yellow-and-blue 'Correios' sign. Post offices sell cardboard boxes for sending packages. Rates and rules for sending vary from post office to post office and whim of the clerk. The quickest service is called SEDEX.

BUSINESS

The Geert Hofstede sociological analysis of Brazilian business culture shows that Brazil is a risk-averse culture where 'uncertainty avoidance' ranks very high (resulting in a very bureaucratic and controlling structure), and where there is a large power distance between employers and employees (and within Brazilian society in general). Brazil is regarded by Hofstede as a collectivist rather than an individualistic society, but unlike in many Asian societies, this collectivism is based around family and bonds of friendship, rather than group loyalty.

Here are a few tips on business culture and etiquette:

- Appearances count. In general three-piece suits are worn by executives, two-piece suits by workers. Do not use ties with drawings or too much colour. In Brazil they give the impression that you are not serious. Women in the workplace dress more ostentatiously and stereotypically femininely than in Northern Europe or North America and spend more attention on manicured nails and make-up. Never wear green and yellow (the national colours).
- Stay in a good hotel. Entertain in a top class restaurant.
- Gifts are not important in establishing a business relationship.
- Touching on arms, shoulders or the back are common and after first acquaintance so is kissing on the cheek between men and women and women and women.
- The American 'OK' hand signal (the same as the OK signal used in diving) is extremely vulgar and offensive in Brazil.
- Never refer to Brazilians or Brazilian culture as Latin or Latinos. This has very negative, 'American imperialist' connotations.
- A thumb placed between the index and middle fingers while making a fist signifies good luck. Flicking the fingertips underneath the chin indicates that you have no interest in what's being discussed.
- The 'self-made' businessperson is not admired in Brazil. Inherited wealth and a good family background are much more important.
- Never make impromptu calls at business or government offices.
- Relationships are the key to business success in Brazil. Be prepared to commit long term resources (both in time and money) toward establishing them.
- Business and personal matters are mixed in Brazil and to establish good relationships you will have to spend a great deal of your private time socialising with Brazilian business movers and shakers.
- Time-keeping and responses to email are lax in Brazil. Make appointments at least two weeks in advance, confirm them and follow an email with several more to elicit a reply.
- Naming is a mixture of the formal and informal. Surnames are rarely if ever used, but titles are very important; so much so that they are often given when they are not due and those regarded as important can be referred to as 'Douto' (Doctor) even if they have no PhD.
- Whilst Brazilians are very informal and always refer to each other by first names and as 'voce' (you), they have a very strong sense of hierarchy that includes a very high power concentration and acceptance of inequality within companies. Try and gauge this hierarchy.
- Business in Brazil is conducted face to face. Only very limited business is undertaken by phone and almost none by email.
- Business meetings begin with casual 'chatting' first, this can last for some time. Launching into a business conversation before this ritual is complete is regarded as impolite. Favourite topics include football (soccer), food and family. Bad conversation topics include Argentina, politics, corruption and environmentalism.
- Conversations are frequently interrupted. This is regarded as enthusiastic rather than rude.
- When a negotiation process is already in place, do not change the team members. Relationships are crucial for success and changing the negotiation team in the middle of the process will be a setback.

- Brazilians are fond of eye contact and prolonged, warm handshakes. When leaving a small group, be sure to look them in the eye and shake hands with everyone present.
- Always get a written agreement with starting date, time of delivery, payment details, etc. Bill in advance.
- Hire a local lawyer.
- The drinking toast is 'Saude' (pronounced *Sah-OO-jee*)
- Brazilians do not deal well with criticism, which is usually taken personally and not perceived as directed to the executed task.

CULTURAL ETIQUETTE

Bahians, and Brazilians in general, are some of the most relaxed, informal and forgiving people in the world and are difficult to offend. However, there are a few matters of etiquette that should be borne in mind:

- Those in a hurry will be miserable in Bahia, where, if you arrive ten minutes late, you will be at least half an hour early.
- Complaints about the Bahian relaxed attitude to time will be received with consternation. Repeated complaints will have you treated like a pariah.
- Foreigners who like to see their glass as half empty will find themselves without a drinking buddy in Bahia. Bahians are private about negative feelings and do not like to moan even with reason.
- Bahians are unhurried in life except when in a tearing rush in a car. They drive fast, aggressively and make ample use of the horn and flashing headlights.
- Never insult an official or a policeman. Up until the 1980s Brazil was a military dictatorship; you are asking for trouble.
- Bikinis may be small but public nudity or toplessness on beaches is not only deeply offensive to Bahians, it is an arrestable offence.
- Bahians are very touchy-feely and they dance close. Do not confuse this with a sexual come-on.
- In Brazil spirituality is not a belief one assents to; it is part and parcel of life itself. Atheists are regarded with a mix of puzzlement and pity in Bahia and will be invited enthusiastically to church, terreiro, temple or other place of worship.
- Public drunkenness is regarded as vulgar and distasteful. Brazilians drink socially but seldom to get drunk.
- Silence is not golden in Bahia. It is rude. Bahians talk loudly, warmly and all the time. Bear this in mind when booking your birding trip or nature walk.
- Brazilians can be very proud of their country and are easily offended by foreigners' criticism.

TRAVELLING POSITIVELY

Increasing numbers of travellers are choosing to become more deeply involved in the destinations they visit – rather than merely using them for beach, sun and a spot of adventure, they wish to learn more about them, interact more with local people and give something back to local communities. Much positive travelling is common sense. But here are a few tips, some of which are specific to Bahia or Brazil.

BEFORE YOU GO
- Learn some Portuguese. Few Baianos speak more than a few words of English and you will get so much more from your visit.

- Read up on Brazilian and Bahia culture and sport and listen to some local music. This will immediately earn you local friends.
- Plan to visit community initiatives like Jaqueira Pataxó village, Carlinhos Brown's African music or the Ilê Aiyê centre. These and other such ventures are fascinating and vibrant.
- Learn something about the wildlife and visit areas where it is threatened.
- Plan ahead to visit local conservation or wildlife projects with local rather than international tour operator guides (these are indicated in the text).
- Remove all excess packaging – waste disposal is poor in Bahia.

WHILST IN BAHIA

- Buy local produce rather than imported goods – insect repellent, soap, shampoo, flip-flops, bathing costumes and so on are available at the same or better quality in Bahia as they are back home.
- Stay in a small local hotel rather than a big international chain
- Bring your rubbish in and out of national parks.
- Refuse plastic bags in shops where possible – North Eastern Brazil has a severe problem with wind-blown plastic waste.
- Book tours through local operators rather than one central office in Salvador. This distributes income more evenly.
- Do not buy products made from hardwoods, feathers (which are often taken from parrots) or coral.
- Baianos have different habits and different ideas of punctuality – try and prepare yourself for this psychologically. Getting angry and frustrated will earn you few supporters in Bahia.
- Try and leave a CD of pictures of local people with the local operator.
- If you visit communities, discreetly give pencils, paper or similar to the head of the family rather than openly giving sweets or money to children.
- Always ask about the local wildlife – with specific questions addressed to local guides and the request of a species list from hotels and operators which package themselves as practising ecotourism. This greatly increases awareness and the sense of economic importance of the wildlife itself which is often indiscriminately killed in Bahia.
- Avoid touching coral when diving.

WHEN YOU RETURN If you've promised to send pictures to people remember to do so.

GETTING INVOLVED
Environment and wildlife

BirdLife International www.birdlife.org. A global partnership of conservation organisations that strives to conserve birds, their habitats & global biodiversity, working with people towards sustainability in the use of natural resources. They work extensively in Bahia in partnership with SAVE (see page 20). BirdLife partners operate in over 100 countries & territories worldwide.

Conservation International www.conservation.org. Campaigns to protect the Atlantic coastal forests & the cerrado in Brazil & is actively involved in community-based ecotourism worldwide.

Earthwatch www.earthwatch.org. Ecological & conservational research placements in countries worldwide, with an average cost of around US$2,000 for a 1–3-week team duration. Projects in Brazil & occasional projects in Bahia.

Greenpeace International www.greenpeace.org. Campaign to prevent the export of mahogany & other hardwoods from Brazil.

International Institute for Peace through Tourism www.iipt.org. Bring together leaders from tourism industry, general public, private sector, academics & NGOs to respond to issues & crises.

Rainforest Action Network, http://ran.org/. Campaign to save forests worldwide.

World Rainforest Movement www.wrm.org.uy. Campaign to preserve rainforests & support forest peoples (including the Pataxó) to control the use of their lands & resources through their Forest Peoples' Programme. Work with the United Nations.

WWF International www.panda.org. One of the world's largest environmental & conservational agencies campaigning throughout Brazil & in the Atlantic coast rainforest.

Responsible tourism
International Ecotourism Society (TIES)
www.ecotourism.org. An international campaigning organisation for genuine ecotourism who publish & distribute ecotourism information, organise workshops & encourage (though do not monitor) best practice from their members & the tourism community at large.
International Centre for Responsible Tourism
www.icrtourism.org. A post-graduate training &

research centre at the University of Leeds encouraging & researching responsible tourism & hospitality worldwide.
Tourism Concern Stapleton Hse, 277–281 Holloway Rd, London N7 8HN; 020 7133 3800; www.tourismconcern.org.uk. Information about responsible tourism & links with other organisations.

Community support and *campesinos*
Ashoka www.ashoka.org. A large NGO supported by McKinsey & Co amongst others & supporting grass-roots projects like local radio stations & ecotourism projects aimed at rejuvenating poor communities.
Movimento Sem Terra (MST) www.mstbrazil.org. Brazilian land reform movement, fights for land equality & other basic social rights such as education. They controversially occupy land owned by *coroneis* & other landowners & comprise the largest social movement in Latin America & one of

the most successful grass-roots movements in the world. Often portrayed very negatively in the Brazilian press.
Sociedade para a Conservação das Aves do Brasil (SAVE Brasil) www.savebrasil.org.br. One of the most stalwart campaigners for the protection & preservation of bird-rich habitats throughout Brazil. They work extensively in Bahia & are partnered by BirdLife International.

ECOTOURISM OR NOT ECOTOURISM?
TEN QUESTIONS TO ASK BEFORE YOU DECIDE

1 Does the establishment or operator have a written policy regarding responsible activity towards the environment and local communities?
2 What exactly do they do to support the local community? How do they measure it?
3 How many of their employees are locals?
4 Do they train locals to enable them to work as guides or management?
5 If the hotel is based in nature, do they have a species list for birds or mammals? What endangered or threatened species live in their area?
6 What exactly do they do to support the environment? How do they measure it?
7 Do they recycle? If an operator, how do they deal with rubbish and do they make an effort to work with hotels etc who recycle? If a hotel, do they recycle water and/or rubbish and how do they treat their sewage?
8 Do they use solar power or make an effort to work with those who do so? Ask them what % of produce and services are sourced from within 25km of the lodge.
9 What percentage of their food and chattels are locally sourced?
10 How do they help tourists to become more involved in local conservation or community projects?

The more these questions are asked, the more awareness is increased in Bahia.

www.stuffyourrucksack.com is a website set up by TV's Kate Humble which enables travellers to give direct help to small charities, schools or other organisations in the country they are visiting. Maybe a local school needs books, a map or pencils, or an orphanage needs children's clothes or toys – all things that can easily be 'stuffed in a rucksack' before departure. The charities get exactly what they need and travellers have the chance to meet local people and see how and where their gifts will be used. The website describes organisations that need your help and lists the items they most need. Check what's needed in Bahia, contact the organisation to say you're coming and bring not only the much-needed goods but an extra dimension to your travels and the knowledge that in a small way you have made a difference.

Indigenous peoples

Cultural Survival 215 Prospect St, Cambridge, MA 02139; www.culturalsurvival.org. The leading US NGO campaigning for the protection of the rights of indigenous peoples worldwide.

Indios Online www.indiosonline.org.br. Information about Brazilian indigenous peoples from Brazilian indigenous people. With news, campaigns & general information. In Portuguese.

Instituto Socioambiental www.socioambiental.org. The leading Brazilian NGO campaigning for rights for traditional & indigenous peoples. Their website is an excellent resource of information on all of Brazil's indigenous groups, & on the latest news & issues.

Survival International 6 Charterhouse Bldg, London EC1M 7ET; 020 7687 8700; www.survivalinternational.org. An NGO that campaigns for indigenous peoples' rights in Brazil & throughout the world.

General

Latin America Bureau www.lab.org.uk. An information database for all things Latin American. Very good book list, particularly current affairs & politics.

Part Two

THE GUIDE

3

Salvador

Telephone code 071

> About eleven o'clock we entered the Bay of All Saints, on the northern side of which is situated the town of Bahia or San Salvador. It would be difficult to imagine before seeing this view anything so magnificent. It requires, however, the reality of nature to make it so. If faithfully represented in a picture, a feeling of distrust would be raised in the mind.
>
> Charles Darwin, 1832

Like Lisbon and Rio, Salvador is proof that more than any European imperial power, the Portuguese knew how to choose the perfect location for a city. Basking under a brilliant sun but cooled by a perpetual sea breeze, Bahia's capital clambers over a series of craggy cliffs and low dune hills at the tip of a finger that divides a bottle green Atlantic from a vast ocean bay. Brazil largely began here in the 16th century, as a mission – a few houses built from middens and thatch, gazing wistfully back across the sea to Portugal. Through the indigenous, and later the African, slave trade, the city grew to become a major port and stopover *en route* between Europe and Africa, before becoming the capital of a Portuguese captaincy and briefly a country.

Salvador was a Brazilian cultural capital until the latter half of the 20th century, giving Brazil many of its unique cultural colours, and providing much of the nations' quotidian soundtrack. Candomblé (belief system) and capoeira (dance), the rhythm that became samba, and the novels of Jorge Amado were developed largely here, as was the tropicália music of Caetano Veloso, Tom Zé and Gilberto Gil, the batucada beats of Olodum and Ilê Aiyê and the innovative films of Glauber Rocha, iconic leader and theorist of Cinema Novo. Modern Salvador remains vibrant, especially during its frenetic and fervid Carnaval which vies with Recife's as the largest in the world, and the city remains an important repository of African-Brazilian culture. However, it is only in recent years that Salvador has once more begun to reclaim its place at Latin America's cultural cutting edge and begin to vie with Belém and Recife as one of the great musical centres of northeastern and northern Brazil.

ORIENTATION

The skyline and waterfront are dominated by neighbourhoods of Lego-coloured apartment blocks. Close to the beach and relatively safe, with wonderful views and good restaurants, are the neighbourhoods of modern Salvador (Campo Grande, Barra, Ondina and Amaralina). Wealthy and predominantly white Salvadoreans play here – in mock-Miami clubs and wharf-front restaurants and bars – deliberately oblivious to the largely African old Salvador which lies behind. Old Salvador provides the city with its depth of culture and the architectural heritage that has earned it UNESCO World Heritage status. Old Salvador sits around the docks and atop the clifftop behind them. Almost all the tourist sights are in the upper, clifftop section, of Old Salvador – the **Cidade Alta** (Upper City). This clusters around the

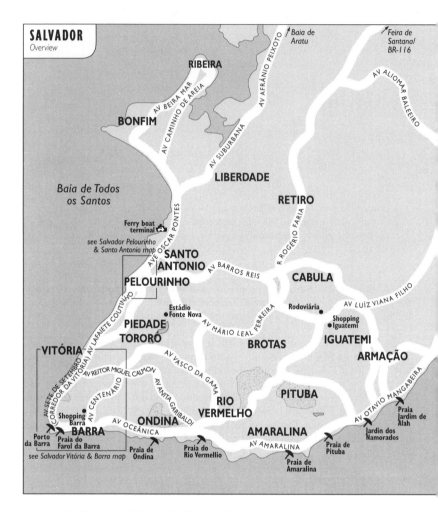

Praça da Sé (dominated by the hulking cathedral), and spreads in a series of long, steep cobbled streets colloquially referred to as the Pelourinho, into the neighbourhood of Santo Antônio. The decrepit colonial buildings, bustling markets and stately churches of the **Cidade Baixa** (Lower City) crumble below, next to a shimmering, turquoise sea. The Pelourinho is named after the spot where thousands of Africans were pilloried and in a quirk of fate it is now one of the cultural centres of African Brazil. Streets of grand, if crumbling, ochre and sky- blue townhouses stretch around, secreting churches whose interiors are covered with gold leaf, and leading to little alleys and handsome squares that peter out and merge with breeze-bloc favelas as the city sprawls inland. Highlights here include the opulent Convento de São Francisco church – with some of the finest Baroque carving and *azulejos* (painted, tin-glazed, ceramic tilework) in Latin America, nightlife on Tuesdays, and the Museu Afro-Brasileiro.

A handful of Salvador's other neighbourhoods preserve their traditional characters. **Candeal** favela has one the liveliest musical communities in the city, focused on the cultural centre founded by illustrious percussionist, Carlinhos Brown (see box on page 135). Beachside **Rio Vermelho** is an important sacred site in the

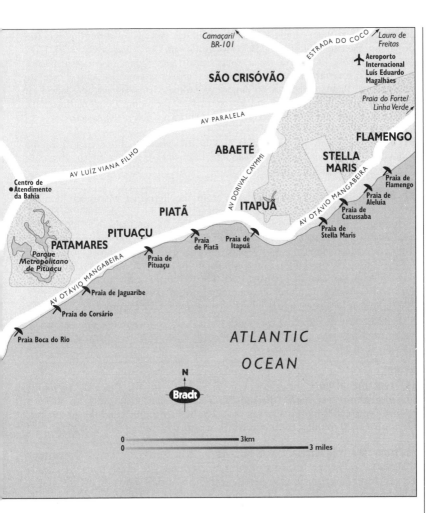

Candomblé religion (see *Chapter 1*, page 46), the locus of the Festa de Yemanjá (see page 95) and an alternative nightlife and traditional culinary centre to the Pelourinho. **Bonfim** in the Baía de Todos os Santos, and the church of the same name, is another key Candomblé centre, hosting another important African-Brazilian festival – the Lavagem do Bonfim (see page 94).

A DAY IN SALVADOR FOR CRUISE-SHIP PASSENGERS Allow a long morning or afternoon for walking around the Pelourinho, seeing the sights here and browsing in the shops. This should include at least an hour for the area's most impressive site – the Convento de São Francisco. Spend around two hours shopping in the Mercado Modelo and if there is time left over have a sunset drink or meal at one of the waterfront restaurants in Barra or Campo Grande.

GETTING THERE

BY AIR Salvador's Deputado Luís Eduardo Magalhães International Airport (*Praça Gago Coutinho;* ☏ *3204 1010; www.infraero.com.br*) lies 28km northeast of the city centre. There are flights to all the other Brazilian state capitals and direct flights to Rio de Janeiro, São Paulo, Brasília and Belo Horizonte with Gol (*www.voegol.com.br*), TAM (*www.tam.com.br*), Ocean Air (*www.oceanair.com.br*) and Webjet (*www.webjet.com.br*). See page 86 for further details on domestic carriers serving Salvador. There are international flights to Miami on American Airlines (*www.aa.com*), to Madrid on Iberworld (*www.iberworld.com*) and European cities including London, Barcelona, Frankfurt, Rome and Amsterdam on Condor/Thomas Cook (*www.condor.com*).

BY BUS Buses from all over Bahia and Brazil arrive at and depart from the rodoviária (*Av Antônio Carlos Magalhães 4362, Pernambués;* \ *3616 8300*) which lies 5km from the historical centre.

BY BOAT Boats and catamarans leave from the Terminal Marítimo Mercado Modelo next to the Mercado Modelo for the islands of the Baía de Todos os Santos, including Bom Despacho on Itaparica every 30 minutes (\ *2105 9800; www.travessiasonline.com.br for the latest timetables*), and catamarans to the islands of Tinharé via Morro de São Paulo, five departures daily (see *www.morrodesaopaulo.com.br* for the latest ferry timetable). When catamarans to Morro de São Paulo are full it is possible to go via Valenca (see page 157). The terminal is a five-minute walk from the Lacerda lift. Another ferry terminal, São Joaquim (*Av Oscar Pontes 1051;* \ *3254 1020*), known locally as 'fair-hee bort', has car ferries for Itaparica (\ *2105 9800; www.travessiasonline.com.br*).

GETTING AROUND

BY BUS
To/from the airport Buses connect the airport with the Praça da Sé in the historical centre via Barra (marked Praça da Sé/Aeroporto) and with the bus terminal (marked Rodoviária/Aeroporto). The best are the air-conditioned services, leaving every 30 minutes from outside the terminal between 05.00 and 22.00.

To/from the rodoviária Local bus RI or RII (marked Centro–Rodoviária–Circular) departs from the foot of the Lacerda public lift which links the Cidade Baixa (Lower City) of Salvador directly with the historical centre on the cliff above. This lift is not safe after dark. Others buses run from the Praça da Sé or Barra to the Iguatemi Shopping Centre which is next to the rodoviária. Allow at least 90 minutes for either journey during rush hour. Upstairs, on the Cidade Alta (Upper City), you can buy the tickets at booths with destinations clearly marked on placards. Downstairs is reserved for shops and cafés.

Coastal neighbourhoods to/from the historical centre The Praça da Sé /Aeroporto bus links Barra, Campo Grande, Ondina and Rio Vermelho with the Praça da Sé in the city centre. The Flamengo bus also links all the southern beach neighbourhoods with the Praça da Sé. It leaves roughly every 40 minutes. Both buses cost about R$4 per ride.

BY CAR There are Avis, Budget, Europcar and Hertz rental car counters in the aiport terminal building, together with other local companies. There is car parking near the terminal building. To drive to the city from the airport or vice versa it is easiest to follow the BA099 road that runs close to the coastline and follow the signs marked Centro.

BY TAXI Taxis are numerous in Salvador but should only be caught from ranks (*postos*). Taxis from the airport to the city centre will cost around R$50 and about R$45 to Barra.

TOURIST INFORMATION

The state tourism authority, Bahiatursa (*www.bahiatursa.ba.gov.br*) has information booths throughout the city at the following locations:

i Aeroporto Internacional Dep Luís Eduardo Magalhães, Praça Gago Coutinho s/n, São Cristovão; ✆ 3204 1244/ 1444; ⏰ 07.30–23.00 daily.

i Centro de Convenções da Bahia, Jardim Armação s/n, Armação; ✆ 3370 8494; ⏰ 08.30–18.00 Mon–Fri.

i Instituto Mauá, Praça Azevedo Fernandes, 01, Porto da Barra; ✆ 3264 4671; ⏰ 09.00–18.00 Mon–Fri, 10.00–15.00 Sat.

i Mercado Modelo, Praça Visconde de Cayru 250, Comércio; ✆ 3241 0242; ⏰ 09.00–18.00 Mon–Sat 09.00–13.30 Sun.

i Pelourinho, Rua das Laranjeiras 12, Pelourinho; ✆ 3321 2133/ 2463; ⏰ 08.30–21.00 daily.

i Rodoviaria, Av Antônio Carlos Magalhães 4362, Iguatemi; ✆ 3450 3871; ⏰ 07.30–21.00 daily.

LOCAL TOUR OPERATORS

TATUR Av Tancredo Neves 274, Centro Empresarial Iguatemi II, Salas 222–224B; ✆ 3114 7900; www.tatur.com.br. Run day tours in & around the city.

WHERE TO STAY

Most visitors choose to stay in the city centre, either on or around the Pelourinho, which has a broad choice of rooms, from hostels to small hotels, or in Santo Antônio, which is quieter and has some pretty boutique hotels set in old colonial buildings. Barra – on a not-so-clean beach – is increasingly popular for those craving sea air and caters for all budgets and offers plenty of nearby restaurants. It is a 15-minute taxi ride from the Pelourinho. All of Salvador is potentially dangerous at night; it is best to take a taxi back to your room rather than walk, especially if you're alone.

Unless otherwise stated, prices are based on doubles at high-season rates (December–February and July). They can more than double over Carnaval weekend.

Most hostels, though not all, offer double rooms as well as beds in dormitories.

CENTRO HISTÓRICO AND SANTO ANTÔNIO

🏠 **Pestana Convento do Carmo** (79 rooms) Rua do Carmo 1; ✆ 3327 8400; www.pousadas.pt. Salvador's grandest hotel is a beautiful colonial convent in the historic centre. Gilt cherubs watch over the cloister cocktail bar & the award-winning restaurants, the pool is built around an 18th-century fountain, & there's a spa & even a private Baroque chapel. The building itself is a UNESCO World Heritage Site – there's priceless art at every turn, from stunning *azulejos* to ecclesiastical Rococo flourishes. Service can be Baroque too – full of effusive flourishes but as slow as a Dark Ages ritual. Web discounts. $$$$$

🏠 **Villa Bahia** (17 rooms) Largo do Cruzeiro de São Francisco 16–18, Pelourinho; ✆ 3322 4271; www.hotelvillabahia.com. A pleasant, airy little boutique hotel with rooms decorated in the style of former Portuguese colonies from Goa to Nagasaki. The best are on the 3rd floor & overlooking the Pelourinho & the São Francisco church. The rooftop has a tiny pool & a jacuzzi. The environs are delightful by day but dangerous by night. $$$$$

🏠 **A Casa das Portas Velhas** (15 rooms) Largo da Palma 6, Santana; ✆ 3324 8400; www.casadasportasvelhas.com. A boutique hotel in a smart townhouse overlooking the square, featured in Jorge Amado's *Dona Flor and Her Two Husbands*. Rooms are ostensibly furnished in Portuguese colonial style & decorated with Afro-Brazilian art. In reality they look like a pale imitation of the Ritz Carlton in New York – frowsty, closed to the world behind heavy drape curtains built for a northern winter rather than tropical Bahia & furnished with the kind of mock-European, mock antiques that would look just right in an aspirant country club somewhere in the American Midwest. The streets between the Pelourinho & the hotel are not safe at any time. Take a taxi. $$$$–$$$$$

🏠 **Villa Santo Antônio** (14 rooms) Rua Direita de Santo Antônio 130, Santo Antônio; 📞 3326 1270; www.hotel-santoantonio.com. Another of Santo Antônio's tastefully converted townhouses, owned by a diffident German fashion photographer & his less diffident wife. Public areas are tiled in raw stones, decorated in neutral colours & furnished with comfortable sofas & easy chairs. The upper floor AC rooms with a shared balcony have huge French windows which offer views to the bay from the queen-sized beds, whilst the master suite with its lavish marble bathroom occupies almost half a floor. Others have street views. $$$$–$$$$$

🏠 **Pousada Baluarte** (5 rooms) Ladeira do Baluarte 13, Santo Antônio Além do Carmo; 📞 3327 0367; www.pousadabaluarte.com. This snug, 1960s-built guesthouse lacks the colonial charm & views of its neighbours & it's a longer walk to the Pelourinho. But it's quiet, very well kept, pleasantly decorated with local art & a personal touch & the owner Zelina is friendly & serves a generous b/fast on the sunny little patio. $$$

🏠 **Pousada das Flores** (9 rooms) Rua Dureita de Santo Antônio 442, Santo Antônio; 📞 3243 1836; www.pflores.com.br. Fan-cooled rooms, with optional portable AC, in a pretty 18th-century house 10 mins from the Pelourinho. Each has heavy wooden floors & high ceilings & is decorated in colonial style, with heavy Gauguin colours on the window frames, wooden floors & white walls, & filled with heavy antique furniture. The smartest & largest are the veranda suites 7, 8 & 9. $$$

🏠 **Pousada do Pilar** (12 rooms) Rua Direita do Santo Antônio 24, Santo Antônio; 📞 3241 6278; www.pousadadopilar.com. Large, modern AC rooms furnished in dark wood & whitewash & housed in a converted colonial mansion house. Those on the upper floors have verandas with views over the Baía de Todos os Santos. B/fast is a cornucopia of fruit & pastries, served on the open-air top-floor deck which doubles up as a bar in the evening. $$$

🏠 **Pousada Villa Carmo** (10 rooms) Rua do Carmo 58, Santo Antônio; 📞 3241 3924; www.pousadavillacarmo.com.br. A range of simple but elegant fan-cooled & AC rooms decorated with Brazilian art & ceramics chosen by the owner Ana Luz. Some are fairly small with barely room for more than 2 twin beds. The best 3 have private balconies with views over the bay. $$$

🏠 **Solar do Carmo** (14 rooms) Rua Direita do Santo Antonio 108, Santo Antônio; 📞 3323 0644; www.solardocarmo.com.br. A converted town mansion with a series of AC rooms furnished & decorated in the aesthetic spirit of a doctor's waiting room. Guests should opt for an upper-floor room with a terrace, affording breathtaking views of the Baía de Todos os Santos bay, which shimmers below. B/fast on the balcony also comes with a wonderful view, & the owner Flavia is warm & friendly. $$$

🏠 **Hotel Pelourinho** (49 rooms) Rua Alfredo Brito 20; 📞 3243 2324; www.hotelpelourinho.com. Jorge Amado once lived in this stately house right on the Pelourinho itself. Rooms are now plain & simple – painted white, with tiled floors & furniture that would have looked dated when K-Tel were producing vinyl. But this is more than made up for by the location in the heart of the Pelourinho & the sweeping bay views from the upper floors. Children under 5 stay for free. $$–$$$

🏠 **Hotel Quilombo do Pelô** Rua Alfredo Brito 13, 📞 3322 4371; http://quilombodopelo.vilabol.uol.com.br. A Jamaican-themed guesthouse hotel in a converted mansion in the heart of the Pelourinho. The best room is the delightfully cheesy 'Rei Zumbi' suite on the top floor with a jacuzzi & views over Salvador. The hotel restaurant serves Jamaican food. $$–$$$

🏠 **Pousada do Boqueirão** (15 rooms) Rua Direita do Santo Antônio 48, Santo Antônio; 📞 3241 2262; www.pousadaboqueirao.com.br. The magical play of open space, simple, understated, elegant Italian decoration & warm natural light has made this 18th-century townhouse hotel a popular choice for photo & film shoots. The views over the bay from the b/fast patio & upper-floor rooms are some of the best in Salvador, although the attic rooms are a little small. Be sure to look at the hotel's shop – with objects hand-picked by the owners & crafted by some of the best traditional artisans in the northeast. Great value from R$90 (with shared bathroom). $$

🏠 **Albergue das Laranjeiras** (17 rooms) Rua Inácio Acciolli 13; 📞 3321 1366; www.laranjeirashostel.com.br. This busy IYHA hostel in the noisy heart of the Pelourinho is a great choice for those looking for a short walk to their dorm & a relatively sleepless night. The dbl rooms are very plain, with little more than a bed. Those with the luxury of a private bathroom cost a steep R$130 or more. You'll find better value in Santo Antônio. The hostel also offers internet access, tour booking services & a crêperie restaurant. Dorm beds from $–$$$

🏠 **Albergue dos Anjos** (4 rooms) Rua Gregório de Matos 15; www.alberguedosanjos.com.br. This colourful, well-appointed hostel offers a quieter alternative to the Albergue das Laranjeiras for travellers who wish to be in the heart of the Pelourinho. The hostel was fully refurbished in 2009. The well-kept, tiny rooms are freshly painted & decked out in heavy wood furniture & the tile-floor dorms are spick & span. Services include tour booking, internet, laundry & a small library of books. $-$$

🏠 **Albergue do Peló** (7 rooms) Rua Ribeiro dos Santos 5; ☎ 3242 8061; www.alberguedopelo.com.br. A friendly, brightly coloured little hostel with a series of simple but well-kept stone-floor dorms segregated by sex & with space for 4–12 people. Quieter than the larger hostels in the Pelourinho & unlike most, with b/fast included in the price. Discounts for groups. $-$$

🏠 **Albergue São Jorge** (5 rooms) Rua Alfredo de Brito; ☎ 3266 7092; www.saojorgehostel.com. A friendly hostel with brightly-painted communal areas decorated with Bahian art, WiFi access in the lobby & a broad range of services including tour booking. Little English is spoken & even lashings of bright paint can't disguise the pokiness of the dorms & individual rooms. Dorm beds from R$25. Dbls from R$60 with a shared bathroom. $-$$

VITÓRIA AND BARRA

🏠 **Grande Hotel da Barra** (116 rooms) Av Sete de Setembro 3564; ☎ 2106 8600; www.grandehoteldabarra.com.br. This 1960s dame, with some of the largest rooms in Barra, has recently been refurbished. It still looks ungainly — with character-free tiling & anonymous patent leather furniture — but the best rooms are no longer unkempt. The best are on the upper floor, with ocean views. Good web prices. $$$

🏠 **Monte Pascoal Praia** (83 rooms) Av Oceânica 591; ☎ 2103 4000; www.montepascoal.com.br. The little tiled boxes stacked one on top of the other in this tower hotel — with their ugly patent leather furnishings, flat-screen TVs & twin or dbl beds — are bearable only because of the fabulous views over the Atlantic from the large windows, & the access to the rooftop pool — which offers the best view of all. The hotel is in a superb location for Carnaval (which passes right below) & the accompanying fireworks. Wi-Fi in rooms for a price. $$$

🏠 **Porto Farol** (39 rooms) Rua Engenheiro Milton de Oliveira 134; ☎ 3267 8000; www.portofarol.com.br. A big 1990s seafront block with a range of anonymous rooms with tiled floors, fitted laminate-top wall desks, a chunky wooden b/fast table & large windows letting in plenty of light. The best are the aparamentos standard & duplex, with their own kitchenettes. Standard rooms are a little pokey. The

🏠 **Hotel Arthemis** (19 rooms) Praça da Sé 398, Edifício Themis 7th Flr. Rooms are very basic, with little more than spongy sgl & dbl beds & rickety bedside tables. But the b/fast views from the rooftop terrace, over the Cidade Baixa & Baía de Todos os Santos to Itaparica island, make the hotel better value than many of the hostels for those looking for a room rather than a dorm. The best rooms have 3 beds, bay views through rickety aluminium windows & en suites. Look at a few. $-$$

🏠 **Nega Maluca** (7 rooms) Rua Dos Marchantes 15, Santo Antônio; ☎ 3242 9249; www.negamaluca.com. A popular party hostel 5mins uphill from the Pelourinho; named not according to offensive racial stereotyping but a folkloric character from Carnaval. Staff are friendly to all comers (if a little forgetful), & offer a range of services including free internet & free Wi-Fi in rooms & a great b/fast of fruit & pastries. Rooms & dorms are a little pokey with spongy beds, but there's plenty of lounging space, on the hammock-strewn tiled terrace or in the TV common room. $-$$

duplex quintas are the best value if you're in a group — with room for up to 5 people at just under R$70 each. $$$

🏠 **Sol Barra** (189 rooms) Av Sete de Setembro 3577; ☎ 3264 7011; www.solexpress.com.br. A big block of cement with windows overlooking the sea, whose principal draws are its rooftop sun deck, with a superb view over the Atlantic & the proximity for Carnaval with 2 parades commencing within 5mins' walk of the lobby. Rooms vary in size & quality. All are clean but decorated like an impoverished provincial dentist's waiting room — hospital ward-white Brazilian floor tiles & walls are offset by cheap butterscotch nylon curtains, lime green & custard yellow swirly counterpanes & matching desk chairs, & blocky laminate & MDF furniture. But they're bright, a few offer a glimpse of the sea & the largest have room for 4. Cheapest rates through the website. $$$

🏠 **Bahia Flat** (105 apartments) Av Oceânica 235, Barra; ☎ 3339 4140; www.bahiaflat.com.br. A series of flats in a 5-storey blue & yellow concrete bldg on the waterfront that looks like a cheap apt block from a 1970s cop show. The best of the rooms are ocean facing on the upper floors & are more modern, if plain with tile floors, little wicker tables, flower-print nylon sofas & kitchenettes with microwaves, fridges & small hobs. The hotel has a little pool & sauna. $$$

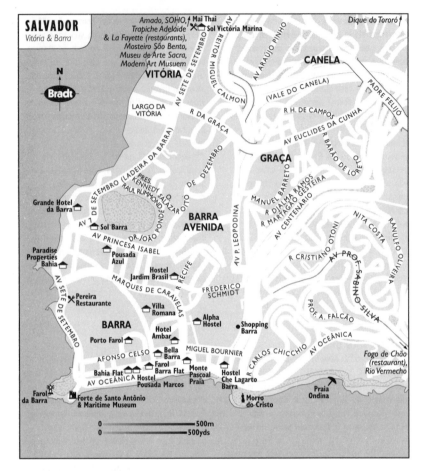

SALVADOR
Vitória & Barra

N

Bradt

Amado, SOHO, Mai Thai
Trapiche Adelaide Sol Victória Marina
& La Fayette (restaurants),
Mosteiro São Bento,
Museu de Arte Sacra,
Modern Art Musuem

Dique do Tororó

VITÓRIA

CANELA

(VALE DO CANELA)

LARGO DA
VITÓRIA

R DA GRAÇA

R H. DE CAMPOS

AV EUCLIDES DA CUNHA

GRAÇA

Grande Hotel
da Barra

Sol Barra

BARRA
AVENIDA

MANUEL BARRETO
R DJALMA RAMOS
R MARTAGÃO GESTEIRA
AV CENTENÁRIO

NITA COSTA

Paradise
Properties
Bahia

Pousada
Azul

R CRISTIANO OTONI

AV PROF SABINO SILVA

Hostel
Jardim Brasil

Pereira
Restaurante

FREDERICO
SCHMIDT

Villa
Romana

PROF. A. FALCÃO

BARRA

Alpha
Hostel

Shopping
Barra

Hotel
Ambar

MIGUEL BOURNIER

AV OCEÂNICA

Porto Farol

Fogo de Chão
(restaurant),
Rio Vermelho

AFONSO CELSO

Bella
Barra

CARLOS CHICCHIO

Bahia Flat

Farol
Barra Flat

Monte
Pascoal
Praia

Hostel
Che Lagarto
Barra

Praia
Ondina

Farol
da Barra

AV OCEÂNICA Hostel
Pousada Marcos

Forte de Santo Antônio
& Maritime Museum

Morro
do Cristo

0   500m
0   500yds

🏠 **Farol Barra Flat** (80 apartments Av Oceanica 409; 📞 3339 0000; www.farolbarraflat.com.br. Newly refurbished rooms in a range of different comfort levels & prices. The best are the VIP suites, which are about as good as a standard European 3 star or a Days Inn & which come with medium-sized rooms dominated by a bed with a mirror headrest, a TV with Brazilian shows stapled to the wall, sofas & assorted sturdy furniture that looks like it was bought in a job lot from a TV shopping channel during a bout of insomnia. The worst are similar but smaller, on lower floors & without the view. Look at a few. $$$

🏠 **Sol Victória Marina** (165 rooms) Av Sete de Setembro 2068, Vitória; 📞 3336 7736; www.solexpress.com.br. With its ugly old-fashioned furniture & brown tiling, tired 1990s décor & grandiose cocaine-baron marble-faced lobby, this tower hotel has certainly seen better days. But it's

worth considering if only for the wonderful bay views (especially from the upper rooms), the cable-car ride that links to the hotel restaurant & daytime lounge deck Mai Thai (see page 115) & the plum location between Barra & the Pelourinho. $$$

🏠 **Paradise Properties Bahia** (43 rooms) Av Sete de Setembro 3743; 📞 3264 5588 (US +1 917 477 0798); www.pp-bahia.com. A broad range of rental apts from budget accommodation cheap enough for backpackers (especially when sharing) to the luxurious AC modern condominiums with wonderful Atlantic (& Carnaval) views. Most are in & around Barra & the excellent website allows for browsing by availability & online reservations. Extra services include mobile phone rental, maid service & airport pick-up. $$–$$$

🏠 **Pousada Azul** (13 rooms) Rua Praguer Froes 102; 📞 3011 9798; www.pousadaazul.com.br. A large, townhouse whose entire exterior has been drowned in

Prussian blue, sitting garishly in a quiet residential street a few blocks back from the sea. With a range of simple, well-kept rooms furnished with little more than beds, a simple chest of drawers & blocky foam-mattress sofas. These are set against whitewashed walls & stand on polished wood floors. Blue predominates as a decorative theme in the interior though thankfully not with the enthusiasm displayed outside. $$–$$$

🏠 **Villa Romana** (50 rooms) Rua Lemos Brito 14; ☎ 3264 6522; www.villaromana.com.br. An old-fashioned, if well-kept family hotel a 10min walk uphill from the beach, with heavy faux-belle époque furniture in the public areas, acres of brightly polished wood & plain rooms just about wide enough for 2 beds & a door leading into a little box of a bathroom. $$–$$$

🏠 **Hotel Ambar** (12 rooms) Rua Afonso Celso 485; ☎ 3264 6956; www.ambarpousada.com.br. Tiny, very plain tile & white-walled rooms with little room for more than a bed & a bag, cooled by fans & clustered around a courtyard. Internet available in reception. A narrow sliver of water serves as a swimming pool in the garden out back. $$

🏠 **Alpha Hostel** (15 rooms) Rua Eduardo Diniz Gonçalves 128; ☎ 3237 6282; www.alphahostel.com. The Salvador branch of a popular Rio hostel is tucked away down a little alley near the beach. The hostel is quiet & well kept & not a location for partiers. Private rooms are very hot, but dorms are airy & staff attentive. Tours can be a little pricey. $–$$

RIO VERMELHO AND THE OTHER BEACH NEIGHBOURHOODS

🏠 **Zank** (17 rooms) Av Almirante Barroso 161, Rio Vermelho; ☎ 3083 4000; www.zankhotel.com.br. Judith Pottecher's overpriced little boutique is built in homage to the world of Ian Shrager & situated in a belle époque house (& an undistinguished modern annexe) 10mins' (uphill) walk from Rio Vermelho's bars & restaurants. There's little novel or original but all is easy on the eye. Colours are largely sombre & duo or tritone – as in so many boutiques. Bathrooms are open plan & glass-fronted, looking chic but offering no privacy even if you'd like it. Some rooms (notably number 10) have ocean views but sadly none have balconies or terraces. The modernist furniture throughout is sourced from contemporary Brazilian designers. $$$$$

🏠 **Pestana Bahia** (513 rooms) Rua Fonte de Boi 216, Rio Vermelho; ☎ 3453 8000; www.pestana.com. The most exclusive of Salvador's many tall tower-block hotels is housed in its own gated compound on a little rocky peninsula (with no access to the

🏠 **Hostel Albergue do Porto** (14 rooms) Rua Barão de Sergy 197–207 ☎ 3264 6600; www.alberguedoporto.com.br. A popular, eye-dazzling lemon yellow IYHA hostel in a large early Republican townhouse a couple of blocks from the beach. Large rooms come with high ceilings, wooden floors & ceiling fans – ensuring that they remain fairly cool. & there are several communal areas including TV & games rooms, hammock-strung corridors & a kitchen. $–$$

🏠 **Hostel Pousada Marcos** (40 rooms) Av Oceânica 281, Barra, 3264 5117, www.pousadamarcos.com.br. A basic but well-kept hostel guesthouse at the lighthouse end of the beach & offering a flat rental service. $–$$

🏠 **Bella Barra** (20 rooms) Rua Afonso Celso 439; ☎ 3264 3260; www.hotelbellabarra.com.br. Monastically simple cells in brown tile & whitewash, with firm wooden beds. Some have partially stained-glass windows & many are in need of repainting. $

🏠 **Hostel Che Lagarto Barra** (7 rooms) Av Oceânica 84B; ☎ 3235 2404; www.chelagarto.com. A big, colourful party hostel in the largest Brazilian hostel chain. Dorms are somewhat musty & not very well kept & the staff a little offhand but the waterfront location close to the Carnaval parade is enviable. $

🏠 **Hostel Jardim Brasil** (10 rooms) Rua Recife 4; ☎ 3264 9637; www.hostelbrasil.com.br. The most popular of the Barra hostels, with a busy, young partying crowd. Dorms are very plain, small, well kept & sex segregated. $

beach). Rooms are large but dull, furnished with bland items that look catalogue or middle-class car-boot sale in origin. But the views through the large French windows are stunning. $$$$

🏠 **Pestana Bahia Lodge** (90 rooms) Rua Fonte do Boi 216, Rio Vermelho; ☎ 2103 8000; www.pestana.com. Views from this newly built cliff-top hotel over the Atlantic & beach from the infinity pool, & Salvador itself spreading along a series of bays to the right. Rooms are modern, well appointed & decorated in a mock-Philippe Starck boutique style & are housed in inelegant, garishly coloured 3-storey mock-colonial buildings with large balconies. $$$–$$$$

🏠 **Catharina Paraguaçu** (32 rooms) Rua João Gomes 128, Rio Vermelho; ☎ 3247 1488; www.hotelcatharinaparaguacu.com.br. This was Salvador's 1st attempt at a boutique hotel & has rooms in a modern & an older wing. The former are musty & dark with ugly blue counterpanes & brick walls. The latter, gathered around a pretty little tropical garden are brighter & airier, especially the duplex rooms with hardwood ceilings, heavy antique furniture & crochet or knitted cotton bedspreads & decorations. The best have sea views. Staff are friendly & accommodating. $$$

🏠 **Cocoon Spaceship Hotel** (27 rooms) Rua Haeckel José de Almeida 238, Jaguaribe; ✆ 3368 8100; www.hotel-cocoon.com. This selfconsciously sci-fi hotel aims to feel as cool as a Kubrik moonbase but falls short of a *Torchwood* film set. Especially in the rooms: beds are mattresses stuck on off-white concrete slabs moulded (along with the side tables) into off-white concrete walls in cubes of rooms whose windows double up as doors — meaning that you need to have curtains constantly drawn for privacy. Aside from the bar, public areas are little better. The pool may change colour but it's so small you could almost leap over it,

service is inattentive & the hotel is stuck behind a 4-lane highway in a residential neighbourhood a taxi ride from a decent restaurant. $$$

🏠 **Blue Tree Premium** (200 rooms) Rua Monte Conselho 505; ✆ 2103 2233; www.bluetree.com.br. This 1990s hotel is the best situated for the Dia do Yemanjá festivals which take place on the beach immediately in front. The spacious if anonymous rooms decked out in beige tile & with fitted hardwood desks & king-sized beds are surprisingly good value, especially if booked online, & the hotel has a decent pool & deck overlooking the sea. $$–$$$

🏠 **Ibis** (252 rooms) Rua Fonte do Boi 215; ✆ 3330 8300; www.accorhotels.com.br. A chunky slab of characterless steel-reinforced concrete with plain cubes for rooms, decorated with bargain-basement, anonymous-hotel furniture. The best have sea views. $$

✕ WHERE TO EAT

With its fusion of Africa, indigenous America and Portugal, Bahia boasts Brazil's most inventive and distinctive cooking and Salvador is its culinary capital. The historic centre boasts restaurants at every turn, but with a few notable exceptions, very little beyond second-rate local cooking and comfort food. Baiano gourmands (with money) tend to head for the swankier establishments along the coast, the best of which are concentrated in Campo Grande.

CENTRO HISTÓRICO: PELOURINHO & SANTO ANTONIO

✕ **Encontro dos Artistas** Rua das Laranjeiras 15, Pelourinho; ✆ 3321 1721. An arty little restaurant decorated with faux-Da Vinci *Last Supper* with Baiano disciples & serving some of the best traditional Bahian seafood in the historic centre. The *moquecas* are especially recommended. $$$$

✕ **O Nilo** Rua das Laranjeiras 44, Pelourinho; ✆ 3321 0073. Chef Nohad el Kadre learnt traditional cooking from his Lebanese parents. & when he opened a restaurant combined those recipes with a love of Brazilian & Asian food to produce a fusion menu which includes dishes like *filé sultão* (lamb fillet cooked almond sauce, garnished with nuts with grilled vegetables & basmati rice). The dining room is low lit & decorated with contemporary Middle Eastern art collected by Nohad & his family. Options for vegetarians. $$$$

✕ **Sorriso de Dadá** Rua Frei Vicente 5, Pelourinho; ✆ 3321 9642. The restaurant takes its name from the perpetual smile of the former queen of traditional Bahian cooking, Aldaci 'Dadá' dos Santos. She began her career selling *acarajé* on the streets of Salvador. In her heyday Tropicalista & culture minister, Gilberto Gil was a fan of her *moquecas* & Dadá was serving

her spicy, Afro-Brazilian dishes to distinguished visitors to Bahia, including Hillary Clinton. But when we ate here last, Dadá had either taken her eye off the ball or was busy in one of her other restaurants in Salvador or on the Costa do Sauipe. The food was bland, lukewarm & over-priced. $$$$

✕ **Olivier** Rua Direita de Santo Antônio 61, Santo Antônio; ✆ 3241 3829. This intimate garden restaurant tucked away near the boutique hotels in Santo Antônio offers French-Brazilian fusion cooking strong on seafood, served with icy beer or cocktails & accompanied by live bossa nova or MPB most w/end evenings. $$$–$$$$

✕ **Restaurante-Escola do Senac** Praça José Alencar 13–19, Pelourinho; ✆ 3324 4557; wwwba.senac.br. A catering school right on the Pelourinho with 2 AC restaurants both offering food cooked by the students (overseen by the professors). The upper floor dining room serves Bahian cooking whilst downstairs serves 40 different Bahian dishes, payable per kilo & served at lunchtime only. Table decoration is by Goya Lopes (see page 121). Options for vegetarians. $$–$$$$

✕ **Al Carmo** Rua do Carmo 66, Santo Antônio; ✆ 3242 0283. It's not only the boutique hotels of

Santo Antônio that boast a magnificent bay view. Even though the Italian food is a little heavy, this is a great spot to watch the sunset over Itaparica island, perhaps accompanied by a light salad & a chilled glass of wine or *batida*. $$$

✕ **Ponta Vital** Rua das Laranjeiras 23, Pelourinho; ☎ 8828 8983. Chef Dom Vital has assembled a menu of traditional recipes from the Bahian Recôncavo, typical of the food that would have been cooked by African Bahians at home in colonial times. House specialities include the spicy seafood *moqueca de mapé*. $$$

✕ **Quincas Berro d'Água** Largo Quincas Berros d'Água s/n, Pelourinho; ☎ 8844 3816. A Bahian food restaurant-cum-art gallery & live music venue offering local favourites like casquinha do Siri (crab paté) & mariscada (fried seafood) with rice & *farofa* manioc flour. $$$

✕ **Churrascaria Gramado** Praça da Sé 18, Pelourinho; ☎ 3322 1727. Together with SENAC, this place is the best value & cleanest of the Pelourinho per-kilo restaurants, with a broad choice of Bahian & Brazilian food. Lunch only. $–$$

☕ **Bahiacafe** Praça da Sé, 20, Pelourinho; ☎ 3322 1266. Great, European-style coffee, a range of bar snacks & cakes & an internet café out back. $

☕ **Coffee Shop** Praça da Sé 5, Pelourinho; ☎ 3322 7817. Cuban cigar shop-cum-café serving sandwiches, snacks & strong Portuguese coffee, in china cups rather than polystyrene vats. $

BARRA, VITÓRIA, CAMPO GRANDE, RIO VERMELHO AND THE INNER CITY BEACH NEIGHBOURHOODS

✕ **Amado** Av Lafayete Coutinho 660, Comércio, Campo Grande; ☎ 3322 3520; www.amadobahia.com.br. Award-winning Bahian food from chef Edinho Engel, who had a celebrated restaurant on the beach in São Paulo for many years. The food is patchy — opt for the seafood *moquecas*, but the view out over the Baía de Todos os Santos is magical. $$$$$

✕ **LaFayette** Av Contorno 1010, Bahia Marina, Comércio, Campo Grande; ☎ 3321 0800. Grills & seafood in another chic waterside space. The best spot is on the veranda lounge deck, dotted with brightly coloured cushions & with a wonderful bay view. Try the fish of the day in lime sauce. $$$$$

✕ **SOHO** Av Contorno 1010, Bahia Marina, Campo Grande; ☎ 3322 4554. The restaurant's long bar is where Salvador's 'A' List drink their *caipirinhas*. Great sushi & sashimi combinations from Paulistano chef Marcio Fushimi. The best tables are on the open-air veranda overlooking the ocean. Come for a late dinner — say about 21.30–22.00. $$$$$

✕ **Trapiche Adelaide** Praca Tupinmabas 2, Av Contorno, Campo Grande; ☎ 3326 2211; www.trapiceadelaide.com.br. This glass-walled, modernist cube sitting over the water on the Baía de Todos os Santos is another popular posing spot in rich Salvador's 'Vanity Fair'. The crisply dressed tuck into the house favourite — king prawns in Dijon sauce or sip cocktails in the equally selfconsciously chic Bar da Ponta Bar next door. $$$$$

✕ **Pereira Restaurante** Av Sete de Setembro 3959, Porto da Barra; ☎ 3264 6464. Raw brick & glass-walled rustic chic restaurant & bar with an ocean-view patio (which attracts a young & well-dressed crowd most evenings). Main courses include glutinous pastas & risottos, large slabs of meat & a smattering of Bahian dishes. It's possible to come just for a beer & a bar snack. $$$$_$$$$$

✕ **Fogo de Chão** Praça Colombo 4, Rio Vermelho; ☎ 3555 9292. The best *churrascaria* (spit-roast restaurant) in the city. Black-tie waiters rush around the dining room brandishing spits thick with cuts of beef, pork, lamb, sausages, & a buffet bar serves salads & pasta. Come with a carnivore's appetite & an empty stomach. $$$$

✕ **Mai Thai** Av Sete de Setembro 2068, Hotel Sol Victoria Marina, Vitória; ☎ 3336 7736. A daytime lounge deck, evening restaurant & after-hours lounge bar sitting on a covered pier jutting into the emerald water of the Baía de Todos os Santos. To get to Mai Thai take the cable car from the Hotel Sol Victoria — it's worth coming for a beer just for the journey, especially around sunset. Non-Brazilians used to the real thing will find the Thai food heavy & under-spiced. Very busy at w/ends with families & teenagers roaring as they plunge into the water off the zip line. $$$

OTHER REGIONS

✕ **Paraiso Tropical** Rua Edgar Loureiro 98-B, Cabula; ☎ 3384 7464. This simple, family restaurant run by eccentric many-times widower Beto Pimental is well worth the cab ride from the centre. The menu is perhaps the best in the city, with superb *moquecas* flavoured with organic fruits & condiments from Beto's garden. Many, like *biri biri* are unique to northeastern Brazil. Staff are very friendly & welcoming. $$$$$

✕ **Jet Set Dining Club** (see page 117)

Salvador's nightlife has long been stratified by race and class, with the wealthy white elite and middle classes tending to frequent clubs and bars in the beach suburbs – from Campo Grande to Barra and beyond. But the increase of tourism is changing things, particularly around the Pelourinho (which is traditionally a lower middle class entertainment neighbourhood), where most foreign visitors tend to spend their time. Every Tuesday live bands play in Terreiro de Jesus Square in front of the church of São Francisco de Assis – ostensibly to celebrate the giving out of alms to the poor by the parishioners, but in reality to kick off the week's biggest knees-up. Crowds spill from the square down the Pelourinho and adjacent streets and by 21.00 the whole area is bustling with people from all over the city – eating grilled cheese from makeshift barbecues, quaffing cans of beer sold by wandering vendors or sitting at rickety plastic tables in the myriad street-corner bars. There are live bands playing in all the key venues on the Praça Beco d'Água and the Praça do Reggae. Much of the music is dull axé pop, MPB or international reggae but there are occasional samba de rodas and more experimental acts. Look out for names like Mariene de Castro and Tiganá – and for the irritatingly insistent touts around the Terreiro de Jesus. The party begins to wind down from about 23.00 after which it's best to catch a taxi back to the hotel unless you're in a group. A smaller party takes place on Fridays and Saturdays. Salvador's other nightlife area worthy of attention is Rio Vermelho – an eclectic, artistic, middle-class neighbourhood which nonetheless has strong African-Brazilian heritage. Friday and weekend nights see the little bars gathered around the Largo da Mariquita, the neighbourhood's main square, buzzing with life. Bands frequently play shows here. Adjacent streets like the Largo de Santana are home to popular *botecos*.

BARS

♀ Boteco do França Rua Borges dos Reis 24-A, Rio Vermelho; ✆ 3334 2734. A spit & sawdust rustic beer & snacks bar with black-tie waiters & a buzzing local crowd. Great *batidas* (alcoholic fresh fruit juice mixes), caipirinhas & bar snacks including *abusadinho* (sun-dried meat with cream cheese & spinach).

♀ Cantina da Lua Praça Quinze de Novembro (Terreiro De Jesus) 2, Pelourinho; ✆ 3322 4041. A popular spot to drink chilled bottles of beer & people-watch. The *comidinhas* (bar food) is edible but avoid the main dishes.

♀ Cravinho Praça 15 de Novembro 3; ✆ 3322 6759. Very popular little bar just off the Terreiro de Jesus serving an enormous range of *cachaças* stored in barrels behind the bar. Occasional live music.

♀ Cruz do Pascoal Rua Direita de Santo Antônio 2, Santo Antônio; ✆ 3243 2285. Great bar snacks & cold bottled beer served on a little veranda with a view over the Baía de Todos os Santos.

♀ Praça do Reggae Ladeiro do Pelourinho (next to the church of Nossa Senhora do Rosário dos Pretos). A string of bars with live Brazilian & international reggae every Tue & more frequently around Carnaval. Be wary of pickpockets, especially in the toilet areas. There is usually a cover charge of R$8–10 for the band.

TIGANÁ SANTANA RECOMMENDS

Tiganá Santana (*www.tigana.com.br*) is one of Bahia's most exciting new musical talents with an effortlessly beautiful resonant voice and a unique compositional style fusing African and Brazilian rhythms and languages. Here is his tip for what to see and do in Salvador:

On Saturday night (at 20.00) you can watch the unique and beautiful 'opening sacred ritual' at the Ilê Aiyê cultural centre in Curuzu on the outskirts of Salvador. You really shouldn't miss it. The traditional drumming by powerful drum troupes in exuberant costumes and the accompanying dancing are incredible and the culural centre lies in the heart of the most important Afro-Brazilian district in Salvador.

♀ **Praça Beco d'Água** Off Rua J C Rabelo, Pelourinho. & with a similar set-up to the Praça do Reggae with beery bars surrounding a central stage that plays host to live bands & dancing.

♀ **Santo Antônio Botequinho** Av Otavio Mangabeira 2323, Jardim dos Namorados, Pituba; ✆ 3240 1491. Formerly the French Quartier Music restaurant this faux-New Orleans jazz & blues bar & restaurant offers a bizarre menu (ostrich steaks & Bahian snacks) & live bossa nova, jazz & blues. One of the best bars for dancing to live music in the city.

♀ **World Bar** Rua Dias Dávila 26, Barra; ✆ 3264 5223. Basic beer bar with a mix of students, locals & backpacker tourists.

♀ **Zauber Multicultura** Ladeira da Misericórdia, Edf. Taveira s/n (reachable via the street next to the Prefeitura); ✆ 9983 0313. A busy bar with an outdoor lounge terrace which doubles up as a trance club at w/ends. Great *caipirinhas* & *mojitos* & an eclectic boho-chic crowd. Take a cab here — it's an unsavoury area.

CLUBS

☆ **Jet Set Dining Club** Rua Guadalajara 09, Morro do Gato; ✆ 3235 4107. A Salvador version of London's Lounge Lover, mixing cocktails & a limited food menu with a lounge bar & DJ-driven dance floor. The music is mock-European & North American electronica & the crowd wealthy 20 & 30 something. The kitchen closes after midnight — after which it's dancing & drinking only.

☆ **Korunn** Rua Ceará 1240, Pituba; ✆ 3248 4201. A bar complex with a lounge area, stage & dance floor. Music is mostly rock & MPB but DJs spin modern club sounds. Bar food available.

☆ **Madre Disco e Evento** Av Otávio Mangabeira 2471, Boca do Rio; ✆ 3346 0012. As Fashion Club, this location was a mainstay on the upper middle-class Salvador nightclub scene for years. In 2008 it was gutted & refurbished with a long Technicolor bar, huge dance floor & thumping sound system which pumps out cheesy European house & techno to over 1,000 20-something Salvadoreans nightly. The themed party night every month sees a change of décor & occasionally, fancy dress. R$35 entry.

☆ **Mercado do Peixe** Rio Vermelho (on the beachfront opposite the Blue Tree Towers Hotel). A popular semi-open-air after-club & bar spot on the beach where

waiters continue to dish out cold beer & bar snacks at the plastic tables almost until dawn; when it reverts to being a seafood market with snack-bar restaurants.

☆ **Off Club** Rua Dias D´Ávila 33, Barra (next to the lighthouse); ✆ 3267 6215. The city's longest-established (& still busiest) gay club. Brazilian DJs from the city, São Paulo, Rio & Recife play techno, hard house; skimpily clad go-go boys dance on little stages & chef Murilo Brochini serves bar snacks from *croque messieurs* to stuffed mud crabs.

☆ **Praça Pedro Arcanjo** Near the Pelourinho. Look out for the Santo de Casa cultural group who play here most Sats. Together with singer Mariene de Castro they are one of the few upholders of traditional Bahian samba. They're full of raw energy & verve.

☆ **Quereres** Rua Frei Vicente 7, Pelourinho; ✆ 3321 1616. Sweaty, tiny & popular bar/club in an old Pelourinho townhouse offering live & DJ-fuelled MPB, Rio funk & cheesy Bahian axê. Busiest on Tue & Fri.

☆ **Santo Antônio alem do Carmo** There are often live shows with traditional Bahian samba & African Brazilian music at w/ends in the fort or around the square in front of it.

☆ **Terreiro de Jesus** Live music on Tue (see above, page 116).

LIVE MUSIC VENUES

🎭 **Rock in Rio** Shopping Aeroclub Plaza Show, Av Otávio Mangabeira 6000, Boca do Rio (on the road to the airport 30mins from the centre); ✆ 3462 8000. One of Salvador's largest concert venues, inspired by the mock-Glastonbury Rock in Rio, with bands playing on a huge stage through one of northeast Brazil's best PA systems. Music ranges from frenetic axé to heavy rock & MPB. DJs play between shows & the venue attracts Soterpolitanos of all classes. R$10 entrance.

🎭 **Casa do Ilê Aiyê** Rua das Laranjeiras 16; ✆ 3321 4193; www.ileaiye.org.br. The HQ of another of Salvador's established batucada drum troupe who parade at Carnaval. Like Olodum their aim is to

preserve & honour African Bahian culture. There are often live performances.

🎭 **Casa do Olodum** Rua Gregório de Matos 22; ✆ 3321 5010; http://olodum.uol.com.br. The home of the famous batucada drum troupe who found international fame playing on Paul Simon's *Rhythm of the Saints* & who perform live every Tue & Sun at 19.00.

🎭 **International Center for Black Music** & **Museu Du Ritmo** Rua Torquato Bahia, 84 Edificio Mercado do Ouro; ✆ 3353 4333. The premier spot for African-Brazilian music in the old city centre. It's worth visiting just to see the giant space pod on stilts that towers over the colonial courtyard, housing the DJ.

CINEMAS For cinema listings see www.guiadasemana.com.br/salvador/cinema.
Unlike in Rio and São Paulo, in Salvador most English-language films are dubbed. For subtitled films look or ask for 'legendas' (subtitled) rather than 'dublada' (dubbed). The listings website above specifies this. The best screens are in the shopping malls.

Blockbuster cinemas

🎬 **Shopping Barra** Av Centenário, Shopping Barra; ✎ 3264 5795
🎬 **UCI Shopping Aeroclube** Av Otávio Mangabeira, Boca do Rio; ✎ 3535 3030

🎬 **Multiplex Iguatemi** Av Tancredo Neves 148, 3rd Flr Shopping Iguatemi, Pituba; ✎ 3533 0880
🎬 **Cinemark Salvador** Av Tancredo Neves 2915, Loja 300; ✎ 3443 1870

Art cinemas

🎬 **Cinema do Museu** Museu Geológico, Av Sete de Setembro, Corredor da Vitória; ✎ 3338 2241
🎬 **MAM** Solar do Unhão, Av Contorno s/n, Solar do Unhão; ✎ 3329 5727. In the Museum of Modern Art complex, housed in a beautifully converted historical

building with an unpleasant past – it was used as an auction house for slaves until the late 19th century.
🎬 **Cine Vivo** Av Rubens Guelli 135, Shopping Paseo Itaigara; ✎ 2223 9700

SPORT

Football (Soccer) Salvador follows football with religious fervour. The city has two principal teams: Esporte Clube Vitória and Esporte Clube Bahia.

Esporte Clube Vitória (*www.ecvitoria.com.br*) is one of the oldest in Brazil. Aside from Pernambuco's Náutico and Sport club it is the only team from the Brazilian northeast to play in Brazil's top Série A league. The club was founded as a joint cricket and football club in 1899 by Artur and Artêmio Valente, brothers who discovered the games when studying in England. They play at the Manoel Barradas stadium (aka Barradão) and were Brazilian runners-up in 1993.

Esporte Clube Bahia (*www.esporteclubebahia.com.br*), often known simply as Bahia, are the city's second team, currently playing in Brazil's Série B (second division). The club was founded in 1931, and has as strong a fan base as Vitória, gained through an illustrious career. Highlights were wins in the Campeonato Brasileiro Série A in 1988, and the Taça Brasil (the predecessor of the modern Brazilian League) in 1959 – the latter in a thrilling final with Pelé's Santos.

Bahia play in the Roberto Santos stadium (aka Estádio Pituaçu), which is located in a conservation area in Pituaçu. Their official ground, Otávio Mangabeira (aka Fonte Nova), next to the Dique de Tororó park, is currently undergoing complete renovation in preparation for the 2014 World Cup and the football tournaments of the 2016 Olympic Games. Work is expected to be complete in 2011.

How to buy a ticket Games are advertised on the club websites and in the local papers. Tickets can be bought up to 72 hours before a game at the Vitória club headquarters (*Estádio do Barradão, Av Artênio Castro Valente 01, Nsa da Vitória;* ⊕ *09.00–17.00 Mon–Fri*), the Sede Social Headquarters (*Av Otávio Mangabeira s/n Boca do Rio;* ⊕ *09.00–17.00 Mon–Fri, 09.00–17.00 Sat & 09.00–12.00 Sun*) or Estádio de Pituaçú (*Av Prof Pinto de Aguiar s/n, Pituaçu;* ⊕ *09.00–17.00 Mon–Fri*). They can also be bought online through the club websites (see above) up to 48 hours before a game, but only with a Brazilian credit or debit card.

Capoeira The spectacular martial art dance capoeira was born in Bahia and remains the most popular 'sport' in Salvador after football. The fighting technique fuses acrobatics with high kicks and punches all based in a rhythmic two-step called the *ginga*. There are always capoeira touts around the Pelourinho and the Mercado Modelo performing often inferior shows for tourists and charging for photos. Some now tout lessons too. For the real McCoy head for one of the capoeira schools where you can both watch a show or class and learn capoeira from those who represent the living traditions. The following schools are recommended by *capoeiristas*, and though English is not always spoken, teaching seldom suffers as a result.

Capoeira classes There are a number of capoeira schools in the **Forte de Santo Antônio Alem do Carmo** (↳ *3117 1488; www.fortesantantonio.blogspot.com;* ⊕ *09.00–18.00 Mon–Fri – later for capoeira students; entry to the fort free*) offering both regional and Angola capoiera. All are almost unknown to tourists. These schools include: Pele da Bahia (↳ *3387 6485; www.mestrepeledabahia.blogspot.com*) and Mestre Boca Rica (↳ *3401 3019*).

Capoeira regional
Associação de Capoeira Mestre Bimba Rua das Laranjeiras 1, Pelourinho; ↳ 3322 0639; www.capoeiramestrebimba.com.br; ⊕ 09.00–12.00 & 15.00–20.00 Mon–Fri. This school is the inheritor of the teaching of Mestre Bimba who was the first master to define a system for teaching capoeira. With men & women teachers including well-known names.

Capoeira Angola
CECA Rio Vermelho Rua Raimundo Viana 61-E, Rio Vermelho; ↳ 3345 2311, 8813 9060; www.ceca-riovermelho.org.br (new students must attend for an initial session 19.30 & 22.00 Tue or Thu). A large school aimed at locals & founded by Mestre João Pequeno, another alumnus of the legendary Pastinha. Most classes are conducted by his pupil, Mestre Faísca.

Escola de Capoeira Angola Irmãos Gêmeos Rua Gregório de Mattos 9, Pelourinho; ↳ 3321 0396, 9963 3562; http://ecaig.blogspot.com (also on Facebook). A school founded by Mestre Curió, an alumnus of another legendary capoeirista, Mestre Pastinha. Classes are broad & not just aimed at the young & fit male.

They are also excellent for women, kids & older people & in Curió's absence classes are conducted by the mestre's pupil, Mestra Jararaca (the first woman to earn the Mestra tiltle in Capoeira Angola).

Grupo Cultural de Capoeira Angola Moçambique Rua Gregório de Mattos 38, Pelourinho; ↳ 8113 7455, 8811 4815, 3356 7640; ⊕ 12.00–14.00 Mon–Fri. Teaching is very flexible, with options for either day classes or full semesters & it also offers berimbau & percussion lessons. Some of the most illustrious teachers work here, including Mestres Boca Rica & Neco – alumni of Canjiquinha & Waldemar – 2 of the most celebrated teachers of the 20th century.

SHOPPING

Salvador offers the best shopping in Bahia. The bulk of the tourist-orientated shops are on and around the Pelourinho. Here you will find bead jewellery, musical instruments, clay figures and knick-knacks, alongside music, fashion and tourist miscellany. Similar items can be found below the Pelourinhos in the Cidade Baixa – at the Mercado Modelo. The various shopping malls (*shoppings* in Portuguese) – notably Shopping Barra and Iguatemi – are the best locations to buy brand fashion (both international and Brazilian), books, perfumes and suchlike.

ARTS AND CRAFTS
Arte e Vida Rua Alfredo de Brito 41, Pelourinho; ↳ 3322 0580. General arts & crafts from home decoration & paintings to musical instruments. **Brasil Açu** Rua da Misericórdia 07, Portal da Misericórdia, Pelourinho; ↳ 3266-3099. Contemporary

art, decorative pieces, sculpture & painting inspired by Bahian culture. There are often exhibitions by local artists in the shop's front space.

Casa da Mulher Rendeira Rua Gregório de Matos, Pelourinho; ↳ 3321 3012. Northeast Brazilian stitch

& crochet knitwork, cotton garments, tablecloths & other such items.

Coisas da Terra Rua Maciel Baixo 19, Pelourinho; ☎ 3322 9322. Contemporary objets d'art for the home with designs drawing on traditional Bahian themes.

Fundação Pierre Verger Galeria Rua da Misericórdia 9, Loja 9 (off the Pelourinho); ☎ 3321 2341; www.pierreverger.org. An art gallery showing the black & white pictures of French naturalist photographer & long-time Salvador resident Pierre Verger & occasional exhibitions by other photographers of Bahia, & selling books, postcards & other items related to their work.

Galeria Atelier Totonho e Raimundo Ladeira do Carmo, Pelourinho. Two galleries showcasing & selling the work of some 28 naive artists. Mostly painting & all at attractive prices. See also *Mercado Modelo*, page 121.

Instituto de Artesanato Visconde de Mauá Largo do Porto da Barra 2, Barra; ☎ 3264 5501, & on the Pelourinho: Rua Gregório de Matos 27, Pelourinho; ☎ 3321 5501; www.maua.ba.gov.br. A state-supported arts & crafts shop selling traditional & contemporary ceramics, carved wood, glass & silverware, lace, leather & musical instruments. Products are made by artisans from all over the state & the institute runs courses from R$30.

BOOKSHOPS

Graúna Bons Livros Usados Ltda ☎ 3286 0455; www.graunalivros.com.br. Excellent Salvador-based online source of used Portuguese books, including many out of print, technical & rare titles.

Livraria Brandão Livros Usados Rua Ruy Barbosa 4 loja B; ☎ 3322 4809. A broad range of secondhand books including some titles in English, Italian, French & German.

Livraria Saraiva Megastore 2nd Flr, Shopping Barra; ☎ 3264 2191; www.livrariasaraiva.com.br. Brazil's answer to Waterstone's or Borders sells 2 floors of books, CDs & magazines with some English language titles & a large kids' section.

Livraria Siciliano 3rd Flr, Shopping Iguatemi, Av Tancredo Neves; ☎ 3450 7728. Large well-stocked bookshop with contemporary Portuguese titles (including plenty of travel & reference books), CDs & magazines. Some English-language newspapers, magazines, novels & business books.

CIGARS

Tabacaria Rosa do Prado Rua Inácio Acioli 5, Pelourinho; ☎ 3322 1258. Bahians will try to convince you that their soft, spicy cigars are the equal of Cuba's. The best are reputedly Danneman & Menendez Amerino (from the same family who manufactured Cuba's Upmann cigars) — made in the Recôncavo.

MUSIC AND MUSICAL INSTRUMENTS

Bazar Musical Rua Marquês de Caravelas 609, loja 8, Barra; ☎ 8873 5233. Hundreds of rare Brazilian vinyl LPs. Discounts for bulk buys. Very knowledgeable, friendly proprietor.

Cana Brava Records www.bahia-online.net/brazilian-music.htm

Casa do Ilê Aiyê Rua das Laranjeiras 16; ☎ 3321 4193; www.ileaiye.org.br. Ilê Aiyê's headquarters & shop — where you can find information about their shows & Carnaval events — buy music, T-shirts & percussion instruments.

Oficina de Investigação Musical Rua Alfredo Brito 24, Pelourinho; ☎ 3322 2386. One of the best places in the historical centre to buy percussion instruments. The proprietor has made berimbaus for famous musicians including Carlinhos Brown.

FASHION

Blue Man 3rd Flr, Shopping Barra; ☎ 3264 1332, Iguatemi Shopping; ☎ 3450 0117 & Salvador Shopping; ☎ 3878 2051; www.blueman.com.br. Super-sexy, beautifully made bikinis & swimming shorts for young & well-toned bodies. One of Rio's top 20-something labels.

Bob Store 3rd Flr, Shopping Barra; ☎ 2105 9669 & Shopping Iguatemi; ☎ 3431 3033; www.bobstore.com.br. Light, smart, casual young fashion for women from one of São Paulo's leading upper- to mid-market labels.

Carlos Miele www.carlosmiele.com.br. One of Brazil's leading international boutique designers for women — with shops alongside those of Stella McCartney & Alexander McQueen in New York's meatpacking district. Vivacious, young, sophisticated & making use of light, flowing fabrics, bright colours & Brazilian artisan techniques like patchwork, stitching, crochet, &

leatherwork. A favourite of celebrities like Keira Knightley. Many of the cuts available in Brazil are not available internationally.

Didara Goya Lopes Rua Gregório de Mattos, Pelourinho; ☎ 3321 9428; www.goyalopes.com.br. Goya is an African-Brazilian artist & designer whose work has been exhibited at the Glass Curtain Gallery in Chicago. Her Didara label features simple cotton clothing & beach shawls stamped with intricate motifs from Candomblé & Brazilian cultural life.

Folic 3rd Flr, Barra Shopping; ☎ 3264 1386; www.folic.com.br. Light, summery dresses, skirts, tops & shoes for 30- & 40-something women from a leading Rio de Janeiro label.

Iodice 3rd Flr, Shopping Barra; ☎ 3267 2848; www.iodice.com.br. A São Paulo brand famous for its sexy 20-something figure-hugging clothing & funky jeans. For women.

Maria Bonita Extra Shopping Iguatemi; ☎ 3450 1122; www.mariabonitaextra.com.br. Bright, upmarket urban wear & lush gowns for young women, from a Rio label increasingly popular in the USA.

Osklen ShoppingBarra; ☎ 3237 4973. Brazil's answer to Ralph Lauren offers cool, stylish, sophisticated beach & casual wear that's more surf than sailboat.

Rosa Chá Iguatemi Shopping; ☎ 3450 2172; www.rosacha.com.br. Amir Slama's famous label is one of the world's leading top-end beachwear brands; beloved of New York fashion week & supermodels from Naomi Campbell to Isabeli Fontana. The cuts available in Brazil are not sold in the US or Europe.

Salinas Moda Praia, 3rd Flr, Shopping Barra; ☎ 3332 2936. Together with Lenny Niemeyer & Rosa Chá, Salinas are the most internationally sought-after Brazilian beach fashion label. Sophisticated sexy (but never vulgar) bikinis & swim suits are considerably cheaper than the Salinas beachwear you'll find in top-end department stores in the US & Europe.

Toulon Shopping Iguatemi; ☎ 3432 8110; www.toulon.com.br. Great-value jeans, jackets & casual wear for men. Brazil's Primark.

SOUVENIRS

Projeto Axé Av Estados Unidos 161, Edf Suerdieck 9 Andar, Comércio. T-shirts, kangas & other items of clothing sold by an organisation which works to help the street children of Salvador.

Lembranças da Fé Rua João de Deus 24, Pelourinho; ☎ 3321 0006. Kitschy Catholic saint figures & their associated *orixás* in gaudy colours in wood, plaster & plastic.

SHOPPING MALLS The city is replete with *shoppings* ('shawpeengs') – US-style shopping malls of varying quality. These are good, safe places to visit an ATM, buy general consumer goods (books, CDs, clothing, shoes, toys, etc) but they are poor for arts and crafts. Most of the malls have travel agents (for buying internal plane and bus tickets), cinemas and a wealth of fast-food restaurants. Most malls open 09.00–22.00 Monday to Friday and 12.00–21.00 on Sunday.

Shopping Aeroclub Plaza Show Av Otávio Mangabeira 6000, Boca do Rio; ☎ 3461 0300. This mock-Miami semi-outdoor mall overlooking the beach in the far east of the city is one of the newest – with a bowling alley, cinemas, live music venues & a broad range of shops.

Shopping Barra Av Centenário 2992, Chame-Chame, Barra; ☎ 2108 8288; www.shoppingbarra.com. The largest shopping mall in easy access of the tourist centres is one of the oldest. Together with a good range of mid to top-end boutiques, it also boasts the best cinemas – a short walk from the Barra lighthouse.

Shopping Iguatemi Av Tancredo Neves 148, Caminho das Árvores; ☎ 2126 1111; www.iguatemisalvador.com.br. A large, modern, upmarket mall with a broad range of boutiques & one of the best multiplexes in the city, sitting directly opposite the rodoviária.

Salvador Shopping Av Tancredo Neves 2915; ☎ 3878 1000; www.salvadorshopping.com.br. A large, modern mall in east Salvador (just under a km east of the rodoviária) with cinemas, many restaurants & mostly mid- to upper-market boutiques.

MARKETS

Mercado Modelo Praça Cairu, Cidade Baixa; ⏲ 09.00–19.00 Mon–Sat, 09.00–14.00 Sun. A large covered market next to the boat terminal for Morro de São Paulo, selling all manner of tourist-orientated items. Look out for woodcarvings, bags made out of ring pulls, leather & ceramics.

OTHER PRACTICALITIES

BANKS There are plenty of banks in Salvador's city centre (and in the airport terminal, the rodoviária and every shopping mall) – far too many to list. You are rarely likely to be more than 500m from an ATM. It is best to avoid using ATMs after dark. Bradesco and HSBC offer cash advances on Visa and MasterCard. In addition to shopping malls, addresses include:

$ **Banco Bradesco** Rua Chile 23, Centro; ☏ 3321 3154 & Lad Praça 2, Centro; ☏ 3322 8022 (both near the Praça da Sé, a couple of blocks south of the

Pelourinho), & at Rua Alm Marques Leão 5489, Barra; ☏ 3264 8300
$ **HSBC** Rua Marq Caravelas 355, Barra; ☏ 3264 3244

HOSPITAL
Hospital Espanhol, Av Sete de Setembro 4161, Barra; ☏ 3264 1500; www.hospitalespanhol.com.br.

PHARMACIES Pharmacies (*drogarias/farmácias*) are even more abundant than banks. Hours vary from 09.00–18.00 to 08.00–20.00 and 'Farmácias 24 horas', which never close. Most pharmacies will have a notice giving the address of the nearest open alternative.

POST OFFICES The main office is at Avenida Alm Marques Leão 20 (*Barra;* ☏ *3264 0222*) and there are other branches in the major shopping malls, including Shopping Barra (see page 121).

WHAT TO SEE AND DO

OLD SALVADOR
Praça Tomé de Sousa and the Praça da Sé Salvador grew from a collection of buildings hastily constructed on a cliff top in March 1549, above the shimmering Baia de Todos os Santos (Bay of All Saints). Tomé de Souza (see page 28), a seasoned soldier and minor nobleman, had been chosen by King João III of Portugal to lead a thousand new settlers across the Atlantic and found the capital of a new outpost of empire. The site of the new city was chosen by Diogo Álvares 'Caramuru' – a merchant who had failed to found a settlement in Tupinambá territory some years earlier, and who had only been spared his life because of his long-standing trade relations with the Indians. De Sousa and his troops cleared three indigenous villages from the cliff top and set about building the city. In the square which still bears his name – the Praça Tomé de Sousa (aka Praça Municipal) – the first buildings were constructed from indigenous shell middens that had accumulated over 2,000 years prior to the founding of Salvador. Tupinambá were paid to help with the construction and the governor himself hauled logs up the hill. The square and those adjacent to it form the crown of what became the capital of Brazil, and what is now the UNESCO World-Heritage colonial centre of Salvador. It's a delightful sprawl of colourful Renaissance houses, glittering Baroque churches and eclectic civic palaces that stretch north from the Praça Municipal, in narrow cobbled streets, to the district of Santo Antônio. Most of the sights of interest in Salvador, and many of the hotels lie here.

The Old City is largely pedestrianised, but the **Praça Tomé de Sousa** receives buses from the rodoviária, airport and the beach suburbs and is therefore the logical place to begin a visit. The praça sits at the historic centre's southern extremity. None of the original buildings remain on the square, which is dominated by post-18th-century edifices. The most eye-catching is the **Palácio Rio Branco** (*Praça Tomé de*

Souza, Praça Municipal; 71 3176 4200; ⏲ *09.30–17.00 Tue–Sat; free admission*) an eclectic fusion of neoclassical and French Baroque, covered in wedding cake-coloured stucco and topped by a creamy cupula. It's the fourth building to stand on the site of de Sousa's original modest, wattle-and-daub governor's palace – built in the 1920s as one of the first architectural fruits of the bombastic new republic. The palace was the seat of state government until 1979 and is now home to little more than bureaucrats and filing cabinets, but it's worth a peek inside to see a motley assortment of state-commissioned paintings, a statue of Tomé de Souza and glorious views of the bay.

On the west side of the square is the 72m-high **Elevador Lacerda** lift (*Praça Tomé de Souza, Praça Municipal s/n, R$0.50*), which connects the Cidade Alta (Upper City) and Cidade Baixa (Lower City). It takes its name from its engineer designer Antônio Lacerda, an early Bahian transport magnate who built the original hydraulic lift from steel imported from Britain in 1874. The current Art Deco construction, which dates from the 1930s, looks at its most impressive when seen at dusk from Cidade Baixa when the elevator – set against the cliffs and the peacock-blue sky – is illuminated with low light in gradually shifting hues. The lift is not safe to use after dark. The praça is also home of the late 18th-century neoclassical **Paço Municipal** (*Praça Tomé de Souza, Praça Municipal;* 71 3176 4200; ⏲ *09.30–17.00 Tue–Sat; free admission*) which stands immediately opposite the Lacerda lift, on the site of another of Tomé de Souza's first buildings. It is still a seat of local government and has a pretty internal courtyard.

A few dozen metres north of the Praça Municipal is the more imposing **Praça da Sé**, reached via the Rua da Misericórdia. There is a fine Baroque church on this street, **Santa Casa da Misericórdia** (⏲ *09.00–12.00 & 14.00–18.00 Mon-Fri; R$10*). It dates from 1774 and has beautiful ceiling panels attributed to Antônio Rodrigues Braga and a series of *azulejos* depicting early Bahian religious processions. There is a small sacred-art museum (entry included in the price for the church). The Praça da Sé itself is dominated by a colossal, bulky cathedral at the far north eastern end of the square. The south side of the praça is lined with pretty cafés, the northwestern open to the bay, with wonderful sweeping views and the praça itself decorated with a sprinkle of modernist fountains. *Capoeiristas* often gather here for impromptu shows and, as if in anticipation of the Pelourinho just to the north, there are increasing numbers of bric-a-brac and arts and crafts stalls. A statue of a stately **Tomé de Souza** in bronze gazes across the square at Mario Cravo Junior's famous *Cruz Caída (Fallen Cross)* sculpture and the bay beyond. The sculpture depicts a cross that has fallen and fractured at its apex, and was inaugurated on the 445th anniversary of the founding of Salvador as a homage to Brazil's principal cathedral which was demolished in 1933, along with a magnificent cluster of Renaissance houses. The cathedral's bones lie up a few steps from the cross, in the form of denuded foundations grown over with wild flowers, and bits of ecclesiastical masonry. The building was one of the finest examples of 17th-century Portuguese ecclesiastical architecture in the world – a striking fusion of neoclassical and Baroque with a towering nave. It was the site of Brazil's first bishopric, the headquarters of the early Brazilian Catholic Church administered by the cruel **Pero Fernandes Sardinha**. He was a bigoted, intransigent old man whose many injustices included having a group of colonists stripped to the waist, bound and gagged as a forced penance for imitating the Indians by smoking tobacco. He and several hundred early Baianos were shipwrecked off the coast of Pernambuco on their way back to Lisbon where they were massacred by the Caeté Indians, an act the Jesuit Manoel de Nóbrega saw as divine punishment for the cruelty meted out by the settlers on the Tupinambá of Bahia. A few metres west of the church is the **Memorial da Baiana do Acarajé** (*Praça da Sé s/n;* ⏲ *09.00–12.00 & 14.00–18.00*

3

Mon–Fri; R$10), a small museum devoted to Bahian women who wear traditional large swirling dresses, with displays and photos showing the history of Baianas since colonial times, customs, African traditions and religion. An adjacent café serves Bahian snacks like *acarajé* and small souvenirs.

Terreiro de Jesus and Largo Cruzeiro de São Francisco

After the 1933 demolition another Jesuit church was appointed the city's cathedral. The **Catedral Basílica de São Salvador** (aka Catedral da Sé) separates the Praça da Sé from the **Terreiro de Jesus** (aka Praça 15 de Novembro) square, a long rectangle of dragon's tooth black-and-white cobbles surrounded on all sides by beautiful colonial buildings. It was originally delineated by Manoel de Nóbrega (see below). It's a lively place – always bustling with little stalls selling everything from coconut juice to Bahian musical instruments. Every Tuesday and most weekends there are live concerts here – the former led by Afrobeat and Olodum jazz-band leader Geronimo – and on Sundays an **arts and crafts market** which spills down into the streets of the adjacent Pelourinho. The praça takes its name from the Candomblé word for sacred ritual site, and it is aptly named: for several hundred years this praça and the adjacent Praça da Sé were the centre of Christianity in Brazil, with the Jesuit order as the dominant power. The Jesuits arrived with Tomé de Sousa on the beach not far from the praça in 1549, under the leadership of **Manoel de Nobrega**. It was an arrival they saw as imbued with auspicious symbolism. 'I saw with my own eyes,' Nobrega declared, 'four footprints, very clearly marked with their toes.' They were set in stone – like Buddha footprints in southeast Asia, and like other medieval peoples who made sense of the world through symbols as much as syllogisms, Nobrega regarded them as signs from God that St Thomas had preceded them. Nobrega and many other early Iberian Catholics believed that the American indigenous people were descendants of one of the lost tribes of Israel, and as such they were protected by the Church. At least in theory, fighting to ensure this protection against abominable cruelties and the rigorous control through which the fathers de-culturalised and commanded the Indians would lead to the Jesuit order being thrown out of the Portuguese colonies and eventually altogether disbanded.

Salvador's present **cathedral** (*Catedral Sé; Praça da Sé s/n;* ⏲ *09.00–12.00 & 14.00–18.00 Mon–Fri; free admission*) was built largely between 1657 and 1672. It is one of the earliest examples of Baroque architecture in Brazil, with a vast vaulted interior crowned with an altarpiece covered in a filigree of gold leaf and rooms covered in beautiful paintings and some of Brazil's finest statuary. The grand and imposing façade self-consciously remembers the imperial Portuguese church of São Vicente de Fora in Lisbon, one of the most important Mannerist buildings in Portugal and the burial site of the Portuguese Bragança kings. The cathedral's cavernous nave, chapels and tombs are filled with ghosts of Brazil's brutal past. Before becoming the city's principal church the cathedral was – like São Vicente – a monastic church, used by the city's Jesuit college. Early Latin America's most celebrated orator, the African-Portuguese Jesuit **Antônio Vieira**, spent much of his life here – in between trips to the Amazon to fight against the genocide the Portuguese were inflicting on the Indians and to Europe to plead with kings and popes for protection. Even though he was paternalistic and a proselytiser, he was as close as the Portuguese came to protecting indigenous welfare and his campaigns were deeply unpopular with the early Brazilians most of whom wanted the Indians as forced labour on their plantations. He died full of sorrow in one of the chapels in July 1697, close to his 90th year, condemned by the Inquisition and prohibited from either preaching or writing and slanderously accused of conniving at the murder of a colonial official.

If Vieira was one of the most vocal opponents of the cruelty of the Portuguese administration, one of its most powerful and ruthless patriarchs was **Mem de Sá**, who lies buried in an adjacent room. This seasoned soldier administered Brazil as Bahia's third governor from 1558 until his death in 1572 and like Vieira was one of the political and ideological fathers of the country. But he was of an altogether different sort. On becoming governor he made it clear that the Portuguese rule of law would not apply in Brazil, declaring that 'This land should not and cannot be regulated according to the rules or norms of the Kingdom' – a dual reference, perhaps, to the kingdom of God and the papal bull which demanded that indigenous life be respected. He ruled with an iron rod and military efficiency and was responsible for transforming a string of tiny Portuguese colonies into an incipient Brazilian nation. He fought and defeated the French, dispelling them from their colony of France Antarctique on Guanabara Bay – founding what would become the city of Rio de Janeiro. He worked closely with José de Anchieta the Jesuit founder of São Vicente and São Paulo, turning them from religious settlements into fledgling towns. And he massacred or enslaved the Caeté nation of Pernambuco, who had killed Bishop Sardinha and quelled the Tupinambá who had fought the Portuguese since the arrival of Tomé de Sousa. Mem de Sá proclaimed liberty for peaceful Indians, on the condition that they abandoned cannibalism and inter-tribal wars and lived in compounds governed by Nobrega's Jesuit priests. And he massacred those who resisted him. Contemporaneous Jesuit chronicler Simão de Vasconcellos records that he razed and burnt some 160 indigenous villages. Another Jesuit wrote that Mem de Sá 'undertook with many men, to subjugate them and make them appreciate the only path by which they can arrive at an understanding of their Creator' would be to 'tremble with fear of the Governor'. One group of Tupinambá fled the Mem de Sá's forced assimilation, in one of the most remarkable migrations in Brazilian history – wandering through the vast and wild interior of the country and eventually settling on an island in the middle of the Amazon near modern-day Parintins.

Immediately across the square from the cathedral are two more beautiful Portuguese churches. The early 19th-century **São Pedro do Clerigos** (*Praça 15 de Novembro, Terreiro de Jesus;* \ *3321 9183;* ⊕ *09.00–12.00 & 14.00–18.00 Mon–Fri; free admission*) looks lopsided with its solitary tower sitting unbalanced on one side of an unostentatious, if Rococo façade; its modest interior mixes late Rococo decoration with the more sober 19th-century neoclassical. Next to it is the church of the **Ordem Terceira de São Domingos**. This classic example of Portuguese Baroque, dates from 1731 and houses a striking late 18th-century *trompe l'oeil* ceiling attributed to José Joaquim da Rocha, the father of what has come to be called the Bahian school of painting. This was an ecclesiastical art movement which specialised in illusions of perspective and which da Rocha had probably learnt in Portugal. The church was the seat of power for Antônio Vieira's enemies, the Dominicans, who administered the Inquisition introduced into Portugal in 1580 when the Portuguese crown passed by marriage from the Braganças to the more aggressive Spanish Hapsburgs, and Philip I of Spain also became Philip II of Portugal.

The Terreiro de Jesus also hosts two of the city's best museums. The most interesting is the **Museu Afro-Brasileiro (MAfro)** (*Terreiro de Jesus s/n, Prédio da Faculdade de Medicina;* \ *3283 5540; www.ceao.ufba.br/mafro;* ⊕ *09.00–18.00 Mon–Fri, 10.00–17.00 Sat/Sun; R$5 for a joint ticket with Museu de Arqueologia e Etnologia*) housed in the historic building that was home to the Jesuit college itself and subsequently the first Brazilian School of Medicine, and opened in 1982 as a joint project between the state government and a coalition of west African nations. The museum's exhibits include several rooms of Brazilian artefacts of African cultural origin, from the technological to the theological and others from west Africa. There are many outstanding pieces of secular and ritual art, including numerous masks, garments, ceramic objects, items of jewellery, musical instruments, sculptures, paintings and textiles. A large display compares and contrasts the iconography and clerical aspects of Candomblé with parallel traditions from west Africa. The museum's showpiece is the gallery of 27 two-metre by three-metre stele of the major *orixàs* carved from single blocks of tropical cedar by the Brazilian-Italian artist Carybé. They are perhaps the most important pieces of modern art in the city. Carybé was born Héctor Julio Páride Bernabó in Argentina to a Brazilian mother and an Italian father, spent his early years as an illustrator for the Argentinean press and before moving to his mother's homeland when he was in his 20s. In 1938, he travelled to Bahia for the first time. He returned in 1950 with the mission of sketching the city, at the request of the Education Secretary, Anísio Teixeira, and set up his definite residence here, taking on Brazilian and Bahian citizenship some years later. Whilst living in Bahia he illustrated books by amongst others Jorge Amado and Gabriel Gárcia Márquez and produced some 5,000 paintings, ceramics, drawings, sculptures and woodcarvings, and an authoritative book on African-Brazilian spirituality *A Iconografia dos Deuses Africanos no Candomblé da Bahia* (An Iconography of the African Gods of Bahian Candomblé). He is said to have been an *obá de xangô*, an honorary position in Candomblé and to have died of a heart attack during a session in a Candomblé *terreiro*.

The **Museu de Arqueologia e Etnologia (MAE)** (*Terreiro de Jesus s/n, Prédio da Faculdade de Medicina;* ☎ *3283 5530; www.mae.ufba.br;* ⊕ *09.00–18.00 Mon–Fri, 10.00–17.00 Sat/Sun; R$5 for a joint ticket with MAfro*) in the basement of the same building and administered by the same body as MAfro has recently undergone extensive renovation. It holds priceless indigenous artefacts, from giant funeral urns to ritual costumes, musical instruments and sacred art, gleaned from all over Brazil by the Jesuits and subsequent anthropologists. These sit alongside a handful of modest exhibits devoted to Bahian prehistoric rock painting. A little museum shop sells replicas of some of the ceramics.

Facing the Terreiro de Jesus and the cathedral, completely conjoined with that praça, and separated from it by a towering, iconic Franciscan cross is the **Largo Cruzeiro de São Francisco**. This little square is the gilt-covered heart of Portuguese Salvador and is dominated by one of Latin America's most lavish Baroque churches – the **Igreja e Convento de São Francisco** (*Largo do Cruzeiro de São Francisco;* ☎ *3322 6430;* ⊕ *08.00–17.00 Mon–Sat, 08.00–16.00 Sun; R$4*). The convent was founded by Franciscan friars, an order whose members had said the first mass on Brazilian soil on 26 April 1500 and had friars martyred in Porto Seguro in 1516, but who only arrived on the continent in earnest well after Nobrega's Jesuits, in Pernambuco in 1585 and in Salvador two years later. Like all the Catholic monastic brotherhoods at that time, they were in competition with the other orders – who jostled like political parties for the greatest influence in Iberia and ultimately in Rome. Franciscans became heavily involved in farming in Bahia, particularly in the plantations of the Recôncavo. African slaves had made the sugar plantations and *engenho* mills highly profitable, and after their initial, modest, monastery was destroyed by the Dutch attack in the 17th century, the Franciscans had both the personal resources and the support from Salvador's increasingly wealthy elite to build a far grander church.

The church is reached through the monastic cloisters enclosing a courtyard garden whose walls are covered with glorious *azulejo* tiles, painted by renowned Portuguese master Bartolomeu Antunes de Jesus and imported from Lisbon. They are inspired by the humanistic Emblem books of illustrated sayings from Horace by the 17th-century Flemish humanist and teacher of Peter Paul Rubens, Otto Venius. Each of Antunes's *azulejos* depicts a Christian virtue, captioned below with a pithy epigram. 'Quem e Rico? Quem nada ambiciona', proclaims one – 'Who is rich? He who is ambitious for nothing'. The picture shows a man crowned from behind by a bare-breasted glory whilst simultaneously pushing away the golden crowns of the monarchical state. This feels like irony when you walk into the church itself, whose nave is encrusted with almost a tonne of pure gold. The Franciscans certainly didn't acquire such wealth by denouncing the secular powers of contemporaneous Salvador, or the slave trade they grew fat on. The irony is felt even more sorely on scrutinising the *azulejos* in the sacristy which show scenes from the life of St Francis of Assisi himself, the nobleman turned mendicant who founded the Franciscan order, and who in doing so prayed to God: 'Grant me the treasure of sublime poverty: permit the distinctive sign of our order to be that it does not possess anything of its own beneath the sun, for the glory of your name, and that it have no other patrimony than begging.'

In fact most of the lavish interior decoration was not paid for by the Franciscans, but by the wealthy Bahian elite, who with consciences pummelled by preaching from the pulpit, donated vast amounts of money to decorate Salvador's churches – to assuage their sins and purchase a place in heaven. São Francisco was built at the height of Salvador's wealth. Church communities like São Francisco's and the Carmelite churches' in nearby Santo Antônio competed furiously for the best decoration, leading to the development of a thriving artisan guild, many of whose members were descendants of African and indigenous slaves – individuals whose families and friends would have been prohibited from worshipping in the churches they decorated. African-Brazilian craftsmen were dispatched to Portugal to study the new Baroque styles and artistic techniques, and they returned to work on Salvador's fabulous churches, including São Francisco. The finest work in the church's interior dates from the early 18th century. The painting on the wooden ceiling at the entrance to the church, displaying the illusionist perspective characteristic of the Bahian school, is by José Joaquim da Rocha. The nave itself is completely covered in hexagonal-, diamond- and star-shaped religious paintings. These descend into an opulent sacristy whose every square millimetre is rich with minutely carved giltwood. Statues of saints seem to be perched in ornate foliage and decorative Rococo and Baroque motifs burst from the organically swirling shapes like fruits on a vine. The overall effect is of shimmering burnished gold. It must have been even more magnificent when the church was lit only by candlelight.

Little is known about the artists who created this magnificence. What is certain is that many were of African origin (look out for the two African masks on either side of the sacristy, high up at the altar-end of the nave), and that the effigies they created met with controversy at the time – all the genitals of the cherubs have been clumsily removed. Records and rumours would have us believe that many of the statues within the church, including a haunting, naturalistic figure of São Pedro de Alcântara holding a cross, are by Manuel Inácio da Costa – born in the beautiful Bay of Camamu and nicknamed 'Six Fingers' by his contemporaries for his ability to mould wood. Other unspecified statues are known to be by Bento dos Reis, the child of African slaves, who is celebrated for the emotion he imparts to his figures. These may include a wonderfully serene Saint Benedict, the patron of African-Brazilians and himself born to Ethiopian slaves in Messina, cradling the Christ Child in his arms. The names of the painters remain unknown.

Another magnificent Franciscan church sits alongside the Igreja e Convento de São Francisco. Until the installation of electricity in 1919, the ornate façade of the **Igreja da Ordem Terceira de São Francisco** (*Ladeira da Ordem Terceira de São Francisco 3;* \ *3321 6968;* ⊕ *08.00–17.00 Mon–Sat, 08.00–16.00 Sun; R$4*), inaugurated in 1702, was hidden by plaster. One legend has it that this was because the Franciscans were angered by the inclusion of Masonic symbols in the design or that they feared that on hearing of the church's magnificence, Bonaparte would cross the Atlantic and ransack Salvador. But it is more likely that the church facade's overtly Spanish churrigueresque style offended the Portuguese of 18th-century

Salvador after their country became increasingly bitter enemies with Spain in the decades subsequent to the abandonment of the Union of Iberian crowns in the 1640s. The church is one of only two examples of the style in Brazil, the other being the Igreja de Nossa Senhora da Guia in the state of Paraíba. The interior of the Igreja da Ordem Terceira de São Francisco is more modest than either its façade or the interior of the neighbouring convent church, but there are striking ceiling paintings and panels by two of Jose Joaquim da Rocha's students, respectively Antônio Joaquim Franco Velasco and José Teófilo de Jesus (see page 137 and page 153 for respective biographies), and a series of *azulejos* showing scenes of Lisbon before the devastating earthquake of 1755. In June 2009, the complex of the two Franciscan churches was voted to be one of the Seven Wonders of Portuguese Origin in the World at a spectacular gala ceremony in the city of Portimão, in the presence of New Seven Wonders founder and president, Bernard Weber.

The Pelourinho Ruas Alfredo Brito (also confusingly called Portas do Carmo), João de Deus and Gregório de Matos drop in steep, rough-hewn cobbles northeast from the Terreiro de Jesus to the Largo do Pelourinho square itself – a distance of some 400m. Strictly speaking, it is only the square itself which is the Pelourinho, named after the pillory which once sat here, and where African slaves were whipped for disobedience, but in local parlance the name is given to all these streets and the grid of alleys which connect them. Like most of the historic city centre, the area was run-down and destitute until the mid-1980s when a full restoration began under the supervision of the distinguished Brazilian architect Lina Bo Bardi. This was consolidated by another restoration programme which began in 1991 and saw the state government renovate or rebuild over 1,350 houses, churches, monuments and museums. The streets around the Pelourinho are now lined with refurbished and magnificent colonial and early Republican houses converted into shops, bars, restaurants and hotels – and together they make up the centre of tourist Salvador. The best way to see the Pelourinho is simply to wander slowly through, browsing in the shops, stopping for a juice or a snack and using the various attractions as points on your navigational compass. There are many sights of note, most of them clustered around the Largo de Pelourinho itself.

At the corner of Rua Alfredo Brito and the Largo do Pelourinho is the **Fundação Casa de Jorge Amado** (*Praça Jose Alencar s/n, Largo de Pelourinho;* ☏ *3321 0070; www.jorgeamado.org.br;* ⊕ *09.00–18.00 Mon-Fri, 10.00–16.00 Sat; free admission*), a big red townhouse looking out over the square offering exhibitions, courses and events related to Bahia's most famous novelist. Amado's stories are a fusion of the bawdy and the bombastic, the picturesque and picaresque – a kind of cross between 18th-century episodic romps like *Tom Jones* and contemporary Latin American magic realism. He is perhaps Brazil's most internationally successful and most widely translated novelist, and all his books – whose covers adorn the ground-floor walls – are on sale in the Casa Jorge Amado. But he is not without controversy. One literary critic accused him of 'melodramatic over-sentimentalisation of the wretched plight of the Bahian masses'. Others have accused him of sexism, largely for his portrayals of African-Brazilian women as hyper-sexualised projections of male fantasy. Although he was born in Ilhéus, he lived for many years in this house in Salvador and many of his books are set in and around the Pelourinho, including *The War of the Saints* and *Dona Flor and Her Two Husbands*. In the latter Amado takes the reader on a journey through his favourite bits of Salvador – from Fat Carla's house, where the would-be intellectuals gather to talk about trash poetry to the port-side favelas, where street kids dance to *sambas de roda* beaten out on dustbins and the Palace casino, where the elite and the down at heel gamble side by side. A pot pourri of Bahian life permeates the novel – a glimpse of a Candomblé ceremony, a capoeira

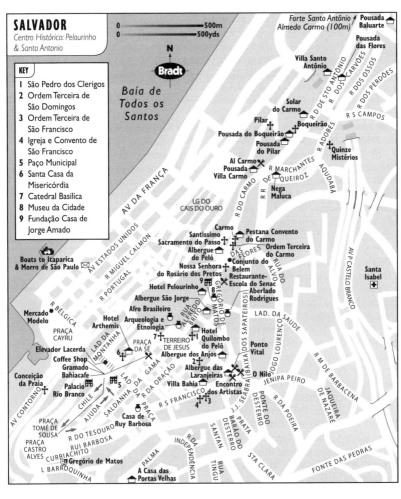

SALVADOR

Centro Histórico: Pelourinho
& Santo Antonio

KEY

1 São Pedro dos Clerigos
2 Ordem Terceira de
  São Domingos
3 Ordem Terceira de
  São Francisco
4 Igreja e Convento de
  São Francisco
5 Paço Municipal
6 Santa Casa da
  Misericórdia
7 Catedral Basilica
8 Museu da Cidade
9 Fundação Casa de
  Jorge Amado

Baía de
Todos os
Santos

fight, recipes for a successful crab *moqueca* given by Dona Flor and repeated allusions to and descriptons of Bahian music. *The Capitaes de Areia* – which is perhaps his finest novel – is also set in Salvador. This tells the story of a group of 50 or so Salvador street children who are abandoned by their parents, neglected by the authorities, abused by the police and forced to endure inhumane conditions in a state borstal. It is one of his few books which transcend the sentimental and stereotyped to enter a more Dickensian world of poignant social critique.

Next to the Casa Jorge Amado in two conjoined 18th-century houses is the **Museu da Cidade** (*Praça Jose de Alencar 3, Largo de Pelourinho;* ✎ *3321 1967;* ⊕ *09.00–18.30 Tue–Fri, 13.00–1700 Sat, 09.00–13.00 Sun; free*). The collection is a mishmash of fascinating paintings and old photographs showing the growth of the city, artefacts gleaned from 450 years of Salvador history and ritual objects from the city's various African-Brazilian religions. These include papier mâché effigies of the *orixás* made by the artist Alecy Azevedo, ritual costumes and ornaments. One of the rooms is devoted to the life and work of the 19th-century romantic poet and abolitionist Castro Alves, whose most celebrated work, *Navio Negreiro*, begins as an epic eulogy to the great sailors of Europe and ends as a tirade against the disgrace of slavery:

Ontem plena liberdade (Yesterday full liberty),
A vontade por poder ... (The will to carry on ...)
Hoje... cúm'lo de maldade (Today an accumulation of bitterness),
Nem são livres p'ra morrer (They aren't free even to die)
Prende-os a mesma corrente (Caught as they are in the same current)
— *Férrea, lúgubre serpente* (Iron-clad, lugubrious serpent)
Nas roscas da escravidão (In the nuts and bolts of slavery).

Just around the corner from the Museu da Cidade is the **Museu Abelardo Rodrigues** (*Rua Gregório de Matos, 45 – Solar Ferrão, Pelourinho;* \ *3320 9383;* ⊕ *13.00–18.00 Tue–Sat; R$5*). This is one of the best small sacred-art museums in Brazil, with a series of beautiful, and beautifully displayed, ecclesiastical objects – from paintings to vast, shimmering monstrances, intricately carved reliquaries and colourful oratories. These are housed in one of the Pelourinho's prettiest 18th-century mansions. Behind the museum is a tiny little praça with stone steps leading to a secret, hidden bar which has live music most weekend evenings.

Halfway down the Largo do Pelourinho, and unmissable – with its chubby towers and Prussian-blue façade – is the **Igreja da Nossa Senhora do Rosário dos Pretos** (*Praça Jose Alencar s/n, Largo do Pelourinho;* \ *3241 5781;* ⊕ *08.30–18.00 Mon–Fri (with African-Brazilian mass every Tue at 18.00), 08.30–15.00 Sat/Sun; free admission*). This splendid blue-and-cream, late-Baroque church was built by the Brotherhood of the Black Men of the Pelourinho, a slave brotherhood who devoted their meagre spare time to building a church for a community forbidden by virtue of their colour from entering the lavish churches many of them had built in colonial Salvador. Construction took around a hundred years, beginning in 1704. The church remains a centre for Catholic–Candomblé syncretism. Many of the effigies inside the church are as much *orixás* as they are Christian saints and every Tuesday evening during mass the church resonates with African-Brazilian choral singing and reverberates to intricate percussion.

From here the Pelourinho drops steeply some 50m to the taxi ranks on the Ladeira do Taboão and Rua Padre Agostinho Gomes. On the corner of the latter street is the **Casa do Benin** (\ *3241 5679*), which together with the nearby **Casa da Nigéria** (*Rua Alfredo Brito 26, Pelourinho;* \ *3328 3782*) provides a space for African art and culture in central Salvador, also offering language courses and providing a library resource.

Morro do Carmo and Santo Antônio Opposite the Largo do Pelourinho is another steep hill covered in rough cobbles and lined with pastel-paint houses that climbs just under a kilometre to the **Morro do Carmo** – another hill with a cluster of magnificent colonial Portuguese churches. The first you come across on the steep climb is the **Igreja de Santissimo Sacramento do Passo** (*Ladeira do Passo s/n; currently closed*), which crowns a series of vertiginous stone steps called the Escadas do Passo. Modern Brazilian cinema was born here. Many of the most important scenes from the first *cinema novo* movie and cult classic, *O Pagador de Promessas* (aka The Keeper of Promises, The Given Word or The Promise) were shot here in 1962 by Paulistano director Anselmo Duarte. It is the only Brazilian film to have won the Palme d'Or and was the first Latin American film to be nominated for an Academy Award. Its intense melodrama, strong political theme and dreamy mood paved the way for the films of later tropicália directors like Glauber Rocha and its themes have much in common with early liberation theology. The screenplay was adapted from a famous Brazilian drama by Salvador-born playwright Alfredo de Freitas Dias Gomes. This tells the story of Zé do Burro (Donkey Joe), a naive land holder and holy fool from the Bahian sertão whose best friend is a donkey. When his donkey falls terminally ill, Zé makes a pledge with a Candomblé priestess: if the donkey recuperates, he will give away his land and bear a heavy wooden cross through the desert to Salvador, where he will present it to the priests of the Igreja de Santa Barbara. The donkey recovers and Zé keeps to his pledge only to be turned away by the Catholic Church for making a pact with paganism. Everyone along the way attempts to manipulate Zé: Candomblé devotees use him as a figurehead for a campaign against discrimination by the Catholics; and newspapers interpret his promise as the first fruit of a communist-driven redistribution of land rights. The film ends with Zé shot by the police and subsequently carried into the church by Candomblé devotees.

The Morro do Carmo continues uphill from the Escadas do Passo to the Largo do Carmo, a little praça faced by the magnificent **Convento do Carmo** (see page 109) – which is now a luxurious five-star hotel – and two adjacent Carmelite churches. The Carmelites were the fourth of the powerful Catholic monastic orders to found monasteries and convents in early Salvador. From the first days of the Brazilian colony, the order were in the main content to accept the establishment status quo, proselytising indigenous people without complaining about their ill-treatment by the Portuguese slave traders and bandeirantes and at times participating in that exploitation themselves. In 1699, Carmelites, Franciscans and Mercedarians were accused by the King of Portugal of 'using their Indians for their service and convenience, in an impious way, with great dishonour in their behaviour, living very scandalously and abandoned to sensuality, to the great discredit of their [monastic] habits'. They were thus the arch-political enemies of Jesuits. The malicious publication by a Carmelite of a private letter sent by Father Antônio Vieira (see page 124) to the Prince Regent of Portugal in 1661 – complaining vocally of the indigenous slave trade in Maranhão and Para – largely led to the Jesuits being expelled from those states, paving the way for the eventual disestablishment of the order. Like the other Salvador churches the convent, **Igreja da Ordem Terceira do Carmo** (*Morro do Carmo s/n;* ⏱ *08.00–11.30 & 14.00–17.30 Mon-Sat, 10.00–12.00 Sun; R$2*), built by the order's lay brotherhood and inaugurated in 1703, and the adjacent **Igreja do Carmo** (*Morro do Carmo s/n;* ⏱ *08.00–12.00 & 14.00–17.30 Mon-Sat, 08.00–12.00 Sun; R$2*) were built by skilled African-Brazilian artisans who were not allowed to worship in the churches. The Igreja do Carmo retains a beautiful painted ceiling by the freed slave, José Teófilo de Jesus (see page 153), but the Igreja da Ordem Terceira was badly damaged by a fire in the late 18th century – which destroyed much of the intense gold work which once covered the church – and restored more modestly in the 19th century. A handful of Salvador's greatest sculptural treasures survived, all of them carved by a mixed-race slave, Francisco Xavier Chagas – O Cabra (the goat or bandit). The most famous are two statues of Christ which formed part of a series depicting the Passion. The most famous is housed in a glass case and lit with fluorescent strips as stark and unflattering as lights in a morgue. This is strangely appropriate – Christ lies on his back, covered in a varnish of blood and sweat (whose visceral sheen was obtained through a mix of whale oil and tiny rubies, whose recipe is probably unique to Chagas). His body is mutilated and twisted by suffering and there is a gaping wound in his breast, yet his face is calm and serene and his head looks as if it is falling gently back as if into sleep. The overall effect is powerfully immediate as death itself – as physical as Mel Gibson's *Passion of the Christ*. It is almost an apotheosis of suffering – with a dignified Christ transfigured by pain. In *Blind Memory: Visual Representations of Slavery in England and America, 1780–1865* Marcus Wood suggests, as others have, that it is both an allegory and documentation of the tortures and whippings inflicted on African slaves, with Christ 'not a God suffering for man, but a human beaten beyond humanity .... The back, texturally and colouristically, has become a thing apart, a landscape of pain … [it] is both disgusting and beautiful, the drops of blood which glisten upon the surface consisting of hundreds of rubies set into gesso.' Chagas's other statue is more serene – a lifelike effigy of the Madonna and Child – both physical and present and innocent and other-worldly, in the sacristy.

Rua do Carmo continues to climb after the Carmelite churches into the neighbourhood of Santo Antônio, where it becomes the Rua de Santo Antônio. This street is lined with dozens of charming little pousadas, built in the converted interiors of tall 18th- and 19th-century townhouses, many of which have wonderful views over the Baía de Todos os Santos. After a little over a kilometre it enters a large square, the Barão do Triunfo (Largo de Santo Antônio), which is watched over by an impressive one-towered Rococo-meets-19th-century neoclassical church, the **Igreja de Santo Antônio Além do Carmo** (*Barão do Triunfo s/n, Santo Antônio;* ❧ *3242 6463;* ⊕ *09.00–12.00 & 14.00–17.30 Mon–Sat, 08.00–12.00 Sun; free*) and crowned with the **Forte de Santo Antônio além do Carmo** (*Barão do Triunfo s/n, Santo Antônio;* ❧ *3117 1488; http://fortesantoantonio.blogspot.com; R$4*) fort at its northeastern end. The church stands on the site of one of the city's first chapels, built in 1584. But the current structure is a fusion of an old Rococo church and the newer building into which it was incorporated, dating from 1842. The fort dates from the last decade of the 17th century and is known locally as the Forte da Capoeira as it is home to half a dozen capoeira schools. It was restored at the turn of the 20th century and there are beautiful views over the bay from its bulwarks.

Cidade Baixa Clustered around the Lacerda lift and the base of the cliff which drops away from the Pelourinho and Santo Antônio is Salvador's Cidade Baixa or lower city. It grew together with Tome de Souza's new capital, from the first makeshift jetties, to become the most important trading hub in colonial Brazil – until it was eclipsed by Rio de Janeiro when the country's capital moved south in 1763. Thousands of boats laden with sugar, tobacco and cacão beans from Bahia's Recôncavo and Atlantic coast plantations left here annually and thousands arrived laden with human cargo. Up until abolition in 1850 Portugal and post-independence Brazil made some 30,000 voyages to Africa, transporting 4,650,000 slaves (see page 30). Many of these ships brought their prisoners to the Cidade Baixa – especially in the early years of the Brazilian colony.

As Salvador became wealthier, the Cidade Baixa grew in magnificence. From 1736 the Portuguese shipped an entire church from Lisbon, brick by brick, tile by tile and slab of exquisite pink-tinted *lioz* marble by slab. Even church-weary visitors find it hard not to be impressed by Manuel Cardoso de Saldanha's **Igreja de Nossa Senhora da Conceição da Praia** (*Rua da Conceição da Praia s/n;* ❧ *3241 2507;* ⊕ *07.00–11.00 Mon, 15.00–17.00 Tue-Fri, mass at 08.30 & 09.00 Sun; free*). It preserves what is probably the finest José Joaquim da Rocha ceiling painting in the city – showing the Lamb of God surrounded by the Madonna and saints – in a beautiful octagonal nave behind two unique, diagonally set towers. Brazil was five years off independence when the grandson of the Bahian first commissioned to piece together the ecclesiastical jigsaw completed the building, in 1820.

When Rio de Janeiro became the capital, Salvador's entire historical centre, including the Pelourinho, began to deteriorate. The city's wealthy moved south to the beach, a tendency which was consolidated by an ambitious 1935 city plan and the subsequent construction of the airport and the main bus station. By the 1980s many of the colonial mansions and churches were falling to pieces, a process which was reversed in the Pelourinho from 1985 (see page 127), but which continues in the Cidade Baixa. Streets of handsome municipal and commercial buildings have been left to crumble into mere shells, with their *azulejo* tiles cracked by tree roots and with their façades and interiors overgrown with vines, and the area as a whole has long had a tawdry reputation, especially at night. There are few signs of changes for the better.

The area around the **Terminal Marítimo Turistico** ferry port (for boats to the Ilha de Itaparica and Morro de São Paulo, see page 161) and the large covered market – the terracotta-tile roofed **Mercado Modelo** (*Praça Visconde de Cayru;* ✎ *2241 2893;* ⊕ *09.00–19.00 Wed–Mon, 09.00–13.00 Sun, closed Tue*) – has been cleared up in the last decade. And the market itself is now a delight, with some of the best souvenir shopping in Salvador. Come here to browse stalls proffering everything from musical instruments and herbal remedies to *orixá* effigies and textiles. The handbags made from colourful ring pulls sewn together with fishing thread, and sold in markets throughout the world, originate here and can be purchased at a fraction of their American or European price. There are often planned and improptu capoeira shows here (especially in the late morning and early afternoon on weekdays) and a handful of little cafés and makeshift market eateries offer Bahian snacks (and cooling juices as a relief from the heat). A few streets north of the Mercado is Carlinhos Brown's **International Center for Black Music** and **Museu Du Ritmo** (*Rua Torquato Bahia, 84 Edifício Mercado do Ouro;* ✎ *3353 4333*) which opened in late 2009. This complex is built around a 1,000m² concert arena with a state of the art sound system housed in a giant courtyard formed from the shell of a huge colonial building. The courtyard cloisters are decorated with allegorical artworks drawn from African-Bahian spirituality and the whole arena seems alive with Candomblé energy – especially during one of the frequent live shows. The museum of black music and culture has plans for over 100 multi-media installations by 2011, and there's also a a cinema, art gallery, school and recording studio on the site.

NEW SALVADOR
Campo Grande and the modern city centre
The tower apartments and broad avenues of modern Salvador stretch to the south of old Salvador; immediately south of the Praça Municipal and the Cidade Baixa – in a string of sprawling neighbourhoods which stretch around the peninsula and extend along the beaches all the way to the airport and Stella Maris. But the locus of commercial activity stretches between the wealthy beachside neighbourhood of Campo Grande and the **Dique do Tororo**, a fountain-filled lakeside park sacred to Candomblé (and with *orixá* sculptures by Tatti Moreno). This area is the epicentre of middle-class Salvador and the city's commercial heart – home to the biggest banks and offices, to many of the city's most distinguished museums and to its best restaurants.

As Rua Chile leaves the Praça Municipal the shops and offices along its length become increasingly less dilapidated until the street reaches **Praça Castro Alves**, where the abolitionist poet looks over Salvador from high on a plinth, with his back to the bay and right arm outstretched in grand gesture. This area is usually referred to as the Novo Centro – or simply the Centro, or city centre. Salvador's raucous Carnaval reaches its climax here, but otherwise there is no real reason to visit. Two broad avenues, Carlos Gomes and Sete de Setembro, descend from Praça Castro Alves through the city centre to the Praça 2 de Julho which marks the beginning of the neighbourhood of Campo Grande, home of Bahian celebrities like Ivete Sangalo. There are a few interesting sites along the way.

The **Mosteiro São Bento** (*Largo S Bento 1, Avenida Sete de Setembro;* ✎ *3322 4749;* *www.saobento.org;* ⊕ *09.00–12.00 & 13.00–16.00 Mon–Fri; R$5*) is another of the city's beautiful monastic churches, established in 1582 by Benedictine monks. It was one of the few Renaissance churches in the city to be built outside the original city walls, originally sitting eyrie-like over a Tupinambá village on a high, forest-fringed hill overlooking the bay. It was the first church to be damaged in the Dutch invasion of 1624 after which it was partially rebuilt over a long period – accounting for the simple interior and the eclectic but largely successful mixing of Baroque and neoclassical styles in the building as a whole. The church museum has some beautiful statues by famous ecclesiastical artists like Frei Agostinho da Piedade, Frei Ricardo do Pilar, Frei Agostinho de Jesus and paintings by José Joaquim da Rocha together with exhibitions of contemporary Bahian art. And the Torre de Santa Escolástica church tower affords some of the best and least known of any of the city centre views – out over the Baía de Todos os Santos to the distant, glimmering beaches of the Ilha de Itaparica. Nearby is the **Museu de Arte Sacra da Bahia** (*Rua do Sodre, Rua Carlos Gomes s/n;* 3243 6511; *www.mas.ufba.br;* 11.30–17.30 *Mon–Fri; R$5*), in the 16th-century Discalced Carmelite Convento de Santa Teresa de Ávila, named after the order's mystical co-founder. The convent played an important role in the history of Bahia, serving as a garrison for Bahian troops during the war for independence against the Portuguese in the early 19th century. The building is one of the largest historic Discalced Carmelite convents outside the Spanish world and is protected by Instituto do Patrimônio Histórico e Artístico Nacional (IPHAN) as one of Brazil's most important religious buildings. It was in ruins until 1958 when it was renovated by the Universidade Federal da Bahia, who installed the museum. It preserves one of the largest collections of priceless sacred art in South America, with some 2,000 pieces, including work by Aleijadinho as well as most of the important artists of the Bahian school such as José Joaquim da Rocha's exquisite, agonising, carved Christ on a jacaranda crucifix. There are also superb bay views from the peaceful cloistered gardens.

Sitting on the bay a kilometre west of the museum is the **Modern Art Museum (MAM)** (*Av Contorno s/n, Solar do Unhão;* 3117 6139; *www.mam.ba.gov.br;* 13.00–19.00 *Tue–Sun, 13.00–21.00 Sat; free admission*) which, since being moved to this new location in 2008, has begun to establish itself as one of the finest modern art museums in the country. Together with pieces by Bahian artists like Mario Cravo Jr, Carybé, Pancetti and the Franco-Bahian photographer Pierre Verger, the collection includes work by most of Brazil's important artists like Emiliano di Cavalcanti, the abstract painter Alfredo Volpi, social-expressionist Cândido Portinari, the founder of the antropfagismo Tarsila do Amaral (whose paintings have fetched the highest price at auction of any Brazilian artist) and contemporary artists like Jose Bechara, Siron Franco and the photographer Mario Cravo Neto. The building itself – the Solar do Unhão – is an important historical monument. It was built in the 17th century and was occupied by a series of influential Bahians over the following centuries, all of whom left their mark on the building – from late Baroque chapels to exquisite *azulejos*. The gallery also has temporary exhibitions, an arts cinema (*www.saladearte.art.br*) and a bar/café with live jazz on Saturdays from 18.30. There are many good restaurants within a five-minute cab ride (see *Where to eat,* page 115).

A kilometre or so to the south along Avenida 7 de Setembro are two more art museums, the **Museu de Arte de Bahia** (*Av 7 de Setembro 2340;* 3117 6903; 14.00–19.00 *Tue–Fri, 14.30–18.30 Sat–Sun; R$5*) and the **Casa Carlos Costa Pinto** (*Av 7 de Setembro 2490;* 3336 6081; *www.museucostapinto.com.br;* 14.30–19.00 *Mon & Wed–Sun; R$5*). The former is a collection of art and period furniture – from a superb and beautifully displayed gallery of sacred art by the Bahian school artists including José Joaquim da Rocha (see page 125) and José Teófilo de Jesus (see page 153) to reproduction rooms of 18th-century Bahia, complete with period furniture and curios like a strange antique miniature piano that doubles up as a sewing machine. The latter museum houses an eclectic private collection which includes some exquisite jewellery, small sculptures and medals, 1,000 tea sets which once belonged to the writer Eça de Queiroz and solid gold *balangandã* baubles worn by slaves in the colonial period to show off the wealth of their owners. The museum has a lovely little garden café with excellent comfort food – quiches, little tarts and

Carlinhos Brown is one of Bahia's greatest musicians. As a percussionist and producer he is sought after by the biggest names in the Brazilian and international music business. As a composer and bandleader of the Afoxé group *Timbalada*, he has done more than any other musician to shape the sound of modern, sophisticated Bahian music. He was born Antônio Carlos Santos de Freitas – poor and marginalised in a Salvador *favela* in the early 1960s. Initially he made a living selling bottled water on the beach, but his passion was music and after changing his name in homage to James Brown he began to work tirelessly on songwriting and perfecting a flawless percussion technique. By the late 1970s his exuberant and virtuoso drumming and unique, catchy compositions earned him stints in local bands, and in the early 1980s a spot as a jingle composer on local radio station WR. His jingles became instant hits and before long Brown was working with the cream of Bahian musicians, including Caetano Veloso and Gilberto Gil. This gave him the opportunity to launch his own band, *Timbalada* – an afoxé percussion group, who still perform at Carnaval. In the 1990s he launched his solo career with a string of classic albums, the best-selling of which was the lively, quirky *Alfagamabetizado*, which bursts from the speakers from its first track Pandeiro-deiro and takes the listener through a tour of mesmerising Bahian soundscapes. Since the 1990s he has gone from strength to strength – recording albums with Marisa Monte, performing to stadium crowds in Spain and serving as a symbol and a guide to a generation of African Brazilian Bahians. In 2010 he opened the first centre in Bahia devoted to the state's African musical heritage, the Museu do Ritmo, where you can hear him and the best of Brazil's African-Brazilian musicians perform. You can hear his music and find out where he is performing next on his website: www.carlinhosbrown.com.br

strong, thick coffee. **Palacete das Artes and the Museu Rodin** (*Rua da Graça 284, Graça;* ❧ *3117 6986;* ⏲ *10.00–18.00 Tue–Sun; free admission*) This museum opened in 2009 with a grand exhibition of 62 Rodin pieces (including The Thinker and The Kiss) which will remain in Salvador until 2012. Rodin is one of the most admired and prolific modernist sculptures, celebrated for his trademark powerful, expressive figures whose faces are remarkable for their liveliness.

Barra and the beach suburbs (Cidade da Praia)

Avenida 7 de Setembro continues south from Campo Grande to Barra, a fashionable beach suburb sitting on the tip of the peninsula that is becoming an increasingly popular base for foreign tourists. There are many hotels and restaurants here, a large shopping centre with cinema, Western-style bars and clubs and the first beaches south of the city centre – though the water is far from clean. From here Salvador spreads east towards the airport in a series of mostly anodyne beach suburbs, characterised by tower apartment blocks and busy two- or three-lane avenues facing long, broad beaches – Ondina, Rio Vermelho, Amalina, Pituba, Armação, Corsário and eventually Stella Maris near the airport. There are only a few sights here, none of them worth a special visit; most tourists come or stay to be close to the beach. In Barra is the **Forte de Santo Antônio da Barra** fort (*Farol da Barra;* ❧ *3264 3296;* ⏲ *08.00–10.00 Mon, 08.30–19.00 Tue–Sun; R$6*), dominated by a big lighthouse where hundreds gather to watch the daily Baía de Todos os Santos sunset. The fort itself (which dates from the late 17th century) houses the city's nautical museum with some 400 items salvaged from caravels and galleons – including the *Sacramento*, a Portuguese ship which sank in 1688. The lighthouse itself is closed to visitors. Rio Vermelho – 9km east of the city centre – has the best alternative nightlife scene outside the

Whilst the Baía de Todos os Santos city beaches are generally not fit for swimming the city has a series of ocean-facing beaches that get progressively cleaner as you go away from the city to the east. Pickpockets are always on the lookout for tourists. Leave your valuables in the hotel during the day and avoid the beaches after dark. In order (west to east), the beaches are as follows.

BARRA A busy strip of hotels and restaurants overlook a narrow stretch of much-trodden sand which forms small rockpools as the tide retreats. Very popular, especially at weekends. Plenty of beach snacks and sunshades available.

ONDINA A spit of narrow, dirty sand busy with beach barracas and broken by rocky shoreline and chunks of long-dead exposed reef. Very popular at weekends.

RIO VERMELHO A narrow, urban and none too clean beach with coarse sand and a few beached fishing boats. The numerous street bars and clubs behind draw lively crowds most evenings.

AMARALINA Surfers come here for the strong waves that break on the patches of jagged reef. But intermittent smelly algae can make sunbathing unpleasant. A kiosk on the beach serves great *acarajés*.

PITUBA A long straight stretch of broad greyish sand shaded by a few coconut palms and with dozens of *barracas* selling Bahian snacks, beers and drinks. Numerous offshore reefs break the waves and form pools at low tide. Swimming is unsafe around the Chega-Nego/Jardim dos Namorados stretch of Pituba.

JARDIM DE ALÁ Together with Jaguaribe and Pituaçu, the best stretch of sand close to Salvador city centre – long, broad, shaded by coconut palms and with gentle waves and good swimming. Very busy at weekends. Plenty of *barracas* offer beach snacks, sunshades and cold drinks.

ARMAÇÃO The continuation of Jardim de Alá, with better surf and marginally fewer people.

BOCA DO RIO Long, broad and backed by a big shopping mall, stretches of grassland and suburban plots.

JAGUARIBE Long, broad and washed by strong waves. Very popular with weekenders with plenty of facilities.

PITUAÇU A long, wide bay of silky sand backed by coconut palms, grassland and a solid line of *barracas* selling beer, cold coconuts and snacks and very busy at weekends.

ITAPUÃ A fine white-sand beach broken by rocks and watched over by a lighthouse. Low tide reveals natural swimming pools formed in the dead coral reef. Very popular.

STELLA MARIS Many of the city's middle class have beach houses on this long broad stretch. Good surf, plenty of beach facilities and big crowds on the weekends.

FLAMENGO A long bay pounded by strong waves that are safe only for strong swimmers. Very popular with surfers and backed by legions of gated communities.

Pelourinho (see *Entertainment and nightlife*, pages 116–17) and is developing as an alternative beachside place to stay, even though the beaches here are very poor. Safe, clean beaches are far from the city centre at Piatã (25km from the Pelourinho), where there are many beach barracas; Itapuã (27km) with good nightlife and a Projeto Tamar sea turtle centre (*www.tamar.org.br*), the surf beach at Stella Maris (near the airport and 31km from the Pelourinho) and the cleanest and wildest Flamengo (33km).

Bonfim, Ribeira and the Baía de Todos os Santos suburbs

A series of bay suburbs stretch north from the Cidade Baixa, many fronted by beautiful beaches lapped by little waves. But they are far too polluted for a swim. Most tourists come here to see the **Igreja de Nosso Senhor do Bonfim** (*Praça Senhor do Bonfim s/n,* 📞 *3316-1673;* ⏰ *06.00–12.00 & 14.00–20.00 Tue–Sun; free admission*), the most sacred African-Brazilian church in Salvador and the site of one of the country's most spectacular annual religious festivals, the Lavagem do Bonfim. This festival, which takes place every third Sunday in January, is when up to a million pilgrims gather from 09.00 to process from the Igreja de Nossa Senhora da Conceição da Praia (see page 132) to Bonfim. They are blessed by Baianas along the way, dressed in traditional clothes and with vases on their heads, and at the end of the walk they wash the steps of Bonfim church with perfumed water in a cleansing and purification rite which is dedicated to the creator divinity of Candomblé, *oxalá* as much as it is to Christ. *Fitas* – little ribbons – are tied around the pilgrims wrists by Baianas. Pilgrims then make three wishes, which are said to be fulfilled when the fita falls of its own accord through wear and tear. The church itself was built in 1772 and has a Rococo façade covered in Portuguese *azulejo* tiles. The ceiling painting in the nave and the panels in the sacristy showing the Passion of Christ are by another Bahian school artist, Joaquim Franco Velasco. Franco Velasco was one of the more experimental artists of the Bahian school. He was born and died in Salvador but after tutelage with da Rocha travelled widely within Brazil, making his name as a portrait painter with a series of portraits of now forgotten dignitaries and a few of the emperor Dom Pedro I. He absorbed French stylistic influences whilst in Rio de Janeiro (where he is said to have painted the interior of the Fundação Castro Maya). A few kilometres from Bonfim in the suburb of Ribeira is another magnificent late Renaissance church, **Nossa Senhora da Penha** (*Av Beira Mar s/n, Ribeira*) and the city's northernmost fort **Monte Serrat** (*Rua Santa Rita Durão s/n;* 📞 *3313 7339;* ⏰ *09.00–17.00 daily; R$1*) built to guard the entrance to the port of the Baia de Todos os Santos in 1583 and complemented by the fort in Barra – which lay at the city's southernmost limits in colonial times.

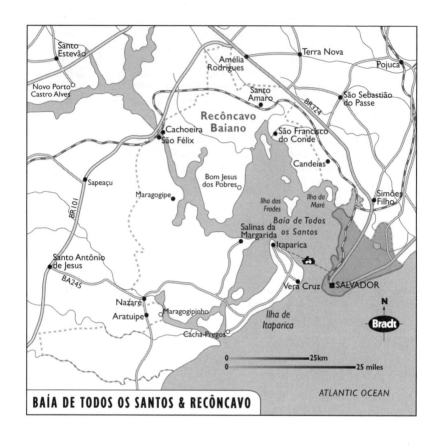

BAÍA DE TODOS OS SANTOS & RECÔNCAVO

Baía de Todos os Santos had such great mythological importance for the Tupinambá people that it had its own creation myth. In the beginning of time, after flying for days and nights without stopping over a vast ocean, a great white-feathered bird finally saw the shore of an immense country. He fell dead from exhaustion on its shores. His white wings lay open and were transformed into long beaches of brilliant sand. Where his heart pulsed its final beats a great depression opened in the earth and the waters of the ocean poured in. His spilt blood fertilised the land all around him where he fell. And the bay came to be known as Kirymuré-Paraguaçu or 'the great interior sea'.

The Rua das Portas do Carmo runs steeply uphill from the Pelourinho to Santo Antônio in the heart of old Salvador (AR) page 130

left   The Costa do Dendê coast is dotted with tiny, very simple shack-like restaurants serving fresh rock lobster caught daily off the reef (AR) page 163

below   The coast of Tinharé island is backed by swaying coconut palms and fringed with pearly white coral beaches (AR) page 159

left There are no cars on Caraíva's sand streets — just flip-flops, and horses and carts (AR) page 203

below Tropical beaches, like this one at Ponta do Corumbau, see more fishermen than tourists — even in high season (AR) page 204

bottom Masked boobies and other tropical ocean birds find a refuge in the Parque Nacional Marinho dos Abrolhos off the Costa da Baleia (AR) page 215

above The Pataxó kept the Portuguese out of southern Bahia for centuries, but were cruelly conquered in the end. At the Reserva Pataxó da Jaqueira, near Porto Seguro, their culture is making a resurgence with the help of ecotourism (AR) page 205

right Pataxó children sell hand-crafted bead and seed jewellery on beaches along the Costa do Descobrimento (AR) page 205

below Much of the Bahian coast is lined with mangrove forests, which provide a haven for waterbirds and juvenile fish (AR) page 7

above The Mucugezinho River cuts through pristine cerrado forest and plunges over rocky cliffs at the Cachoeira do Diabo waterfall near Lençóis in the Chapada Diamantina (AR) page 239

left The waters of the Gruta Pratinha flow into an inky-black cave in the heart of the Chapada Diamantina mountains (AR) page 241

below Locals fish for dourado in the Marimbus wetlands in the Chapada Diamantina (AR) page 241

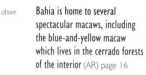

above Bahia is home to several spectacular macaws, including the blue-and-yellow macaw which lives in the cerrado forests of the interior (AR) page 16

above right Agami heron: these shy reclusive birds live in varzea and gallery forests along Bahia's numerous coastal rivers (AR) page 17

right Brown capuchins are a common sight in the rainforests of the Costa do Descobrimento (AR) page 8

Morro de São Paulo's Quinta Praia is pretty much deserted at any time of the day (AR) page 159

Baía de Todos os Santos and Recôncavo

Telephone code 71

Salvador sits on a peninsula that juts into the northern portion of the Baía de Todos os Santos, or All Saints Bay, the biggest in Brazil and one of the largest in South America. It extends over 1,100km², its calm, warm waters dotted with dozens of little islands and its edges lined with little sandy beaches, little inlets that lead to secret coves, large tracts of mangrove and small but still wild patches of Atlantic coastal rainforest. Numerous rivers drain here – the Subaé, Jaguaripe, Cobre and the Paraguaçu which originates high in the Chapada Diamantina mountains deep in the drylands of the Bahian sertão, and whose course was used by the early cattle and gold-prospecting pioneers when opening up Brazil's interior. Their floodplains have made the hinterlands of the Baía de Todos os Santos fertile. The tobacco, sugar and cacau plantations that sprung up on these plains in colonial times produced not only a series of pretty and prosperous little sugar towns, but the first riches of the Brazilian Empire. And the region came to be known as the Recôncavo.

Many of Bahia's enslaved Africans were put to work in the Recôncavo, giving the region a rich African-Brazilian culture. Samba de roda was born here and its mix of dance, music and poetry would give rise to Carnaval samba in Rio when people from the region migrated to that city in the late 19th century. Colonial towns like Cachoeira and São Felix, which lie opposite each other on the banks of the Rio Paraguaçu, and Santo Amaro where the singer Caetano Veloso was born, remain centres of Candomblé and capoeira.

Opposite Salvador and at the southern mouth of the Baía de Todos os Santos is Itaparica island, the largest in the bay. Once it was the beach resort of choice for wealthy Soteropoletanos (natives of Salvador). It has fallen from grace in the last few decades but still retains some beautiful, unspoilt beaches and has two sleepy little seaside villages. It is connected to Valenca, which sits at the north of Costa do Dendê and has fast connections to the resort of Morro de São Paulo.

HISTORY

> The other … came to a fazenda where he was not looked for, and there beheld what he did not expect – a Negro about to be boiled to death for some act of insubordination. His owner had incited, according to custom in such cases, neighboring proprietors to witness the tragedy.
>
> Thomas Ewbank commenting on a visit to inspect the treatment of slaves
> on the Bahian *engenhos* whilst on a trip to Brazil in the 1850s

The Baía de Todos os Santos was a sacred place for the Tupinambá people, who knew it as Kirymuré-Paraguaçu (see box, *A Creation myth*, opposite). They lived in large numbers around the bay – on its shores, on the 56 different islands and principally on the Ilha de Itaparica before the arrival of the Portuguese. The first

European to see the bay was almost certainly the Portuguese explorer, Gaspar de Lemos in 1500. On that voyage de Lemos was one of the captains in Pedro Alvares Cabral's fleet which 'discovered' Brazil. De Lemos returned the following year with the Florentine navigator Amerigo Vespucci. Although the voyage was captained by the Portuguese sailor and the boats and money for the expedition were Portuguese, it became famous because of Vespucci and his name is forever connected to the Baía de Todos os Santos. It was on this voyage that – as a cartographer – he became the first European formally to identify the New World of North and South America as separate from Asia. And on his return he published a series of letters which became the 16th-century equivalent of best-sellers, ensuring that he became remembered whilst his captain was forgotten, and that two continents came to bear his name. It was Gaspar de Lemos who named the bay, however, after the day on which he and Vespucci arrived – 1 November or All Saints' Day.

Commerce with the Tupinambá in the Baía de Todos os Santos was initially peaceful, with the Portuguese and the French exchanging foreign goods for wood which produced a red dye much sought after by the Flanders textile industry. The wood was called Pau-Brasil; and it was to give its name to the new colony – which was at that time called Terra de Santa Cruz (the land of the true cross). The Tupinambá preferred the French. The Portuguese were brutal and seemed intent on establishing a colony. But in the spirit of Rousseau (who would write about noble savages after Brazil's indigenous people visited France), the French treated the Tupinambá more like equals and wanted merely to trade. Concerned that they would lose their nascent colony, the Portuguese carried out a sustained campaign against the French over several decades, which reached its culmination in the Baía de Todos os Santos in 1526 when a fleet of Portuguese battleships defeated three French trading vessels after a day-long sea battle at the mouth of the Rio Paraguaçu – a location still called the Ilha dos Franceses today. This was followed by a further fleet in 1531, captained by Martim Afonso de Sousa and dispatched from Lisbon to establish colonies and sugar-cane plantations. Afonso most famously founded São Vicente in modern São Paulo state, but soldiers from his fleet also settled the Recôncavo, some 18 years before Salvador – the capital of the new country would be founded at the mouth of the bay.

The campaign against the French failed to suppress their Pau-Brasil trade – they merely employed Portuguese smugglers. The most famous was Diogo Álvares Correia or Caramuru, who was shipwrecked during what was probably a French-funded voyage and captured by a tribe of Tupinambá. He spent some 47 years with them, eventually marrying Paraguacu, the daughter of the powerful cannibal-chief of Itaparica – Taparica (after whom the island is named) – in a ceremony in France in which the princess took a European name, Catharina. The couple settled opposite Itaparica island at what is today Porto da Barra in Salvador, a move that would lead to the founding of Salvador. In 1535 a Portuguese expedition was sent to establish colonies in Bahia, setting up sugar plantations around the Recôncavo and a fortified settlement in Caramuru's village from where they began to trade and to enslave Tupinambá. This led to all-out war, with the Brazilians gathering some 6,000 warriors to attack the Portuguese whose plantations were burnt and people driven away, killed or ritually eaten.

The Portuguese responded by sending a larger fleet commanded by Tomé de Souza in 1549, with the title 'Captain of the people and lands of Bahia and Governor of the land of Brazil' and orders to quell the Tupinambá. De Souza founded Salvador (see page 28) and a series of forts around the Baía de Todos os Santos. It was Caramuru who negotiated peace with the Tupinambá, leading to their enslavement by the Portuguese who put them to work on the sugar and tobacco plantations of the Recôncavo. Those who resisted were slaughtered, initially by

Tomé de Souza's troops and later in far greater numbers by his successor Mem de Sá. By the end of the 16th century there were prolific numbers of sugar-cane *engenhos* or factory-plantations in the Recôncavo and far too few enslaved Tupinambá to work them. The Portuguese began transporting Africans (see page 30). In Bahia most of them went to the Recôncavo.

By 1700 the Recôncavo had some 150 *engenhos* and many had grown from manor houses to villages whose populations were predominantly enslaved Africans working 18 hours a day and suffering repeated torture just to ensure that they did so. There were a minority of indigenous Brazilians, Portuguese and *caboclos* – or rural people of mixed race. The *engenhos* and villages clung to the bay's shore and the riverbanks: there were no roads to speak of. Transport was almost entirely fluvial. By the 1800s the *engenhos* had proliferated further and the villages had become towns. Santo Amaro and Cachoeira's streets boasted opulent churches. São Felix had a cigar factory. Roads and bridges were finally built only in the 19th century, just as Bahia's sugar was beginning to lose competitiveness to the producers in the British Empire like Guyana and Mauritius.

GETTING THERE AND AROUND

BY BUS, MINIVAN AND TAXI Buses leave every other hour from the Bom Despacho bus terminal for Valença, taking two hours and also to Camamu for Barra Grande on the Peninsula de Maraú (from where there are buses on a very rough road down to Itacaré). There are frequent buses between Salvador and all the towns referred to in this chapter. Connections to southern Bahia are via the town of Santo Antônio (for Valença, Ilhéus, etc). There are buses every other hour from Cachoeira/São Felix to Santo Antônio. Minivans (*combis*) run from the boat jetties at Mar Grande and Bom Despacho around Itaparica island calling at Itaparica town, Conceição, Barra Grande, Cacha-Pregos and stopping at all the beaches along the way on request from 06.30 until 19.30, charging R$10. There are taxis on Itaparica island and bicycles can be rented in either Bom Despacho or Mar Grande.

TOURIST INFORMATION AND LOCAL TOUR OPERATORS

For general information on the Recôncavo and Baía de Todos os Santos see **Brazil Max** (*www.brazilmax.com*). The Salvador-based, Irish-run tour operator **Tatur** (*Av Tancredo Neves 274, Caminho das Árvores, Salvador;* ✆ *3114 7900; www.tatur.com.br*) offers day tours around the Recôncavo and to Itaparica island. **Trip Brasil** (*Vila 14, Loja 50, Rua Odilon Santos 14, Rio Vermelho, Salvador;* ✆ *3015 2235; www.tripbrasil.com*) offer a one-day tobacco tour of the Recôncavo visiting the Danneman tobacco plantation and factory (see page 154) in Cachoeira/São Felix, a colonial *fazenda* (for a huge traditional Bahian lunch) and the factory itself where the cigars are still hand cut and rolled.

ILHA DE ITAPARICA

This bean-shaped island 14km from Salvador across the mouth of the Baía de Todos os Santos has long been a favourite weekend escape for Soteropolitanos, many of whom have built holiday homes here. They come for the beaches. The two towns on the island are barely hamlets. Itaparica's ocean-side is fringed with some 29km of beautiful palm-shaded white-sand beaches. And its bay-side – 12km to the west – preserves broken mangrove swamps and marshy inlets with once rich, but now sadly depleted birdlife. The island is busy at the weekends but it's still a sleepy place during the week – when it is easy to have a beach almost to yourself.

GETTING THERE AND AROUND

By ferry Passenger ferries leave regularly from the Terminal Marítimo ferry dock in front of Salvador's Mercado Model for Mar Grande on Itaparica island every 45 minutes. The journey takes about 25 minutes. A big new wide-bottomed car ferry (appropriately called *Ivete Sangalo*) takes 30 minutes to cross from Salvador's São Joaquim terminal (*Av Oscar Pontes 1051;* \ *3254 1020; www.twbmar.com.br*) for Bom Despacho on Itaparica island every 45 minutes between 06.00 and 22.00, though schedules vary according to the season and are subject to change.

Overland A bridge on the south side of Itaparica connects to southern Bahia via Valença (see page 157); this is often the quickest route from Salvador to Morro de São Paulo.

TOURIST INFORMATION There are no tourist information offices or booths on the island. The municipal website (*www.itaparica.ba.gov.br*) is in Portuguese only. The website http://ilhaitaparica.com/blog/ has information on hotels and services in Portuguese only.

WHERE TO STAY

Club Med (334 rooms) BA-001 to Nazaré 19km south of town, Praia da Conceição; \ 3681 8800; www.clubmed.com.br. Club Med Itaparica was the first resort ever opened in Bahia, in 1978. Minimum stays in high season are for 7 days. Some rooms are scruffy, the best have been renovated with hardwood floors, rattan chairs & contemporary decoration in neutral colours offset by colourful bed linen with stripes or polka dots. Rooms have views either over the garden or the adjacent lake. Stays are all-inclusive with everything from rooms & food to night-time entertainment taken care of on site. The resort even attempts (illegally) to restrict the beach to guests. The result is an anaesthetised Bahian experience on (what by Bahian standards) is an average beach. Good perhaps if booked at a discount rate through an online travel agent & used as a base, but just another resort otherwise. $$$$$

Pousada Canto da Praia (32 rooms) Travessa do Coqueiral 20, Praia de Ponta de Areia; \ 3631 4237; www.pousadacantodapraia.com.br. A 3-storey building ringed with wooden verandas & with exposed wooden

ITAPARICA'S BEACHES AT A GLANCE

Amoreiras Good swimming, calm, a 30–40-minute beach walk from Ponta de Areia.
Aratuba Rock pools at low tide.
Barra do Gil Long, broad with fine white sand and many condos.
Barra Grande Condos, many beach *barracas*, fluffy sand and a rougher sea.
Barra do Pote Good swimming in calm waters off a white-sand beach.
Berlinque Good swimming in clear, calm waters and many beach *barracas*.
Cacha-Pregos A village with boatbuilding, boat rentals and a busy beach.
Conceição The Club Med guards don't like visitors but the beach is not private.
Coroa Wild, unspoilt and with difficult access by foot only or at low tide.
Forte In the Itaparica village; good swimming, safe water, historic monuments.
Gameleira Fronting a little fishing village and very popular at weekends.
Manguinhos Small beach, good swimming, gentle waves.
Mar Grande In front of a string of condos and next to the boat dock.
Penha Surfing, views of Salvador, offshore reefs, a little chapel and exclusive crowd.
Ponta de Areia The island's most popular; good swimming, very calm, many *barracas*.
Porto do Santos Swimming, slight waves.
Tairu Fine white sand and shady coconut palms. Romantic.

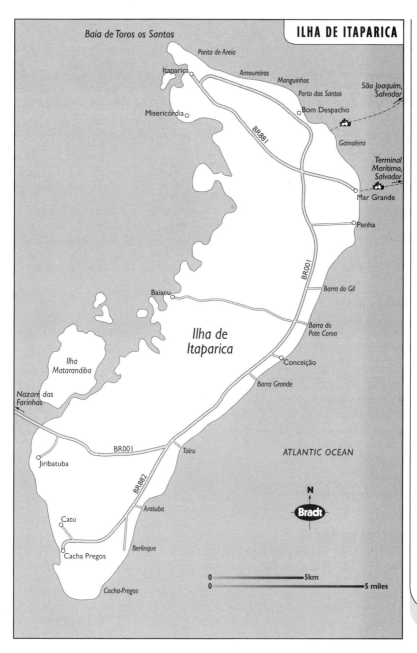

Baía de Toros os Santos

Ponta de Areia

Itaparica

Amoureiras

Manguinhos

Misericórdia

Porto dos Santos

São Joaquím, Salvador

Bom Despacho

BR881

Gamaleira

Terminal Marítimo, Salvador

Mar Grande

Penha

BR001

Baiacu

Barra do Gil

Barra do Pote Coroa

Ilha de Itaparica

Conceição

Ilha Matarandiba

Barra Grande

Nazaré das Farinhas

BR001

Tairu

ATLANTIC OCEAN

Jiribatuba

BR882

N

Bradt

Aratuba

Catu

Berlinque

Cacha Pregos

0   5km

0   5 miles

Cacha-Pregos

beams & a terracotta-tile roof. Rooms are small but bright, attractively decorated in terracotta & cream & hung with paintings of marine creatures, & large wooden windows let in plenty of natural light. Each is furnished with a wooden bed with white linen stamped with blue fish, TV & minibar & have a small balcony. The front rooms face the sea, the back rooms face the mangroves. The restaurant sits in front of the main building in thatched-roof gazebos with 2 buffets of hot food & a table of salad. The service is courteous & attentive. Many guests use the hotel as a comfortable base from which to explore other islands in Bahia de Todos os Santos such as Frades & Maré where there the accommodation is quite basic. In a good location, just across the street from the calm waters of Ponta de Areia beach. $$–$$$

🏠 **Pousada Arco-Íris** (15 rooms) Estrada da Gamboa 102, Mar Grande; ☎ 3633 1130; www.parcoiris.na-web.net. This spacious late 19th-century house sits in the grounds of an old mango farm & is still surrounded by some 1,500 stately mango trees. These sit in a large orchard alongside cashew, jenipapo, sapoti, pitanga, banana & coconuts, all of which are free for guests to pick in season. The house is just 100m from the beach. The interior is decorated with period furniture, sitting on patterned, dark red & terracotta tiles alongside large pottery vases & contemporary dark wood chairs. Room rates vary according to type. The priciest are the cabins set in the garden & with a veranda & hammocks. The cheaper rooms have shared bathrooms & sit in the

house. The hotel restaurant, Manga Rosa, is considered one of the best in Itaparica (see below). $$

🏠 **Jardim Tropical** (13 rooms) Estrada da Rodagem, Ponta de Areia; ☎ 3631 1409, e jardim-tropical@click21.com.br; www.jardim-tropical.com. As the name indicates the pousada, is set in a tropical garden. The partially shaded lawn is dotted with white beach chairs & colourful hammocks. Rooms are in little cottages pleasantly arranged along the garden beyond the lawn. There are 3 categories varying according to comfort level. The chalet is not much more than an empty room with a bed. The cabana is in a wooden cottage with a loud chequered vinyl floor. The apts are more solid, brighter & have larger rooms with either black or white tiled floors, half-covered stone walls, a comfy chair & a coffee table. All rooms have dbl bed, private bathroom, mosquito nets & fan; only some have AC. Rate includes b/fast. Kids under 5 don't pay. Free transfer to Ponta de Areia beach & Itaparica town. $–$$

✘ WHERE TO EAT

✘ **Manga Rosa** Pousada Arco-Íris Estrada da Gamboa 102, Mar Grande; ☎ 3633 1130; www.parcoiris.na-web.net; ⏱ 12.00–16.00 & 18.00–24.00. The restaurant is attached to Arco-Íris (see above) by the garden in a wooden cabana with a tiled roof & exposed beams. It's prettiest at night when candles give a romantic feel & the bar serves great caipirinhas & batida cocktails. Food is regional & international, with grilled fish wrapped in banana leaf & cooked in a wood-fired oven a speciality. Modest wine list. $$–$$$

✘ **Phillippe Restaurante** Largo de São Bento, Mar Grande; ☎ 3633 1060; ⏱ 11.00–24.00. Close to the docks this unpretentious restaurant serves both French & Bahian cuisine at an affordable price. Dishes include escargots & salads & well-prepared moquecas. Try moqueca siri mole. $$–$$$

✘ **Volta ao Mundo** Largo de São Bento 165, Mar Grande; ☎ 3633 1031; ⏱ 12.00–23.00 Mon–Fri. A simple but good-value buffet restaurant with a fixed price giving as many helpings as diners want. Good variety of hot dishes including fish, meat & salads. Regional, international & oriental food. $–$$

OTHER PRACTICALITIES There are no banks on Itaparica. Come with money from Salvador.

WHAT TO SEE AND DO

Itaparica town and the northern beaches There are two little towns with colonial and early Republican architectural remnants and many beaches. The prettiest is **Itaparica** at the northern tip of the island. In Portuguese times this was called the Ponta da Baleia – whale point on account of the large numbers of humpback whales which used to enter the Baía de Todos os Santos to calf. It was also a logical strategic point. The Dutch built a fort (*Rua do Matriz* s/n) here in 1647, and after they took the land back, the Portuguese built another on its ruins in 1711, alongside a small Baroque church, the **Igreja Matriz do Santissimo Sacramento** (*Rua do Matriz* s/n). In 1847 the Bahians built a public drinking fountain, the **Fonte da Bica** (*Av 25 de Outubro at Cais do Oeste*), covered in impressive *azulejos* and topped with a navy blue Portuguese Rococo pediment. The water is said to be medicinal. The town has a few beaches, the Praia do Forte – which extends away from the fort – and the Praia do Boulevard, which is in reality a cobblestone promenade, shaded by tamarind trees, and with beach sand exposed only at the lowest of tides. The most popular beach, **Ponta de Areia**, lies 1km east of the town on the road to Bom Despacho. It's an almost waveless family beach with everything from stalls and parasols to jet skis and floating bananas.

The island's main road, the BA-532 runs in a loop south from Itaparica, with the easternmost arm reaching **Bom Despacho** after 7km. There is little more than a ferry jetty, manmade harbour and a cluster of touristy restaurants, shops and pousadas in this tiny village. But there are beaches within a few minutes' walk. **Manguinhos** is the closest – a 300m-long, slender stretch of yellow sand lapped by tiny waves. **Porto dos Santos** lies next to the ferry boat jetty and all but disappears at high tide; but it offers more gentle swimming. **Amoreiras**, 2km to the north of Bom Despacho, is a continuation of Ponta de Areia, but with coarser sand, fewer people and beach *barracas* offering sea food and cold beer and *batidas*. Some 4km south of Bom Despacho is the popular beach of **Gameleira** with many beach huts and busy with people at the weekends.

Veracruz and the central beaches Itaparica's other colonial town, **Veracruz** (aka Mar Grande), lies 13km south of Bom Despacho. It is the island's principal ferry port and location for many Salvador condominium holiday homes. The town is fringed with beaches – particularly running south – such as **Mar Grande** itself (which is lined with a mix of colonial and Republican buildings and modern condo houses) and **Penha** (the most exclusive beach on the island backed by expensive holiday homes and attracting a yuppie weekend crowd). This beach is watched over by a little colonial chapel, the **Igreja Nossa Senhora da Penha** (*Praia de Penha* s/n), from where there are great views of distant Salvador. The town itself was built around a *fazenda* called Congo, whose ruins were purchased and renovated by Antônio Carlos Pereira (known to his friends as God), an entrepreneur from São Paulo some 30 years ago. He converted the *fazenda* into a pousada – one of the first on the island. It lies in the centre of the town and both the main building and the little chapel can be visited.

Igreja Nosso Senhor de Vera Cruz (*Estrada Baiacu* s/n) Some 20km south and across the island from Veracruz is the municipality of Baiacu, lost in mangroves and looking out over a series of tiny islands in the bay. It's worth coming here just to see the ruins of the church of Nosso Senhor de Vera Cruz. This is said to be the third oldest in Brazil and was built by the Jesuits when they founded a mission to Tapiraca's Tupinambá in 1560. The entire building has been propped up by a gigantic gameleira tree, whose massive roots extend around the masonry like gaudiesque organic flying buttresses. The gameleira is a sacred tree to Candomblé and the ruins have gone from being Catholic to a site frequented by devotees of the *orixás*. They are not signposted. To arrive, drive to km8 on the BA-001 to Baiacu (the turn-off is some 11km south of Veracruz), cross through the hamlet of Baiacu and carry on for 3km more. The ruins are next to Fazenda Baiacu do Mundo. Or take a *combi* to Baicu and walk, or take a cab the whole way.

The Southern Beaches The island's best beaches begin just south of the turn-off to Baiacu. **Barra do Gil** is long, broad and palm-shaded and stretches for over a kilometre. **Coroa** is a wilder stretch reachable only at low tide along the coast or by dirt road at other times. **Barra do Pote** and **Conceição** are contiguous, the latter with a pretty 18th-century colonial chapel overlooking a glorious stretch of beach guarded by security guards from the adjacent Club Med resort, who attempt to dissuade non-paying guests. But all beaches in Brazil are public and they can only appear to impede entry. There is another long fine beach south of Conceição at **Barra Grande** (washed by more turbulent oceanic waves and backed by many holiday homes) before the island reaches its southernmost tip via three beautiful white-sand beaches: **Tairu** (with fine talc soft sand and coconut palms), **Aratuba** (which forms large rock pools at low tide) and **Berlinque** (with calm waters and good swimming). The southern tip of the island, **Ponta Cacha Pregos**, has the largest concentration of condos south of Veracruz, and offers swimming in the sea and the Jaguaripe River which runs out from the Recôncavo at this point. It's a popular yachting point; with boats bobbing behind a long spit of sand and there are a number of little boatyards here where locals build and repair fishing boats.

Western Itaparica The western bay-side of Itaparica remains semi-wild, broken by mangrove swamps and deserted beaches. There are a number of protected areas – the **Parque Ecológico de Baiacu** (where the Igreja de Nosso Senhor de Vera Cruz lies), the **Proteção Ambiental Recife das Pinaúnas** (protecting a unique form of reef that forms around the mangrove forests) and largest of all the **Santuário Ecologico da Contracosta**. This sanctuary protects a series of mangrove forests which run up the southwestern side of the island. The water here is brackish – a mix of the salty Atlantic and fresh water from a string of little rivers that flow out of the Recôncavo. The birdwatching in the wilder patches is fair. It's easy to spot two or three kingfisher species and four or five heron species. But there should be far more birds. Boats can be rented to all these locations in Cacha-Pregos.

FRADES AND MARÉ ISLANDS

After Itaparica, these two islands in the north of the bay are the largest in the Baía de Todos os Santos. Ilha dos Frades is wedge-shaped and about 10km long by 5km wide at its widest point. There are small settlements at Ponta Nossa Senhora do Guadalupe in the far south and Paramana on the north. Ilha da Maré is about 10km long by 3km at its widest point. There are small villages at Vila de Santana on the far south west of the island and Praia Grande roughly 1km to the north of Santana. Both are partially covered with Atlantic coastal rainforest and fringed with long white-sand beaches and remnant mangrove swamps. Frades is wilder and less visited whilst Maré has a handful of small fishing villages where locals make colourful *renda de bilro*, knitted lace shawls and spreads.

HISTORY Despite their exuberant tropical beauty the islands have an ugly past. According to locals the Ilha dos Frades is named after two friars who were captured and ritually eaten by Tupinambá in the late 1500s. But like the rest of Bahia the indigenous people were eventually conquered – converted and Westernised by the Jesuits (who were 'owners' of the island until the order was expelled from Brazil by Pombal) and subsequently enslaved by the Portuguese. Frades then became a slaving port and then a leper colony – there are ruins of a small hospital here and a fort where African slaves were kept in vile cramped conditions before sale. During the colonial sugar boom, Maré was dominated by a large *engenho* whose ruins still stand, together with a cluster of religious buildings, which once served the workers.

GETTING THERE AND AROUND Tatur (*Av Tancredo Neves 274, Caminho das Árvores, Salvador;* \ *3114 7900; www.tatur.com.br*) offer bespoke **cruises** around the Baía de Todos os Santos which can include one or both of the islands. Schooners leave when full on weekends and in high season from the Terminal Marítimo behind the Mercado Modelo in Salvador. Passenger **boats** (used by the islanders) for Ilha do Maré leave from the Terminal Marítimo in the city of São Tomé de Paripe, 25km north of Salvador (and reachable from Salvador's rodoviária). Passenger boats for Paramaná on Ilha dos Frades leave from the quays at the little town of **Madre de Deus**. This tiny town, with a lovely white-sand beach and a hilltop church with bay

Idyllic though it may seem, the interior of the Baía de Todos os Santos is not safe for swimming. Eighty percent of all the state's sewage drains here – directly into the sea, with no treatment. Nor do the sugar refineries and factories that dot the Recôncavo adequately treat their effluent. By 2009 the problem had become so grave that members of the Bahian Environmental Institute (IMA) and the water board (Ingá) met with government officials in a special summit, to discuss a plan for the treatment of organic and industrial waste destined for the Baía de Todos os Santos. They took the first tentative steps towards organising a management plan for the region. But for now the pollution continues.

views is worth spending a few hours in along the way. It lies 70m north of Salvador on the shore of the Baía de Todos os Santos, and is also reachable from Salvador's rodoviária, with ten buses daily. On Frades, boats can be hired at Ponta Nossa Senhora do Guadalupe in high season and at any time in Paramana, and rough walking trails lead around the island, though much of it can be walked at low tide along the coast. On Maré *jegue* **sail boats** can be hired at Vila de Santana and Praia Grande, and exploring the island at their tranquil pace is a delight.

TOURIST INFORMATION There are no tourist information offices on either island. Information is available in Portuguese and English on the Visit Bahia website (*www.visiteabahia.com.br*).

WHERE TO STAY

Pousada Farol de Maré (10 rooms) Praia de Itamoabo s/n; 3297 6084. A small concrete & terracotta-tile-roofed blocky guesthouse backed by forest & overlooking its own tiny pool & patio a few mins' walk from the beach. All rooms are fan-cooled & price includes b/fast & the owners can help with boat tours. $

Pousada Paramaná (12 rooms) Vila Paramaná s/n, Ilha dos Frades; 3297 7084, 8716 8403. Very simple fan-cooled rooms in a little family-run pousada near the waterfront in the fishermen's village. All rooms have fans & no AC. From R$40–80 with b/fast. $

WHERE TO EAT There are very simple makeshift *barraca* restaurants in the villages on both islands serving fried or grilled fish.

OTHER PRACTICALITIES There are no banks on either island.

WHAT TO SEE AND DO Even though the waters of the Baía de Todos os Santos are not very clean, both islands are visited principally for their **beaches** and stretches of remnant forest. The best beaches are Praia da Ponta de Nossa Senhora de Guadalupe (long broad bay of white sand visited by the day cruises) and Praia da Viração (which is visited by the day cruises on request or by hiring a boatman at the village of **Paramana)**. The best beaches on Maré are Praia Grande – a long, fine white-sand beach – Neves, Santana and Itamoabo. There are tiny villages at each. Both islands are dotted with Jesuit buildings, many of them in ruins. The miniature, simple whitewash and terracotta-tiled Baroque **church** of **Nossa Senhora do Loreto** (*Ponta do Loreto;* none; ⊕ *irregularly*) sits on a tiny plinth overlooking a white-sand beach backed by palms and forest at the far north of the Frades. It was built in 1640. There's another larger 17th-century church at the opposite end of the island – **Nossa Senhora de Guadalupe** (*Praia da Ponta de Nossa Senhora de Guadalupe* s/n) – and ruined Jesuit buildings near both. There's

Baía de Todos os Santos and Recôncavo   FRADES AND MARÉ ISLANDS

4

another pretty little church with a view on Maré – **Nossa Senhora das Neves** (Our Lady of the Snows, a strangely inappropriate name for such a sweltering tropical location) sits on a hill above the beach of the same name, and is reachable by a little forest trail. It's worth climbing up to the building just for the view. Senhora Santana on the Santana beach is 19th century. The locals on **Praia Grande** still speak to each other in west African dialects.

SÃO FRANCISCO DO CONDE AND CAJAÍBA ISLAND

São Francisco do Conde was once the most illustrious city on the Recôncavo, as its full name (the count's city of St Francis on the beach of Sergi) would suggest. It's a sleepy, little-visited backwater today, sandwiched between a palm-covered hill, farmlands and the mangrove swamps and looking out towards the pristine beaches of Cajaíba island – immediately offshore. The city's environs are dotted with dozens of crumbling Baroque and colonial monuments, which rarely receive a visitor and whose eerie ruins, gradually reclaimed by the tropical landscape, seem forgotten by all but time.

GETTING THERE AND AROUND There are eight **buses** a day from Salvador's rodoviária to São Francisco do Conde, the first at 05.15, the last at 19.00. The journey takes an hour. There are 11 buses a day to Santo Amaro – where it is possible to change buses for Cachoeira/São Felix (see pages 151–2).The journey takes just under 30 minutes, with the first bus leaving at 07.10 and the last at 18.00. The centre of São Francisco do Conde is small and easily negotiated on foot. A **taxi** to the ruins at the Imperial Instituto will cost around R$15, though it is possible to walk in under an hour. Bring a hat, water and sunscreen. Cajaíba island lies 5km offshore of São Francisco and can only be visited by chartering a **fishing boat**. Expect to pay at least R$100–150 for a half-day round trip for up to eight people.

TOURIST INFORMATION For tourist information the Prefeitura de São Francisco do Conde (*Rua Espírito Santo at Praça de Independencia;* \ *3651 8599; www.saofrancisco doconde.ba.gov.br*) can help with guides and boat hire to Cajaíba island. No English spoken, however.

 WHERE TO STAY AND EAT There are a few simple restaurants around the Praça da Independencia in the centre of town. Most are open at lunchtime only. There are no hotels or pousadas.

WHAT TO SEE AND DO
Convento de Santo Antônio (*Rua João Florêncio Gomes 1, Praça Artur Sales;* \ *3651 1074;* ⊕ *08.00–12.00 & 14.00–17.00 Mon–Sat, 08.00–11.00 Sun; free*) São Francisco was the third town to be settled in the Recôncavo. After the third governor Mem de Sá had massacred or enslaved the indigenous people he gave this land to his son Francisco, after whom the town is named. His daughter Felipa inherited the land and married the Portuguese count Fernando de Noronha Linhares (whose family included the governor-general of Goa). And it was Fernando who paid for the construction of this opulent church and convent in 1618. The façade is typically Portuguese Baroque, with twin towers aside a façade decorated with ornamental pilasters and with scroll-like flourishes above and beneath the windows and on top of the elaborate pediment. There is a small sacred art museum in the interior. The town has another fine Baroque church, the **Igreja Matriz de São Gonçalo**, which is usually closed.

Imperial Instituto Baiano de Agricultura (*Estrada para São Bento km3; no tourist infrastructure*) In the 19th century São Francisco's sugar wealth and aristocratic prestige was such that Emperor Dom Pedro II stayed here during a state visit to Bahia, announcing plans to establish Bahia's first agricultural institution whilst in the city. The building is an impressive ruin nowadays, on a bluff with sweeping views over the river and mangroves and with its imperial crest overgrown with epiphytes, its stately stone steps broken by weeds and its 365 paneless windows framing nothing but blue sky.

Cajaíba island This mangrove and scrub forest-swathed island 20 minutes boat ride offshore of São Francisco makes a delightful day trip from the town. Foreign tourists are almost never seen and the local fishermen are very friendly and welcoming. Little trails run through the forest, to ruined Portuguese buildings and to a small, hidden beach. In colonial times this island was home to one of the largest and wealthiest *engenhos* on the Recôncavo. And the mansion house, sugar factory and workers' quarters remain relatively well preserved.

SANTO AMARO

Pedacinho mais antigo do Recôncavo Baiano. Do seu massapê nasceram as canas mais doces e as mais doces estórias.
You are the oldest part of the Recôncavo. The sweetest sugar cane and the sweetest stories were born from your soil.

Mabel Velloso

The Vila de Nossa Senhora da Purificação e Santo Amaro, or simply Santo Amaro as it is called by the locals, is one of the most distinguished towns in the Recôncavo. The city centre lies 70km from Salvador and is littered with handsome colonial and early Republican buildings, from a past when this was one of the most prosperous locations in Bahia – with some 60 *engenhos*. Santo Amaro played an important role in the liberation of Bahia from the Portuguese and in the Revolta dos Alfaiates fought for emancipation of Bahian slaves in 1798. Many important Bahians were born here: the legendary capoeira master Besouro Cordão de Ouro (whose body was said to be impermeable to bullets), Popó (who popularised the Bahian martial art stick dance of maculelê), the modernist painter Emanuel Alves de Araújo and the co-inventors of tropicália Caetano Veloso and his sister Maria Bethânia. And the area around Santo Amaro is one of the prettiest in the Recôncavo – with clear-river waterfalls and little-visited beaches. Yet despite all these draws few tourists make it to Santo Amaro. The glorious days seem long gone, the grand mansions decaying and whilst the town still bustles with people – especially at morning market – even the churches are almost invariably closed.

GETTING THERE AND AROUND There are more than 20 buses a day from Salvador's rodoviária to Santo Amaro, many of them continuing to Cachoeira/São Felix. The journey takes from 45 minutes to an hour. There are at least 15 buses a day to Cachoeira/São Felix, 45 minutes away. The city centre is small and easily negotiated **on foot**, meaning that Santo Amaro can easily be visited on a day trip or *en route* to Cachoeira/São Felix and other places in the Recôncavo.

TOURIST INFORMATION There are no tourist information offices in Santo Amaro.

WHERE TO STAY AND EAT

⌂ **Enseada do Caeiro Eco Resort** (32 rooms) Rodovia BA-878 km14, Praia de Itapema; ☎ 3264 3000; www.enseadadocaeiro.com.br. Two-storey AC bungalows overlooking the beach in a child-friendly eco-resort 14km from Santo Amaro. The area is quiet with beautiful sea views & tufted-eared marmosets &

tanagers visit the little palm-filled lawns & gardens. The ecotourism amounts to little more than walks in nature but there are pony rides on the beach, boat trips & a big pool for the kids. $$$

OTHER PRACTICALITIES There is a branch of Bradesco bank (*Sampaio 2E;* ❧ *075 3241 2621*) in Santo Amaro at Praca.

WHAT TO SEE AND DO
Igreja Matriz de Nossa Senhora da Purificação and the engenhos (*Praça da Purificação s/n;* ❧ *075 3241 1172;* ⊕ *08.00–12.00 & 14.00–17.00 Mon–Sat, 08.00–11.00 Sun, in practise most often closed; free*) This towering, massive-walled church was built in 1706 at the height of Baroque Bahia's wealth and power. The magnificent *azulejos* that decorate the interior were imported from Portugal and the ceiling painting is by José Joaqim da Rocha. Between 23 January and 2 February every year the town celebrates the Lavagem da Purificação when celebrants wash the church's steps after parading through the streets of Santo Amaro. The streets around the praça are filled with crumbling *engenhos* and colonial mansions.

Museu do Recolhimento dos Humildes (*Praça Frei Beto s/n;* ⊕ *09.00–13.00 Tue–Sat; free*) A sacred art museum housed in a beautiful but sadly dilapidated 18th-century cloistered convent on the outskirts of the city. The museum's collection of 500 pieces includes some magnificent reliquaries, monstrances and icons (some of which show an Indian influence – presumably through Goa). To reach the museum take a motorbike taxi from the Praça da Purificação (R$3).

Cachoeira do Urubu (*Arrange a guide through the Prefeitura de Santo Amaro Rua Gal Argôlo 59;* ❧ *75 3241 8600*) A 15km walk on jungle trail from the city's railway station via Ferrea Santo Amaro-Cachoeira railway. The Urubu Falls are formed where the Sergi River drops through a series of cascades into a deep green pool in a little Atlantic coastal rainforest glade outside Santo Amaro. It is a popular spot for canyoning abseilers, who drop the entire length of the falls, often roaring and frightening away the otherwise abundant birdlife. Come during the week for a quiet swim in nature and a delightful half-day trail walk.

Praia de Itapema (*Vila de Itapema, BA-878; 20km from Santo Amaro*) A series of little rivers and creeks break up mangrove forests and pearly white-sand beaches on the shores of the Baía de Todos os Santos just outside Santo Amaro. Few tourists – even locals – make it here. R$50 round trip in a taxi or take a local bus from the rodoviária via Acupe (7km from Itapema).

CACHOEIRA AND SÃO FELIX

Cachoeira and its twin town São Felix sit opposite each other on the banks of the Rio Paraguaçu 110 km north west of Salvador, preserving between them the greatest repository of Baroque buildings in Bahia after the capital. In the 17th and 18th centuries these were two of the richest towns in the country with a population greater than Salvador's. It's hard to believe this today. Between them the cities are so tiny that you could walk from the outer limits of one, across the Paraguaçu River and to the outer limits of the other in well under an hour. It is a sobering realisation that so large a country as Brazil (with a population of millions of indigenous people) was conquered and established from such meagre means. Most visitors to Cachoiera take an early bus from Salvador and spend just a day here.

HISTORY Incursions by the French along the Brazilian coast and alliances forged by them and the Tupinambá forced the Portuguese to turn their Brazilian trading venture into a proto-colony. And in 1531 Martim Afonso Sousa, a humble but experienced sailor, set off with a crew of brigands and minor noblemen to found colonies in Brazil. Like most of the early settlers, Afonso's sailors were mostly marginalised, poor or criminal. Brazil was seen as a desperate venture. The imperial money was in the spice trade with the East, in Goa or Africa. Many of the marginalised were New Christians – non-Catholics who had voluntarily converted from their original Jewish or Muslim faith. They suffered heavy persecution in contemporaneous Portugal – some 3,000 were murdered in riots in 1506, incited by two Dominican friars (who were executed by the king, together with 45 mobsters), and they lived under the threat of the Inquisition, which was due to legislate on its findings in 1536. One of the New Christians, Paulo Dias Adorno, settled on the banks of the Paraguaçu River in the Recôncavo, using all the money he had saved in Portugal to construct a home, chapel, sugar factory and slave quarters. He was accompanied by another Portuguese, Rodrigues Martins, and assisted in making friendly contact with the Tupinambá by Caramuru. The Adorno and Rodrigues families, together with the descendants of Caramuru and his Tupinambá wife, would be instrumental in the conquest of the rest of Bahia in the following century. Their first settlement prospered and grew quickly to become Cachoeira, and as it grew it was afforded increasing protection from the new capital in Salvador. By the time the third governor, Mem de Sá, had risen to power it was a substantial size. So much so that Mem de Sá decided to clear the Tupinambá from the opposite bank, killing most of their men, enslaving their women and children and establishing a further settlement – São Felix.

The twin towns boomed in the 17th century, with tobacco, sugar cane and cattle eating up the forested surrounds. By the 18th century the towns had outgrown Salvador and tobacco from São Felix was smoked by people the world over – from merchants in London to mandarins in China. When gold and diamonds were discovered in the interior of the Minas Gerais and Piauí states, expeditions for both often left from Cachoeira and the mining riches were shipped to Portugal from the city or from Rio de Janeiro or Paraty far to the south. The ferocious Tapuia people of the Bahian sertão were conquered from Cachoeira after they began to hunt the Portuguese cattle, and then, when ranchers and *garimpeiros* chanced upon diamonds in the Chapada Diamantina, the Cachoeira and São Felix became busier still with a Bahian mineral rush, which prompted still more growth.

The two cities were the principal bases for the revolutionary armies who liberated Bahia from Portugal in the 1820s and the city was one of the first outside the southeast to proclaim Dom Pedro I emperor of an independent Brazil. The town was twice the capital of Bahia: once in 1624–25 during the Dutch invasion, and once in 1822–23 while Salvador was still held by the Portuguese.

With the introduction of roads and the decline of river transport and steam, the cities declined in importance after Brazil became a republic in the 20th century. And like much of the Recôncavo they seem lost in time – quiet provincial towns, surrounded by the decaying ruins of colonial *engenhos* and old Portuguese churches, and famous to Bahians more for their African culture than an illustrious past which enslaved them. The towns remain centres for Candomblé, capoeira and samba de roda.

GETTING THERE AND AROUND Cachoeira and São Felix are 108km from Salvador. The Cachoeira/São Felix bus terminal lies next to the bridge in Praça Manoel Vitorino. There are buses every half-hour to Cachoeira from Salvador's rodoviária, the first at 05.15, the last at 19.00. The journey takes 2–2½ hours. Faster and more frequent buses (every 15–30 minutes, taking under one hour), can be flagged down on the BR-101 federal highway 4km outside town (reached via motorbike taxi for R$5). There are eight buses a day to Santo Amaro – where it is possible to change buses for Salvador. The journey takes 45 minutes. All the sights in both cities are easily visited on foot.

TOURIST INFORMATION
Tourist office Rua Ana Néri 4; 📞 75 3425 1123. No English spoken & nothing but a few pamphlets.

WHERE TO STAY
Aclamação Apart Hotel (14 rooms) Praça da Aclamação, Centro; 📞 75 3425 3428; www.aclamacaoaparthotel.com.br. Another 19th-century building in the historic centre with rooms converted into flats & fully restored in 2008. The best are on the 2nd floor with a view over the main praça (noisy at night), the Praça da Aclamação (quieter) or the river (quietest). $$
Pousada Convento do Carmo (21 rooms) Rua Inocêncio Boaventura, Praça da Aclamação, Centro; 📞 75 3425 1716; e pousadadoconvento@hotmail.com; www.pousadadoconvento.com.br. Simple rooms with wooden floors in a slightly run-down old convent with crumbling 17th-century furniture, a frowsty chapel & a little sacred-art gallery. The best in town though, & with a pool. $$

Pousada La Barca (6 rooms) Rua Inocência Boaventura 37, Centro; 📞 75 3425 1070; http://labarca.zip.net/indexc.htm. Set on the 1st floor of a 19th-century colonial house. All rooms have a private bathroom, fan, window overlooking Paraguaçu River. B/fast included. The Argentine owner is an artist with a particular interest in Afro-Brazilian culture. His paintings proliferate throughout. $

SHOPPING There is a great woodcarving tradition in Cachoeira and many of its artists can be seen at work in their studios. Best are

Davi Gonçalvesi J J Seabra 68, Centro; 📞 75 3425 2686
Doidãoi R Ana Nery 42; 📞 75 3425 2764

Foryi R Treze de Maio 31, Centro; 📞 75 3425 1142,
Louco Filhoi R Treze de Maio 18, Centro; 📞 75 3425 4310

OTHER PRACTICALITIES
$ Bradesco Bank Praça Dr Aristides Milton 10. Has a Visa ATM.

WHAT TO SEE AND DO
Casa da Câmara e Cadeia (*Praça de Aclamação s/n, Cachoeira;* 📞 *75 3425 1018;* ⏱ *08.00–12.00 & 14.00–18.00 daily; adult/child R$5/free*) For a brief period (during the insurrection against the Portuguese in 1822), this modest but handsome 17th-century colonial building was the seat of Bahian government. Today its whitewashed façade hides government offices on the upper floors – with polished wooden floors and ranks of desks – where even casual male visitors are expected to wear long trousers and proper shoes. Downstairs is a slavery museum, which has a frowsty and oppressive, heavy-walled dungeon. In the 17th century *quilombo* villages were numerous on the Paraguaçu, founded by escaped Africans and oppressed indigenous Brazilians who practised syncretistic Christianity – mixed with African spirit religions and indigenous shamanism. Many of them were members of the messianic *santidade* cult. Under crown sanction, *bandeirantes* left from the Praça de Aclimação to burn such settlements to the ground and recapture the escaped Africans. They were dragged back to rot in misery in the Casa de Câmara before being returned to their owners. The contrast between the heavy air in the dungeon (and the modest collection of vile instruments of slavery in the adjacent room), with the small town bureaucracy in the offices above is bathetic.

Museu Regional de Cachoeira (*Praça da Aclamação 4, Cachoeira;* \ *075 3425 1123;* ⏲ *08.00–12.00 & 14.00–17.00 Mon–Fri & 08.00–12.30 Sat/Sun; adult/child R$5/free; book ahead*) Another of the city's grand old mansion houses whose stately, high-ceilinged rooms preserve a dusty collection of 400 years of furniture from Portuguese to Republican times, together with Catholic miscellany and documents related to the history of the town. The dark mark on the walls near the staircase at the entrance shows where the waters of the Paraguaçu reached during the 1989 flood.

Igreja da Ordem Terceira do Carmo (*Praça da Aclamação s/n, Cachoeira;* ⏲ *09.00–12.00 & 14.00–17.00 Tue–Sat, 09.00–12.00 Sun; adult/child R$3/free*) The grandest religious complex in the city was built when Cachoeira and São Felix were at the zenith of their powers in the early 18th century. The church's façade is covered with Rococo flourishes as elaborate as a wedding cake – from the florid pediment to the ornate window boxes. The interior is no less elaborate, with galleries of *azulejos* and a lavish Baroque altar. The effigies of Christ dripping with blood are from Macao and the faces which were probably carved by Chinese artisans show marked oriental features.

Igreja Matriz de Nossa Senhora do Rosário (*Rua Ana Nery s/n, Cachoeira;* ⏲ *09.00–12.00 & 14.00–17.00 Tue–Sat, 09.00–12.00 Sun; free*) Whilst there have been chapels in Cachoeira since the 1500s, the city's first grand church was not built until 1698. The interior is lined with some of the finest *azulejos* in Bahia – stretching 5m towards the ceiling of the nave – painted in Lisbon and shipped to Bahia as balast. And the ceiling painting is attributed to one of the most important artists of the Bahian school, **José Teófilo de Jesus**. Teófilo de Jesus was a freed slave and José Joaquim da Rocha's star pupil, learning his craft assisting with the painting and gilding of secondary figures of ceilings and panels in Salvador's Baroque churches. Aided by da Rocha, he became one of the first black Brazilian artists to train in Europe, studying in Portugal from 1794 at the Academia do Desenho in Lisbon with the painter Pedro Alexandrino de Carvalho. After his return to Brazil he painted panels in the Igreja da Ordem Terceira de São Francisco in Salvador and the ceilings of the naves of the Igrejas da Ordem Terceira de Nossa Senhora do Carmo as well as the magnificent ceiling of Nossa Senhora do Rosário. The church's upstairs museum contains religious artefacts from the Convento de São Francisco do Paraguaçu.

Igreja de Nossa Senhora da Ajuda (*Largo da Ajuda s/n, Cachoeira;* ⏲ *09.00–12.00 & 14.00–17.00 Tue–Sat, 09.00–12.00 Sun; free*) This is the city's oldest church, constructed as a simple (if fortified) adobe and stone chapel in 1595 when Cachoeira was beginning its transformation from remote *engenho* to sugar port town. Despite the official opening hours, it's often closed to visitors.

Santa Casa de Misericórdia (*Praça Doutor Milton s/n;* ⏲ *09.00–12.00 & 14.00–17.00 Tue–Sat, 09.00–12.00 Sun; free*) This also dates from the city's golden period (it was built in 1734), when it served as the colonial hospital.

Museu da Boa Morte (*Rua 13 de Maio s/n, Cachoeira;* ⏲ *10.00–18.00 Mon–Sun; free*) This society of African-Brazilian women has strong roots in Candomblé and originally started as a slave sisterhood that publicised ritual events on the sly and served as a point of contact for the slave community. Their museum is a sacred Candomblé terreiro with a small chapel with *orixá* effigies inside. There are usually sisters hanging around and happy to converse, if you speak Portuguese.

Ponte Ferroviaria (*Rio Paraguaçu*) This iconic 300m railway and passenger bridge was built by the British in the 19th century to link the two towns over the muddy Rio Paraguaçu to São Felix.

Fundação Hansen Bahia (*Rua 13 de Maio, São Felix;* \ *075 3425 1453;* ☉ *09.00–17.00 Tue–Fri, 09.00–14.00 Sat/Sun; adult/child R$5/free*) This houses a collection of powerful engravings by the German artist Karl Meinz Hansen, who was born in Hamburg and lived in Salvador in the 1950s. His xylographs bring a European eye to the lives of everyday Baianos that contrast sharply with the jolly, carefree stereotype proffered by writers like Jorge Amado. The beggars and downtrodden women who prostituted themselves for pennies are almost Dostoyevskian in their portrayal of both destitution and transcendence through suffering. The museum is housed in the former home of Ana Néry – the Florence Nightingale of Brazil who nursed Brazilians in the Paraguayan War.

Fabrica Danneman (*Av Salvador Pinto 29, São Felix;* ☉ *08.30–12.00 & 13.00–16.30 Mon–Fri; free admission*) A large warehouse showcasing contemporary Bahian art where Baianos dressed in green satin dresses hand-roll what are said to be Brazil's best cigars, which can be purchased at knock-down prices in the factory shop.

Igreja de Nossa Senhora de Belém (*8km from Cachoeira, just off the road to Conceição de Feira*) The flying priest, Father Bartolomeu Lourenço de Gusmão, attempted some of the world's first aviation experiments at this pretty Baroque church overlooking the Rio Paraguaçu in the first decades of the 18th century. The church is closed and falling down nowadays, but it's worth coming here for the beautiful views and swimming off the little river beach on the banks of the Paraguaçu.

MARAGOJIPE AND THE BAÍA DO IGUAPE

There's little to this tiny colonial town at the junction of the Paraguaçu and Guaí rivers – just a scattering of rather undistinguished colonial churches and buildings and a few streets of pre-20th-century painted worker's houses. But it sits in some of the most impressive landscapes of the Recôncavo.

GETTING THERE Maragojipe is 131km from Salvador. Buses run from Salvador and Cachoeira to Maragojipe.

 WHERE TO STAY AND EAT There are only a few very simple hotels and restaurants in Maragojipe.

⌂ **Hotel Flor de Liz** (12 rooms) Rua Doutor Rodrigues Lima 55, Centro; \ 75 3526 2193. A very simple town hotel within easy walking distance of the Paraguasçu River & with plain fan & AC rooms. B/fast included. $$–$

OTHER PRACTICALITIES There is a Banco do Brasil (*Avenida Maragojipe s/n;* \ *075 3526 1010*) but it will not take international cards or change travellers cheques. The nearest international ATM is in Cachoeira.

WHAT TO SEE AND DO The **Rio Paraguaçu** The only reasons to come to Maragojipe are the scenery in general and the River Paraguaçu in particular. Where the latter meets the Guaí it forms a bay within the Baía de Todos os Santos – a long sleeve of shimmering blue water lined with mangrove wetlands known as the Baía do Iguape. A long day's kayaking or touring the bay's uninhabited islands, beaches and backwaters by fishing launch is a delight. There's a moss- and bromeliad-covered ruin at every turn – from the imposing Convento dos Franciscanos do Paraguaçu (which must have been almost as impressive as the Baroque churches of Salvador in its heyday and which now sits like a Brazilian Fountains Abbey between the river and a lush rainforest-swathed hill) to the jungle-covered, dripping ruins of the grand *fazenda* and *engenho novo*. Boats and drivers can be hired at the quay in Maragojipe for around R$80/hour.

5

Costa do Dendê and the Costa do Cacau

Before the arrival of tourism and the boutique beach resort, the Bahian coast between the Recôncavo and distant Porto Seguro was one of the wildest and most romantically beautiful stretches of beach in the tropical Americas. Long strands of silky sand were deserted but for tiny fishing hamlets, broken bays and the mouths of dozens of winding rivers. They were watched over by ruined mansions; overgrown with lianas and sitting in untidy groves of plantation trees, whose crop gave the coast its name – dendê brought from Ghana and planted for palm oil in the north of the region, around **Valença**, and the native cacau or chocolate tree, farmed around the city of Ilhéus. And offshore the coast fragmented into myriad, mangrove-lined islands populated more by little blue herons and ringed kingfishers than people. Then in the 1970s Brazilians from São Paulo discovered the surf beaches at **Itacaré** to the north of the region's main city, **Ilhéus**, and the lonely palm-fringed beauty of the islands off the coast of Valença at **Morro de São Paulo**, and fishing villages swiftly turned into resort towns and roads grew and were coated with asphalt. And in the 1990s the world began to notice the Costa do Dendê and Cacau. Europeans bought up the land by the hectare but much of it lies fallow, awaiting the hotel boom that has infected so much of southeast Asia, but which may never come to Bahia. For now there are still many silent stretches and hidden bays on the Costa do Dendê and Cacau, and whilst the foreign-owned rapacious resorts on Morro de São Paulo have begun the inevitable process of de-characterisation and environmental destruction that heralds decay, there are still many places where tourists can directly spend their money and make a real difference to the livelihoods of local people who would otherwise struggle to make ends meet.

VALENÇA *Telephone code: 75*

This hot and sweaty fishing town on the banks of the River Una is the largest settlement on the Costa do Dendê, though it is seldom visited by tourists except in transit to Morro de São Paulo. There's little reason to stop except to visit the boatyard where they still build traditional *saveiro* fishing boats or wander through the streets, which have a smattering of colonial architecture. There are some beautiful beaches nearby where there is very little tourism and even less infrastructure.

GETTING THERE

By road Valença is well connected to Salvador via Bom Despacho on the Ilha de Itaparica, with at least one bus an hour from 05.00 to 21.00 daily. The journey takes two hours. The bus station is 10km from the city centre.

By sea Ferries leave from Bom Despacho for Salvador (see page 142). There are daily services to Porto Seguro (nine hours), thrice-daily services to Ilhéus (five

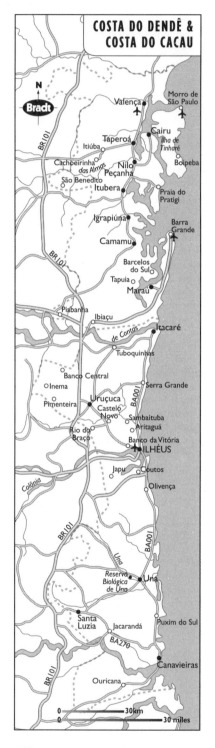

**COSTA DO DENDÊ &
COSTA DO CACAU**

hours) and hourly buses to Camamu (90 minutes). Boats leave for Morro de São Paulo at least every hour (and every half-hour in high season), from 06.30 until 17.00 daily, taking 35–90 minutes to make the journey depending on the class of boat.

By air There are flights between Valença and Salvador on air taxi only. The airport is 15km from the city centre.

Tourist information and practicalities
The town no longer has a tourist office. A Bradesco bank at Rua Governador Gonçalves 178 (◊ *3641 3821*) has a Visa ATM.

WHERE TO STAY AND EAT
⌂ **Aguas do Guaibim** (10 rooms) Av Taquari, Guaibim beach (18km from Valença city centre); ◊ 3646 1047; www.aguasdoguaibim.com. A series of tiled AC apts in a rather ugly long block overlooking the beach. Facilities include a sauna, swimming pool & football pitch. Very popular with families. $$$$

⌂ **Recanto Brasilissimo** (6 rooms) Av Taquari, Guaibim beach (18km from Valença city centre); ◊ 3646 1136; www.recanto-brasilissimo.com. A lovely little beachfront pousada with chalets gathered around a pool in a palm-shaded, lawned tropical garden. The hotel organises a range of light adventure activities including horseriding, sailing & mountain biking as well as tours of the region. $$$

⌂ **Gaivota Praia** (19 rooms) Av Taquari, Guaibim beach (18km from Valença city centre); ◊ 3646 1206; www.gaivotapraia.com.br. A standard motel-like Brazilian hotel in a concrete block 5mins' walk from the beach. Rooms make more than the usual concessions to aestheticism — with exposed brick walls, cream & ochre paint & terracotta amphorae in the little space between the room & bathroom. $$–$$$

⌂ **Hotel Valença** (15 rooms) Rua Doutor Guedes 15; ◊ 3641 3807. A basic blocky hotel in the centre of Valença, offering very simple fan-cooled or AC rooms with little more than a bed, TV & wardrobe. $

WHAT TO SEE There are good views out over the city from the hilltop colonial church of **Nossa Senhora do Amparo** (*off Rua do Pitanga;* ⊕ *usually 08.00–12.00 & 14.00–18.00 daily*) with the sluggish river behind. There are **beaches** some 15km outside town. **Praia de Guaibim** is the most frequented and is especially busy on weekends. Buses run from the old rodoviária in the town centre near the Praça da Independencia. The beaches get less busy the further north you go – from **Praia de Taquari** to **Barra do Jiquiriçá** at the mouth of the river of the same name, where there is no accommodation.

MORRO DE SÃO PAULO AND BOIPEBA Telephone code: 75

Offshore of Valença, the Bahian coast fragments into a series of 36 broken islands divided by the organic bends and swirls of muddy rivers and mangrove swamps and fringed, on the Atlantic seaboard, with a succession of long, white pepper-fine beaches. Taken together the bays, beaches and inlets are known as the islands of Tinharé (in the north), Cairu (in the west) and Boipeba (in the south). Most visitors come to stay in **Morro de São Paulo** – a tourist village at the northern tip of Tinharé which has become so popular that it has lent the Tinharé and the region as a whole its name. Like many of the Bahian resort towns, Morro was a remote fishing village, perched on the first of many beautiful beaches below a colonial fort and a huddle of Portuguese buildings, which became a hippie enclave in the 1970s and then a refuge for Paulistanos on vacation from university in the 1980s. It was discovered by Italians in the 1980s, the rest of the outside world at the turn of the millennium and shortly after by Spanish property developers who have yet to turn it into another Ibiza. Whilst Morro's tourism remains low-scale by Thai or Spanish standards, it can still feel very crowded in high season and is one of the few places in Bahia where foreigners are beginning to outnumber Brazilians. Despite a tourist tax levied on every visitor when they arrive at the town pier or airport, the surrounding Atlantic coastal forests, pearly beaches and the local people are beginning to become compromised by unsustainable development.

Boipeba island, which lies some 25km south of Morro town across the Rio do Inferno, promises a quieter alternative. Together with much of Tinharé and

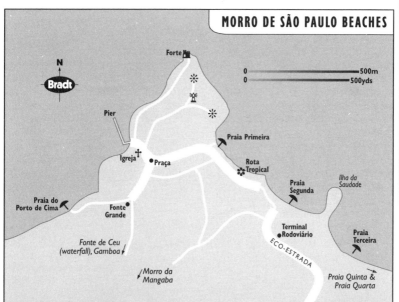

MORRO DE SÃO PAULO BEACHES

5

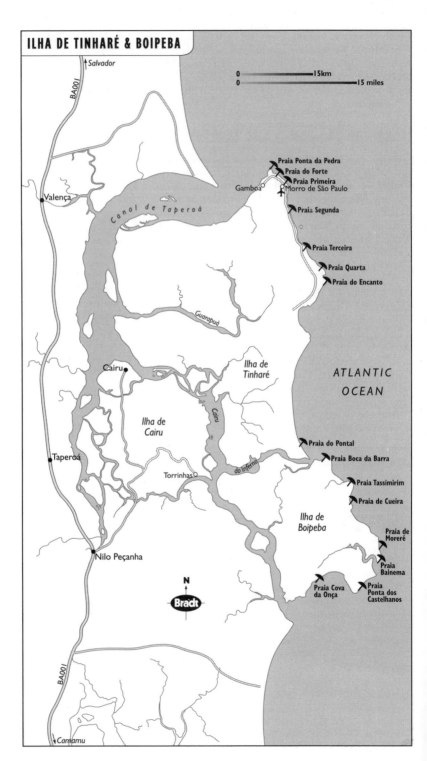

ILHA DE TINHARÉ & BOIPEBA

↑Salvador

0 ————— 15km
0 ————— 15 miles

BA001

Valença

Canal de Taperoá

Guarapuá

Cairu

Ilha de
Cairu

Ilha de
Tinharé

ATLANTIC
OCEAN

Gamboa

Praia Ponta da Pedra
Praia do Forte
Praia Primeira
Morro de São Paulo

Praia Segunda

Praia Terceira

Praia Quarta

Praia do Encanto

Taperoá

Torrinhas

Cairu

do Inferno

Praia do Pontal

Praia Boca da Barra

Praia Tassimirim

Praia de Cueira

Ilha de
Boipeba

Praia de
Moreré

Praia
Bainema

Nilo Peçanha

N

Bradt

Praia Cova
da Onça

Praia
Ponta dos
Castelhanos

BA001

↓Camamu

160

neighbouring **Cairu** island (which has no beaches and only mangrove), it is theoretically protected as an Environmental Protection Area (Área de Proteção Ambiental – APA Ilhas de Tinharé/Boipeba), created under Bahian state law 1240 in June 1992 to protect 43,300ha of as yet unspoilt forests, reefs and beaches. But what has saved Boipeba so far is not the unmonitored and un-policed paper park but the local people who have formed an association to conserve both the environment and their low-key way of life. There are two places to stay on Boipeba – **Boipeba village** in the north of the island, where boats and tractors from Morro de São Paulo arrive, and the fishing village of **Moreré** 90 minutes walk to the south.

GETTING THERE

By air There are three direct 20-minute flights daily from Salvador airport to the little airstrip behind Morro's third beach, operated by **Addey** (✆ *3652 1242; www.addey.com.br*) and **Aerostar** (✆ *3652 1312; www.aerostar.com.br*) and costing around R$225 one-way. See www.morrodesaopaulo.com.br for the latest flight timetables.

By sea Fast catamarans run from Salvador's Mercado Modelo ferry terminal (see page 132), taking around 120 minutes and costing around R$80 one-way. Times vary according to the season and weather but there are usually at least six a day between 08.30 and 14.00 (with the last boat returning from Morro to Salvador at 16.00). See www.morrodesaopaulo.com.br for the latest boat timetables. There are also numerous water taxis, fishing and speedboats running between Valença and Morro and with connections to and from Salvador via Itaparica. There is a port tax of R$10 payable at the prefeitura on arrival at Morro and R$1 on leaving the island. And despite its ostensible raison d'être it seems to do little to protect Morro or sustain the disenfranchised locals, and is resented by many.

GETTING AROUND Five beaches – named prosaically according to number (Primeira, Segunda, Terceira, Quarta and Quinta, sometimes referred to as Encanto – run south from Morro town over a distance of around 15km. They all but disappear at high tide. The town itself is very small and is easily negotiated **on foot**. At a steady pace, a walk from the town to each beach up until Quarta takes a successive ten minutes (with the Quarta taking between around 40 and 60 minutes and accessible at low tide). Quinta is separated from the others by a cape and takes around 90–120 minutes to reach. Bring a sun hat for the walk.

Until 2008 all roads were unpaved sand or dirt tracks but there is now a partially paved section between the town and the beaches, and this is covered by regular *combis*, **motorbikes** and **beach buggies**. These leave from the Receptivo – a café/restaurant marking the beginning of the road just behind the end of the second and beginning of the third beaches.

Old Toyota *bandeirante* **jeeps** or **tractors** leave Morro at 09.30 daily for Boipeba. They are easily bookable through even the simplest hostel or the plague of little tour agencies on the island. These also offer **boat trips** with optional snorkelling for around R$70. Most of these go in a clockwise direction around Tinharé, visiting Boipeba town and the villages to its south (including Moreré), the offshore reef pools for snorkelling and the mangroves and tiny colonial town of Cairu on the Ilha de Cairu southwest of southern Tinharé.

TOURIST INFORMATION AND LOCAL TOUR OPERATORS

Ⓩ Centro de Informações ao Turista (CIT) Praça Aureliano Lima s/n; ✆ 3652 1083; www.morrosp.com.br.

Tours can be organised through any of the hotels or through one of the many tour agencies along the main street in Morro town.

WHERE TO STAY IN MORRO DE SÃO PAULO Unless there is no alternative in the price bracket, we have tried to promote hotels which are either locally (or at least Brazilian) owned, or which make some attempt at best practice. But as ever in Bahia, genuine ecotourism (see box on page 101) is difficult to find. There are clusters of cheap rooms in Morro town – especially around Fonte Grande (near the main praça) – but as there are few trees the area is hot even at night. Morro's beaches become quieter and less developed the further you go from town. Quinta beach is less developed even than Boipeba. Primeira and Segunda beaches are raucous in high season, pulsating with bars and makeshift discos by night and bustling with beach volleyball and bikinis by day. There is only one way out of town – by foot. Morro's high street becomes a path as it runs south. Turning right as it finishes will take you to the beaches. Wheelbarrow-wielding porters can be hired to cart luggage to a hotel on one of the first three beaches or to the Receptivo café/restaurant for a ride to Quarta or Quinta beach.

The website www.morro.travel lists most of the hotels on the island – including those that don't have their own sites. Information is in Portuguese but the site is easy to navigate.

Vila dos Orixás (10 bungalows) Quinta Praia, in the south; 3652 2055; www.hotelviladosorixas.com. The most expensive & upmarket hotel on the Island do Encanto is priced similarly to far superior hotels in Trancoso, but it sits in an enviable location, in a lawned palm-tree garden with a deep blue 25m-long pool on the quietest beach. Rooms are spacious faux-Asian beach palm-thatched concrete cabins with wood deck floors & verandas. The hotel restaurant-bar serves decent seafood & cold *caipirinhas*; a good thing as anywhere else is a 10–15min *combi* ride away & transport has to be booked. Popular with the Spanish. $$$$–$$$$$

Pousada da Torre (24 rooms) Segunda Praia; 3652 1038; www.pousadadatorre.com.br. A Brazilian-owned family boutique hotel right on the beach with a small palm-shaded pool & rooms decked out in jaqueira wood & raw stone. The best (on the top floor) have balconies with sea views. Those in the back annexe are plainer, hotter (with AC for cooling instead of Morro's wonderful sea breeze) but are well appointed with king-sized beds & warm wood walls. $$$$

Farol do Morro Primeira Praia; 3652 1036; www.faroldomorro.com.br. A charming little Bahian-owned pousada with a tiny infinity pool & a series of cabins spread up a steep hill, gathered around a lighthouse & reached by a miniature funicular railway. $$$–$$$$

Catavento Praia Hotel (20 rooms) Quarta Praia; 3652 1052; www.cataventopraiahotel.com.br. Large & vaguely mock-colonial-era tile & whitewash rooms in bungalows gathered around a large, sculpted pool in a shady garden. The hotel restaurant serves decent food, including a sumptuous *moqueca*. $$$

Fazenda Vila Guaiamú (22 rooms) Terceira Praia; 3652 1035; www.vilaguaiamu.com.br. Seven pretty little cabins in a large garden which backs onto a little forest reserve. The Italian owners support an ecotourism project which protects the guaiamú – a species of crab, which depend on Morro's extant original mangrove forests for their survival & which are therefore an important indicator species for the island's natural welfare. Guaiamú live in the river which runs through the hotel. Guided rainforest walks available. The simple restaurants serve perhaps the best food of any hotel restaurant on the island. Great massages available. $$$

Vistabella (14 rooms) Primeira Praia; 3652 1001; www.vistabelapousada.com. The hotel lives up to its name, with wonderful sea views from the best of a range of cosy, fan-cooled rooms. Opt for those at the front of the pousada – which come with hammocks for whiling away the hottest part of the day in the shade. $$$

Agua Viva (15 rooms) Terceira Praia; 3652 1217; www.pousadaaguavivamorro.com.br. A simple pousada owned by local fishermen offering tile & whitewash rooms decorated with art painted by the owners. The best sit at the front of the building & have small verandas. $$

Grauça (15 rooms) Terceira Praia; 3652 1099; www.pousadagrauca.com.br. A range of modest but well-maintained AC & fan-cooled rooms with concrete cabins 5mins from the beach. $$

Ilha do Sol (20 rooms) Primeira Praia; 8871 1295; www.pousadailhadosol.com. A big concrete block perched on the hillside on the edge of town & with very simple whitewash & tile rooms, 15 of which have some of the loveliest sea views on Primeira beach. The owners are friendly & the b/fast one of Morro's more generous. $$

🏠 **Hostel Morro de São Paulo** (10 rooms) Rua Fonte Grande at the end of Beco dos Pássaros; ☎ 3652 1521; www.hosteldomorro.com.br. An airy, well-kept, backpacker-packed little hostel on the outskirts of the town on the pathway leading to the spring. Rooms & dorms overlook a small garden & public spaces are strewn with hammocks. But you can find AC options for a lower price than the most basic fan-cooled rooms in the hostel at the locally owned guesthouses listed below & on the www.morro.travel website. $–$$

🏠 **Tia Lita** (10 rooms) Terceira Praia; ☎ 3652 1532; www.morro.travel/turismo/pousada_tia_lita.htm. A locally owned, very friendly guesthouse offering very simple AC tiled rooms with TVs & fridges. The restaurant serves very good *moquecas*. $–$$

🏠 **Coqueiro Do Caitá** (26 rooms) Terceira Praia; ☎ 3652 1194; www.coqueirodocaita.com. A little guesthouse tucked away down a leafy alleyway at the back of the beach. AC rooms are simple & basically appointed but come with Brazilian TVs & fridges & the suites even have a jacuzzi. The guesthouse has a tiny pool. $

🏠 **Grauçá** (16 rooms) Terceira Praia; ☎ 3652 1099. A bright red 3-storey house with boxy but bright AC rooms, some with balconies & a sea view. The owners are local evangelical Christians. $

🏠 **Pousada Tia Preta** (9 rooms) Rua da Fonte Grande 144; ☎ 8129 2061. A very basic little guesthouse in an arcade of shops with some of the cheapest rooms in southern Bahia. But even at this price the rooms are AC, if otherwise pretty airless, have fridges & come with b/fast included. The owner Tia Preta herself is friendly & welcoming. $

🏠 **Timbalada** (13 rooms) Segunda Praia; ☎ 3652 1366. A bright guesthouse close to the party scene but sufficiently far down an alley to be quiet(ish). Rooms are simple little boxes, good for dumping a bag, but the guesthouse serves a generous b/fast. $

✕ **WHERE TO EAT IN MORRO DE SÃO PAULO** Morro de São Paulo town is packed with restaurants, from Bahian establishments serving *moquecas* to pizzerias & per-kilo places. Many are overpriced. The cheapest options are the *barraca* grills & *acarajé* vendors who ply the beaches, profferring their wares principally on Segunda Praia. Look out for Pulcinella here – where an ever smiling Luciana serves delicious *beiju de tapioca*, juices, coffee and snacks.

✕ **Sabor da Terra** Rua Caminho da Praia; ☎ 3652 1156. A good-value lunchtime per-kilo & à la carte evening restaurant with regional-cooking seafood. $$

✕ **Tia Dadai** Praça Aureliano Oliveira Lima; ☎ 3652 1621. A great little family restaurant overlooking the main praça in town & selling delicious *casquinha de siri* (baked crab in its shell) & *badejo a Portuguesa* (fillet of bream in tomato & onion sauce). $$

✕ **Tinharé** Down a little set of steps off Rua Caminho de Praia. Some of the best Bahian & seafood cooking in Morro. Try the *peixe escabeche* – fresh fish cooked in coconut milk & served in a sizzling cast-iron pot. The portions are big enough for 2 or even 3. $$

🏠 **WHERE TO STAY AND EAT IN BOIPEBA** Boipeba (http://ilhaboipeba.org.br) is far quieter than Morro and isn't a good place for those looking for a party – or for air-conditioned rooms. Rooms in Boipeba are simple, but they are often elegant and almost no matter where you are on the island – even in pocket-sized Boipeba town – you can fall asleep to the sound of the sea and the light of the moon. Accommodation and restaurants are split between Boipeba town, where all but the day-tour transport from Morro arrives; its next door beach, the Boca da Barra; and the fishing village of Moreré, a half-hour boat ride or 90–120 minutes' walk (high tide only) to the south. Details on accommodation (with pictures of the hotels) and other tourist concerns can be found in English on the island's website. Restaurants are simple beans, rice and fish/chicken/beef affairs unless indicated below.

🏠 **Pousada Tassimirim** (15 rooms) At the far end of Boca da Barra beach, 15mins' walk from the village; ☎ 3653 6030. A delightful pousada with mock-colonial, terracotta-roofed cabins & rooms in a garden filled with flowering trees. The hotel has its own restaurant & pool; & a lovely sundeck overlooking the beach. The price includes b/fast & dinner. The hotel can organise transfers from Salvador. $$$

Santa Clara (7 rooms) Boca da Barra beach; 3653 6085; www.santaclaraboipeba.com. Two brothers from California's Bay Area offer a range of large, tastefully decorated duplex bungalows 3mins' walk from the beach, together with the best restaurant on the island & great therapeutic massages. $$$

Vila Sereia (8 rooms) Boca da Barra beach; 3635 6045. Elegant shutter-board duplex bungalows sitting in the sand with a cosy upstairs cabin (which is great for kids) & a larger bedroom below leading to an open-air (but privately screened) shower. $$$

Colibri (4 rooms) Moreré; 9981 2286. A handful of very simple bungalows in a lush & semi-wild tropical beach garden 5mins from the sea & on the edge of Moreré village. $$–$$$

Dos Ventos (7 rooms) Praia do Moreré town; 3653 8913. Rustic chic cabins with whitewash walls, colourful counterpanes & palm-thatched roofs. Right on the beach. $$–$$$

Horizonte Azul (10 rooms) Boca da Barra beach; 3653 6080. This friendly guesthouse run by a Brazilian & her French partner has a range of bungalows in a large sloping garden visited by hummingbirds & tufted-eared marmosets in the late afternoon & with great views out to sea. $$–$$$

Sete (3 rooms) Praça Santo Antônio, Boipeba village; 3653 6135. Pretty much the cheapest option in the main village, with small but very well-maintained AC tile floor & whitewash rooms decorated with floral prints & a popular restaurant offering Brazilian & Bahian staples. $–$$

OTHER PRACTICALITIES There is a Bradesco cashpoint in Morro town, but no banks or money changing facilities in Boipeba.

WHAT TO SEE AND DO People come to Morro to do little but party, or just relax. And but for walking and sunbathing on beaches, snorkelling and sipping a caipirinha there is indeed little to do. For views, climb the hill on Morro to the lighthouse, from where you can look out over coconut palms and the first three of the island's beaches. The rocky hill which gives Morro de São Paulo its name was the site of a Portuguese fort (dating from 1630) which is now largely a ruin. Tourists arriving by boat from Salvador pass through the stone arch which was once the fort's main gateway. The battlements are barely visible, perched above on the rocky crags. The path from the pier fans into a series of tiny streets that branch off to a small colonial praça with a little church. Another path runs north to the lighthouse and a ruined lookout with a cannon and panoramic views. A trail runs from here inland to the Fonte de Ceu waterfall via Gamboa village. It is best to take a guide from Gamboa and it is possible to return to Morro from Gamboa by boat. On 7 September there is a big fiesta with live music on the beach. Tours run around the island visiting offshore swimming pools (those who worry about damaging the coral might use a T-shirt rather than sun protection whilst swimming), beaches, mangroves and Cairu town where there are some colonial remains.

PENINSULA DE MARAÚ AND THE BAÍA DE CAMAMU   *Telephone code: 73*

South of Boipeba the Bahian coast makes a glorious crescent-shaped sweep before fragmenting once more into Brazil's third-largest bay (after Todos os Santos and Guanabara in Rio) – the **Baía de Camamu**. The bay is a filigree of inlets, estuaries and islands nestled in calm, warm water which was once rich in fish, cetaceans and manatees. Its mouth opens to the north – shielded from the broadside of the Atlantic winds and the open sea by a 25km-long finger of scrub forest and sand, the **Peninsula de Maraú**. Long, broad dune-backed and wind-blown continental beaches fringe this peninsula's entire length, and at the northern tip there is one tiny town, **Barra Grande**, with a smattering of concrete and shutterboard hotels. This is connected by passenger boat to the only other town of any touristic note in the area, **Camamu** – a huddle of terracotta roofs around a fine 17th-century church that lies sleepy on a sluggish river amidst mosquitoes and muddy mangroves.

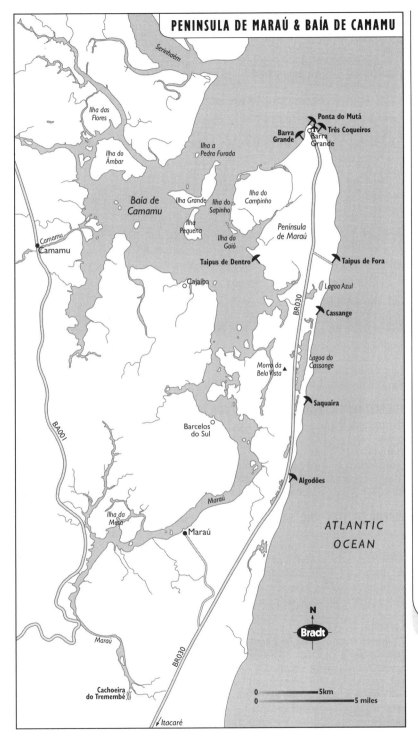

Serinhaém

Ilha das
Flores

Ilha do
Âmbar

Ilha a
Pedra Furada

Ponta do Mutá

Barra
Grande

Três Coqueiros

Barra
Grande

Baía de
Camamu

Ilha Grande

Ilha do
Sapinho

Ilha do
Campinho

Ilha
Pequena

Península
de Maraú

Ilha do
Goió

Camamu

Camamu

Taipus de Dentro

Taipus de Fora

Cajaiba

Logoa Azul

Cassange

Morro da
Bela Vista

Lagoa do
Cassange

BR030

Saquaíra

Barcelos
do Sul

BA001

Algodões

Ilha da
Mesa

Maraú

Maraú

ATLANTIC
OCEAN

Maraú

BR030

N

Bradt

Cachoeira
do Tremembé

Itacaré

| 0 | 5km |
| 0 | 5 miles |

5

GETTING THERE

By boat Twelve slow boats a day run from Camamu to Barra Grande between 06.00 and 17.30 Monday to Saturday, taking 90–120 minutes and costing around R$7 per passsenger. Eleven sail on Sunday. The same number return from Barra Grande and the last return boat is at 17.00. Speedboats (*lanchas rapidas*) leave four times daily between 07.00 and 16.30 and twice daily on Sunday with the last boat at 11.00. They take 30 minutes, cost R$25 and luggage is restricted to 15kg (after which a tax of about R$1/kg is imposed).

By bus Camamu has several daily buses to and from Salvador, Bom Despacho on Itaparica island (for connections to Salvador) and daily buses to Valença and Ilhéus. Buses also run regularly to Itabuna (100km to the south) from where there are connections to these cities and the rest of Bahia – without necessitating travel through Salvador. One bus daily makes the gruelling dirt road trip to Ilhéus (some 120km to the south) via Itacaré.

By plane Barra Grande has charter flights sporadically to Salvador via Morro de São Paulo with Aerostar (*3377 4406; www.aerostar.com.br*), which run according to demand and season. Check the website or ring the company for the latest information.

GETTING AROUND Camamu is easily negotiated on foot; you could crawl across it in half an hour and it's hard to get lost – the river and church of Nossa Senhora de Assunção on the hill are omnipresent reference points. It would be easier to get lost in your own house than in Barra Grande – the town barely has a street. Tractors and Toyotas leave from the junction of two sand trails in the centre of Barra Grande (known locally as the Praça Principal) – when full – for the various beaches along the Peninsula de Maraú.

TOURIST INFORMATION AND LOCAL TOUR OPERATORS There are excellent two–five-day tours of the Baía de Camamu and the peninsula with Ilhéus-based tour operator Orbita (see page 175). Jeeps leave from that city or Itacaré – or the company can meet you in Barra Grande or Camamu – given warning and a down payment. For further information on Camamu and its environs (in English) see www.camamu.net. There are plenty of pousadas in Barra; see www.portaldemarau.com.br and www.barragrande.net for a list beyond our recommendations.

WHERE TO STAY AND EAT There are a number of cheap and cheerful seafood restaurants and cafés in both Barra Grande and Camamu, but nothing that deserves special recommendation.

Beach hotels on Maraú are not good value – their expense justified by the location far more than the quality of the hotels themselves. If you want beach chic and are prepared to pay for it, head south to Trancoso. For the best value on the peninsula stay in Barra and walk to the beach. Or camp.

Camamu

 Hotel Rio Acaraí (22 rooms) Praça Dr Francisco Xavier, Camamu; *255 2315; www.hotelrioacarai.com.br. A hotel sitting on a pretty bluff by a bend in the river with corridors of small plain rooms (with little in but twin beds, a TV & writing desk) overlooking a small pool & the bay beyond. Decent b/fast & internet. $$–$$$

Pousada Costa do Dendê (14 rooms) Rua Djalma Dutra 22, Camamu; *3255 1624; www.pousadacostadodende.com.br. Plain AC peach & orange cubes near the waterfront, internet access, a generous b/fast & helpful staff who can organise boat trips throughout the bay & transfers to Barra Grande. $$

🏠 **Green House** (10 rooms) Av Djalma Dutra 61, Cidade Baixa, Camamu; 📞 3255 2178. A very basic

Peninsula de Maraú

🏠 **Kiaroa** (28 rooms) Praia de Bombaça; 📞 3258 6213; www.kiaroa.com.br. The most luxurious accommodation on the peninsula, with a variety of well-appointed rooms, the best of which are the bungalows – those in the annexe can feel rather crowded together. The resort has a spa, tour & beach activities & the best restaurant in Maraú, decent enough for seafood. But there is little competition elsewhere. $$$$$

🏠 **Taipu de Fora** (24 rooms) Praia Taipu de Fora; 📞 3258 6278; www.taipudefora.com.br. Intimate low-key hotel aimed at couples. The situation is beautiful, but bungalows close to the beach are expensive for what you get – simply if elegantly decorated (with raw cotton counterpanes & floral prints offsetting plain walls & tiled floors). A range of outdoor activities including diving, horseriding & kayaking. $$$$$

🏠 **Lagoa do Cassange** (15 rooms) Praia do Cassange; 📞 3255 2348; www.maris.com.br. A small-scale beach resort popular with families, who often opt to stay in the larger beach house rather than the smaller chalets. The price includes dinner. $$$$

but friendly pousada in the centre of town next to the rodoviaria with b/fast & a small restaurant. $

🏠 **El Capitan** (20 rooms) Av Vasco Neto s/n, Barra town; 📞 3258 6078; www.elcapitan.com.br. Basic cabins in tile & concrete, topped by terracotta-tile roofs & with hammock-slung terraces. These are clustered around a pool in a small-lawned & palm-shaded garden decorated with rusting anchors. The pousada is at the mainland end of the town, 200m from the pier. $$–$$$

🏠 **Porto da Barra** (12 apts) R Beira Mar, Barra town; 📞 3258 6349; www.pousadaportodabarra.com. A beachside guesthouse, each apt with 2 long corridors of plain concrete AC rooms. Those on the upper floor have partial sea views & the friendly owner serves a generous b/fast of fruit, pastries, rolls, juice & coffee. $$–$$$

🏠 **Meu Sossego** (19 rooms) R Dr Chiquinho 17, Barra town; 📞 258 6012; www.meusossego.com. Plain AC rooms with a bed, desk, fridge & little else, a stroll from the beach. $$

⛺ **Camping Cantinho da Ivete** Caminho para praia, Barra Grande; http://cantinhodaivete.blogspot.com. Crusty wooden bungalows & a little lawn with space for tents, including a little shade. $

OTHER PRACTICALITIES There are no banks in Camamu or Barra Grande.

WHAT TO SEE

Islands Aside from the bobbing fishing boats in the harbour at Camamu and the adjacent boatyard (where shipwrights still build *saveiro* yachts), the attractions in the Baía de Camamu and along the Peninsula de Maraú are all natural. The bay is dotted with islands, many of which can be visited, and all of which are washed by far cleaner waters than those to the north in the Baía de Todos os Santos. Boats to all the islands can be chartered at the port in Camamu for about R$150 an hour, tours operate in high season and bespoke itineraries can be organised through Orbita (see page 175). **Ilha Grande**, or big island, lies 10km upstream of Camamu and is fringed by glorious beaches. The rocky **Ilha da Pedra Furada** – named after twin limestone arches which cut through part of the island – lies 12km offshore of Camamu and is also fringed with pretty beaches, whilst the **Ilha de Quiepe**, which is 4km from Barra Grande, has the finest beach of all – a long spit of fine white sand next to a shallow coral bay. The island is privately owned and can only be visited with prior permission through an organised tour.

Waterfalls The **Cachoeira do Tremembé** waterfall is one of two in the Baía de Camamu (and only a few in South America) that plunge directly into the sea. It sits in a small patch of Atlantic coastal forest at the mouth of the Rio Baiano near the tiny village of Tremembé (which lies off the BR-030 highway and is served by infrequent buses from Ubaitaba on the BR-101 federal highway). The other waterfall is the **Cachoeira da Pancada Grande** at the opposite northern end of the bay, which has a similar setting near the tiny village of Itajaí (*combis* or taxis from Igrapíuna town which is itself reachable from Camamu). Alternatively the waterfalls can be visited on an organised tour with Orbita or on a chartered boat from Camamu town.

Beaches There are beaches throughout the bay, with the best being towards the northern end near the mouth. **Praia de Tubarão** sits opposite the Ilha da Pedra Furada and the long, dune-swept **Praia da Boca da Lagoa** at the northern head of the bay. Both are readily reachable by boat only. But the best beaches are on the Peninsula de Maraú, around Barra Grande. The entire ocean-side of the peninsula is in reality one long, broad beach – all the way to the Rio de Contas some 45km to the south near Itacaré, though it has a series of different names. **Praia de Três Coqueiros** is the closest to Barra Grande village where the bay mouth meets the sea. It has coarse sand and strong waves and lies a kilometre southeast of town. **Praia de Bombaça** is a better beach a further 3km south, with calmer waters, broken by offshore reef and little rock pools at low tide. **Taipu de Fora** with swimming pool-sized rock pools lies beyond this beach some 500m out at low tide. There are pousadas and shady palms on all these beaches.

The coast gets wilder south of Taipu de Fora – **Cassange** (5km from Taipu de Fora and with talcum powder-fluffy sand), **Saquaíra** (8km beyond, with some good surf) and **Arandis** (4km from Saquaíra, with large rock pools) are almost deserted. The final beach **Algodões** (1km from Arandis) runs long and broad some 20km to the mouth of the Rio de Contas where a raft-ferry crosses the river to Itacaré (see below). There are beaches on the bay-side too – notably **Praia de Barra Grande** (2km from the town, with a little fishing village and calm waters), **Campinho** (with bobbing yachts, a few simple pousadas and restaurants and a jetty reached by boats from Camamu) and **Praia da Ilha do Goió** (a gorgeous spit of sand on a tiny island a few hundred metres offshore). All of the bay beaches can be reached by tour or by boat from either Camamu or Barra Grande.

ITACARÉ *Telephone code: 73*

Itacaré was a fishing village with *saveiros* and wooden boats bobbing up and down on the Rio de Contas until the 1980s. It had changed little in a century. Then surfers began to arrive, drawn by a series of pretty rainforest-backed coves with pounding breaks. And slowly the town grew into one of Bahia's first surf resorts. Today it has spread its wings further; the most secluded beaches to the south of the town have attracted a spate of exclusive spa hotels, of the sort that appear in coffee-table books and articles on beach chic in lifestyle magazines. Itacaré town itself remains rustic – with just a few streets spreading back from the old harbour area next to the river. But like its hotels, Itacaré's handful of restaurants and bars are the best south of Salvador and north of Porto Seguro.

GETTING THERE AND AROUND Itacaré can be reached from Ilhéus (to the south) or Barra Grande to the north. If coming from either the south or Salvador to Ilhéus by plane or bus the former option is the easier.

Itacaré has at least three buses daily to Ilhéus taking 45–60 minutes. The quickest way to get to or from Salvador by bus is via Ubaitaba (3hrs from Itacaré; R$10). There are at least four buses between Ubaitaba and Salvador (6hrs; US$20). Buses leave Itacaré from a bus stand 1km from the centre of town on the road to Ilhéus. There are irregular buses up the dirt road to Barra Grande – a long and uncomfortable three–four-hour trip. But the road is impassable much of the year.

Cars can be hired in town through **Fertur** (*Av Castro Alves 92;* ☏ *3251 3463*). The town is small and easy to negotiate on foot. Taxis and, in high season, *combis* run to the main town beaches, all of which are less than an hour's walk away.

TOURIST INFORMATION AND LOCAL TOUR OPERATORS There is no Itacaré tourist office, but www.itacare.com has plenty of useful information.

Orbitá R Marquês de Paranaguá 270, Ilhéus; ✎ 3234 3250, 9983 6655; www.orbitaexpedicoes.com.br. Offer trips & adventure activities from kayaking to canyoning throughout the Costa do Dendê & Cacau region & can organise transfers to the Chapada Diamantina, Porto Seguro & Salvador & to/from Ilhéus airport.

Nativos Rua Pedro Longo 215, Pituba; ✎ 3251 3503; www.nativositacare.com.br. Organise dive trips, white-water rafting, kayaking, whale watching & light adventure throughout the region & can also organise airport transfers.

WHERE TO STAY Itacaré is a burgeoning resort and, with demand outpacing supply, prices are rising every year and bookings becoming ever more necessary in the mid- and upper-range hotels and beach houses.

Txai (40 bungalows) Praia de Itacarezinho; ✎ 2627 6363; www.txai.com.br. The most self-consciously luxurious resort in the region comprises large thatched bungalows with 4-poster beds & wooden sun decks set in a palm grove on what is effectively a private beach. The spa is one of Brazil's best. As in most luxury hotels in Bahia the staff receive a minute fraction of the room fee & tips are much appreciated. $$$$$

Art Jungle (7 bungalows) ✎ 9944 4700; www.artjungle.org. Seven individually designed tree & stilt houses in a tropical garden 10km from Itacaré on the Rio de Contas. A favourite with international celebrities. $$$$

Villa Ecoporan (51 rooms) Praia da Concha; ✎ 3251 2470; www.villaecoporan.com.br. Between the town & Praia da Concha. Brightly painted, rather ungainly large terracotta-roofed huts overlooking a jewel-like pool (set in a wooden deck) or dotted around a hammock-filled garden. Good Bahian restaurant & live music & dancing in the bar some nights in high season. Big & busy enough to generate its own party. $$$$

Vira Canoa (13 rooms) Praia da Concha; ✎ 3251 2525; www.viracanoa.com.br. Plum-coloured bungalows with all-white interiors, with big beds heavy with quality cotton, plasma-screen TVs & iPod docking stations looking over a pool & garden. Chunky Indonesian furniture in the public areas. Decent seafood in the restaurant & massages. $$$$

Villa Bella (12 rooms) Praia da Concha; ✎ 3251 2985; www.pousadavillabella.com.br. A newly opened beach hotel with large, bright & comfortable modern rooms with wood-panel floors & uncluttered tasteful interiors housed in duplex garden bungalows & sitting in a large lawned garden around a Prussian blue pool. $$$–$$$$

Maria Farinha (16 rooms) Rua Louro Amarelo 240, Conchas do Mar II, Itacaré; ✎ 3251 3515; www.mariafarinhapousada.com.br. Pretty family-run pousada arranged around an *oca*-like circular reception & b/fast area. Rooms are plain, in a 2-storey L-shaped concrete annexe overlooking a little pool. Ten mins' walk to the beach. One of the few establishments with disabled access. $$$

Nainas (5 rooms) Praia da Concha; ✎ 3251 2683; www.nainas.com.br. Brightly painted cabins & rooms with verandas & little decks set in a lush garden a stroll from the beach. The rooms are simple concrete & white floor-tile affairs but are brightened up with colourful bedspreads & bright arts & crafts on the walls. Decent b/fast. Very tranquil. $$$

Sage Point (8 rooms) Praia de Tiririca; ✎ 3251 2030; www.pousadasagepoint.com.br. Individually decorated cosy wooden rooms overlooking the beach & decorated with chunky wooden furniture, beds & surf-chic driftwood arts & crafts. Each cabin has a hammock-strewn terrace. Check the website for pictures before booking as some rooms are smaller than others. The staff speak English & can organise trips, tours & surfboard rental. $$$

Sitio Ilha Verde (9 rooms) Rua Ataide Seubal 234; ✎ 3251 2056; www.ilhaverde.com.br. Unlike so many of the bland resorts in Bahia, bungalow-rooms in this pousada are decorated with artistic flair – bathroom mirrors are set in cracked-tile mosaic, bedrooms are painted in warm peaches & oranges & have matching or complementary bed linen. They sit in a delightful little heliconia & orchid filled garden with a secluded little pool & relaxing lounge areas. Families can opt for the larger *casita*. Great b/fast. $$$

Pousada da Lua (6 bungalows) Praia da Concha; ✎ 3251 2209; www.pousadadalua.com. Simple mock-colonial whitewash & terracotta-tile roof chalets (some of which are large enough for 4 people) in a patch of forest filled with birds & tufted-eared marmosets (which bite if you try to feed them). Great b/fast. $$–$$$

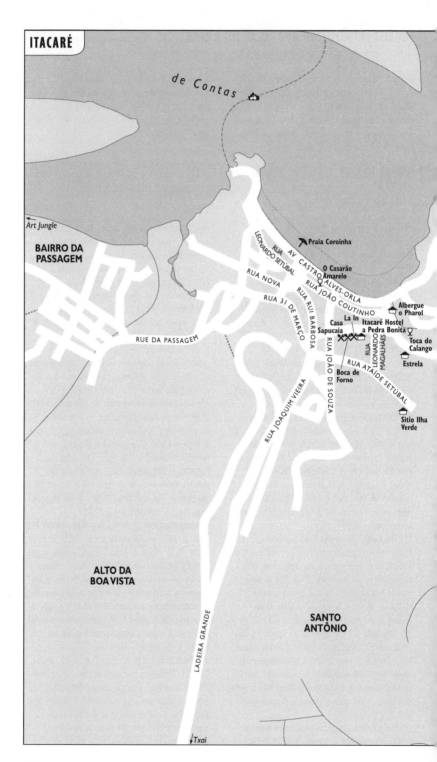

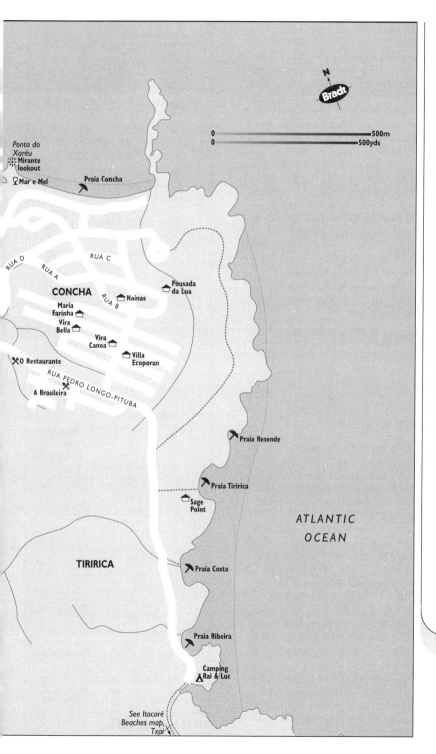

Ponta do
Xaréu
☼ Mirante
lookout
☐ Mar e Mel

Praia Concha

RUA C

RUA D

RUA A

CONCHA

RUA B

☐ Nainas

Pousada
da Lua

Maria
Farinha ☐
Vira
Bella ☐

Vira
Canoa ☐

☐ Villa
Ecoporan

✕ O Restaurante

RUA PEDRO LONGO–PITUBA

✕ A Brasileira

Praia Resende

Praia Tiririca

☐ Sage
Point

ATLANTIC
OCEAN

TIRIRICA

Praia Costa

Praia Ribeira

Camping
Rai & Luc

See Itacaré
Beaches map,
Txai

N

Bradt

0   500m
0   500yds

5

🏠 **Albergue o Pharol** (6 rooms & dorms) Praça Santos Dummont 7, Itacaré; ☎ 3251 2527; www.albergueopharol.com.br. A smart, well-decorated hostel with very simple, spartan rooms & pleasant public areas with heavy wooden furniture & lacy hammocks. There are plenty of rooms to choose from – private dbl & trpl AC apts, fan-cooled dorms for 4–6 people & a room with full disabled facilities. Five hundred metres from the bus stop. $–$$

🏠 **Estrela** (12 rooms) Rua Pedro Longo 34, Itacaré; ☎ 3251 2006; www.pousadaestrela.com.br. A range of nicely decorated rooms in chunky hardwood & pastel colours. Staff friendly & offer a good homemade b/fast with a huge choice. Wi-Fi access. $–$$

🏠 **Itacaré Hostel a Pedra Bonita** (8 rooms) Rua Lodonio Almeida 120; ☎ 3251 3037; www.itacarehostel.com.br. A central hostel with tiny dbls & dorms, a pocket-sized pool, internet & a TV area. Staff are friendly & helpful. $–$$

⛺ **Tropical Camping** Rua Pedro Longo 187, Itacaré; ☎ 3251 3531. Small, safe palm-shaded campsite in the centre of Itacaré town. $

🍴 **Where to eat** Most of the restaurants in Itacaré are on the town's main drag, Rua Lodônio Almeida. There are plenty to choose from – pizzerias, per-kilo restaurants, juice bars and more sophisticated establishments offering reasonable wine lists.

🍴 **Casa Sapucaia** R Lodônio Almeida; ☎ 251 3091. Regional & international fusion cooking strong on seafood, from 2 ex-round-the-world sailors. $$$$

🍴 **A Brasileira** Rua Pedro Longo 175; ☎ 8825 3560. Elegant, well-cooked seafood dishes served with organic & wholefood sundries. $$$

🍴 **Boca de Forno** Rua Lodônio Almeida 134; ☎ 3251 2174. The busiest restaurant in Itacaré, with large wood-fired pizzas served by model-like staff in raw cotton outfits to diners sitting at heavy wood tables in a large, open-air dining space. $$$

🍴 **La In** Rua Lodônio Almeida 116, Centro; ☎ 3251 3054. Bahian & seafood serving well-priced, generous lunches & dinners including the house speciality – fish in prawn sauce baked in a banana leaf. The restaurant is decorated with colourful art by the owner, Marcio. $$–$$$

🍴 **O Casarão Amarelo** Praia da Coroinha, old town; ☎ 9996 0599. Swiss-owned restaurant-bar & nightclub in one of the town's few pre-20th-century buildings. The large international menu includes some reliable options. $$

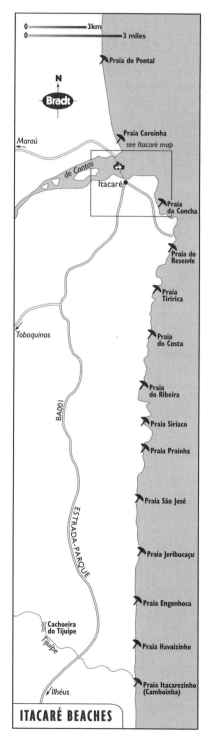

ITACARÉ BEACHES

✕ O Restaurante Rua Pedro Longo 150; ☏ 3251
2012. Value set lunches & dinners (*prato feito*) &
large but economical à la carte seafood & pastas. **$**

ENTERTAINMENT AND NIGHTLIFE In high season there's always a bar pulsating with forró or pagode music somewhere in Itacaré. But what's in fashion one season changes the next. As this book went to press, the most popular bars were **Toca do Calango** (*Praça dos Cachorros*) and **Mar eMel** (*Praia das Conchas*). The **Casarão Amarelo** restaurant becomes a dance club after 23.00 on weekends.

SHOPPING Small shops and stalls along the main street, Rua Lodônio Almeida, sell attractive seed jewellery and beach items including a good (and good-value) choice of Brazilian-cut swimwear and cool, light beach items. Pharmacies sell plenty of (expensive) suncream and insect repellent.

OTHER PRACTICALITIES There are plenty of internet cafés throughout the town. There is a Banco do Brasil (for changing money) at Rua 31 de Março in the centre and a Bradesco ATM in the Praça do Forum.

WHAT TO SEE There is nothing to see in Itacaré but the beaches. From north to south they are as follows: **Do Pontal** is some 20km long, deserted and stretches all the way to the beaches of the Peninsula de Maraú. Take a tent and plenty of water and walk – it's some 30km for the nearest hotel and shop, with rivers to ford along the way. The beginning of the beach is immediately across the Rio de Contas from town and is reached by passenger ferry. **Coroinha** runs around the harbour urban area and is far from clean but offers pretty views of both the town and the 18th-century church of São Miguel. It's especially pretty at sunset. **Da Concha** is the main town beach, backed by Itacaré's equivalent of suburbs – a tiny grid of dirt streets filled with pousadas. Beaches to the south are better. **Do Resende** runs around a little bay and has white, fluffy sand, swaying coconut palms and a handful of pousadas. It is ten-minute walk from Da Concha. **Tiririca** is Itacaré's surf beach. The town became a resort from here. It lies ten minutes' walk from Resende and has a handful of surfer pousadas which have turned increasingly chic over the years. **Do Costa** is another little bay beach, with strong waves and good surf. It sits ten minutes' walk from Tiririca. **Do Ribeira** is the best beach for families, sitting in a small bay surrounded by tropical forest and with a little stream (beware *bicho do pé*) and gentler waves. It lies at the end of the road from town, ten minutes' walk from Do Costa. **Prainha** is far more private, with more intrepid visitors who arrive here by trail from Ribeira. It has good surf and sits in a protected area (US$1.50 entry fee), 20–30 minutes' walk from Do Ribeira. Don't take valuables along the path if walking alone or in groups of less than four; there have been robberies of late. There are many other beaches further south accessible only via the BA-001 to Ilhéus.

ILHÉUS AND THE FAR SOUTH OF COSTA DO CACAU *Telephone code: 73*

The region's largest city, **Ilhéus**, sits on a broad bay at the mouth of the muddy Rio Cachoeira river some 75km south of Itacaré. It is most famous as the birthplace of one of Brazil's most famous – if not most illustrious – novelists, Jorge Amado (see page 128) who was born in the city in 1912 and who set a number of his most famous bawdy novels here, including *Gabriela, Cravo e Canela* (Gabriela, Clove and Cinnamon), *Cacau* and *Terras do Sem Fim* (The Violent Lands) the last two of which chronicled life on the region's cocoa plantations. There's little to see of the torrid atmosphere and colour of Amado's novels in modern Ilhéus. It's a quiet provincial

The coastal mountains of Bahia preserve some of the most biodiverse and little-studied rainforests in the world. They have suffered centuries – from brasilwood felling by the Tupinambá (for the Europeans), sugar plantations and exploitation from large- and small-scale farming. Cocoa was traditionally one of the major crops in this area and has long been cultivated under the *cabruca* system, whereby canopy trees are maintained and cocoa trees are planted in the shaded understorey. But crisis in the cocoa market (caused by a combination of disease and fluctuating prices) has led to many *cabrucas* being abandoned or turned over to less environment-friendly agricultural practices. As a result deforestation is accelerating rather than diminishing in the second decade of the new millennium, leaving a landscape which is a patchwork of plantations, pastures, second-growth jungle and primary forests whose cover is too small to preserve unique animal species.

Studies undertaken since the 1990s around the Serra das Lontras and Serra do Javí near Una have shown that the mountains have an exceptionally high biodiversity. Many new species have been discovered, including higher vertebrates. In the 1990s, two bird species entirely new to science, the Bahia spinetail (*Synallaxis whitneyi*) and the Bahia tyrannulet (*Phylloscartes beckeri*) were discovered in the early days when the surveys were focusing on an area called Boa Nova, to the northwest of Serra das Lontras. In less than two decades this has been entirely destroyed. However, more recent surveys further into the mountains themselves have discovered 11 globally threatened bird species. Four of these species are new to science and a fifth represent a new genus, which is dependent on the canopy trees within the *cabrucas* for its survival, demonstrating the importance of this plantation system for conservation. Even more species are as yet uncatalogued. The threats that the forests currently face, and the recent destruction of Boa Nova, make it imperative that they are preserved as a matter of urgency.

With this in mind, BirdLife International (*www.birdlife.org*) in conjunction with SAVE (*www.savebrasil.org.br*) have set up a private reserve encompassing a core area of forest to establish a state-level conservation unit, ensuring the maintenance of the *cabruca* system of farming that surrounds the forested area, and sustainably managing the remnant forest areas within the Serra das Lontras/Javí complex. You can support them through their websites.

The Serra das Lontras can be visited with Ciro Albano or with Orbita (see page 175).

town at heart – albeit with a minor crime problem, which makes its port area and (nocturnally) semi-deserted centre a little dangerous after dark. Beyond Ilhéus the Bahian coast stretches for over 100km towards Porto Seguro and the Costa do Descobrimento, broken by another labyrinthine bay at the old colonial village of **Canavieiras**. The beaches along the way are superb, with good surf at the tiny town of **Olivença** and tracts of remnant Atlantic coastal rainforest, some of which is protected around **Una** at a sanctuary for very rare **golden-headed lion tamarin** monkeys. But there is little to no infrastructure for tourists, even in the smattering of fishing villages *en route*. Most tourists use Ilhéus as a transport hub, spending a half-day or a day here before heading north towards Itacaré or south towards Porto Seguro.

HISTORY Ilhéus began as a settlement in the earliest days of Portuguese colonisation, and was elevated to a captaincy by King João III in 1534. As commerce from the plantations increased, the town became wealthy first on sugar and tobacco and then – much later – after the invention of confectionary chocolate from

Mexican and Brazilian cocoa beans on Cacau. The 19th- and early 20th-century Cacau boom around Ilhéus was like the rubber boom to the north – sudden, exploitative and violent. Workers were all but enslaved through systems of debt peonage administered by ranch-owning patriarchs who ruled ruthlessly through their hired guns or *jagunços*. Today workers are still paid a pittance though they have considerably better workers' rights – particularly after Lula's terms in government. And Ilhéus's port still exports 65% of all Brazilian cocoa. Cargo freighters can be seen entering the bay and docking at the port on the southern shore, from the Convento de Nossa Senhora da Piedade viewpoint, which also affords the best views of the city.

GETTING THERE AND AROUND

By air The airport is 8km away from the city centre, in Pontal on the south bank of the Rio Cachoeira, and reachable from Ilhéus by bridge. Gol and TAM have flights to Salvador and São Paulo (with TAM also offering connections to Belo Horizonte) and Trip has flights to Salvador.

By bus The rodoviária lies 4km from town on Rua Itabuna, but the Itabuna–Olivença bus goes through the centre of Ilhéus. Itabuna is very well connected to most of the major centres in Bahia via fast bus (including Salvador, Porto Seguro and Feira de Santana for onward connections to the Chapada Diamantina). Several buses run daily to Salvador (7hrs; R$40). The 06.20 bus goes via Bom Despacho on Itaparica. There are four buses to Itacaré (45–60mins; R$15). Four buses a day leave for Eunápolis for onward connections to Porto Seguro (5hrs; R$35) and there are also direct buses to that city – though check that yours is a faster express service – which take six hours (R$40) as opposed to around ten on a slower bus. There are two buses daily to Valença (5hrs; R$25). Buses to Olivenca, its beaches and mud baths leave from the city centre and the rodoviária. Any São Jorge or Canavieiras bus will stop at the beaches and there are very frequent buses to Olivença itself.

By taxi and car Taxis (be sure they use the meter), tour companies or hire cars will be needed for trips further afield. Cars can be hired through agencies at the airport or through Hertz (*www.hertz.com*). The city centre is manageable on foot.

TOURIST INFORMATION AND LOCAL TOUR OPERATORS The tourist office is on the beach opposite Praça Castro Alves, a few minutes' walk from the cathedral. Staff are friendly and helpful and have up-to-date city maps. But they speak little English. **Orbitá** (*R Marquês de Paranaguá 270;* ☏ *3234 3250, 9983 6655; www.orbitaexpedicoes.com.br*) offer trips and adventure activities from kayaking to canyoning throughout the Costa do Dendê and Cacau region and can organise transfers to the Chapada Diamantina, Porto Seguro and Salvador and to and from Ilhéus airport. They are an excellent, English-speaking source of knowledge about the city and offer good half- to one-day city and regional tours as well as trips to the Tamarin Centre in Una and to ruined *fazendas*, beaches and waterfalls near Ilhéus.

WHERE TO STAY For those passing through and on a budget, there are clusters of dirt-cheap hotels near the local bus station. Not all charge by the night. The best option is in the city centre.

⌂ **Jardim Atlântico** (55 rooms) Rodovia Ilheus–Olivenca km2, Jardim Atlantico, Ilhéus; ☏ 3632 4711; www.hoteljardimatlantico.com.br. This old-fashioned self-contained package resort sitting in a sprawling beachfront complex 10mins south of the city is one of the best hotels in southern Bahia for

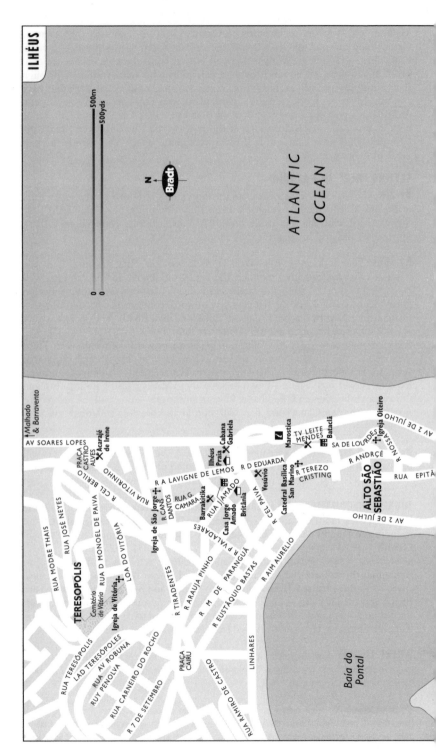

ILHÉUS

ATLANTIC OCEAN

500m
500yds

N

Malhado & Barravento

AV SOARES LOPES

PRAÇA CASTRO ALVES

Acarajé de Irene

TERESOPOLIS

RUA MODRE THAIS

RUA JOSÉ NEYES

RUA TERESÓPOLIS

LAD TERESÓPOLES

RUA AV ROBUNA

RUY PENOLVA

RUA CARNEIRO DO ROCHO

R 7 DE SETEMBRO

RUA RAMIRO DE CASTRO

Cemitério de Vitória

Igreja de Vitória

R CEL BERILO

RUA D MONOEL DE PAIVA

LOA DO VITÓRIA

RUA VITORINHO

Igreja de São Jorge

R CANS DANTOS

RUA G. CAMARA

Barrakitika

RUA J AMADO

Casa Jorge Amado

R TIRADENTES

R ARAUJA PINHO

R M DE PARANGUÁ

PRAÇA CAIRU

LINHARES

R EUSTÁQUIO BASTAS

R AIM AURÉLIO

P VALADARES

R A LAVIGNE DE LEMOS

Ilhéus Praia

Cabana Gabriela

Britânia

R CEL PAIVA

R D EDUARDA

Vesúvio

Catedral Basilica San Marino

R TEREZO CRISTING

Marostica

TV LEITE MENDES

Bataclã

SA DE LOURDES

R ANDRÇE

RUA EPITÃ

ALTO SÃO SEBASTIÃO

AV 2 DE JULHO

Igreja Oiteiro

R NOSSA

AV 2 DE JULHO

Baía do Pontal

176

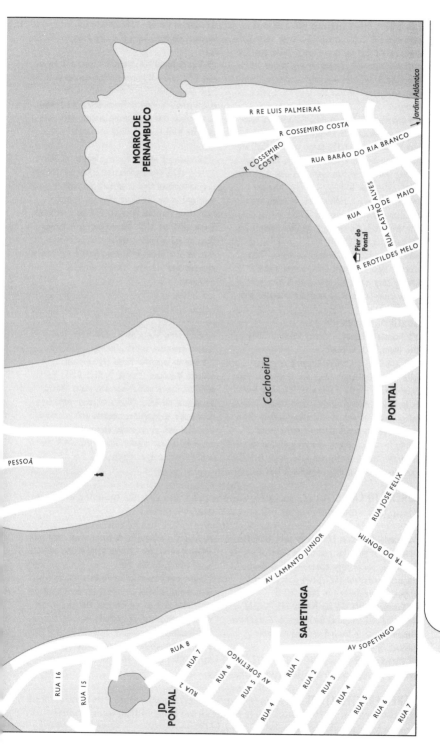

MORRO DE PERNAMBUCO

R RE LUIS PALMEIRAS

R COSSEMIRO COSTA

R COSSEMIRO COSTA

RUA BARÃO DO RIA BRANCO

Jardim Atlântico

RUA 130 ALVES

RUA CASTRO DE MAIO

Pier do Pontal

R EROTILDES MELO

PONTAL

Cachoeira

PESSOÁ

RUA JOSE FELIX

TR DO BONFIM

AV LAMANTO JUNIOR

SAPETINGA

AV SOPETINGO

RUA 8

RUA 7

AV SOPETINGO

RUA 6

RUA 5

RUA 1

RUA 2

RUA 3

RUA 4

RUA 5

RUA 6

RUA 7

RUA 4

RUA 2

JD PONTAL

RUA 15

RUA 16

kids. It offers child-friendly stays with a series of supervised kids' clubs, activities & a small water park. Adults have run of the tennis courts, sauna, gym & a handful of excursions. Rooms are airy, decked out in lush wood & decorated with bright paintings & have their own garden terraces. The hotel has a decent restaurant. $$$$

⌂ **Barravento** (25 rooms) Praia Malhado, Rua Nossa Senhora das Graças 276, Ilhéus; ⍁ 3634 3223; www.barravento.com.br. This jagged concrete block with tinted glass windows is the best hotel in Ilhéus itself, offering small but modern rooms with little more than a bed, coffee table & writing desk. Most have tiny terraces & there is a rooftop pool. The urban beach is not clean enough for swimming. $$$

⌂ **Ilhéus Praia** (56 rooms) Praça Dom Eduardo (on the beach), Ilhéus; ⍁ 2101 2533; www.ilheuspraia.com.br. Another anonymous 1980s concrete block of a hotel sitting behind a pool & offering boxy rooms, the best of which have views out over the sea, & all of which are decorated with

the standard Brazilian white floor tiles & MDF furniture. The hotel has a 20m-long pool. Free Wi-Fi. $$$

⌂ **Pier do Pontal** (26 rooms) Av Lomanto Jr, Pontal km3.5; ⍁ 3632 4000; www.pierdopontal.com.br. A small beach hotel 20mins' drive south of the city centre across the river in Pontal. Rooms are housed in a modern, concrete, 3-storey building overlooking a pool. The hotel has a Japanese restaurant. $$–$$$

⌂ **Britânia** (15 rooms) Rua Jorge Amado s/n, Ilhéus; ⍁ 3634 1722; www.brasilheus.com.br/britania_por.htm. This old-fashioned hotel in an early 20th-century townhouse in the city centre offers the best-value rooms (with the most character) away from the beach. Rooms which are simple but well kept have wooden floors as well polished as the assembly room in a Victorian prep school. B/fast is generous & the hotel is in a safe area with easy access to plenty of restaurants. $$

South of Ilhéus

⌂ **Fazenda da Lagoa** (14 rooms) Rodovia BA 001, Una, Ilhéus; ⍁ 3236 6046; www.fazendadalagoa.com.br. A super-luxury beach hotel with 100m² beach bungalows designed by Mucki Skowronski, sitting on a 50m-wide, 10km-long beach in front of a winding mangrove-lined estuary. This is full of birdlife – with at least 3 kingfisher species & many smaller herons & there are ocelot in the nearby forest. But despite advertising itself as an eco-hotel, the staff (& owners) can barely name even the commonest bird. But the *caipirinhas* & food are

excellent. Bring binoculars & a field guide. The tamarin sanctuary at Una is nearby. $$$$$

⌂ **Fazenda Tororomba Hostel** (100 rooms)Rua Eduardo Magalhães, Olivença; ⍁ 8125 0293; www.fazendatororomba.com.br. This chalet hotel & hostel near the beach offers a range of rooms, from comfortable AC bungalows complete with Jacuzzis & king-sized beds to fan-cooled dorms with space for up to 6. Staff can organise airport pick-ups & tours around Olivença & the region. $–$$$

✗ **WHERE TO EAT** Stalls and snack bars on the praça and near the cathedral offer safe, cheap eats – including *acarajé* and prawn kebabs.

✗ **Vesúvio** Praça Dom Eduardo; ⍁ 3634 4724. This Arabic restaurant & bar next to the cathedral was featured in one of Jorge Amado's novels & always attracts literary fans. The ice-cold draught beer & *caipirinhas* are the best in Ilhéus. $$$

✗ **Cabana Gabriela** Rua Rui Penalva 109; ⍁ 3632 1836. The best restaurant for *moquecas* & traditional Bahian cooking in Ilhéus. Come with an empty stomach. $$

✗ **Marostica** Av 2 de Julho 966; ⍁ 3634 5691. Ilhéus is not a gourmand's town. The best restaurant

in the city is popular for its pizzas, which come with oodles of sticky cheese. Stodgy pasta is also available. & the beer is ice-cold. $$

✗ **Acarajé de Irene** Praça Castro Alves s/n. Irene has been serving delicious *acarajé* at her market stall for many years & is a local favourite; with long queues of hungry office staff at lunchtime. $

✗ **Barrakitika** Praça Antônio Muniz 39; ⍁ 3231 8300. A lunchtime per-kilo restaurant & night-time bar with live music on Fri & Sat nights. $

OTHER PRACTICALITIES There are plenty of internet cafés in the city centre – look out for signs for LAN House. There is a Bradesco bank with an international ATM at Rua Marques de Paranaguá 8 (⍁ *3234 5233*).

WHAT TO SEE

Ilhéus Ilhéus has a handful of interesting historical buildings and the modest Baroque **Igreja do São Jorge** (*Praça Rui Barbosa* s/n), is the city's oldest, dating from 1556. It has a small sacred-art museum (⊕ *09.00–12.00 & 14.00–17.00 Tue–Fri*). The city skyline is dominated by the towers of the **Catedral de São Sebastião** (*Praça Dom Eduardo* s/n), an imposing but unremarkable early 20th-century construction. The stately American Art Nouveau house in the city centre where Jorge Amado grew up and wrote his first novel is now a museum, **A Casa de Jorge Amado** (*Rua Jorge Amado 21;* ⊕ *09.00–16.00 Tue–Sun; R$5*) with historical artefacts, manuscripts and books as well as information panels about the writer's life. The **Bataclã** cultural centre (*Av 2 de Julho 75;* \ *3634 7835*) was once a famous whorehouse and poker palace, frequented by the Cacau *coroneis* and linked to other parts of the town by a series of secret tunnels through which the patriarchs and their *jagunços* would flee should their wives come searching for them in the establishment. The club was immortalised in Jorge Amado's *Gabriela, Cravo e Canela*.

Beaches The city beach itself is polluted but the beaches around the town are splendid and increasingly deserted the further south or north you go. **Praia do Marciano**, 4km north of the city, has reefs offshore and good surfing. South of the river, the beaches at Pontal (reachable on the 'Barreira' bus which leaves from the city centre just after the Hotel Jardim Atlântico) include the 100m-long **Praia da Concha** (with coral) and the long, broader **Praia do Sul**, shaded by coconut palms, busy with barracas and with strong waves. There are better beaches still 20km south of the city at **Olivença**. Between Ilhéus and Olivença, from north to south the beaches are **Cururupe** (long, broad and straight with strong waves and coarse sand), **Back Door** and **Batuba** (both with some of the best surfing in Bahia, with waves of up to 2.5m, and exposed rock pools at low tide), **Cai n'Água** in Olivença itself (another surf beach but with more *barracas* and sunbathers – particularly at weekends). At the **Balneário de Tororomba** on the Rio Batuba, 3km north of Olivença, there is a series of iron-rich medicinal mudbaths.

Rio do Engenho At the village of **Rio do Engenho** on the river of the same name there is a series of ruined *fazendas*, including Sant'Ana, one of Brazil's first, whose tiny, squat terracotta-roofed church dates from 1537, making it the third-oldest in Brazil. The village can be visited on a day tour with Orbitá (see page 175), which can include a boat journey through the bird-filled mangroves on the river.

The Reserva Biológica de Una and beyond Beyond Olivença the coast gets remoter and wilder. At Una there is an important wildlife sanctuary – the **Reserva Biológica de Una** (*www.ecoparque.org.br*) – set up to protect the golden-faced lion tamarin (*mico-leão da cara dourada*) one of the world's tiniest and rarest monkeys. Visits are available through Orbitá or on jeeps which leave from the rodovíaria in Ilhéus. Note that this is the wettest part of Bahia (most notably in October).

The road continues through the **Ilha de Comandatuba**, a spit between the River Una and the Atlantic with a scattering of ugly resorts, and ends at **Canavieiras**, a picturesque town which benefited from the cocoa boom and which has several fine beaches but few hotels. A very rough dirt track continues from here to the big estuary at **Belmonte** (passenger ferries across the estuary cost around R$10) from where there is a paved road through to Porto Seguro. No public transport takes this route – heading inland instead to the federal highway and then south.

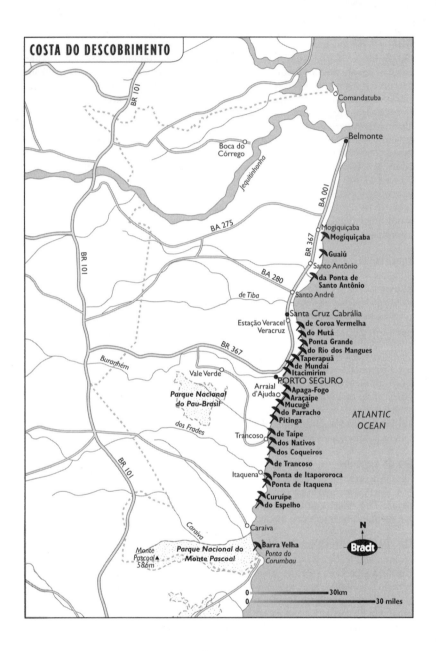

6

Costa do Descobrimento

Around vespers we caught sight of land: at first a great mountain, wide and high and other, lower mountains to its south, then we saw level land covered with trees. The tall mountain was given the name Mount Pascual.

Pero Vaz de Caminha on first sighting Brazil, 21 April 1500

Long, sweeping beaches with sand as fine as white pepper and barely a soul in sight. Coral coves backed by steep sandstone cliffs that glow golden in the warm light of the tropical dawn. Sandy bays, swaying palms, myriad greens of shallow reefs, rainforest, and restinga and a string of little villages that have swelled into tourist towns. The Costa do Descobrimento has been luring tourists to Bahia since 21 April 1500 when a 30-year-old Portuguese nobleman and his retinue of caravels and carracks became the first white men to see Brazil. This is the best of beach in Bahia – a mix of vibrant party towns and quiet villages, beaches with chic boutique hotels and strands of deserted sand walked only by egrets. And there are real wild areas, too – clinging on in the midst of encroaching eucalyptus plantations. The largest eagle in the world – the harpy – nests here at its only recorded site in the Atlantic coastal forests, and jaguars still hunt within the region's scant patchwork of national parks and protected areas.

Coming south from Salvador, the Costa do Descobrimento begins quietly in **Belmonte**, barely a village on the southern bank of Bahia's wildest great river – the Jequitinhonha – before getting slowly busier at **Santa Cruz Cabrália**, a forgotten little colonial town slowly becoming revitalised through beach tourism. It is an important centre for the **Pataxó** indigenous people, the descendants of those Indians who watched whilst the Portuguese celebrated the first Brazilian mass, on the Santa Cruz's Coroa Vermelha beach and planted a cross in the sand appropriating their land for Portugal. **Porto Seguro**, 22km to the south on the north bank of the Rio Buranhém, is the Costa do Descobrimento's biggest tourist draw, with its cobbles and colonial buildings and its vast beaches, most of which are backed by equally vast resort hotels. Across the river from here is **Arraial d'Ajuda**, perched on a hill and surrounded by even better beaches and offering low-key, backpacker luxe. Things get chic in **Trancoso**, 15km beyond Arraial, which has the kind of hotels that grace the pages of *Wallpaper* and Taschen coffee-table books and a clientele that can spot a brand name on a bikini. And they stay chic all the way to tiny Caraíva, which is little more than a collection of sandy streets and a long, magnificent beach. **Corumbau**, which sits in the shadow of Monte Pascoal, is smaller still and marks the end of the Costa do Descobrimento.

The Costa do Descobrimento preserves some of Bahia's best wildlife destinations and three national parks: **Parque Nacional do Descobrimento**, **PN Monte Pascoal** and **PN Pau Brasil**. Bizarre as it might seem, these are off most tour operator itineraries which are still shaped to predominantly Brazilian tastes and focus on driving fast in beach buggies and romping on ropes in nature. But it is possible to visit using hired transport, or to organise a bespoke tour.

Few tourists make it to Belmonte. And herein lies its charm. It's a provincial fishing town with a few Portuguese buildings which still feels largely like a provincial fishing village and not a tourist attraction. And whilst the sea is muddied by the waters of the Jequitinhonha River for much of the year the beaches to the south of the town are still fluffy, white and palm-shaded and some offer the sea and the river for bathing. The Jequitinhonha itself is magnificent. It is a broad, powerful stream which begins in the diamond-mining villages of Bahia's neighbouring state to the southwest, Minas Gerais. And it meanders across the depths of the remote sertão and the forests of Bahia before disgorging into the Atlantic in Belmonte – in a delta of gallery forests, islands, marshes and mangroves. The river itself has unique fauna (a new species of fish was discovered as recently as April 2009), and the delta itself offers some of the best coastal birdwatching in Bahia – especially when visited in conjunction with the **Estação Veracel Veracruz** just to the south. For more information on the birding, with species, see the box on pages 20–1. The scenery is as magnificent as the birds – a labyrinth of forested waterways, mudflats covered in crabs and with scores of wading birds and tiny beach-fringed islands, stretching 20km along the coast to the little village of Canavieiras on the Costa do Cacau.

GETTING THERE AND AROUND Regular buses connect Belmonte with Santa Cruz Cabrália and Porto Seguro. Whilst fishermen on the quay offer one–two-hour trips on the Jequitinhonha, it is also possible to traverse the delta to or from Canavieiras by private launch. Prices can be negotiated in Belmonte or Canavieiras. Expect to pay around R$120 for a boat for four. The journey can also be organised through Portomondo travel (see page 193) who can arrange transfers from Canavieiras, or with Órbita Turismo e Expedições in Ilhéus (see page 175). There are daily connections between Canavieiras and the other towns on the Costa de Cacau.

Belmonte has a small grid of streets and is easy to find your way around on foot.

LOCAL TOUR OPERATORS

Associação de Barqueiros m 73 9966 8758. A co-op of 10 boatmen who offer trips on the river & connections to Canavieiras from R$70. Belmonte is famous for its beautiful sunsets over the river & sunset tours are very popular. Boats take a max of 6 people. Snacks, water & insect repellent are inclusive.

WHERE TO STAY

Pousada Galápagos (15 rooms) Av Celso Jorge Guimarães 351, Centro; 3287 2223. About 1.5km from the beach. The small rooms are spartan, with little more than a TV, fan & optional AC & hammock. Pousada amenities include internet access, safe, b/fast & parking. Popular with Brazilian backpackers. $–$$

Pousada Rio (9 rooms) Av Presidente Getúlio Vargas 127, Centro; 3287 2202;

e pousadariojequitinhonha@hotmail.com; www.belmontebahia.com/pousadario. A very basic & simple but clean pousada by the riverside with bright rooms with windows overlooking the river & famous Belmonte sunset. They have a small pool in a shaded area of the courtyard. Rooms have bathrooms & AC. B/fast is included & the staff do all they can to be friendly & attentive. $–$$

WHERE TO EAT

O Açougue Av Rio Mar 251, Centro; 3287 2041; ⊕ 10.00–22.00 daily. The atmosphere is very informal at this popular eatery, with tables on the pavement & locals drinking cold beer & coconut-flavoured _cachaça_ served in the coconut. There is live music on Fri. _Petiscos_, fried fish & other bite-size savouries, go well with cold beer. For main course try _camarão com mandioca à moda cabral_. If you're brave enough you could try their secret recipe speciality: aphrodisiac soup, with _mocotó, camarão e sururu_. Accepts Visa.
$$–$$$

✗ **Restaurante do Diogo** Av Rio Mar 2020; ☎ 3287 2221; e rspbelmonte@hotmail.com; ⊕ 09.00–20.00 daily. This popular Belmonte restaurant is well known for its specialities: blue mangrove mud crabs or guaiamun and moqueca de robalo (sea bass *moqueca*). $$

SHOPPING

Ceramica 14 Irmaos Rua São Domingos, Visgueira; ☎ 73 3287 2624; ⊕ 08.00–17.30 daily. A local, family co-op of 14 siblings, their partners & children all working together to produce large & small terracotta urns, vases, statuettes & sundry items. It's possible to visit their studio to watch them work & see your item being made in front of you.

OTHER PRACTICALITIES There are no banks with international credit card ATMs in Belmonte.

WHAT TO DO

Capoeira A local capoeira group – Academia de Capoeira Relâmpago – with an excellent mestre, practise in a large bungalow near the centre of town, following mestre Bimba capoeira regional style.

SANTA CRUZ CABRÁLIA AND AROUND *Telephone code: 73*

With its whitewashed Portuguese Rococo church set on a cliff-top lawn, its ramshackle town centre busy with terracotta-roofs and its fishing boats bobbing up and down in a natural harbour, Santa Cruz looks like a scruffy hybrid of Arraial d'Ajuda and Trancoso. Yet it receives a fraction of their tourists. There are strands of long talcum powder-fine beaches stretching all the way to Porto Seguro and close to Santa Cruz they remain resort-free.

GETTING THERE AND AROUND Hourly buses connect Santa Cruz Cabrália and Porto Seguro 22km to the south. Santa Cruz Cabrália is easily negotiated on foot.

⌂ WHERE TO STAY

⌂ **A Toca do Marlin** (10 rooms) BA-001 to Belmonte km40.5 (Ponta de Sto Antônio); ☎ 3671 5009; www.tocadomarlin.com.br. Plush & very spacious beachside cabins gathered around a large pool right next to the sea on a converted stud farm breeding Andalusian horses. Cabins have huge windows allowing the intense natural light to warm the raw wood beams, whitewash & the deep ochre of the terracotta floor tiles. A range of tours include galloping along the beach & boat trips on the nearby mangrove-lined waterways. Excellent restaurant & service. $$$$$

⌂ **Pousada Victor Hugo** (10 rooms) Enseada Jacumã, Vila do Santo André km3; ☎ 3671 4064; www.pousadavictorhugo.com.br. Rooms in this pousada range from the small & monastic to large luxe suites with hammock-strung balconies & sofa beds. All are elegantly, if simply decorated with rustic wood furniture & lamps made from half coconut shells. The location is fabulous, on the long sweeping Enseada Jacumã bay – backed by restinga & in a small protected area & there is a lovely outdoor garden restaurant. $$$–$$$$

⌂ **Marlin Azul** (13 rooms) Rodovia BR-367 km81, Praia dos Lençóis, Santa Cruz Cabrália; ☎ 3282 1225; www.pousadamarlinazul.com.br. An ungainly concrete guesthouse on the beach with 2 storeys of concrete & tile balconied rooms overlooking a small pool (with a long slide for kids). Family friendly (children under 5 stay for free) & with a generous b/fast. The English on the website is gloriously nonsensical. $$–$$$

⌂ **Hostel Maracaia** (30 rooms) Rodovia BR-367 km77.5, Praia Coroa Vermelha; ☎ 3672 1155; www.maracaiahostel.com.br. A big, busy IYHA hostel 5mins' walk from historic Coroa Vermelha beach. Unlike many this is a great option for families; with dbl rooms as well as dorms (both spruce & well kept with polished brick floors, wooden beds & cream walls) & a larger-than-usual hostel swimming pool, a shady garden, restaurant & bar. Trips can be organised to the Jaqueira reserve & to offshore coral atolls for snorkelling or even diving. Transfers from Porto Seguro docks or airport available. $–$$

✗ WHERE TO EAT

✗ **Tropical** Av Cristal 100 Mirante da Coroa; 📞3282 1411; ⊕ 10.30–22.00 daily. Good fish of the day & traditional Portuguese dishes including a good Bacalhau tropical which is big enough for 2 people. **$$$**

✗ **Vanda** Rua Frei Henrique de Coimbra 75; 📞 3282 1384; ⊕ lunchtimes only Mar–Dec. Dona

Vanda Ramos has been cooking some of the best *moquecas* on the northern Costa do Descobrimento for over 25 years – spiced with the endemic *biri biri* berry & made with freshly caught fish. Come with spare belly & plenty of time; service is slow. **$$$**

OTHER PRACTICALITIES There are no banks in Santa Cruz Cabrália.

WHAT TO SEE AND DO

Buildings Santa Cruz preserves a handful of Portuguese buildings, the best of which is the early 17th-century, Jesuit-built Igreja da Nossa Senhora da Conceição, with Rococo flourishes on the façade. There are great views out over the coast and the town from here.

Beaches and atolls Brazil's first mass was celebrated on the sheltered bay at **Praia Coroa Vermelha** some 5km south of town, watched by groups of Tupiniquin indigenous people. A big cross marks the spot. Vaz de Caminha, the Portuguese fleet's chronicler, recorded that 'when mass was finished and we sat down for the sermon, many of them stood up and blew a horn or trumpet and began to leap and dance for a while'. The Portuguese carpenters built and erected a large cross and the Tupiniquin were transfixed by the iron tools. Cabral had the Portuguese 'kneel and kiss the cross ... we did so and motioned to them to do the same: they at once all went to kiss it'. Brazil was named after the cross itself – christened A Terra da Veracruz – the Land of the True Cross, a name which never stuck. There is a small tourist village here and another simpler one with wilder stretches of sand at Santo André across the river from Santa Cruz and next to the small environmental **reserve of Santo Antônio**. Schooners leave early for snorkelling trips to offshore coral platforms and atolls including Ilha da Carolina (with snorkelling and bathing in natural pools) and Ilha Paraíso. Most of the coral itself is dead but there are plentiful (common) reef fish.

Estação Veracel Veracruz (*Reserva Particular do Patrimônio Natural Estação Veracel; Rodovia BR-367 km37;* 📞 *3166 1535, 8802 0161;* e *estacaoveracel@veracel.com.br; www.veracel.com.br/veracruz;* ⊕ *08.30–16.30 Tue & Thu, 08.30–11.30 Sat; advanced bookings only; special arrangements can be made for scientists & researchers, inc groups of accredited birders – members of a scientific organisation*) This 6,000ha private reserve between Santa Cruz Cabrália and Porto Seguro is one of the highlights for wildlife lovers visiting southern Brazil. It is a haven in the tourist tide for some 307 species of birds (with 21 threatened or endangered species and 32 endemics) and 40 mammals and myriad reptiles and amphibians. There is good birdwatching on a weekday out of season (during high season the crowds get too big), with rarities like red-billed curassow and banded and white-winged cotingas. Harpy eagles nest in the reserve – the only place in the Atlantic coastal forests where they have been recorded doing so. This is also one of the last refuges for tapir, jaguar, thin-spined arboreal porcupine and primates including brown howler monkey, Geoffroy's marmoset, crested capuchin and coastal black-handed titi monkey.

Jaqueira (*BR-367, Porto Seguro-Santa Cruz Cabrália; http://reservapataxojaqueira. blogspot.com;* ⊕ *09.00–17.00 daily*) The **Pataxó**, who moved to the coast after the Tupiniquin were displaced by the Portuguese, now sell arts and crafts on the same beach. And they personally run this inspiring tourism project. Jaqueira (named after a hardwood tree which grows on the reserve) is an ethno-tourism project which funds a living community. The project was conceived and instigated by Pataxó sisters who, despairing at the loss of indigenous culture in the Pataxó communities of southern Bahia, resolved to do something about it. If we don't, they thought, no one will and our culture will die. The Jaqueira tourism and cultural recuperation model has completely rejuvenated local Pataxó culture, with young indigenous people speaking their own language again and restoring their identity after decades of refusing to speak Pataxó and cultural loss. It is possible to visit and to stay in the village in Pataxó houses in the heart of a stand of native-owned rainforest. All the food is grown or hunted using traditional techniques. And a small craft shop selling beautiful ceramics, sacred incense and art provides extra revenue. Visits with Portomondo (*www.portomondo.com*).

PORTO SEGURO *Telephone code: 73*

Bahia's beach tourist explosion began in Porto Seguro in the 1980s and, since then, what was a colonial village has swelled to become the biggest coastal town between Ilhéus and Espírito Santo. This is where much of Brazil comes to have fun in the sun; big, brash resorts that wouldn't look out of place on Spain's Costa del Sol or the Mexican riviera line the beaches north of town next to booming *barracas* and the airport receives charter flights from all over Brazil. Yet for all its bombastic growth Porto itself remains a pleasant town. Forward-thinking town planning has ensured that there are still no buildings over two storeys high in the town itself; Porto has retained its attractive colonial centre and much of its charm. Paradoxically whilst it's the most developed tourist town in southern Bahia, it's the only one on the Costa do Descobrimento that feels like it has a life of its own beyond tourism. And whilst the beaches are more developed than they are in Arraial d'Ajuda a five-minute ferry ride across the water, accommodation in Porto's town centre is better value.

HISTORY It wasn't merely cordiality and curiosity that led the Tupiniquin to welcome Pedro Alvares Cabral so warmly. From the first sight of the swords, cannons and muskets and the marvellous metal tools wielded by the Portuguese carpenters they recognised both their technological superiority and a potential ally. Cabral had arrived at a propitious moment. The Tupiniquin were involved in a low-level war with their neighbouring linguistic brothers, the Tupinambá. So when Gonçalo Coelho arrived to erect a stone marker at the crest of the hill above the river, claiming the land for Portugal, he too was welcomed as were the first settlers who named the town Veracruz and set about enslaving their indigenous friends. By 1535, when the first captain Pero de Campo Tourinho arrived to claim the land he had been granted by the Portuguese crown (and which extended south to the present-day border with Espírito Santo and north to Ilhéus) the Tupiniquin had already realised their mistake in allowing the Portuguese to settle and were on the offensive. But by the 1550s the Europeans and their *mameluco* offspring had defeated the Tupiniquin. However, a more formidable foe stepped in to replace them.

Tribes of fierce Gê-speaking Cariri people and Gueren-Gueren who the Portuguese erroneously called Aimoré (after a Tupi word for enemy or evil person) left the forests of the interior and returned to the coast – their ancestral homelands which they had lost to the Tupi-speakers before the Portuguese arrived. They were fearsome, athletic warriors, tall, gainly and experts in guerrilla warfare; they struck horror in the Portuguese and Tupiniquin alike. 'They are extraordinarily agile and great runners,' wrote Gabriel Soares de Sousa in his *Tratado Descriptivo do Brasil* of 1587, 'afraid of no sort of people or weapons.' A successive wave of attacks from the 1550s limited the Portuguese to the immediate environs of Porto Seguro (and all

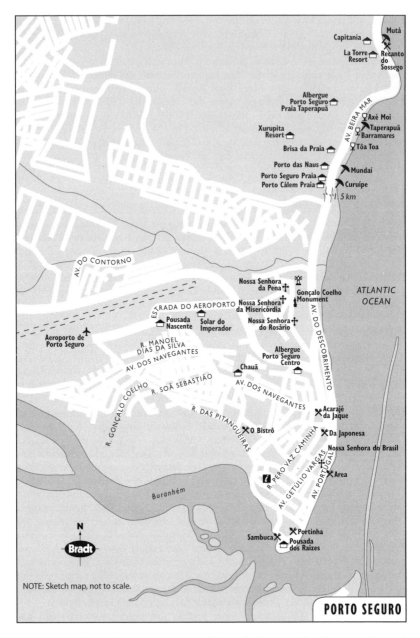

PORTO SEGURO

NOTE: Sketch map, not to scale.

the way north to the Recôncavo), and forced them to abandon *engenhos* and settlements along the Costa do Descobrimento and Cacau. By the 1580s Soares wrote that 'the captaincy of Porto Seguro and that of Ilhéus are destroyed and almost de-populated from fear of these barbarians'.

The Aimoré prevented Porto Seguro developing into anything more than an outpost – one of a string of tiny isolated missionary ports along the Costa do Descobrimento. It was their resilience that prevented agriculture spreading to the area in the time of the *engenhos* and kept Porto Seguro a backwater until the coming of roads and tourism in the 20th century. That most of Bahia's remaining coastal forests are in the south is due to the Aimoré peoples. They were never defeated, just slowly worn down over centuries by disease and the weight of numbers. And they never called themselves the Aimoré – they survive as the Pataxó to this day.

GETTING THERE

By plane Flights from Rio de Janeiro, São Paulo, Belo Horizonte, Ilhéus, Salvador, Porto Alegre, Brasília, Curitiba and Vitória operated by Gol (*www.voegol.com.br*), Tam (*www.tam.com.br*) and Webjet (*www.webjet.com.br*) arrive at the airport 2km north of town (*Estrada do Aeroporto s/n;* ☏ *3288 1880*). There are banks and a car rental booth in the terminal. A taxi to the centre (☏ *3288 1880*) costs US$15.

By bus The rodoviária is 2km west of the centre, on the road to Eunápolis, and has direct services to/from Ilhéus (daily 07.30, 4½hrs; R$90), Valença (Águia Branca, daily, 10 hrs; R$140) and Salvador (Águia Branca, daily, 12 hrs; R$160) and further connections via Eunápolis on the BR-101 federal highway (buses every 30 minutes, 1hr; R$10). Buses to most destinations on the Costa do Descobrimento and Baleia also leave for the rodoviária. Some buses for Caraíva go via the federal highway at Eunápolis and Itabela (leaving Eunápolis at 13.30, 2hrs). Direct Porto Seguro to Caraíva buses leave at 07.00, 13.30 (high season) and 15.00 (via Trancoso). To Trancoso, there are two daily buses, but it is easier to take the ferry to Arraial and catch one of the more frequent buses or *combis* from there.

It is also possible to reach Caraíva from Arraial (see page 191). To Curumuxatiba, Prado and destinations on the Costa da Baleia, take a bus to Eunápolis, Texeira de Freitas or Itamaraju and an onward bus from there.

The rodoviária has cafés and snack bars. Taxis charge R$10 to/from the town or ferry (negotiate at quiet times) from the rodoviária.

By car There are car hire companies at the airport, including Localiza (☏ *3288 1488*) and at Ria Cova da Moça 620 (☏ *3288 1488*) and Nacional (☏ *3288 4291*).

By bike Cycles can be hired at Oficina de Bicicleta (*Av Getúlio Vargas e R São Pedro*) at R$30 for 24 hours.

GETTING AROUND
Buses run through the city to and from the old rodoviária near the port every 30 minutes (R$1). Expresso Brasileiro buses run from Praça dos Pataxós along the BR-367, stopping at the beaches north of town all the way to Santa Cruz Cabrália, and from the port.

A **ferry** crosses the Rio Buranhém on demand from Arraial d'Ajuda (10mins; R$1 for foot passengers, R$15 for cars).

Taxis and motor-bike taxis proliferate around the docks and beach areas. **Car hire** is available at the airport, through larger hotels or tour agencies (around the port or at Portomondo).

TOURIST INFORMATION
The tourist office, Secretária de Turismo de Porto Seguro (*Rua Pero Vaz de Caminha 475, Centro;* ☏ *3288 3708; www.portosegurotur.com.br*) offers information on tours and hotels, and maps of the city and region. For tour operators see Arraial d'Ajuda (see pages 191–3).

WHERE TO STAY
Porto Seguro's beaches don't offer intimate comfort. Hotels here are built large and garish and they cater to Brazil's 1970s-style package tourist market which looks for an all-inclusive stay and lots of organised in-house

entertainment. Rates are invariably cheaper through online travel agents (easily found through TripAdvisor.com) and children are nearly always happy in the noisy environments and big pools. Unless of course they crave for nature which, while all around, has to be visited from Porto's resorts. For something lower key head across the river to Arraial or still further south.

⌂ **Brisa da Praia** (153 rooms) Av Beira Mar 1860, Praia de Taperapuã; ☎ 3288 8600; www.brisadapraia.com.br. A huge family resort, just across the street from the beach with live music 3 times a week by the pool & a kids' play area. Guests mostly arrive from São Paulo on all-inclusive packages. Rooms in the cuboid concrete corridor blocks look better from inside than they do out — with lemon & cream walls, prints in a tropicália of colours & large granite-topped workplaces. The lively Tôa Tôa *barraca* is 5mins' walk away. Amenities include a poolside relaxation area with hot tubs a sauna & beauty salon, Wi-Fi, gym & playground. $$$$$

⌂ **La Torre Resort** (170 rooms) Av Beira Mar 9999, Praia do Mutá; ☎ 2105 1700; www.resortlatorre.com. A large resort on one of the shadier portions of Porto Seguro's busy Mutá beach, with diverse rooms — including spacious family suites & there is a romantic, low-lit restaurant area next to the big, sculpted pool. Built on a grand scale but still more intimate & relaxing than Porto's giant towers. Cheapest rates through the OTAs. Rates are all-inclusive with meals, drinks (only Brazilian alcoholic drinks are provided) & sport activities. They provide regular transfer to their own *barraca* at the beach & to the airport. $$$$$

⌂ **Xurupita Resort** (16 rooms) Rua B 25, Taperapuã; ☎ 2105 9500; www.xurupita.com. This low-key hotel sits 1½km from the beach on a low hill affording a sea view. It's surrounded by Atlantic coastal forest busy with hummingbirds & tanagers at dawn & unpolluted by noisy music. Rooms are plain rectangles decorated with big floral murals that add splashes of colour & decked out with uninspiring wicker & hardwood furniture that looks fresh from the Argos catalogue. Amenities include a sports centre with gym coaching, squash & tennis & the hotel offers transfers & car rental. $$$$$

⌂ **Porto Seguro Praia** (149 rooms) Av Beira Mar 1500, Praia de Curuípe; ☎ 3288 9393; www.psph.com.br. Complexes of low bungalow buildings housing minimalist rooms brightened by large windows & blocks of colour from scatter cushions & tropical prints. The hotel sits next to the beach in a large palm-tree garden some distance from the noisy *barracas*. Amenities include restaurant, pools for adults & children, gym & sauna. $$$$

⌂ **Capitania** (160 rooms) Av Beira Mar 12700, Praia do Mutá; ☎ 2105 5533; www.capitaniahotel.com.br. A standard beach 3-star with plain cuboid rooms & catalogue furniture & rows of somewhat drab-looking housing units each accommodating up to 5 people. The complex is surrounded by palm trees & is just across from Praia de Mutá. The hotel promotes sports tournaments on the beach. They keep several tennis & volleyball courts plus swimming pool, restaurant & Wi-Fi. $$$

⌂ **Porto Cálem Praia** (97 rooms) Av Beira Mar 1999, Praia de Curuípe; ☎ 3268 8400; www.portocalem.com.br. The hotel is made of 2 independent mock-*fazenda* wings containing small, simple rooms where floor tiles & plain walls are offset with little floral prints; the new wing offers the same recipe, though rooms are larger. Each block has a swimming pool & the hotel has its own restaurant & gym. $$$

⌂ **Porto das Naus** (129 rooms) Av Beira Mar 4000, Praia de Mundaí; ☎ 3268 8000; www.portodasnaus.com.br. A set of simple 2-storey buildings built in mock-*fazenda* style (with terracotta roofs & ochre façades) overlooking an internal courtyard with kids' & adults' pools. Rooms are bright & have verandas. Poolside music can be intrusive. There's a restaurant & the rate includes b/fast & dinner. $$$

⌂ **Chauã** (40 rooms) Av dos Navegantes 800, Centro Histórico; ☎ 3288 2894; www.hotelchaua.com.br. A hotel at the city centre, close to shops & restaurants. A yellow 2-storey building with balcony faces a small pool. The rooms are basic but with private bathrooms & AC. Paid internet access available. $$

⌂ **Pousada Nascente** (19 rooms) Estrada do Aeroporto 437, Cidade Alta; ☎ 3288 2537; http://pousadanascente.spaces.live.com. The pousada sits behind an ugly breeze-block wall a short walk from both beach & historic centre. Bungalows are spread around palm-shaded garden & pool area (with tamed macaws) looking towards the sea. AC rooms are spartan with TV, & Wi-Fi. $$

⌂ **Pousada dos Raizes** (15 rooms) Praça dos Pataxós 196; ☎ 3288 4717; e pousadaraizes@hotmail.com. A functional but friendly pousada — with very simple but well-kept bed, fridge & wardrobe rooms. Rates come with or without b/fast. $$

🛏 **Solar do Imperador** (100 rooms) Estrada do Aeroporto 317, Cidade Alta; ☎ 3288 8450; www.solardoimperador.com.br. The hotel is set in a lush garden less than 1km from both the beach & the historic centre. It's in an elegant faux-colonial style. The rooms are equipped with AC, TV & minibar & each balcony is provided with a hammock. Dinner is optional at a different rate. Good value. $$

🛏 **Albergue Porto Seguro Centro** (20 rooms) Rua Cova da Moça 720; ☎ 3288 1742; www.portosegurohostel.com.br. A small but welcoming

IYHA hostel in the historic centre near the main bars & restaurants & the ferry for Arraial. Facilities include internet, a pool & tour operator. $

🛏 **Albergue Porto Seguro Praia Taberapuan** (20 rooms) Taberapuan beach ☎ 3288 1742; www.portosegurohostel.com.br. The beachside annexe of the town hostel offers a big games room & leisure area & similar featureless but clean rectangles accommodating dbls or 6-in-a room dorms. Internet, pool & tours. $

✗ WHERE TO EAT

✗ **Area** Av Portugal 246; ☎ 3288 5358; www.areagroup.com.br; ⏰ 17.00–24.00 daily. The restaurant specialises in Italian-Brazilian cuisine. It's set in a colonial house right in the historic centre & caters mainly for Italian tourists who eat fresh barbecued fish & meat & assorted seafood dishes. $$$$

✗ **O Bistrô** Rua Marechal Deodoro 172; ☎ 3288 3940; ⏰ 18.30–24.00 Mon–Sat. Snug & welcoming with an al fresco area. Modern regional cuisine is based on seafood but includes some vegetarian options. Try the *camarão ao molho de pitanga*. $$$$

✗ **Recanto do Sossego** Av Beira-Mar 10130, Praia do Mutá; ☎ 3677 1266; www.recantodosossego.com; ⏰ 08.00–17.00 daily. The restaurant is by the beach with tables both indoors, with sea view, or on the sand under thatched-roof shade. The Italian chef cooks Brazilian with Italian ingredients & Italian with Brazilian. The house speciality is *moqueca italiana*. $$$$

✗ **Sambuca** Praça dos Pataxós 216; ☎ 3288 2366; ⏰ 18.00–24.00 daily. Next door to the ferry port to Arraial D'Ajuda. Outdoor tables also available at the back. Good wood oven-cooked pizza & an à la carte menu of stodgy pasta. $$

✗ **Portinha** Rua Saldanha Marinho 33; ☎ 3288 2743; www.portinha.com.br; ⏰ 12.00–17.00 & 18.00–22.00 daily. One of a popular chain of self-service restaurants with food charged per kilo. Basic well-prepared regional cuisine, with a range of meat, fish & poultry dishes, salads & desserts. Good value. Recommended. $– $$

✗ **Acarajé da Jaque** Av Navegantes cnr with Rua Cidade Fafi; ☎ 9985 6998; ⏰ 16.30–22.00 Mon–Fri. Jaqueline, the cook, sets up a little pavement table in the historic centre to sell her famous *acarajé*. $

✗ **Da Japonesa** Praça dos Pataxós 38; ☎ 3288 2592; ⏰ 07.00–23.00 daily. Sushis, sashimis & some of the Brazilian standard – meat/chicken/fish with rice, beans & unseasoned salad. Excellent value. $

ENTERTAINMENT AND NIGHTLIFE Porto Seguro builds its *barracas* on an industrial scale. They are not the little palm-thatched lean-tos that proliferate on most of Bahia's beaches, but hulking great affairs – some with two storeys of bars and dance floors, others with giant soundstages booming out axé music. Brazilians congregate at the noisiest and Porto Seguro *barracas* pride themselves on being bigger and noisier than anywhere else in Brazil. If you are looking for a peaceful and idyllic beach holiday spot, this is not the place. But it's where beach Bahia loves to party.

♫ **Axé Moi** Av Beira Mar km367, Praia de Taperapuã; ☎ 3679 3237; www.axemoi.com.br; ⏰ from 10.00 daily. Axé Moi is Porto's biggest noise – especially on Mon. Axé bands play day & night on the beach all through the high season. See the website for their schedule. As well as a sound stage the *barraca* has a restaurant, café, bar, toilets & even playground child-minding for when parents want to be free to dance & have fun.

♫ **Barramares** Av Beira Mar km367, Praia de Taperapuã; ☎ 3679 2980; www.barramares.com.br;

⏰ from 10.00 daily. Parties on Wed. Live concerts & DJs throughout the week in high season. Barramares boasts 4 stages presenting different music styles including European electronica & house.

♫ **Tôa Toa** Av Beira Mar km367, Praia de Taperapuã; ☎ 3679 1146; www.portaltoatoa.com.br; ⏰ from 10.00 daily. Live concerts of kitschy axé sung loud & accompanied by big-thighed *dancarinhas* prancing about the stage like pumped-up cheerleaders on amphetamines.

SHOPPING The Pataxó sell beautiful handicrafts at Jaqueira (see page 184).

Arte Indígena da Amazônia Rua Assis Chateaubrian 68, Passarela do Álcool; ☏ 3288 4352. Indigenous art & crafts from the Amazon.

OTHER PRACTICALITIES Bradesco on Avenida Getúlio Vargas and the airport each have a Visa ATM. Banco do Brasil on Avenida Beira Mar (☏ *10.00–15.00*), changes travellers' cheques (big commission) and US dollars and euros cash.

Portomondo can change cash and book flights (see page 193). There are myriad internet shops throughout town. The post office is in the mini-shopping centre on the corner of Jandaias and Avenida dos Navegantes.

WHAT TO SEE AND DO

Cidade Histórica – the colonial centre Portuguese Porto Seguro crowns the highest point of a large grassy knoll fringed with tropical trees and overlooking the river and beaches. This is where Brazil began and it's one of those rare spots where Bahia has taken real care to preserve its history. The colourful single-storey houses are (mostly) freshly painted and they lead to a small square dominated by the 18th-century church of **Nossa Senhora da Pena** (*Praça Pero de Campos Tourinho s/n;* ☏ *3288 6363;* ☏ *09.00–12.00 & 14.00–17.00 daily; free admission*) built over an original and more modest 16th-century structure. Inside is what is said to be the oldest piece of statuary in the country – an undistinguished effigy of St Francis of Assisi. Next to the church is the stately 16th-century Palladian **Casa de Câmara e Cadêia** (*Praça Pero de Campos Tourinho s/n;* ☏ *3288 5182;* ☽ *09.00–17.00 daily; free admission*), from where the Portuguese failed to conquer and rule a captaincy the size of a large European country and where they tried, gaoled and executed their prisoners. It houses a modest sacred art museum today with some gruesome Baroque art and a few touching statues of a suffering Christ. **Nossa Senhora da Misericórdia** (*Praça Pero de Campos Tourinho s/n;* ☏ *3288 5182;* ☽ *09.30–13.30 & 14.30–17.00 Sat–Wed; free admission*), Brazil's oldest church built in 1526, sits on the other side of the Casa de Câmara. Even the twee children's paintbox colours and the little scrolled Rococo pediment can't disguise that it's a functional little building with heavy walls, built to defend the first fathers and fighting farmers against the irate locals whose land they were requisitioning for the Portuguese crown. The Jesuit church of 1549 **São Benedito** (*Rua Dr Antônio Ricaldi s/n*) a stroll away is simpler still and even more heavily fortified and it sits in the ruins of a college conquered by the ancestors of Pataxó in the face of strong casuistry. At the far side of the grassy knoll is a lingam-shaped block of Cantabrian marble inscribed with the Cross of the Order of Christ. This is where – if anywhere – Portuguese Brazil began in 1503 when Gonçalo Coelho thrust into the hilltop in the midst of the Tupiniquin – as formal declaration that the Portuguese were claiming the Indians' land as their own.

Memorial da Epopéia do Descrobimento (*Br-367 km67, Praia do Itacimirim;* ☏ *3268 2586;* ☽ *08.30–12.30 & 13.30–17.00 Mon–Sat*) This memorial was constructed on Curuipe beach during the 500th anniversary celebrations of the discovery of Brazil, in 2000. It includes a replica of a tiny caravel that carried Pedro Álvares Cabral to Brazil – built by a local joiner, Quincas.

Ilha dos Aquários A complex of five aquaria on an island in the river between Porto and Arraial. The largest, with 220,000 litres, houses sharks and morays; the others reproduce marine environments around Porto Seguro from river and reef to mangroves. There's also a small orchidarium and series of overpriced restaurants. At night the island comes alive with live forró bands and gaggles of teenaged Brazilians.

ARRAIAL D'AJUDA *Telephone code: 73*

Porto Seguro's counterpart immediately across the water is altogether more laid-back. Like most of the towns in southern Bahia it began life as a scattering of semi-fortified churches and houses built on a bluff with strategic views out over the river. After the Aimoré began to slacken their attacks on the Portuguese settlers it became a little fishing town with skiffs on the river and *saveiros* on the beaches. And then in the 1970s it was discovered by Paulistanos seeking refuge from the military government and life in tranquil nature and copious amounts of weed. The rest of the world slowly followed and by the 1980s Arraial had become another secret on the legendary Gringo Trail and unlike Porto Seguro it never really lost its hippy heart; it just commercialised it.

Arraial today remains low-rise and for a resort town, low-key. Its beaches are lined with pousadas and not hotels and the further you go south the quieter they become. For much of their length they are backed by golden and ochre sandstone cliffs that look like broken honey and mango halvah in the deep yellow sun. Arraial is a place travellers find themselves getting stuck in. It has long attracted Israelis, many of whom come to see the beach and stay to learn capoiera. At Brazilian holiday times (especially New Year and Carnaval) Arraial bursts at the seams with people.

ORIENTATION The town centre is clustered around the pretty church of **Nossa Senhora da Ajuda** built in 1549 and sitting at the apex of town with views of the palm-covered, beach-fringed coast. The principal streets extend off the square in front of the church. The largest, lined with shops, bars, restaurants and pousadas, is called Bróduei, pronounced Broadway.

There's a party on Bróduei and one or more of the beaches almost every night in high season.

GETTING THERE AND AROUND Ferries from Porto Seguro run across the Rio Buranhém to the south bank, every 10–15 minutes day and night (10mins; R$1 for foot passengers, R$15 for cars).

Arraial d'Ajuda town centre is a further 5km along a dirt road which runs roughly parallel to the beach (R$2 by bus, R$3 by van – which leave when full; taxis cost R$10). There are pousadas all the way along the road – on the beach and inland, with the first literally on the riverbank.

It is not necessary to return to Porto Seguro to reach the rest of Bahia. Arraial is connected by bus to Eunápolis (1hr, with fast connecting services to the north and directly to Salvador) and Caraíva, and Trancoso to the south. Buses for Caraíva leave via Trancoso daily at 07.00 and 16.00; extra bus at 11.00 in high season (*Viação Águia Azul;* ✆3875 1170).

Various agencies in town offer transfers by buggy or Land Rover to Corumbau and beyond all the way to Abrolhos. Portomondo (see page 193) is by far the best and most reliable.

TOURIST INFORMATION The website www.arraialdajuda.tur.br has photos, comprehensive listings of pousadas, restaurants, shops, tour operators and general services (in Portuguese).

LOCAL TOUR OPERATORS There are plenty of tour operators in Porto Seguro and Arraial d'Ajuda offering rough and ready nature-based trips with large (and usually

6

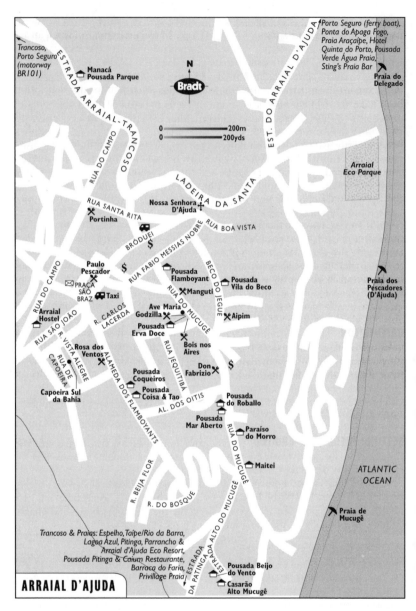

Trancoso,
Porto Seguro
(motorway
BR101)

ESTRADA ARRAIAL-TRANCOSO

Manacá
Pousada Parque

N

Bradt

0 ———— 200m
0 ———— 200yds

EST. DO ARRAIAL D'AJUDA

Porto Seguro (ferry boat),
Ponta do Apaga Fogo,
Praia Araçaípe, Hotel
Quinta do Porto, Pousada
Verde Água Praia,
Sting's Praia Bar

Praia do
Delegado

Arraial
Eco Parque

LADEIRA DA SANTA

RUA DO CAMPO

RUA SANTA RITA

Portinha

Nossa Senhora
D'Ajuda

RUA BOA VISTA

BRÓDUEI

RUA FABIO MESSIAS NOBRE

BECO DO JEGUE

Paulo
Pescador

PRAÇA
SÃO
BRAZ

Taxi

RUA DO CAMPO

Arraial
Hostel

RUA SÃO JOÃO

R. CARLOS
LACERDA

Pousada
Flamboyant

Manguti

Ave Maria
Godzilla

Pousada
Erva Doce

RUA DO MUCUGÊ

Pousada
Vila do Beco

Aipim

Bois nos
Aires

RUA JEQUITIBA

Rosa dos
Ventos

ALAMEDA DOS FLAMBOYANTS

RUA DE
CAPOEIRA

RUA VISTA ALEGRE

Capoeira Sul
da Bahia

Pousada
Coqueiros

Pousada
Coisa & Tao

AL. DOS OITIS

Don
Fabrizio

Pousada
do Roballo

Praia dos
Pescadores
(D'Ajuda)

Pousada
Mar Aberto

RUA DO MUCUGÊ

Paraíso
do Morro

Maitei

ATLANTIC
OCEAN

R. BEIJA FLOR

R. DO BOSQUE

ESTRADA ALTO DO MUCUGÊ

Praia de
Mucugê

Trancoso & Praias: Espelho, Taípe/Rio da Barra,
Lagoa Azul, Pitinga, Parrancho &
Arraial d'Ajuda Eco Resort,
Pousada Pitinga & Caium Restaurante,
Barraca do Faria,
Privillòge Praia

ESTRADA DA PATINGA

Pousada Beijo
do Vento

Casarão
Alto Mucugê

ARRAIAL D'AJUDA

jocular) groups. These are best avoided. When they visit areas with wildlife the animals are gone long before the tourists arrive – such are the noise levels. Serious wildlife enthusiasts and birders should book a specialist guide in advance (see *Birdwatching in Bahia* box on pages 20–1). Those looking for something away from the noisy norm would do well to choose one of the following companies:

Pataxó turismo 9979 5597;
www.pataxoturismo.com.br. Have been working with the local indigenous communities for some 20 years

& offer visits to & overnight stays in a number of villages in the local area. These include Jaqueira. A percentage of profits goes direct to the Pataxó. Maria

Luisa the owner speaks only a little English but can hire English-speaking guides for trips.

Portomondo Ponta do Apaga Fogo 1, Marina Quinta do Porto Hotel; ✆ 3575 3686; www.portomondo.com. The best general tour operator in southern Bahia with a broad range of trips from snorkelling & scuba diving to kayaking along rivers & past beaches,

abseiling waterfalls, rafting & hiking in the national parks. The agency works with the Pataxó & has a marvellous 4–5-day trip all the way south to Abrolhos along the beaches in buggies & boats & can book private homestays & boutique hotels from Trancoso & Corumbau. English spoken & very friendly, knowledgeable staff.

WHERE TO STAY

🏠 **Arraial d'Ajuda Eco Resort** (130 rooms) Ponta do Apaga-Fogo 60; ✆ 3575 8500; www.arraialresort.com.br. Despite its name, this big resort does little to practise genuine conservational tourism, but at least it does encourage guests to explore the region, providing complementary transfer to nearby beaches & free entry to Eco Parque — a theme park with water activities, fun for kids & teenagers. The décor is pleasantly 'eco' with thatched bar by the pool, rattan chairs & decorative effigies of *orixás* (African gods) sculptures. Built in 1990 the hotel has been slowly improved & renovated. The outdoor jacuzzi overlooks the sea & so does the play room for kids. The restaurant Ponta do Apaga Fogo has a very good reputation but although the location is not central it can still be very noisy! Transfer to the town centre is available. $$$$$

🏠 **Maitei** (17 rooms) Rua do Mucugê 475; ✆ 3575 3877; www.maitei.com.br. This luxury hotel boasts that all its AC rooms are fully equipped with king-sized beds, anti-allergenic feather pillows & a sea view. They are also decorated with a tasteful rustic chic with everything from table ornaments to paintings by local artists. Rooms have double jacuzzis, minibar & flat-screen TV with cable channels. No children under 16, so this one's strictly for the grown-ups. It's a stroll away from both town centre & beach. $$$$$

🏠 **Privillage Praia** (20 rooms) Estrada da Pitinga 1800, Praia de Pitinga; ✆ 3575 1646; www.privillage.com.br. A 40min ride from Porto Seguro airport brings guests to this beautiful, secluded beach — free of even dirt roads & beach bars in a tranquil palm-tree glade. Rooms are spread at varying heights around a lush garden overlooking the sea. All have flat-screen TVs with international channels such as Warner & Sony & big cosy beds. There's an excellent restaurant in a thatched hut by the pool; try *caldeirada de frutos do mar*. You could easily spend all your time here but if you would also like to explore the town centre, about 1 mile away, you'll need a cab, a bike or rental car. $$$$$

🏠 **Casarão Alto Mucugê** (8 rooms) Estrada Alto Mucugê; ✆ 3575 1490; www.casaraoaltomucuge.com.

Though small scale there's plenty of space to spare in this farm-style hotel with its high ceilings. There are wonderful sea views, too — rooms sit in a heliconia garden at the edge of a cliff overlooking the sea with a hot tub, comfortable seating & even a massage facility. The main house, where b/fast is served, is full of character & good taste, the decoration is based on objects & holy pictures from the 19th century — it's a pleasant place to hang out, with a pool table, sitting room, Wi-Fi connection. $$$$–$$$$$

🏠 **Pousada Beijo do Vento** (10 rooms) Estrada Alto Mucugê 730; ✆ 3575 1349; www.beijodovento.com.br. On the top of a cliff leaning over Mucugê beach, Beijo do Vento ('Wind's Kiss') deserves its name. There's a constant, refreshing sea breeze & the views from the poolside are breathtaking. The rooms are in a 2-storey terracotta house with the best views available from the Upper storey. There's 1 room with a private outdoor jacuzzi. They only accept children older than 8. $$$$–$$$$$

🏠 **Pousada Pitinga** (17 rooms) Praia de Pitinga 1633; ✆ 3575 1067; www.pousadapitinga.com.br. This pousada is by the beach & sits in a coconut palm-filled rainforest garden embracing the jewel-like pool. Most of the wooden chalets in the garden partially overlook the sea. There's a relaxing atmosphere & great food at the Caium restaurant (see page 195). $$$$–$$$$$

🏠 **Manacá Pousada Parque** (28 rooms) Estrada para Trancoso 500; ✆ 3575 1442; www.pousadamanaca.com.br. The rooms here are simple but the best offer great views — out over the pool deck & canopies of coconut trees to the ocean & at night the twinkling lights of Porto Seguro. The garden is a generous size; the rooms small but functional with hammocks provided in the balconies. $$$$

🏠 **Paraíso do Morro** (13 rooms) Rua do Mucugê 471; ✆ 3575 3330, 3575 2423; www.paraisodomorro.com. This brightly coloured hotel has great sea views from its huge windows. Most rooms include a jacuzzi. There's also a lovely pool deck. It's just a stroll away from Mucugê beach & is popular with couples. $$$$

🏠 **Quinta do Porto** (81 rooms) Ponta do Apaga Fogo; ☎ 3575 1022; www.quintadoporto.com.br. The hotel has a pleasantly shaded garden, deck & pool (right on the riverfront) populated by (clipped-wing) parrots, macaws & parakeets who go for your toes at b/fast given half the chance. Rooms are simple boxy affairs in cream paint & white tile with AC & cable TV but they have good views out over the river. A shuttle bus takes guests into Arraial town every evening. Dinner is included in the rates & transfers to the beach are straightforward as the van & taxi rank is 3mins' walk away, as is the ferry dock for Porto Seguro. Bring earplugs for the terrible pool-side music. $$$$

🏠 **Pousada Coisa & Tao** (14 rooms) Alameda dos Flamboyants 75; ☎ 3575 2425; www.pousadacoisaetao.com.br. Located at the town centre. The pousada has well-maintained air-conditioned rooms, painted in orange & whitewash & decorated with colourful marine prints. Some have space for up to 4 people. There's a relaxing outdoor lounge bar surrounded by lush vegetation & an adjacent small pool. $$$–$$$$

🏠 **Pousada Erva Doce** (15 rooms) Rua do Mucugê 200; ☎ 3575 1113; www.ervadoce.com.br. Good-sized rooms with sense of style. Some take up to 4 people. The pool is situated in a well-kept garden. Lockers & internet access are available to guests. $$$–$$$$

🏠 **Pousada Coqueiros** (28 rooms) Alameda dos Flamboyants 55; ☎ 3575 1229; www.pousadacoqueiros.com.br. There are colourful family rooms (with dbl beds & an optional sgl), & rooms to share with friends (with 2–4 sgl beds) at this popular pousada. The hotel's poolside restaurant-bar, Coqueiros, serves cocktails & decent food, try *file de badejo*, & is a draw for non-guests. Guests can enjoy a sauna on those rare days in Arraial when the temperature plummets to 25°C. $$$

🏠 **Pousada do Roballo** (25 rooms) Rua do Mucugê 436; ☎ 3575 1053; www.pousadadoroballo.com.br. A welcoming, bricked-wall pousada, popular among travellers & very hard to book in high season. It has a small pool & free Wi-Fi. Small rooms with balconies & hammock. Private bathroom, TV & AC. Walking distance to both beach & town centre. Good b/fast. Closed in June. $$$

🏠 **Pousada Verde Água Praia** (11 rooms) Estrada do Arraial 1893, Praia de Araçaipe; ☎ 3575 1453; www.verdeaguapraia.com.br. At Araçaipe beach, with pool & bar, open all day for drinks. There are rooms for up to 3 people & chalets with 2 rooms able to accommodate up to 5 people. No charge for children under 6. Nice garden & restaurant overlooking the sea. $$–$$$

🏠 **Pousada Vila do Beco** (29 rooms) Beco do Jegue 173; ☎ 3575 1230; www.viladobeco.com.br. The beach maybe a 10min walk but there are ocean views from the sculpted pool & shady garden in this town centre pousada. The chalets are in new colonial style, with tiled roofs & white walls. Inside they're spartan – bright white with no ornaments but comfortable, clean & airy & with plenty of storage space. All rooms have bathroom, balcony, fan, TV & minibar. AC is optional. $$–$$$

🏠 **Pousada Flamboyant** (15 rooms) Rua do Mucugê 89 Centre; ☎ 3575 1025; www.flamboyant.tur.br. This cheap & cheerful pousada is a mishmash of varying styles & no style at all. The rooms vary a lot in size; some of them are really well presented & it's conveniently close to shops & restaurants. All rooms with AC, TV & fridge. Good b/fast & pool. $$

🏠 **Pousada Mar Aberto** (14 rooms) Rua do Mucugê 554; ☎ 3575 1153; www.maraberto.arraialdajuda.com. Brick chalets sitting on the crest of a hill & set in lush gardens with a small pool. Good location close to Mucugê beach & the town centre. This pousada is especially popular among Argentinian tourists. AC rooms are basic but decorated with brightly coloured cushions & pictures. $$

🏠 **Arraial Hostel** (16 rooms) Rua do campo 94 Centre; ☎ 3575 1192; www.arraialdajudahostel.com.br. The colourful IYHA 2-storey building has an internal courtyard with a pool in a style they describe as Greco Romano Bahiano. All rooms face the pool. It's central & within walking distance of the beach. Facilities include a bar, internet & good book exchange. Great value. Recommended. $

✖ **WHERE TO EAT** Most restaurants in Arraial open between 12.00–15.00 and 18.00–midnight.

✖ **Aipim** Beco do Jegue 13; ☎ 3575 3222; www.aipimrestaurante.com.br; ⏰ Feb–Dec 18.00–24.00 Mon–Sat, Jan 18.00–01.00. Arraial's most renowned fine-dining restaurant is aimed at couples, with a mood-lit main dining room that works its magic best after dark – despite the tropicália of colours. There's an outdoor second dining too – on a terrace opening onto the garden. The restaurant itself is farmhouse-fashionable, with exposed beams & vines hanging from the walls. Some of the decorations come from a shipwreck. The modern menu is a sophisticated fusion of international & Brazilian flavours. Start with a *caipingibre* drink – vodka, ginger & *pimenta rosa* – a sharp, tangy sertão fruit which tastes like a cross between juniper & chilli without the *picante* burn. To eat, try the seafood degustation with plenty of freshly grilled cuts. $$$$$

✘ **Caium Restaurante** Pousada Pitinga, Praia de Pitinga 1633; ✆ 3575 1067; ⏰ 12.00–22.00 daily. From the large decked area you can dine beachside, overlooking the sea, feeling the night breeze & wondering at the myriad stars. The indoor dining room of this tranquil restaurant is unpretentious, with its thatched roof, small wooden tables & rattan chairs. The cuisine is a mix of Mediterranean & regional. The speciality is *arrastão* – seafood with coconut rice. $$$$

✘ **Don Fabrizio**, Rua do Mucuge 402; ✆ 3575 2407; www.restaurantedonfabrizio.com; ⏰ from 16.00 daily. A candlelit dining room gives an intimate atmosphere which attracts couples to sample Italian-born Fabrizio's homemade pasta, risotto, Tuscan seafood & barbecued meat. The wine list is one of Arraial's best with some 80 bottles to choose from. $$$$

✘ **Rosa dos Ventos** Alameda dos Flamboyants 24; ✆ 3575 1271; ⏰ 16.00–24.00 Mon, Tue, Thu & Sat, 13.00–22.00 Sun. Working since 1991 this charming place, perfect for chilling out, has all its decorations made by local artists & is very much in tune with Arraial's relaxed mood. Maintaining their own vegetable garden & orchard, the proprietors pay lots of attention to the ingredients. Their menu is quite varied. One of their specialities is fish slow roasted in banana leaf. Some dishes like lamb & lobster have to be ordered a day in advance. $$$$

✘ **Boi nos Aires** Rua do Mucugê 200; ✆ 3575 2554; www.arraialdajuda.com/boinosaires. A relaxed Argentinian BBQ with a thatched roof, wooden tables & prime cuts of cow imported from Argentina. The wine list has some respectable *mendozas* & a handful from the republic's arch-enemy across the Andes, Chile. The house speciality is *boi nos aires*, the best cut of loin. $$$

✘ **Manguti** Rua do Mucugê 99; ✆ 3575 2270; www.manguti.com.br. A little yellow house with tables outside fitted into every available nook & cranny. A very busy & bubbling restaurant that owes its success to what they consider a perfect marriage: *nhoque* & meat. The house speciality is *nhoque com filé mignon*. $$$

✘ **Godzilla** Rua do Mucugê 200; ✆ 3575 3302; www.godzillabrazil.com. Korean, Cambodian, Thai, Japanese & Vietnamese fusion cooking (as well as with traditional set menus of sushi & sashimi) from exuberant, bottle-blonde expat Japanese, Fumiaka Yamada. $$–$$$

✘ **Barraca do Faria** Praia de Pitinga; ✆ 3575 3840; www.barracadofaria.com.br. Closed May & June. A bungalow beach bar on Pitinga beach with tables on the sand. The menu is basic seafood tapas including deep-fried fish bites & prawn pastries. To drink there's ice-cold beer, soft drinks & *caipirinha*. There is a space for children with a small play area & pool & live music – though not at the ear-busting decibels of Porto Seguro. Parking is 300m from the *barraca*. $–$$

✘ **Portinha** Rua do Campo 1; ✆ 3575 1289; www.portinha.com.br. One of a popular chain of self-service restaurants with food charged per kilo. Basic well-prepared regional cuisine, with a range of meat, fish & poultry dishes, salads & deserts. Good value. $–$$

✘ **Paulo Pescador** Praça São Brás 116; ✆ 3575 1242; www.paulopescador.com.br. Closed during May. Close to the church on Bróduei. The dining room is filled with wooden tables & the white walls are decorated with nautical pictures. It's busy & lively but relaxed; the clientele dine in their beach clothes on 12 types of PF (*prato feito*) set lunch. All the choices are variations on rice, salad & meat/chicken/fish. $

✘ **Sting's Praia Bar** Estrada da Balsa 1937, Praia de Araçaipe; ✆ 9982 9991; www.stingpraiabar.com. A very popular *barraca* on Araçaipe beach not run by the former lead singer & bassist from the Police. During high season people sit or stand around to listen to the live music in the afternoon. The speciality is grilled *dourado* fillet & vegetables. $

ENTERTAINMENT AND NIGHTLIFE *Barracas* on Mucugê and Parracho beaches offer forró and pagode dancing in high season and are visited by bands from throughout Brazil. Limelight and the Jatobar are the hotspots of the moment.

SHOPPING

Ave Maria Rua do Mucugê 246 Centre; ✆ 3575 3161; www.lojaavemaria.com.br. Good variety of artistic & innovative casual spring & summer dresses, tops & accessories. The work is the result of the association of 2 Brazilian fashion designers who are proud to cultivate both sacred & profane, using appliqué, embroidery & lace.

OTHER PRACTICALITIES Bradesco and HSBC both have ATMs on Broduei (Broadway).

WHAT TO SEE AND DO

Eco-Water Park (*Estrada do Arraial d'Ajuda km4.5*; ✎ *3575 8600; www.arraialecoparque.com.br*; ⊕ *irregularly – see calendar on website or ask in the hotel; adult/child R$60/30*) Despite the name there is nothing eco about this giant water park which is Bahia's equivalent of the WaterWorld franchise; in fact it is quite the opposite with some 60,000m² of treated water, concrete slides and artificial rivers. But it's fun for a noisy afternoon and children especially love it.

Beaches Arraial's beaches begin with Araçaipe at the mouth of the River Buranhem and continue south towards Trancoso. They are invariably splendid and varied and can be reached by walking along Rua da Praia out of town. **Araçaipe** is gentle, pousada-lined and popular with families but the water can be clouded by water from the river. **Mucugê** just to the south of town has good surf and plenty of beach *barracas* for forró and lambada parties in the summer; it's one of the liveliest in Arraial. South beyond Mucugê is **Parracho**, another very lively party beach, which is popular for windsurfing and kayaking (rental available). Next is **Pitinga**, with strong waves breaking on an offshore reef creating some decent surf. After this is **Lagoa Azul**, backed by cliffs, with gorgeous sand and strong surf. Few make it to the beach farthest south, **Taipé**, an hour's walk from Arraial. It is watched over by sandstone cliffs and has glassy water and a handful of *barracas*. At low tide it is possible to walk from Taipé to Trancoso along the beach via the village of **Rio da Barra**; allow two hours from Taipé. A dirt road behind the coast follows the same route and is plied by taxis and cars; it is easy to hitch a lift.

Capoeira

Capoeira Sul da Bahia Rua da Capoeira 57; ✎ 3575 2981; www.capoeirasuldabahia.com.br. Lessons with Mestre Railson; excellent instruction, very popular with foreigners. ⊕ For kids: 09.00–10.00 & 16.00–17.00

Mon, Wed & Fri; beginners: 10.00–11.30 & 18.30–20.00 Mon–Fri; advanced: 20.00–21.30 Mon–Fri; *Rodas* 20.00 Sat.

TRANCOSO *Telephone code: 73*

For the likes of *Vanity Fair* photographer Mario Testino and a generation of label-conscious, tiny Trancoso defines Brazilian beach chic. This is where people who arrive in helicopters and limousines to private parties in São Paulo bump into each other and look surprised, even though only people who attend such parties holiday in Trancoso. And it's where everyone is hip; effortlessly so – in their carefully chosen Havaiana flip-flops, Jack Vartanian diamonds and Lenny bikinis. Trancoso's vanity fair is a pretty parade and great fun to watch whilst sipping one of Brazil's best *caipirinhas* in one of the country's finest restaurants or boutique hotels and enjoying the beauty of the crimson sunset. And it can all be taken in one's stride, for posy though it may be, Trancoso's style is not devoid of substance. Little here comes in poor taste, from the sumptuous cooking to the beachside boho shops. There's no high-rise or cubic concrete, no blaring music and a few of the hotels are making first efforts at conservation. For a quiet, refined comfortable beach stay there's really nowhere better.

Life in Trancoso is simple. There's the beaches which are simply divine and there's the Quadrado. This kilometre-long grassy square ending in another stocky Portuguese church perched on a cliff is lined by pretty painted bungalows - chic shacks housing chic shops and *caipirinha* bars. After beach time, life focuses here, unwinding in a predictable ritual. Just before sunset the locals play football and perform impromptu capoeira. Then the boutiques and bars wake up and the beautiful people begin to wander. After eating they congregate to drink, dance a little and watch each other. Then they retire to a private party in a fashionable beach house or a slick beach hotel – of which Trancoso has many.

GETTING THERE AND AROUND Buses run regularly on the newly paved road between Porto Seguro, Arraial d'Ajuda and Trancoso, at least every hour from Arraial in high season (to Porto Seguro R$8, to Ajuda R$5). Arriving from the south, change buses at Eunápolis from where the newly paved Linha Verde road runs to Trancoso. Buses for Caraíva leave twice daily at 08.00 and 17.00, with an extra bus at 12.00 in high season. Trancoso is easy to get around **on foot**. **Bikes** are the best option for the farther beaches. Most pousadas lend or rent them or can organise someone to do so.

WHERE TO STAY Most of the upper-end Trancoso pousadas do not accept children under 15 either in high season or at any time of the year. Check beforehand.

🏠 **Jacaré do Brasil Casas** (5 houses) Praça São João 9, Quadrado; ☎ 3668 1667; www.jacaredobrasilcasas.com.br. Trancoso's celebrated design & homeware shop has now taken its modish raw wood & rustic formula & applied it to the rental home; with 5 contemporary cliff-top *casitas* in secondary-growth forest around a shared pool & furnished with weather-worn woods, rough & ready refined sofas & chairs & the best of their driftwood & coconut-shell-cool home décor. $$$$$

🏠 **Pousada Estrela d'Água** (28 rooms) Estrada Arraial D'Ajuda, Praia dos Nativos; ☎ 3668 1030; www.estreladagua.com.br. Rows of luxe fishermen's shacks in a long garden lead to a large glass-fronted bar & sitting area overlooking a big, deep blue infinity pool, swaying palms & the beach. Rooms range from the master suite duplex seafront – a 200m², 2-floor *palapa* bungalow & with private bamboo terraces, jacuzzi & ocean views – to the 120m² master suite, which is similar but 1 storey & in the garden; the standard suites out back have twins or kings. All are decorated in minimalist, clean Mediterranean whites & deep blues. Free Wi-Fi throughout. The hotel is one of the few in Bahia to make efforts to practise conservational tourism following the PNUMA UN programme for nature, installing solar power, recycling & engaging in some small welfare programmes. The bar has famous sundowner scene. $$$$$

🏠 **Pousada Etnia** (8 rooms) Rua Principal 25; ☎ 3668 1137; www.etniabrasil.com.br. Andre Zanonato & Corrado Tini's effortlessly chic pousada comprises a series of simple but elegant bungalows. They come with minimalist decoration & are gathered in a hilly

tropical-forest garden filled with brilliantly coloured birds & butterflies & watching over a lush designer pool much photographed by lifestyle magazines. $$$$$

🏠 **Villas de Trancoso** (6 rooms) Estrada do Arraial, Praia dos Nativos; ☎ 3668 1151; www.mybrazilianbeach.com. This American-owned establishment is the best of the beachside hotels, with a run of wooden cabins set around a pool on a large lawn surrounded by remnant forest & mangroves. A boardwalk leads through these to a relaxed private beach bar & rustic wood-weight gym. Cabins are well appointed & decked out in lush polished wood. The duplex suite is perhaps the most luxurious in the town, with a large lower sitting room in polished wood & linens & furnished with long sofas & an upper deck with a bedroom under a thatched-roof *palapa*. Light floods in from huge windows & the cabin is decorated with Brazilian *objets d'art*. $$$$$

🏠 **Pousada Capim Santo** (17 rooms) Rua do Beco, Praça São João, Quadrado; ☎ 3668 1122; www.capimsanto.com.br. Mock-colonial bungalows in a lush garden setting just off the quadrado. Each is bright, light & minimalist in design & décor, with white interiors, açai palm blinds, mosquito drapes & blocks of primary colour from scatter cushions & bed linen. Capim Santo is another of the town's pousadas to take steps towards environmental best practice with water recycling & solar-powered showers. And they run one of the best kitchens in town. $$$$–$$$$$

🏠 **Mata N'ativa Pousada** (8 rooms) Estrada do Arraial, Praia dos Nativos; ☎ 3668 1830; www.matanativapousada.com.br. This warm &

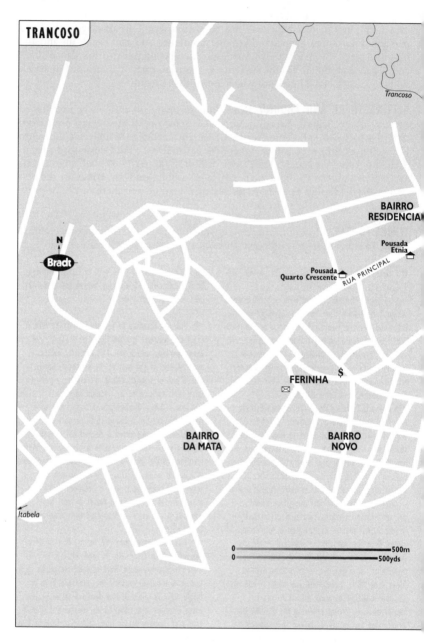

welcoming riverside pousada is the perfect marriage of refined Trancoso taste & Brazil's (customary) lack of pretentiousness. Owners Daniel & Daniela treat guests like old friends rather than clients & offer accommodation in a series of elegant & romantic cabins set in a cool & shady garden visited by numerous birds & butterflies. Daniel offers exuberant light adventure trips – kayaking on the river or nature walking in areas of restinga & Atlantic coastal forest nearby. He is a fount of knowledge about Brazilian flora. The pousada maintains a small collection of nature books in its cosy sitting area. Good English, Spanish & Italian spoken. Great b/fast & children welcome. $$$

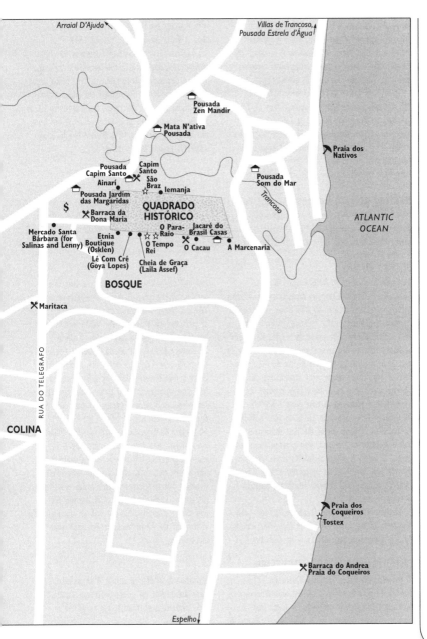

Pousada Jardim das Margaridas (8 rooms) Rua Jovelino Rodrigues Vieira 230; ☎ 3668 1108; www.jardimdasmargaridas.com.br. The dark yellow, mock-hacienda blocks in this pousada are a little ungainly but rooms offer spacious & uncluttered mock-Mediterranean minimalism & unlike most of Trancoso pousadas, children are welcome here. Great massage & treatments from Swiss-trained Taty Calonder. $$$$

Pousada Quarto Crescente (13 rooms or houses) Rua Principal; ☎ 3668 1014; www.quartocrescente.net. Individually decorated, simple rustic apts with tiled floors & concrete walls, a chalet & 2 houses with space for up to 7. The best rooms are Estrela & Lumiar —

where the plainness is offset by colourful linen & attractive abstract ethnic prints. B/fast is generous & varied with fruit, bread rolls, yoghurt & cereals & the pousada has a book exchange, rents bikes, organises excursions (including kayaking & snorkelling) & welcomes kids. Under 3s stay for free. $$–$$$

🏠 **Pousada Som do Mar** (12 rooms) Beco da Praia dos Nativos, Praia dos Nativos; ☎ 3668 1812; www.pousadasomdomar.com.br. Simple rectangles for rooms, all with terraces & hammock & housed in mock-colonial blocks next to a tiny pool & 5mins' walk from the Nativos beach. Internet & Wi-Fi. $$

🏠 **Pousada Zen Mandir** (8 rooms) Estrada do Arraial, Praia dos Nativos; ☎ 3668 1579; www.pousadazentrancoso.com. Comprises 80–130m² orange bungalows next to the beach with echoey large sitting rooms (with futons & TVs), b/fast areas & upstairs bedroom. Furnishings are more minimal than minimalist but the rooms are brightened up by ample light & blocks of primary colour. A km from the Quadrado & 150m from Nativos beach. Good value for groups. Decent b/fast $$

Renting private houses Arraial-based Portomondo (*www.arraialdajuda.tur.br*), São Paulo-based Casas Charmosas (*www.casascharmosas.com.br*) and Matueté (*www.matuete.com*) and the Paraty-based Brazilian Beach House (*www.brazilianbeach.com*) rent a range of villas and beach houses in Trancoso.

✕ WHERE TO EAT

✕ **Capim Santo** Rua do Beco, Praça São João, Quadrado; ☎ 3668 1122; www.capimsanto.com.br. This garden restaurant created by Paulistana expat Sandra Marques is quintessentially Trancoso. Seafood dishes with a Bahian twist like prawn in manioc flour balls or tuna carpaccio are served under star & candlelight in a little tropical garden just off the Quadrado. Be sure to begin the evening with a *caipisake com abacaxi e gengibre* made from sake, crushed ice, fresh crushed pineapple & root ginger. $$$$

✕ **O Cacau** Praça São João 96, Quadrado; ☎ 3668 1266. Doran Mirando serves the best traditional Bahian cooking in Trancoso, with a menu strong on flavour & spices & which includes starters like mini *acarajé* balls with *vatapá* or *caruru* & mains like camarão nativo (local prawns) which are antenna-twitchingly fresh. $$$$

✕ **Maritaca** Praça São João, Quadrado; ☎ 3668 1258. A Marrakesh theme may seem odd in hippy-chic Trancoso. But the sumptuous back deck with its open sky & beautiful drop-off view out to the sea attracts a faithful cocktail crowd & there's a respectable wine list. Take a *caipirinha* or crisp cab sav & watch the sunset or stars. But eat elsewhere. The Italian food is adequate but lacks sparkle & the service slow. $$$$

✕ **Barraca do Andrea Praia do Coqueiros** Coqueiros beach; ☎ none. The *barraca* of the moment for beach-lounge lovers. It's run by a Brazilianised Sardinian who serves great Italian wood-fired pizza, super-fresh *ceviche* & a gamut of fruity *caipirinhas* & tropical juices. $$–$$$

✕ **Barraca da Dona Maria** Quadrado. This Baiana with a warm grin is a Trancoso treasure. She & her 9-year-old grandson sell delicious home-baked bread, tiny prawn, chicken & meat pies (or *empadas*) & steaming hot treacle-sweet black coffee to fishermen (or visiting surfers) who rise with the sun. You can find them on a tiny little tile stall on the Quadrado in front of the Ainarí boutique. But she's gone by mid-morning. $

ENTERTAINMENT AND NIGHTLIFE

☆ **O Tempo Rei** Praça São João, Quadrado 172; ☎ 3668 1472. The Quadrado's current after-dinner watering hole of choice. It takes its name from a song by Bahia's Gilberto Gil & offers great *mojitos* & *caipirinhas*, & live music & dancing, under a panoply of stars.

☆ **São Braz** Praça São João, Quadrado s/n; Plays the liveliest forró in town after 23.00 when the open-air dance floor fills with beautiful couples pressed so close together that they seem grafted at the groin. Forró is Brazil's favourite beachside dance music. It's staccato & pulsating – driven by accordion & hand-held drums & thankfully the steps are kinder on gringo feat than samba. With a little practice even tourists get to gyrate in perfect syncopation.

☆ **O Para-Raio** Praça São João, Quadrado s/n; ☎ 3668 1025. Offers live bands & Euro-American DJ-driven club beats with a smattering of home-grown music from labels like Trama & artists like Patife & Marky – both of whom are Ibiza faves. But if you really want to go Trancoso it's a definite cop-out.

☆ **Tostex** Praia dos Coqueiros s/n. The night-time *barraca* of the moment with guest DJs from São

Paulo & abroad & nothing you wouldn't hear in Ibiza. For Brazilian sounds stick to the Quadrado.

Thousands gather over New Year & at Carnaval when it can feel like a Ko Pha Ngan full moon party.

SHOPPING

A Marcenaria Trancoso Praça São João, Quadrado 12; ✎ 3668 1023. Another rustic chic home décor shop, this one owned by Ricardo Salem, one of pioneer southeastern Brazilian rich hippies who invented the Trancoso scene. It sells a range of raw wood furniture & fittings alongside hardwood & coconut jewellery boxes in gaudiesque organic shapes.
Ainari Praça São João (Quadrado), Trancoso; ✎ 3668 1235. Sissi Prates's casual label is one of the few to have been created in Trancoso itself after the former model & ju-jitsu fighter decided to downgrade from her hectic São Paulo life & move to the beach.
Goya Lopes At Lé Com Cré, Praça São João, Quadrado; ✎ 3668 1180; www.goyalopes.com.br. This African-Brazilian artist & designer has exhibited at the Glass Curtain Gallery in Chicago. Her Didara label features simple cotton clothing & beach shawls stamped with intricate motifs from Candomblé & African-Brazilian cultural life (and Rua Gregorio de Mattos, Pelourinho, Salvador; see *Shopping* on page 121).
Jacaré Do Brasil Praça São João, Quadrado; www.jacaredobrasil.com. One-off contemporary homeware items, furniture & *objets d'art* made from weather-worn wood & natural fabrics & with impeccable, voguish taste. Stuff small enough to pack in a bag includes a coconut wood & silver bracelet for around R$50.

Laila Assef At Cheia de Graça, Praça São João, Quadrado; ✎ 3668 1492. Trashy art. Literally. Laila makes jewel-like household décor, wall sculptures & astonishing light-shades from filigrees of recycled coloured plastic. 'My work is truly ecological,' she says. 'It is for me what Trancoso should represent.'
Lenny Praça São João, Quadrado; ✎ 3668 1408; www.lenny.com.br. The height of Brazilian beach cool with a range of bikinis, swimsuits & post-beach apparel daringly cut & with fabulous prints.
Osklen At Etnia Boutique, Praça São João, Quadrado; ✎ 3668 1137; www.etniabrasil.com.br. Make the most fashionable range of Brazilian men's post-beach apparel in cooling cottons & linens. Men's swimwear – or *sungas* – are rectangles of skin-tight lycra which are (currently) most fashionable in black.
Ramon Lima At Lemanjá, Praça São João, Quadrado; ✎ 3668 2344. A former hip hop DJ who makes eye-catching pop art oratories with Catholic saints and *orixás*.
Salinas Mercado Santa Bárbara, Praça São João, Quadrado; ✎ 3668 1461; www.salinasswimwear.com. Made their name with gorgeous hand-crafted hippy-chic stitch & beadwork bikinis. In bold colours & cuts for Penelope Cruz bodies.

OTHER PRACTICALITIES There is a Bradesco visa ATM on the Quadrado.

BEYOND TRANCOSO

Beaches Below the Quadrado, Trancoso's beaches extend away to the north and south. The closest, most famous and frequented are Praia do Trancoso and Praia dos Nativos, both washed by gentle waves, with coral far off the shore and a cluster of *barracas* which host parties in the summer months with music ranging from café del mar to forró beach bar. Coquieros across the little river to the north is quieter by day but it's the place to come at night-time in mid- and high season. To the south beyond Trancoso beach are Rio Verde, with a little river, and beyond it Itapororoca, a deserted beach with just a few very expensive houses and good clear-water snorkelling.

Praia do Espelho (*Telephone code: 73*) This mini-Trancoso comprises a beautiful curved bay with a broad beach backed by restinga and a cluster of modish pousadas – on the sand and perched on the cliff above. At low tide the sea retreats and the exposed coral forms swimming pool-sized clear-water lagoons at low tide. The only way to get here is by taxi from Trancoso (1hr; cR$100), hire car or to walk the 5km from the Trancoso–Caraíva road – ask the bus to stop at the 'estrada para Espelho'.

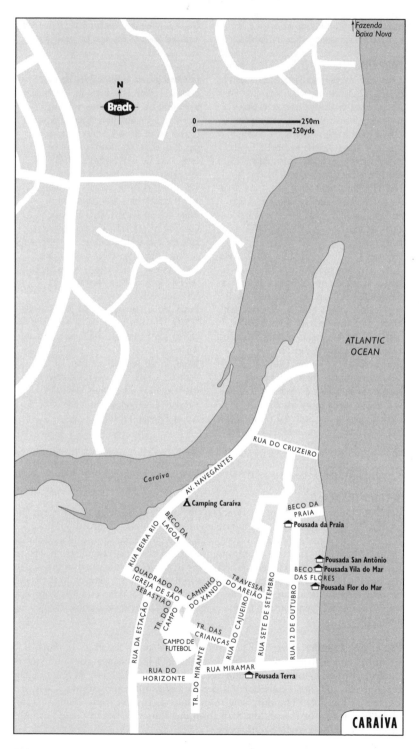

CARAÍVA

Where to stay and eat

Fazenda Cala (8 rooms) Praia do Espelho s/n; 9944 4160; www.fazendacala.com.br. Mock-Mykonos chalets with soft curves & stunning views set on the beach & the cliff above. All the suites have terraces & the hotel has a beach bar that serves appetisers on the beach & a restaurant in the main house. $$$$$

Pousada Vila do Outeiro (12 rooms) Praia do Espelho; 3668 6064; www.pousadadoouteiro.com.br. Rustic rooms in a mock-colonial style & furnished with weather-worn driftwood tables, rattan mats & faux-indigenous *objets d'art*. Large infinity pool. Overpriced. $$$$$

✕ **Sylvinha's** Praia do Espelho; 9985 4157. Those in the know have made special trips from Trancoso to eat the delicious Asian-Bahian cooking at this 2-table *barraca* restaurant on the beach. The oven roasted, ultra-fresh fish is a favourite. By advance booking only. $$$

CARAÍVA Telephone code: 73

Porto Seguro's tourists have yet fully to discover Caraíva – a tiny gem of a town on the banks of a wild river with sandy streets stretching back from a glorious broad and palm-backed beach. And for now at least it still feels remote and relaxed. Electricity and hot water only arrived in 2008 and are still available only during the day. There are walks all around – along the vast beaches all the way to Corumbau some 12km to the south or about half that north to the deserted Praia do Satu (named after its once only resident Senhor Satu who offers fresh and refreshing coconuts).

There are plenty of cheap pousadas and restaurants along the rustic sandy streets. Most bars have live forró in the summer. Flip-flops are best for walking along the sand streets, which can get very hot in the Bahian sun, and take a torch as it is very dark at night.

GETTING THERE AND AROUND **Horses** can be hired through many of the pousadas and **buggy rides** can be organised to Corumbau (from where buses connect to Cumuruxatiba) from the town square with the Pataxó people who have a village nearby (R$100).

Or you can **walk** the 15km along the beach to the river that separates Caraíva's last beach with Corumbau village; there is a boatman here for crossings (10mins; R$5).

Boats can be hired (R$50 per day) at the river port in Caraíva for excursions to Caruípe beach, Espelho, snorkelling at Pedra de Tatuaçu reef or Corumbau (take your own mask and fins), or for trips up the beautiful Rio Caraíva which gets into wild, pristine rainforest some 10km inland. Prainha river beach, about 30 minutes away, and mangrove swamps can also be visited by canoe or launch.

Caraíva is connected to Trancoso and Arraial by two daily **buses** (3 in high season) along a very poor dirt road. The journey involves a river crossing and can take as long as three hours in the wet season (Apr–Jun). If arriving by bus from the south, change buses in Itabela (departs at 15.00), or take a **taxi**, about 50km. The high season is December to February and July.

TOURIST INFORMATION The town website (*www.caraiva.net.br*) has a lot of information, but in Portuguese.

WHERE TO STAY AND EAT

Fazenda Baixa Nova (4 suites) Praia Ponta do Camarão, Nova Caraíva; 9979 6269; flanana@uol.com.br. A simple clifftop hotel with a beachside restaurant in the old *fazenda* farmhouse below, where the owner serves delicious home cooking. Intimate & secluded (some 30mins from Caraíva). Perfect for couples. Prices are for FB & transfers. $$$$$

Pousada Vila do Mar Praia de Caraíva; 3668 5111; www.pousadaviladomar.com.br. The poshest hotel in town is still simple by Trancoso standards. Rooms are spacious, stylish & airy, wooden cabins decorated with fashionable tropical driftwood & coconut shell arts & crafts. The hotel & adults & kids' pool are right on the beach. Under 4s stay free. $$$

🏠 **Pousada Flor do Mar** Praia de Caraíva; ☎ 9985 1608; www.caraiva.tur.br/flordomar. A great little beachside pousada run by a warm & welcoming local & offering bright, simple & airy rooms with hammock-slung balconies & a sea view – the best right at the beachfront. $$–$$$

🏠 **Pousada San Antônio** Praia de Caraíva; ☎ 9962 2123; www.pousadasanantonio.com.br. Brightly coloured faux-colonial cottages with wicker furnishings & breezy public areas right next to the beach. $$–$$$

🏠 **Pousada da Praia** Praia de Caraíva; ☎ 9985 4249; www.pousadapraiacaraiva.com.br. Very simple beachside rooms (with little more than a bed & plain wooden furniture) & an attractive outdoor deck area with hammocks & wicker sofas & armchairs. Good b/fast. $$

🏠 **Pousada Terra** Praia de Caraíva; ☎ 9985 4417; www.terracaraiva.com.br. Rustic chalets on the edge of the town & near the beginning of the Monte Pascoal forest. $$

🏕 **Camping Caraíva** Praia de Caraíva; ☎ 2231 4892, 9993 9087; www.campingcaraiva.com.br. Whitewashed wattle & daub beach *casitas* in rural Brazilian style with polished concrete floors & very simple wooden furnishings & campsites near the beach. $

PONTA DO CORUMBAU *Telephone code: 11*

Corumbau – where the coast forms a pimple in the sea and which is fringed with dying reef – is also where the beaches of the Costa do Descobrimento reach their wildest. Behind are the protected forests of the controversial Monte Pascoal and Descobrimento national parks (see box, *The Pataxó*, opposite). And there are strands of mangroves stretching to the south and the cliffs outside Cumuruxatiba, where the Costa da Baleia begins. Walk half an hour north or south of Corumbau village, which sits on the point, and you'll see fewer than ten people in a morning. At least for now. The chic hotels have begun to move in. Thankfully most of them are tasteful and well run. Corumbau itself is so quiet and so small you could hear someone sneezing on the far side of town. Or you could if it weren't for the crashing of the glassy emerald waves. Just south of the church there's good snorkelling off the beach and a handful of restaurant shacks where it's possible to buy a plate of seafood with rice. Beyond the smattering of small resorts, foreigners are few and far between.

GETTING THERE Corumbau is not easy to reach and any means but helicopter (available through Portomondo, see *Tour operators* page 68) will take you the best part of a day from Arraial or Porto Seguro and not much less than that from Trancoso.

There is one daily **bus** from Itamarajú, which is itself reachable from Eunápolis. And this leaves in the mornings. If you get stuck there are a few pousadas in the town (see below). It is also possible to organise a transfer with an agency like Portomondo or by catching the bus to Caraíva and then either sharing a **buggy** ride from the main square (R$100) or **walking** the 15km to the river and catching the ferry boat (see above).

🏠 **WHERE TO STAY AND EAT** There are a handful of cheap pousadas in town. It's nearly always possible to just turn up and find a room. All the luxury spots have their own restaurants but there are cheapies in town offering seafood. The community is poor and eating in one of these makes a difference.

🏠 **Fazenda São Francisco** (10 rooms) Corumbau village; ☎ 3078 4411; www.corumbau.com.br. Large, well-appointed hardwood & white plaster cabins gathered around a pool in a palm-tree garden 5mins' walk from the beach. $$$$$

🏠 **Tauana** (9 rooms) Praia de Tauá (30mins from town); ☎ 73 3668 5172; www.tauana.com. One of the best small beach hotels in the world for those looking for luxurious seclusion. Rooms are in 100m² + mock-indigenous cabins made to such high standards

Whilst the Tupiniquin people were the first to meet the Portuguese in 1500, it was the Gê people (see page 185) who kept the conquerors at bay around Porto Seguro for well over a century before being slowly worn down by missions and settlements. The Pataxó and the Pataxó Hã-Hã-Hãe (who live in the northwest of the Costa do Descobrimento) are their descendants, but the tribe were still healthy and abundant in the area well into the 20th century and had even been granted land title by the Brazilian government in 1926 – in an inalienable forest reserve around Monte Pascoal. But cattle-ranching and cacau-growing *coroneis* began to infiltrate their forests from the late 1930s, in ever-increasing numbers, and chopped down trees, and the SPI (Serviço de Proteção aos Índios or Indian Protection Service) colluded with them, pushing the Pataxó out of their lands and onto a narrow coastal strip. This caused conflicts with angry protests from the Pataxó. The *coroneis* responded with characteristic brutality – again with the full support of the corrupt SPI.

In 1951 one of their largest villages was (ostensibly) caught in a gun battle between bandits and police. Hundreds of Pataxó, including women and children, were murdered. The Figueiredo Commission on Indian Atrocities appointed by the military government in 1967 to report on the widespread massacres of indigenous people throughout Brazil found that later the Pataxó had had two villages exterminated by being given smallpox-infected clothing. John Hemming in his book *Die If You Must* writes: 'the SPI officials watched Pataxó die one by one, and did it so that "big shots in Bahia's state government" could acquire coveted Indian lands'.

In 1961 the federal government converted 22,500ha of land traditionally occupied by the Pataxó into the Monte Pascoal National Park. The Pataxó were violently evicted and found that overnight they could no longer circulate within their own lands. Much of their territory was later ceded to *coroneis* for farming cacau and planting eucalyptus. On 19 August 1999, numerous indigenous Pataxó people travelled to the foot of the mountain where they declared that 'Monte Pascoal belongs to the Patoxó' reclaiming their territory in order to, as they stated at that time, 'transform what the authorities call Monte Pascoal National Park into an indigenous park, the land of the Pataxó, to preserve it and to rehabilitate it'.

The Pataxó Hã-Hã-Hãe had suffered a similar fate. By the 1970s they had been shunted around from one piece of land to another as successive farmers and land speculators moved into the area. They ended up on a *fazenda* called São Lucas without drinking water or forest and reduced to begging. But their spirit remained unbroken. In 1985, with 60 sick children dying from pneumonia and dehydration and hunger, and *jagunço* gunmen hired by the *coroneis* preventing them having access to river water, they occupied four small farms next to São Lucas. The Bahian police forced them out with tear gas and bullets. Sixteen hundred Pataxó continue to live on the *fazenda* São Lucas today.

The Pataxó continue to lobby for the right to live on their ancestral lands in the second decade of the new millennium.

The World Rainforest Movement have details on their latest effort (www.wrm.org.uy) and provide international support for their campaign. For further information see http://pib.socioambiental.org/en/povo/pataxo-ha-ha-hae and www.indiosonline.org.br/novo.

& with such attention to detail that their carpentry verges on art. They overlook a secluded beach of creamy sand next to a clear-water river. The seafood – which fuses Portuguese & Bahian styles – is good too, especially the grilled fish. Perfect for a honeymoon or a romantic break. $$$$$

🏠 **Vila Naia** (8 rooms) Corumbau; 🕾 3061 1872; www.vilanaia.com.br. Tastefully appointed bungalows set in a little garden across a dirt road from the beach. Popular with fashionable Paulistanos. $$$$$

⌂ **Pousada Corumbau** (8 rooms) Corumbau s/n; ❧ none. Very simple & right on the beachfront. Rooms are fan-cooled. Corumbau is only a collection of houses around a little church so it is easy to find. $

⌂ **Vila Pousada & Camping Segovia** (5 rooms) Corumbau s/n; ❧ none. Very, very cheap even with b/fast; spots for camping out back. $

⋀ **Camping do Lourinho** Campsites 10mins' walk from the beach. Very cheap. $

COSTA DO DESCOBRIMENTO NATIONAL PARKS

This is our land. You have to respect the land you are walking on because it is ours. When you arrived here this land was already ours. And what did you do to us? You stopped our progress with riot squads, gunfire and tear gas. With our blood we commemorate once more the Discovery of Brazil.

Pataxó leader during the indigenous response to the celebration of Brazil's discovery in 2000 in Monte Pascoal National Park

There are three federally protected national parks in the region – Pau Brasil, Monte Pascoal and Parque Nacional do Descobrimento – preserving large stands of Atlantic coastal rainforest. At least on paper. There is no infrastructure, monitoring or even park guards in any of them.

PAU BRASIL Pau Brasil covers some 11,600ha immediately behind Arraial and was created in celebration of 500 years of Brazil in 2000. It is not (officially) open to visitors and the information published by the Brazilian Institute for the Environment and Renewable Natural Resources (IBAMA) states only that the park is home to harpy eagle, 'diverse birds' and many insects. Despite the purpose of the park being to further scientific research, there are no species lists or papers published on the park ten years after its creation. The park office listed by Ibama doesn't man its phones and the email address is incorrect. The park is not officially open to the public but agencies in Arraial organise visits, presumably illegally, and wildlife enthusiasts with a private small group have been known to take advantage of this.

PARQUE NACIONAL MONTE PASCOAL Information on the Parque Nacional Monte Pascoal is of a slightly better quality though still dreadfully vague. The park preserves 22,500ha of Atlantic coastal forest and restinga with patches of inselberg vegetation around the 586m-high Monte Pascoal boulder. IBAMA state that of the endangered species, mutum (a generic name for curassow) are present. A Cites 1 curassow present in the region is the red-billed so we can presume it is this species. BirdLife International confirm that there have as yet been no species surveys in the park. IBAMA also suggest that there are jaguar and puma in the park. And whilst there is no official visitor centre as yet the BR-498 rough road leaves the BR-101 federal highway between Itamaraju and Itabela for Monte Pascoal to the park entrance where there is a small IBAMA headquarters. Trails run from here into the forest and a rough track cuts through the park to Corumbau village 20km away. There are often groups of Pataxó protesting on the park road. Monte Pascoal lies in disputed indigenous territory (see box, *The Pataxó* on page 205).

PARQUE NACIONAL DO DESCOBRIMENTO The 21,213ha Parque Nacional do Descobrimento lies just to the south of Parque Nacional Monte Pascoal behind the

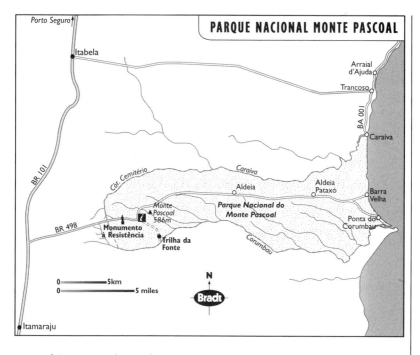

town of Cumuruxatiba on the Costa da Baleia. Its forests are almost contiguous with that park and are linked through tiny corridors in the midst of swaying seas of eucalyptus that are drying out the topsoils in the Rio Cai valley and which are planted to make pulp for toilet paper. Its ecosystem is identical (but for the inselberg vegetation). The park is also the source of the Rio Imbassuaba and has small areas of gallery forest. The small patches of forest that link the two parks allow for movement of fauna. And like Pau Brasil Parque Nacional do Descobrimento has no infrastructure for tourists.

TOUR OPERATORS The parks can be visited through tour operators in Arraial (see pages 192–3), although no one at present offers wildlife guiding. The same tour operators can also organise ascents of Monte Pascoal with notice.

WHERE TO STAY There are a couple of hotels in Itubera town, both offering simple rooms.

🏠 **Hotel Monte Pascoal** Rodovia Br-101 km808; ☎ 73 3294 3334. $–$$

🏠 **Pousada Costa Azul** Rua Joana Angélica 32; ☎ 73 3294 3908. $–$$

COSTA DA BALEIA & COSTA DOURADA

7

Costa da Baleia and the Costa Dourada

> The mountains were so beautiful that I wanted to dance. They go from black to white, passing through all the colours. I marvelled at the convulsive waves of vegetation growing on the rocks. I was moved by the beauty and asked myself how to produce art to reflect this beauty. One feels poor in the face of so much visual wealth.
>
> Frans Krajcberg on Brazil

Bahia's spectacular beaches get muddier and more mangrove-lined on the Costa da Baleia coast, and the towns lose their pastel-paint colours and streets of colonial houses to more provincial and pedestrian architecture. The few tourists who make it here are mostly Brazilian. But the region is well worth a detour from the Discovery coast, if only to take a trip to the **Abrolhos Islands** – little rocky jewels set with pearly-white sand beaches in an aquamarine and deep sapphire ocean. They offer some of the best diving and snorkelling in the southern Atlantic. And sightings of calving **humpback whales** are almost guaranteed between the months of June and December. **Cumuruxatiba** in the far north of the region is a pleasant low-key resort with a pretty beach which offers an antidote both to the Beau Brummel beach set at Trancoso and the tour package and backpacker-age of Arraial and Porto Seguro. It's decidedly Brazilian blue collar here and at the nearby provincial towns of **Prado** and **Caravelas**. The latter sits on a wild mangrove-lined and waterbird-waded river where the ultra-rare Neotropical otter is still a common sight. There are some superb, lonely beaches nearby. Bahia finishes on the **Costa Dourada** in **Mucuri** – with long beaches lined with golden cliffs and sad strands of eucalyptus where once there was tropical forest, and visited by only a handful of tourists.

The remotest stretch of southern Bahia lies between Caraíva and Cumuruxatiba. From here south, towns turn from pretty colonial to prosaic and provincial, and whilst they never reach Costa do Sauípe or Porto Seguro sizes, resorts get bigger and cruder. Tourism on the Costa da Baleia is almost entirely domestic, and it stays that way all the way to Rio, some 600km further south.

CUMURUXATIBA *Telephone code: 73*

Cumuruxatiba is the busiest town between the Costa da Baleia and Arraial d'Ajuda, though itself is small, low-scale and low-key – little more than a few streets of bungalows and shops behind a pretty beach. Tourist accommodatiom here is simple and unpretentious – as is the resort, and therein lies its charm. Cumuru, as it is known to locals, gets lively over Christmas and Carnaval, attracting a Brazil very different from Trancoso. Stepping from one to the other – from the Moët & Chandon to the bread and butter – is fascinating; and whilst the Trancoso set certainly have the style, the Cumuru crowd seem to have much of the fun.

GETTING THERE AND AROUND There are three daily buses to/from Prado and Itamaraju and a bus every other day direct to/from Porto Seguro. One bus a day goes to/from Corumbau via Itamaraju. Getting around is limited to foot or motorbike taxi.

TOURIST INFORMATION The website www.cumuru.com.br has pousada and restaurant listings in Portuguese, real time local climate information and plenty of pictures of the town and beaches.

WHERE TO STAY AND EAT There are restaurants serving the standard and ubiquitous fish, chicken or meat with beans, rice and unseasoned salad all over town but little else.

Pousada Axé (12 rooms) Av Beira-Mar; ☎ 3573 1030; www.pousadaaxe.com.br. Apts with kitchenettes, sitting areas & 1 or 2 bedrooms, with tiny windows & brick walls with all the charm of a prison cell. Furnishings are simple & wooden. But the pousada is good value when apts are shared between several people. Close to the sea. $$$

Pousada Mandala (10 rooms) Alameda Roberto Pompeu, Praia do Rio do Peixe Grande; ☎ 3573 1145; www.pousadamandala.com.br. A 2-storey orange wood & plaster house with corridors of boxy rooms – all with hammocks & terraces outside & a pleasant garden sitting area under a gazebo with wicker sofas. The pousada has a decent sculpted pool & serves a generous b/fast. $$$

Pousada das Cores (5 rooms) Av Atlântica, Praia do Rio do Peixe Grande; ☎ 3573 1180;

www.pousadadascores.com. A colourful pousada in pastel yellows, greens & blues with very simple rooms & disabled access. Next to the sand on one of the town's prettiest beaches. $–$$

Pousada Luana (12 rooms) Rua Bela Vista; ☎ 3573 1090; www.pousadaluana.com. One of the better deals in town with spartan, very simple but airy rooms decorated with colourful-fish wall hangings & tropical prints. The hotel has a small pool in a lawned garden. $–$$

Camping & Pousada Aldeia da Lua (5 rooms) Av Beira Mar, s/n; ☎ 3573 1168; www.campingpousadaaldeiadalua.com.br. A big pink pousada whose AC rooms have little more than a bed & a bedside table, sitting in an extensive coconut grove next to the pier, under which there's a campsite. $

OTHER PRACTICALITIES There are no banks or tourist offices in Curumuxatiba. The nearest are in Prado (see page 212).

WHAT TO SEE

Beaches
Whilst the town beach is long, fine and broad there are some even more beautiful strands north and south of town. Some 19km to the north is the **Barra do Cai** where crumbling ochre cliffs sit high over a 500m-wide beach of pearly sand which seems to stretch for ever and which runs wide and gentle all the way to the Ponta de Corumbau 25km away. Within walking distance of the town, just to the north, are the adjacent beaches of **Rio Peixe Pequeno** and **Rio Peixe Grande** with long stretches of deserted sand and two clear-running rivers. To the south is **Praia Dois Irmãos** with waves that lap rather than crash and a constant breeze, making it a popular spot for kayakers and windsurfers. **Japara Grande** 10km south of town has good snorkelling over rocky reef.

PRADO *Telephone code: 73*

If Porto Seguro (see page 185) is a resort then Prado is a town. And whilst it has a handful of colourful 18th-century houses around the **Beco das Garrafas**, they sit in whizzing traffic surrounded by scruffy commercial streets, and Prado fails to draw the tourist crowds. But dull though the town may be, it sits on a river lined with some of Bahia's more pristine white and red mangrove forest. And boat trips on the **Rio Jurucuçu** from the quays in the town centre are a delightful surprise. In a few minutes the launches take you from untidy urbanity into a wilderness of mudflats and towering trees. Ringed and Amazonian kingfishers flit through the air, there are egrets everywhere, and whilst these birds will have enthusiasts reading their book and muttering 'dime a dozen' or 'common as muck' under their breath, the Jurucuçu is one of the best locations in the state for spotting one of Brazil's rarer mammals – the southern or Neotropical otter. The Neotropical otter shows little fear of humans, which makes seeing it easy. But all over its range the animal has been hunted for its valuable and beautiful pelt, used for coat collars and trimming. One estimate has about 30,000 otters being killed annually in Colombia and Peru alone during the 1970s. Numbers for Brazil are unknown, but the animal is on the IUCN Red List and listed as endangered in CITES appendix one.

Boats ply the river all the way to the mouth where there are a series of wild, completely unspoilt white-sand beaches far prettier than those immediately close to town, backed by Atlantic coastal forest and as yet completely free of hotels. It is possible to walk back to town from here in around two hours. There are still more beaches on the southern side of the river mouth, running wild and mangrove-backed 4km to Guaratiba (where there are condominiums), which continues built-up to Alcobaça 9km to the south.

GETTING THERE AND AROUND Prado is well connected to the rest of Bahia, with direct buses from/to Caravelas (for Abrolhos), numerous daily connections from/to Itamaraju (for the rest of the state) and three daily buses to Cumuruxatiba. Round trips to the beaches for one day cost around R$100 for a boat or around R$40 for a two–three-hour tour on the Rio Jururuçu. Taxis and motorbike taxis are readily available in town.

TOURIST INFORMATION AND LOCAL TOUR OPERATORS

⚡ **Tourist office** Rua Clarício Cardoso dos Santos 100, Novo Prado; ℑ 3298 1047. There are also extensive listings & pictures on www.pradoturismo.com.br.

WHERE TO STAY

🏠 **Ilha da Alegria** Prado; (500 rooms) ℑ 3021 1111; www.ilhadaalegria.com.br. A vast ugly family-orientated resort occupying an entire river island 10mins from Prado town centre, on the Rio Jururuçu, which has little appeal beyond being great for kids. The rooms are functional & inelegant with catalogue furniture & tiny TVs stapled high up on the walls & they sit in a series of annexes gathered around an artificial lake next to the hotel's big pool & water-park area (with slides) which is always packed with delighted children. The hotel runs excursions on the river & to local beaches & tours to the Abrolhos islands. $$$$

🏠 **Casa de Maria** (15 rooms) Rua Seis, Novo Prado, Prado; ℑ 3298 1425; www.casademaria.com.br. Two blocks of rooms in a concrete building built around a pool & next to the beach. Abrolhos excursions organised. Excellent, huge b/fast. $$$

🏠 **Novo Prado** (12 rooms) Praia Novo Prado, Prado; ℑ 3298 145; www.novoprado.com.br. Pleasant

beachside pousada near the town centre, with bright AC & fan-cooled rooms & public areas, a little library, sauna & pool. $$$

🏠 **Abaetê** (20 rooms) Rua IV, Lote 35, Novo Prado; ℑ 3298 1611; www.portonet.com.br/abaete. Tiled, AC rooms with little space for more than a dbl bed & little fridge. These watch over a concrete deck & pool & the hotel is a block from the town beach at the north end of the city. There are many other options nearby. $$

🏠 **Pousada Novo Prado** (25 rooms) Rua Seis 91, Novo Prado; ℑ 3298 1455; www.novoprado.com.br. Bright Mediterranean colours, exposed raw wood beams, relaxing public areas with a little library book exchange, and rooms in lush oranges, blues or whites with scatter cushions & tasteful fittings make this pousada a cut above the rest in this price bracket in Prado. Amenities include a pool & tours. $$

🏠 **Pousada Canto do Rio** (15 rooms) Rua Alfredo Horcades 73; ℑ 3298 1402;

www.pousadacantodoriobahia.com.br. This tranquil, riverside pousada is one of the best deals in town, with leafy public areas. And tastefully decorated rooms with bright bed linen, cushions & wildlife prints. These watch over a wooden deck surrounding a pocket-sized pool. The best have views over the river. $–$$

🏠 **Pousada Hannah** (12 rooms) Av Dois de Julho; ☎ 3298 1385. Rooms here are simple but spruce with low beds, pretty tropical wall hangings & blocks of primary colour. The owners speak a little English & serve a b/fast filling enough to last most of the day. Conveniently located in the centre of town. Wi-Fi access from rooms. $

✖ WHERE TO EAT

Banana da Terra Beco das Garrafas 171; ☎ 3021 1721. One of a string of similar restaurants on this buzzing strip. Seafood & chicken is reliable

accompanied by an ice-cold beer. Decent adjacent options include Tarrafa which is hot on grilled fish. $$

ENTERTAINMENT AND NIGHTLIFE The colonial houses of the **Beco das Garrafas** have been turned into bars and restaurants with outdoor tables. They are very lively at weekends and in high season.

OTHER PRACTICALITIES There is a Bradesco (Agência dos Correios) on Rua Olinto Marcial Cunha (☎ 3298 1087) but the ATM is unreliable and may be permanently removed. There is a Banco do Brasil which will change cash US dollars (at a hefty commission) at Av 2 Julho 484 A (☎ 3298 2111).

WHAT TO SEE AND DO

Beaches **Praia do Prado** and **Praia do Novo Prado** sit in front of the town, backed by throbbing *barracas* and busy as an anthill in the high season. But the sands are silty and not so fine as those 4–5km further to the south at **Praia da Barra** where there are strong waves, white sand, coconut palms and no *barracas*. **Guaratiba** beach (minivans go from Prado town centre – ask at your pousada), 12km from town to the south, is backed by ugly condo houses and a scattering of pousadas. These fade away after a few kilometres at **Coqueiro** (with good surfing) and beyond that there are broad, deserted stretches of sand at **Praia do Farol**, backed by craggy sandstone cliffs and topped with a lighthouse that looks like a sentry tower. This last beach is just a few kilometres from tiny Alcobaça town.

Fazenda Guaíra (*Take the road between Prado & Itamaraju, turn right after the village of Pontinha, some 20km from Prado, onto a dirt road which runs for 9km to the fazenda*) This working farm on the borders of the Parque Nacional do Descobrimento protects a patch of Atlantic coastal rainforest rich in birds (though never to our knowledge birded) with marked trails, lined with orchids leading to the forest and the little river of Japara Mirim. The farm itself grows and sells delicious papaya. Trips only available through local tour operators (the nearest are in Caravelas – see page 214) or local drivers contactable through the pousadas in town.

ALCOBAÇA *Telephone code: 73*

This little town some 20km south of Prado makes up in charm for what it lacks in infrastructure. Its streets are filled with weather-worn, crumbling early 20th-century buildings and 19th-century flour factories. They'd be perfect for a fashion shoot – especially in conjunction with the miles of glorious beaches which spread out from the town to the south in a long spit of honey-coloured icing-sugar sand to the mouth of the Rio Itanhém. The town centre is quiet in the low season, with old men napping on benches and buzzing in the high season when much of Minas

Gerais state seems to empty onto the beaches of the Costa da Baleia, with the 20-something contingent favouring Alcobaça.

GETTING THERE There are at least four buses a day from Prado or Caravelas to Alcobaça.

WHERE TO STAY

🏠 **Brisa dos Abrolhos** (18 rooms) Rua Fernando da Cunha 1657, Praia da Barra; 🕿 3293 2022; www.visanco.com.br/brisadosabrolhos. Rooms here are concrete boxes with beds, TVs & fridges. But they all have balconies & the view over the beach & constant breeze make up for their plainness. Under 5s stay free, 5–10 year olds get a 10% discount & there's a kid-friendly pool. $$

🏠 **Pousada Entre Folhas** (14 rooms) Av Governador César Borges 1133, Praia de Alcobaça; 🕿 3293 2896; www.pousadaentrefolhas.com.br. A delightful set of mock-colonial bungalows set in a lush tropical garden decorated with wooden macaws. Friendly staff & a generous b/fast. $$

WHERE TO EAT

✖ **Maresias** Av Governador César Borges 1041, Praia de Alcobaça; 🕿 3293 2471; ⏰ 08.00–17.00. Serves tasty seafood on the beach accompanied with beans & rice.

OTHER PRACTICALITIES There are no international banks in Alcobaça. The nearest are in Prado or Caravelas.

WHAT TO SEE AND DO

Festivals Alcobaça is Costa da Baleia's festival capital with a calendar choc-a-bloc with festivities.

Folia de Reis (*Nov–6 January*) Celebrates the arrival of the Magi with fancy dress, parades and much traditional music.

Passion of Christ One of the most popular festivals in Alcobaça, lasting from Good Friday to the Ascension of Jesus on Easter Sunday. A stage set is put up in the 19th-century town centre where the passion drama is re-enacted by locals – the miracles of Galilee are re-enacted at the same time.

Feast Day of St Sebastian (*19–20 January*) On the Feast Day of St Sebastian the mostly Afro-Brazilian population re-enacts the battle for southern Portugal fought between the Christian Portuguese and the Moors in the 13th century. It is delightfully incongruous.

Festas Juninas (*First to last weekend of June*) These are Bahia's liveliest festivals after Carnaval and the Candomblé festivals of Salvador and are celebrated with gusto in Alcobaça. There are services in the churches of São Judas Tadeu, São Pedro and São João, and throughout the town selling mulled wine (*vino quente*) and gruel (*canjiquinha*), local food and plentiful live forró music. The highlight of the festivities is the country dancing competition where local and regional groups take part. The festa de São Pedro is organised by the local fishermen, who run a boat procession and firework show, leaving Alcobaça port bearing an effigy of the saint to the mouth of the river. St Peter is their patron and the fishermen believe that they will be protected by honouring him.

Festa do São Bernardo (*11–20 August*) Honours St Bernard, the patron saint of Alcobaça, the parish church being built in his honour. Homage to the saint is paid

7

by all the inhabitants of the town with this very Catholic celebration. There is music and dancing throughout the period. And to conclude the festivities, a mass is held on 20 August at 10.00, followed by a procession through the streets, carrying the image of the patron saint and other venerated Catholic saints. The final event is the procession of Jesus no Santissimo Sacramento (the Host) with another procession on 21 August. During the 11 days of prayer, the inhabitants of neighbouring towns come to the celebrations out of devotion to St Bernard. Every night there are different shows next to the 19th-century Cacimba do Conselho holy well, with a stage, lights and live music and around the square stalls offer local food and drink. Foreigners are a rarity and are heartily welcomed.

CARAVELAS *Telephone code: 73*

Caravelas is named after the caravels that brought the Portuguese to Brazil and was a major trading port in the 18th and 19th centuries. It fell quiet after World War I when the cacau trade grew in Ilhéus and coffee was shipped out of Rio and Santos more with the construction of the Minas railway. Its handsome late colonial and early Republican architecture (with its Portuguese and Macau *azulejos* and late Baroque churches) slowly began to crumble. Tourism began to revitalise Caravelas from the 1980s when Mineiros (from Minas Gerais) poured onto its beaches. They've been coming ever since, and increasingly to visit the Abrolhos islands which are the best location in the southern Atlantic to see humpback whales.

GETTING THERE AND AROUND
By bus Caravelas is 36km south of Prado, on the BA-001, on the banks of the Rio Caravelas and is served by frequent buses from Eunápolis and Itamaraju from where there are connections to the rest of the state. There are two buses to and from Porto Seguro every week and four buses daily to Prado to the north. The town is the departure point for the Abrolhos islands. The best beaches are about 10km away at the fishing village of Barra de Caravelas. Buses leave hourly from the rodoviária.

By boat The Parque Nacional Marinho dos Abrolhos is 70km east of Caravelas. The journey to the islands takes three to four hours depending on the sea conditions. Between July and early December, humpback-whale sightings are almost guaranteed. Boats leave at 07.00 from the Marina Porto Abrolhos some 5km north of Caravelas town centre (around R$80 or cheaper depending on numbers) and they return at dusk. It is possible to dive or snorkel at the islands. If you are coming from Porto Seguro everything including transfers and accommodation in Caravelas can be arranged by Portomondo (see page 193). In Caravelas, book with one of the tour operators (see below) or directly at the Marina Porto Abrolhos.

LOCAL TOUR OPERATORS
Abrolhos Turismo Praça Dr. Emílio Imbassay 08, Central ✎ 3297 1149; www.abrolhosturismo.com.br. Trips to the Abrolhos islands & to locations around Costa da Baleia & scuba diving.

Veleiro Sanuk ✎ 3297 1344; www.catamarasanuk.cjb.net. Trips to the Abrolhos islands.

🏠 WHERE TO STAY AND EAT
🏠 **Marina Porto Abrolhos** Rua da Baleia (5km outside of the town at the port from where boats leave for the Abrolhos islands); ✎ 3674 1060; www.marinaportoabrolhos.com.br. Individual & family suites housed in faux-Polynesian chalets & gathered in a palm-tree garden around a large pool. Activities include trips to the Abrolhos islands. $$$–$$$$

🏠 **Pousada Liberdade** Av Ministro Adalicio Nogueira 1551, Caravelas; ☎ 3297 2076; www.pousadaliberdade.com.br. Spacious, spartan & spruce cabins clustered in a lawned garden area next to a lake & just outside the town centre. Trips to the Abrolhos islands organised. $$$

🏠 **Pousada dos Navegantes** Rua das Palmeiras 45, Centre; ☎ 3297 1830; www.pousadanavegantes.com.br. A small family-run dive shop-cum-guesthouse with corridors of rooms around a pool near the beach. The friendly & helpful owners organise tours to the Abrolhos, dive excursions & dive certification. $$$–$$

OTHER PRACTICALITIES There is a Banco do Brasil on Praça Dr Imbassaí 306 (☎ *3297 1211*) that will change money for a hefty commission.

WHAT TO SEE AND DO
Parque Nacional Marinho dos Abrolhos
(*www.ilhasdeabrolhos.com.br, www.icmbio. gov.br*) The Abrolhos Islands National Park protects some of the most extensive coral reefs in the southern Atlantic with four times as many endemic coral species as the reefs and atolls of the Caribbean. Together with Atol das Rocas and Fernando de Noronha they offer the best diving in Brazil, with giant brain corals, abundant turtles, large shoals of fish as well as many unique smaller animals from nudibranchs to crustaceans. The waters around the islands are some of the best places in the world to see nursing humpack whales who calf here between July and December. In 2002, the Abrolhos region was declared an area of Extreme Biological Importance by the Brazilian Ministry of Environment, based on the Brazilian commitment to the Convention on Biodiversity. The first National Marine Park of Brazil had been created here in 1983 to preserve the coral and the large colonies of noddies and terns which nest on the islands.

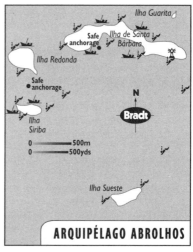

ARQUIPÉLAGO ABROLHOS

Abrolhos is an abbreviation of *Abre os olhos* ('Open your eyes!') an exclamation said to have been shouted by Amerigo Vespucci when he first sighted the reef in 1503. But there are 'Abrolhos' islands all over the world (including in Western Australia) – charted by the Portuguese – and the name probably comes from instructions written on early maps. The Abrolhos marine park consists of five small islands: Redonda, Siriba, Guarita, Sueste and Santa Bárbara. These are volcanic in origin, fringed with brilliant white beaches and shallow water with abundant coral reefs.

Darwin visited the archipelago in 1830 and Jacques Cousteau studied the marine environment here in the 1970s. The archipelago is administered by the Instituto Chico Mendes de Conservação da Biodiversidade (ICMBio) (Chico Mendes Institute of Biodiversity Conservation) (*www.icmbio.gov.br*), a Brazilian government institution created in 2007. And a navy detachment staffs a lighthouse on Santa Bárbara, which is the only island that may be visited. Visitors are not allowed to spend the night on the islands, but may stay overnight on boats.

The Caravelas Delta
Where the Rio Caravelas meets the Atlantic it fans out into a large mangrove-lined wetland with stretches of gallery forest rich in flora and fauna.

Like the blue whale, the humpback, or *baleia jubarte* in Portuguese, is one of the rorquals, a family characterised by having dorsal fins on their backs, and ventral pleats running from the tip of the lower jaw back to the belly area. The shape and colour pattern on the dorsal fin and tail are as individual to each animal as fingerprints are to humans.

IDENTIFICATION Adult males measure 12.2–14.6m in length and adult females 13.7–15.2m. They weigh 25–40 tons (22,680–36,287kg). Humpbacks are black on the dorsal (upper) side, and mottled black and white on the ventral (under) side – a pattern that extends to the tail. When the humpback whale 'sounds' (goes into a long or deep dive) it usually throws its flukes upward, exposing the black and white patterned underside. The flippers are extraordinarily long and usually white ventrally. The humpback's head is broad and rounded seen from above and slim in profile. The top of the head and lower jaw have rounded, bump-like knobs, each containing at least one stiff hair, thought possibly to assist the whale in detecting movement in nearby waters. There are 20–50 ventral grooves which extend slightly beyond the navel.

BEHAVIOUR Humpback whales feed on small shrimp-like crustaceans called krill, and various kinds of small fish, with each whale eating around 1.5 tons a day. These are sieved through 270–400 fringed overlapping plates hanging from each side of the upper jaw called baleen. The whales reach sexual maturity when six–ten years old. Each female usually calves every two–three years and the gestation period is 12 months. Calves are around 3–4.5m long, growing quickly on milk with a 45–60% fat content.

Humpbacks are found in all the world's oceans and follow a regular migration route, spending summer in polar or temperate waters and winter in the tropics when they mate and give birth. At this time they can often be seen breaching, swimming on their backs with both flippers in the air and raising their tails or flippers out of the water and then slapping them on the surface. Males sing incredibly long, complex songs lasting 10–20 minutes, usually repeated continuously for many hours and changing subtly gradually from year to year. Scientists have found that whales in the northwestern Atlantic population sing one song and those in the northeastern Pacific another song. Songs in other areas of the world are uniquely different.

The International Whaling Commission (IWC) gave humpbacks worldwide protection status in 1966. There was extensive illegal hunting by the Soviets until the 1970s and by Japan to this day. It is believed they number about 30,000–40,000 at present, some 30–35% of the estimated original population.

The **Instituto Baleia Jubarte** (*Rua do Barão do Rio Branco 26, Centro, Caravelas;* ✆ *73 3297 1340; www.baleiajubarte.org.br;* ⊕ *08.00–12.00 & 14.00–18.00 Mon–Fri, 08.00–12.00 Sat; free admission*) has information on humpbacks, their conservation in Abrolhos and where else to see them in Brazil.

Boat trips can be taken on seven of the larger waterways: the Macaco, Macangano, Juburuna, Cupido, Poco, Largo and Caribe and two smaller streams – the Perobas and Saco. There are numerous wading birds and a number of sandy islands including Pontal do Sul sitting in blue brackish water, which is crystal clear and full of shoals of little fish in the shallows. There are sandbanks in front of Grauçá Beach and Cassumba Island.

Beaches The best of the town's beaches is **Iemanjá beach** with bars and *barracas* and a long sand spit extending out into the Atlantic to a lighthouse. Big waves give good surf.

Praia Ponta da Baleia to the north is one of the wildest beaches on the Costa da Baleia – deserted and in a small ecological protection area on a cape northwest of Caravelas. Raptors, marmosets and burrowing owls are abundant and the sand is as soft as powder underfoot. The only access is via a rough coastal road that runs northwest out of town for around 15km or along the sand from **Zeloris beach**, itself beautiful, deserted and reachable through *fazendas* by taxis which have to turn right off the BA-001 highway.

NOVA VIÇOSA Telephone code: 73

The Costa da Baleia's last resort town is a pleasant, laid-back place sitting on the banks of the broad Rio do Meio river next to a bottle-green Atlantic. Long, fine strands of white-pepper sand stretch to the south towards the Costa Dourada. And there's good snorkelling around the reefs on Coroa Vermelha island. Like Caravelas and Alcobaça, Nova Viçosa fills with Mineiros in high season. The rest of the year it's a sleepy local place where life focuses on a pretty late colonial town centre of praças, stately, if modest Portuguese churches and broad streets lined with tiny 18th- and 19th-century bungalows in vibrant gouache colours.

GETTING THERE There is no access to Nova Viçosa from Caravelas or Prado along the coast, which is wild and beautiful immediately to the town's north around the Ilha da Cassumba (see page 218). Transport passes through Posto da Mata some 70km to the southeast. This is a forestry station unmarked on road maps where the extensive tracts of eucalyptus that have replaced the Atlantic coastal forest in this region are harvested.

By bus Buses leave from here to Nova Viçosa daily at 09.00, 10.00, 12.30 and 17.00. This is also the quickest way to reach Mucuri (31km to the south), from Nova Viçosa by public transport, as there is only one direct bus a week on Tuesday nights at 22.00.

By boat It is also possible to hitch a ride on a boat from Caravelas or hire a fishing boat for the 25km journey to Nova Viçosa or to take a boat from Caravelas/Nova Viçosa to Barra Velha (about 3km from Nova Viçosa across the water) on the Ilha do Cassumba (aka Ilha da Barra Velha) where there is a fishing village with a few houses where guests can stay if stuck. Expect to pay around R$100 for Caravelas–Nova Viçosa (or vice versa) and half to two-thirds that for Barra Velha.

GETTING AROUND Nova Viçosa itself is small enough to manage on foot. Taxis or motorbike taxis are good for the beaches. Tour operators can organise tours and boats for the islands leave from the town quay on the riverbank.

TOURIST INFORMATION AND LOCAL TOUR OPERATORS The **Secretaria Municipal de Turismo** (*Av Oceânica 2994;* ℡ *3208 1015*) has advice and a few pamphlets, all in Portuguese. The website www.novavicosa.com.br has galleries of photos of the town, river and boat trips as well as lists of hotels and services. **Atobá Agência de Viagens** (*Av Oceânica, 63, Centro;* ℡ *3208 1757*) principally organise trips to the Abrolhos but can help find boats for other destinations, and rent cars.

WHERE TO STAY AND EAT

⌂ **Pousada Costa do Sol** (12 rooms) Av Ocêanica 3436, Bairro Abrolhos, Nova Viçosa; ☏ 3208.1305; www.pousadacostadosol-ba.com.br. Spruce, very well-kept lemon yellow & white tile rooms with beds & little else sitting on 2 storeys overlooking a small pool. The beach is 5mins' walk. B/fast & afternoon tea (with cakes & coffee) included in the price. $$$

⌂ **Recanto dos Corais** (18 rooms) Av Dos Cajueiros 608, Bairro Cajueiro; ☏ 3208 2104; www.recantodoscorais.com. This big, inelegant pousada looks like a mini-shopping mall but offers good value. Rooms are plain & come with no more than a dbl bed or 2 sgls, a brick wardrobe & small TV. They sit around a bare lawn with a pool & a kids' play area 200m from the beach. The hotel has internet. $–$$

OTHER PRACTICALITIES There is a branch of the Bradesco on Praça Vereador Valdomiro A de Jesus 2 (☏ *3208 1145*).

WHAT TO SEE AND DO

Beaches Beautiful beaches run south from the town all the way to the Costa Dourada. The town beach Barra has cloudy waters (turbid and brackish because of the adjacent river). **Pontal da Barra** and **Lugar Comun** are the most popular and busy with holidaying Mineiros in the high season. There are many *barracas* and bars. **Pau Finacado** (with a big weather-beaten tree trunk behind) is long, broad and quieter. And **Sabacui** 16km from town is covered in little shells and lapped by gentle waves. Vans run to the beaches except in the quietest months (Apr–Jun) for a few reais.

Museu Ecológico Frans Krajcberg (*Sítio Natura s/n, Nova Viçosa;* ⊕ *08.00–12.00 & 14.00–18.00 Mon–Fri, 08.00–12.00 Sat; free admission*) Two *maloca*-like indigenous thatch-roofed buildings (one on tree-root stilts) housing scores of Krajcberg's organic sculptures (see box, *Art for nature's sake*, opposite) and set in a beachside garden next to the artist's home. Sculptures range from exposed roots like skeletons, violated trees in shocking red and meditative iconographic effigies of the spirit of nature and its fertility in carefully arranged trunks and husks of bark. It's worth coming to Nova Viçosa just to see the work.

Ilha da Cassumba This 120km² forested island some 20km south of Caravelas (and reachable only by boat) is another gorgeous corner of wild on the Costa da Baleia. The island sits between the mouths of the Caravelas and Peruipe rivers just north of Nova Viçosa and is home to 265 species of trees and 168 birds, all of them catalogued. Mangrove swamps and gallery forest around the rivers lead to extensive tracts of Atlantic coastal forest. The island can be reached through a Caravelas tour company, a cab from Nova Viçosa to Fazenda SPA da Ilha where there are guided walks or by taking a boat to Barra Velha fishing village on a beach on the island's southeast corner – where there are basic pousadas. Boats leave the quay in Nova Viçosa for day trips (from R$60) at 06.30, returning at 16.00.

Ilha de Coroa Vermelha A sandy island fringed with dying reefs and crowned with a big red lighthouse some 90 minutes' boat journey from Nova Viçosa. At low tide long sandy beaches are exposed and large rock pools, some of which are big enough to swim in. Fishing and speedboats leave the quay in Nova Viçosa for day trips (from R$50) at 06.30, returning at 15.30.

MUCURI AND THE COSTA DOURADA Telephone code: 73

Beyond Nova Viçosa, Bahia's beaches stretch into Espírito Santo state along the Costa Dourada (Gold Coast), so named for the honey-coloured and honeycombed cliffs that are gilded by the late afternoon sunlight. Beaches are long, broad and,

Frans Krajcberg is a multi-award-winning artist, Polish Holocaust survivor and protegé of the likes of Chagall and Braque whose powerful art declaims the destruction of Brazil's natural world. He first came to international attention in 1992, when he exhibited at the MAM (Museum of Modern Art) in Rio de Janeiro during the Rio Earth Summit. His organic sculptures, which are rearrangements of natural materials – particularly pieces of tree – can be found in museums and collections all over the world and sell for US$10,000–200,000. His studio is in Nova Viçosa, in a beautiful tree house 12m above the ground in forest just outside the town and he is in the process of constructing an ecological museum on the beach – O Museu Ecológico Frans Krajcberg, two rooms of which are open.

Krajcberg was born in Kozienice, Poland, in 1921, moved to Russia after losing his family in the Holocaust and then to Paris where he was a friend of Sartre and Giacometti and worked as a painter. But he felt stifled by Europe: 'I felt the need to create things that had actual dimension, not paintings. I made impressions, reliefs. Pieces of nature. Soon I could no longer work in Paris. Where to find my land?' He moved to Brazil in the 1970s, initially to Minas Gerais and then to Nova Viçosa.

Here I do not feel stifled by the cultivated woods of Europe or worried by the European intolerances. I was born in this world called nature and I felt its greatest impact in Brazil. Here I feel I was born for a second time; here I became conscious of being a man and of participating in life with my sensibility, my work, my thoughts ... except for the Indians, here we all come from abroad and relate to the wild forests, rich, full of movement, vibrating with colours, growing freely.

Since moving to Brazil he has been a tireless campaigner for the environment and the destruction of nature by man, a violence that for Krajcberg comes from the same root as that of the Holocaust.

I do not write. I am not a politician. I must find the right image. Fire is death, an abyss. Fire has been with me forever. My message is tragic: I show crime. The other face of a technology without control, the abyss. I bring evidence, I put documents together and I add. I want to import to my rebellion the most dramatic and the most violent aspects. If I could spread ashes over everything I would come close to what I feel.

There are evidently in my work cultural reminiscences, war reminiscences, which emerge from my subconscious. With all the racism, the anti-Semitism, I experienced in Europe I could not do any other kind of art. But I live in the present. I express what I saw yesterday in Mato Grosso, in the Amazon or in the State of Bahia. I show the anti-nature violence practiced on behalf of life. I express the rebellion of the planet's conscience. Destruction has shapes, although it speaks of the non-existent.

I do not try to sculpt; I seek shapes for my cry. This burnt husk is me. I feel myself in wood and in stone. Animistic? Yes! Visionary? No! I am a participant in the moment. My only wish is to express all I feel. It is a struggle without truce. To paint pure music is not easy. How to make a sculpture scream as if it had a voice?

Extracts are from the article 'Frans Krajcberg, Brazil's Eco Sculptor' by Leon Kaplan in ARTFOCUS 67, vol 7 no 3, Fall 1999.

beyond Mucuri, almost entirely deserted. Many are nested by turtles. The once extensive Atlantic coastal forests were home to the Aimoré tribes and were recently home to the Pataxó Hã-Hã-Hãe who were displaced – together with the forest itself

– to make way for farms and subsequently eucalyptus plantations that provide pulp paper for the country's toilet rolls. What little forest remains is currently protected by the Area de Proteção Ambiental (APA) Municipal Costa Dourada (Gold Coast Environmental Protection Area). **Mucuri**, the main town on the Bahian stretch of the Costa Dourada some 30km south of Nova Viçosa, has no attractions of its own beyond being the gateway to the region.

GETTING THERE   There is one bus a week to Mucuri from Nova Viçosa. Three daily buses leave for Mucuri from the Posto da Mata (see *Nova Viçosa*, on page 217) and there is a weekly bus from Teixeira de Freitas.

TOURIST INFORMATION AND LOCAL TOUR OPERATORS

Receptivo de Ecoturismo Rua Ponta de Areia (a hut at the end of the road), Porto de Mucuri; ⊕ 08.00–11.30 & 14.00–18.30 Mon–Fri. General information on boat tours from Mucuri on the river estuary (Estuario do Rio Mucuri); trekking along the Costa Dourada & visits to the mangroves on the Passarela Ecológica Gigica boardwalk just out of town.

Boat tours of the Mucuri river estuary leave from the quays on the river. The best time to go is at sunset – for stunning views; expect to pay around R$30 for an hour-long trip. Take insect repellent.

WHERE TO STAY

Pousada Tarumä (33 rooms) Av Central 1629, Sta Monica; 3206 1534; www.pousadataruma.com.br. Located in a large tropical garden 300m from the beach. Room rates vary according with type of building but amenities are all the same. The most affordable ones are chalets set in individual wooden houses in the garden among the trees, and the standards in a 2-storey wooden building with several rooms. The executivo is in an individual bricked house & master in a bricked house with 2 connected rooms, ideal for families. Amenities include AC, TV, minibar, & internet access. $$–$$$

Pousada Fim do Mundo (5 rooms) Rua Copa Setenta 322; e fimdomundo@gmx.de;

http://www.costa-dourada.de/pousada.html. Located on the Costa Dourada 16km south of Mucuri. The name means 'the end of the word', the place is remote. The spacious rooms are in comfortable new colonial houses with verandas in a lush garden, 100m from the beach. Rooms are equipped with fridge, cooker & private parking. No b/fast included. Booking in advance is essential. $$

Pousada Kambuká (27 rooms) Rua Antonio Carlos Magalhães 77, Por do Sol; 3206 1110; www.pousadakambuka.com.br. Located by the beach in a large lawn area with a pool & jacuzzis. A colourful 1-storey building houses the rooms. $$

WHERE TO EAT

Per Tutti Av Central 1599; 3206 1510; ⊕ 18.00–22.00 daily. A varied menu of stodgy pasta & cheesy pizza. $$

OTHER PRACTICALITIES   A branch of Banco Bradesco is at Praça Rui Barbosa 88 (3206 1020).

8

Costa dos Coqueiros

Northern Bahia's beauty can't compare to the south's. The palm-shaded, coral-fringed coves of Itacaré or Arraial d'Ajuda are absent here. Despite their name, the beaches of the Costa dos Coqueiros (Coconut coast) are mostly long and windswept, washed by vast tides that drift in and out of the shallow, slowly shelving sea in flurries of tiny waves. Most visitors to the region are Soterpoletanos, who hop up the coast from the capital for a day or two or over a long weekend. And their habits have led to untidy and ugly development. In some areas beaches are backed by segregated condominiums, with serried ranks of identikit houses that look like beachside, budget versions of Stepford. In others, conglomerations of giant resort hotels look like a bad memory from the early days of European package travel. There are a few pretty, timeless fishing villages, particularly in the far north of the state around **Mangue Seco**. But most – like **Praia do Forte** and **Costa do Sauípe** (both of which were charming and low key only ten years ago) – are being swallowed by the flood of rapacious real-estate development. Yet the appeal of a quick beach still lures visitors with little time.

Beaches on this 193km coastal strip (which is also known as the **Linha Verde**) are busiest near Salvador and at their prettiest some 130km north of the capital, after the town of Sítio do Conde. Transport is excellent, with a good road and regular buses making the northern state border with Sergipe accessible in three to four hours.

AREMBEPE *Telephone code: 71*

The first of the many resorts, just 25km from the airport, comprises a long strip of beaches backed by long rows of condominium houses and small hotels. In the low season the town is deathly quiet in the week and busy at weekends. In high season it heaves with visitors, especially for the post-Carnaval festival of São Francisco de Assis, known to Bahians as **Ressaca da Carnaval** or 'Carnaval hangover', which takes place immediately after the main even in Salvador. Many of Salvador's trio electricos play at this time and the town receives hundreds of thousands of frenzied visitors. Arembepe's 7km of beaches are nothing special by Bahian standards; broken by rocks for much of their length and very narrow at high tide. At the northern end of the town they form a tongue of sand behind a reef of dead coral which exposes rock pools at low tide and provides good sheltered swimming for kids at any time. At **Piruí** there is reasonable surf. And in the late 1960s when fishing boats outnumbered houses, tropicália musicians and a handful of international rock stars (allegedly including Mick Jagger and Janis Joplin) toked copiously on one of Arembepe's northernmost beaches. The town has been selling the area as an *aldeia hippie* (hippy village). It's long lost its flower power and is a rather tawdry area now, huddled on the banks of the Rio Capivara a half-hour walk from town, with little but a few shacks and a lucklustre artisan market. Arembepe has the first of several **Projeto Tamar** turtle hatcheries and visitor centres on the Costa dos Coqueiros (*Estrada da Aldeia Hippie;* \3624 1133; *www.tamar.org.br;* ⊕ *08.00–18.00 daily*) (see box on page 226).

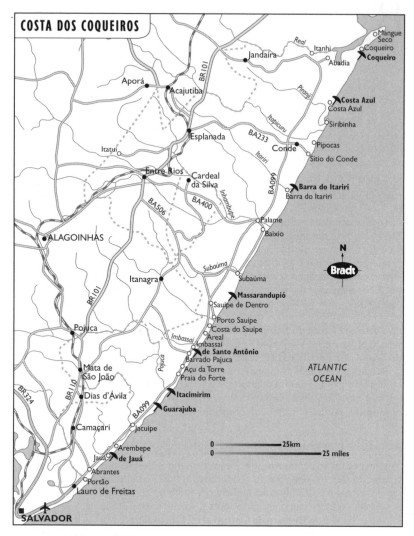

COSTA DOS COQUEIROS

ATLANTIC OCEAN

N

Bradt

| 0 | | 25km |
| 0 | | 25 miles |

GETTING THERE AND AROUND

By bus Buses run between Salvador's rodoviária (as well as the Estação da Lapa and Terminal da França) and Arembepe every half-hour from 05.30–21.00 taking 30 minutes and costing around R$5. Many more can be flagged down at the T-junction on the main BA-099 Linha Verde highway 2km inland of town.

By taxis Taxis charge an exorbitant R$10–15 for the journey between the highway and the beach.

 WHERE TO STAY

⌂ **Gipsy** (40 rooms) Rua Eduardo Pinto km3; ☎ 3624 3266; www.gipsy.com.br. This place next to the beach is good value if unattractive, with simple white-tile AC rooms & a pool with a slide area for kids. $$

⌂ **Arembepe Refúgio Ecológico** (11 rooms) Estrada Aldeia Hippie; ☎ 3624 1031; www.aldeiadearembepe.com.br. Peach-coloured & well-appointed AC cabins & a little pool sitting directly in

222

Antônio Carlos Peixoto de Magalhães, or ACM, governed Bahia with an iron hand, a warm paternalistic smile for much of the latter half of the 20th century and did more to shape the state's fate than anyone had done since colonial times. Magalhães rose to power with the military dictatorship, becoming governor of Bahia in 1970 and clinging onto the reigns of power in Bahia and Brazil until his death in 2007 either overtly or behind the scenes.

After being born into privilege, ACM entered state politics as the private secretary of a relative and was elected state deputy for the União Democrática Nacional (UDN) party in 1954, and federal deputy for Bahia four years later. He was a key player in the US-backed conspiracies against the left-wing president João Goulart that led to the 1964 coup and resulted in 21 years of military rule in Brazil (see pages 40–1).

ACM was a loyal militarist and a leading figure in the pro-government Aliança Renovadora Nacional (Arena) party. He was rewarded with the mayorship of Salvador, in 1967, and was appointed state governor in 1970. ACM brought industry to Bahia, modernised the state capital and regional infrastructure and brokered hard for Bahia in Brasília. But he was ruthless with his opponents, earning the nickname Toninho Malvadeza ('Evil Tony') for his brutal treatment of them. And he had little interest in Bahia's black majority to whom he made grand populist gestures whilst favouring policies which benefited white Bahian businessmen. ACM established a new white, conservative oligarchy in Bahia by steering lucrative contracts the way of those who promised their political support.

After the fall of the military he clung onto power through close ties with fellow northeasterner José Sarney, who appointed him to the important post of Minister of Communications that year. ACM then built up his own network of radio and television stations in Bahia, now owned by his son, Antônio Carlos Jr. A third stint as governor of Bahia in 1990–94 was followed by spells as leader of the right-wing Liberal Front Party and then as president of the Senate, a role in which Magalhães became the kingmaker of Brazilian politics. President Fernando Henrique Cardoso, a sociologist and social democrat, discovered that it was very difficult to get legislation passed without ACM's support. To ensure it he allowed ACM to nominate his supporters to numerous powerful posts in the government. In 1998 ACM lost his beloved son and heir apparent, Luís Eduardo, to a heart attack. He was 43 at the time and president of the lower house of the federal legislature. It was a personal and a political blow.

Another came in 2001 when a money-for-votes scandal forced Magalhães to resign, to much sound and fury. But he won the next election and returned to the Senate as if nothing had happened. It seemed that nothing could hold him back. When arch-enemy Luiz Inácio Lula da Silva was elected president in 2002, Magalhães described himself as coming from 'the Workers' Party wing of the Liberal Front Party'. As a reward he was able once more to slot his supporters into important administrative posts in the new government.

ACM died in 2007, but there are still Magalhães in politics. Antônio Carlos Jr completed his father's term in the federal Senate. ACM's grandson, Antônio Carlos Neto sits in the lower house. But they have to operate in a very different political context. They are less colourful and able than ACM and unable perhaps to operate with his bare-faced impunity. In response to accusations of corruption, ACM once replied, 'I have good and bad friends, but I only govern with the good ones.' And in regard to the passions he aroused among opponents, he said: 'Those who hate are slaves of their hatred, which is why so many of my enemies are my slaves.'

front of one of the quietest & prettiest stretches of beach (just north of the town) & close to Projeto Tamar. $–$$

⌂ **Cores do Mar** (10 rooms) Rua das Flores s/n; ☎ 3624 1155; www.pousadacoresdomar.com.br. A

concrete cube in the middle of town whose very clean AC rooms comprise no more than a bed sitting on floor tiles with a tiny attached shower room. Decent b/fast. $–$$

✗ WHERE TO EAT

✗ **Mar Aberto** Largo de São Francisco 43; ☎ 3624 1257; www.marabertorestaurante.com.br. The only one of the half-dozen restaurants in town worthy of a

mention, with a good menu of seafood dishes & especially tasty & generous *moquecas*. $$

OTHER PRACTICALITIES There is a Banco Bradesco with an international ATM on the Praça das Amendoeiras in the centre of the village.

PRAIA DO FORTE *Telephone code: 71*

The best of the Costa dos Coqueiros's beach resort towns still retains a little of the low-scale fishing village charm which brought locals and then European package holidaymakers here in the first place. The main street is entirely pedestrianised and lined with little boutiques, galleries and cafés, there's a large **Projeto Tamar centre** with many turtles and the **Reserva Florestal da Sapiranga**, a little wildlife reserve focused on a lake and a small area of protected restinga wetland (one of the very few surviving on the northern Bahian coast). The **Castelo Garcia D'Avila**, a 16th-century ruined fort on the outskirts, gives the town its name. Some of the beaches are also protected as turtle-nesting sites, but they are nothing special in themselves – long and coconut shaded but very narrow, with coarse sand and pounded by waves from a cloudy sea. The resort touts itself as an ecotourism destination and whilst it's in the very early stages and plagued by huge unsustainable Spanish resorts, a number of the smaller hotels and businesses are beginning conservational tourism practices.

GETTING THERE AND AROUND

By bus Buses run from Salvador's rodoviária to the crossroads at Praia do Forte every 30 minutes from 05.30–22.00 and five times daily to the town centre itself, continuing on to destinations to the north and Sergipe. They pass south at the crossroads on the main highway BA-099 highway (2km out of town), on their return to Salvador even more frequently. Minivans (*combis*) run between the crossroads and town centre praia every 15 minutes, costing $R0.50.

On foot Praia do Forte itself is almost entirely pedestrianised and small enough to be comfortably seen on foot.

TOURIST INFORMATION AND LOCAL TOUR OPERATORS

☑ **Bahiatursa** http://www.bahiatursa.ba.gov.br; ⏲ 08.00–12.30 & 15.30–18.00 Tue–Thu, 08.00–12.30 & 13.30–17.30 Tue–Sun. Operate a booth at the beginning of Avenida ACM, offering free maps, pamphlets & advice. Some English spoken.
Centrotour Av do Farol, Shopping Armazém da Vila, Loja 19, Térreo Praia do Forte; ☎ 7811 0356; www.centrotour.com.br. Offer trips & excursions

around Praia, including the Reserva Florestal da Sapiranga. The company support the Associação Comunitária Desportiva, Educativa e Social do Litoral Norte (ADESLIN) – an NGO that supports local poor communities & who have initiated a number of successful conservational schemes in & around Praia, including one of Bahia's 1st & largest recycling projects.

 WHERE TO STAY Confusingly, Praia's main street has two names – the official name of Avenida Antônio Carlos Magalhães (aka ACM – named in honour of the state's most famous political patriarch; see box on page 223) and the old, unofficial name, Alameda do Sol. To add to the confusion, the street doesn't have any street numbers marked. As with many of the Costa dos Coqueiros resort towns, rooms are in general overpriced, and in high season Praia the resort is very busy and it can be difficult to find a room without a reservation.

🛏 **Praia do Forte Eco-Resort** (290 rooms), Av do Farol; ☎ 3676 4000; www.praiadoforteecoresort.com.br. A big family resort in the Portuguese Espírito Santo group, whose long annexes of AC rooms overlooking a big pool & the beach sit under palm trees in lawned gardens filled with heliconias. Rooms are spacious & well appointed, b/fast huge & the hotel has a state-of-the-art Thalasso spa, night-time entertainment & a tour agency offering trips around Praia. Far cheaper if booked online or through an international agent. The restaurant serves very ordinary food. Eat elsewhere. $$$$$

🛏 **Aloha Brasil** (7 rooms) Rua da Aurora; ☎ 3676 0279; www.pousadaalohabrasil.com.br. Small but well-kept & tastefully decorated rooms with king-sized beds & verandas in a tranquil tropical garden. No children under 12. $$$$

🛏 **Porto Zarpa** (30 rooms) Rua da Aurora; ☎ 3676 1414; www.portozarpa.com.br. A big, blocky 2-storey building in a small garden, close to the beach, with standard 3-star-hotel AC rooms with cable TV, overlooking a pool. Private parking & family-friendly. $$$$

🛏 **Sobrado da Vila** (27 rooms) Av ACM; ☎ 3676 1088; www.sobradodavila.com.br. One of the best in the village itself (as opposed to beachside), with a choice of individually decorated rooms all with balcony terraces. The hotel has one of the better in-house restaurants. $$$$

🛏 **Ogum Marinho** (20 rooms) Av ACM, ☎ 3676 1165; www.ogummarinho.com.br. An arty little pousada with a gallery showcasing work by local painters & a range of AC & cheaper fan-cooled rooms in a pleasant courtyard garden. Cheaper for stays of more than 2 days. $$$–$$$$

🛏 **Casa de Praia** (21 rooms) Praça dos Artistas 08-09; ☎ 3676 1362; www.casadepraia.tur.br. A tranquil

low-key pousada in rustic-chic raw wood & ochre wash paint with simple rooms, all with balconies overlooking a tidy garden & friendly staff. Free Wi-Fi. $$$

🛏 **Pousada João Sol** (6 rooms) Rua da Corvina; ☎ 3676 1054; www.pousadajoaosol.com.br. Intimate & recently refurbished & tastefully decorated chalets, with colourful en suites, bright *objets d'art* & hammock-slung wooden terraces. The owner speaks English, Spanish & German & serves a generous b/fast. Free Wi-Fi. $$$

🛏 **Pousada Tatuapara** (27 rooms) Praça dos Artistas I; ☎ 3676 1466; www.tatuapara.com.br. Spacious & well-maintained bright AC or fan-cooled rooms with floor tiles & whitewashed walls around a pool. $$–$$$

🛏 **Albergue da Juventude Praia do Forte** (23 rooms) Rua da Aurora 3; ☎ 3676 1094; www.albergue.com.br. A tidy youth hostel with a pretty garden area & plenty of public space. Dorms are better value than the dbls with en suites. All are fan-cooled. The hostel serves a large b/fast, has a communal kitchen & a shop. Cheapest with an IYHA card. $–$$$

🛏 **Pousada Tia Helena** (12 rooms) Just east of Praça dos Artistas at Alameda das Estrelas; ☎ 3676 1198; www.tiahelenapraiadoforte.com.br. Rooms in this bright lilac pousada are simple affairs with little more than wooden beds & bamboo clothes racks. But Helena, the motherly proprietor, ensures that they are scrupulously clean & provides an enormous b/fast. Reductions for 3-day stays & some trpl & quadruple rooms making this cheaper still for groups. $–$$

⛺ **Camping Sapiranga** Estrada para Castela da Torre km3.5; ☎ 3272 0020; www.campingreservadasapiranga.cjb.net. Plots in a shady stand of low forest right near the beach; washrooms, laundry & a communal kitchen. $

✗ WHERE TO EAT

✗ **Bar Do Souza** Av do Sol, on the right as you enter the town. This lively bar & restaurant serves the best seafood in town, with excellent fresh fillets & regional dishes. Live music at w/ends. $$$

✗ **O Europeu** Av ACM; ☎ 3676 0232. Owned & run by a scion of the Wisden cricket almanac family, this restaurant & art gallery serves delicious Brazilian &

British home cooking & some of the best juices in Praia. $$–$$$

✗ **Restaurante Casa da Nati** Av ACM; ☎ 3676 1239. This good-value per-kilo & regional food restaurant is one of the few owned & run by a Praia do Forte native. $$

✗ **Point do Ivan** Av ACM; ☎ 071 9997 1711. One of the better options for Bahian food, with large & well-flavoured good *moquecas*, *bobo de camarão* & a cheap *prato feito* at lunchtimes. $–$$

✗ **Café Tango** Av ACM; ☎ 3676 1637. A lovely little open-air tea & coffee bar serving wholesome pastries & sweet & sticky cakes & snacks. $

ENTERTAINMENT AND NIGHTLIFE There is a string of pulsing dance bars along Avenida Antônio Carlos Magalhães.

SHOPPING

Galeria de Arte Claudia Ferraris Alameda das Estrelas; ☎ 9125 1191; www.claudiaferraris.com. Colourful art from a European artist renowned for her paintings of capoiera which burst with life & movement.
Joia Rara Av ACM; ☎ 3676 1503. Tailor-made jewellery using Brazilian precious stones set in white gold, yellow gold or silver. Customers choose from a range of semi-precious & precious Brazilian rocks, which are polished, cut & set to their own design or

a set of template designs suggested by the shop. Stones include Bahian emeralds, aquamarines, tourmalines & amethysts. The shop doubles up as the artist's studio.
Nativa Av ACM; ☎ 3676 0437. Traditional lace clothing from throughout the northeast with beautiful hand-embroidered shirts, skirts & bags which are smart enough for a night out in a decent Salvador restaurant & cool enough for the beach.

OTHER PRACTICALITIES Bradesco (*Av do Farol s/n*) and HSBC (*Alameda do Sol s/n*) both have banks and ATMs in Praia do Forte.

WHAT TO SEE AND DO

Castelo Garcia D'Avila (aka Casa da Torre) (*Access via a cycle trail or along the beach at low tide, taxis R$20 for the round trip;* ☎ *3676 1403;* ⏱ *09.00–18.00 daily; adult/child R$10/R$5*) The town takes its name from the beach that sits next to this dramatic ruined fort on a bluff overlooking the sea some 4km walk out of town. It was the first big military building in Brazil and is the only late medieval castle in the Americas. The building was largely constructed in 1551 by the wealthy Portuguese settler, Garcia d'Avila, who had arrived in Brazil with Tomé de Souza two years previously. It was intended as an early-warning outpost for Salvador. Much of the extant construction is more recent – the fort was completed in 1624 by Garcia d'Avila's grandson Francisco and expanded and rebuilt in the 17th and 18th centuries. D'Avila was given a huge area of land for his efforts – running from Praia do Forte through to Maranhão – on which he set up the first cattle farm in Brazil, bringing the first coconuts from Goa and mango trees from Angola. The chapel has been fully restored and sits stark and white against the weather-worn honey-coloured battlements. There are plans for further refurbishment and the construction of a museum and indigenous theme-park village.

Projeto Tamar (*Beachside next to the lighthouse;* 🕾 *3676 1403; www.tamar.org.br;* 🕙 *09.00–18.00 daily; adult/child R$10/R$5*) Is home to several species of marine turtles and runs fascinating tours of the hatcheries in season (see box opposite).

Reserva Florestal da Sapiranga (*Praia do Forte;* 🕾*3676 1144;* 🕙 *08.00–17.00 daily; adult/child R$15 – for a guided walk*) A 600ha private reserve of recuperating Atlantic coastal tropical forest with remnant restinga swampland and brackish lakes. Hikes range in length and many include swimming. Abundant birdlife and mammals include ocelot and capivara.

IMBASSAÍ AND THE COSTA DO SAUÍPE Telephone code: 71

Imbassaí means 'the course of the river' in Tupi; it's named after the river which snakes along the coast parallel to the sea for some kilometres – separated from the salt water by a long sandy beach, which is one of the few in Bahia to offer salt- and freshwater swimming. The large Tupinambá village which lay here when the Portuguese arrived has long gone, replaced first by a little fishing village and then with condominiums which now proliferate under the palms next to the river. But the town is still low-key next to its neighbour – the **Costa do Sauípe**, a resort complex of identikit hotels and 'themed' pousadas with names like 'Breezes' and all the charm and personality of an airport restaurant. The hotels and the accompanying sanitised mock-colonial village are aimed at the international tourism market. But they are somewhat old-fashioned, sit on one of the rockiest, roughest stretches of beach in northern Bahia and have so far succeeded in luring only cheaper package tourism. Rack hotel rates are very expensive on the Costa do Sauípe but occasional bargains are available through agencies like First Choice and TripAdvisor.

GETTING THERE
By bus Hourly Linha Verde buses run from Salvador's rodoviária along the BA-099 and will drop visitors at the crossroads for Imbassaí or Sauípe.

By minivan and taxi Minivans (*combis*) and taxis run between the crossroads and the villages, costing R$0.50–15. The hotels on the Costa do Sauípe require pre-booking and can organise transfers from Salvador airport.

WHERE TO STAY
🏠 **Breezes** (324 rooms) Costa do Sauípe; 🕾 2104 8888; www.breezes.com. This hotel aimed at honeymooning couples is in bad need of refurbishment, with tired décor — especially in the rooms & mould growing in the bathrooms. The number of guests means that there is often little space around what is one of the smaller pools in the Costa do Sauípe so it can be a dawn race to place a towel on a sun lounger. The restaurants are bland & the ubiquitous muzak intrusive. $$$$

🏠 **Costa do Sauípe Golf & Spa** (256 rooms) Costa do Sauípe; 🕾 2104 8080. Aimed at a well-to-do senior market, this is the most luxurious of the Costa do Sauípe resort hotels, but it's still decorated like a C-grade Ritz Carlton, with faux-19th-century European furniture & chintzy drapes & bed linen. Rooms are concrete shells with king-sized beds & terraces with wonderful sea views (which are extra) or uninteresting vistas of the resort itself. The intrusive muzak is hard to escape from. The hotel & the golf course are in need of maintenance. $$$$$

🏠 **Grande Hotel** (402 rooms) Costa do Sauípe; 🕾 2104 8080; www.costadosauipe.com.br. Everything about this hotel is big & brash — it has one of the largest convention centres in Latin America, one of the biggest pools, 4 restaurants & a vast coterie of staff trained well in the art of technical courtesy but lacking any genuine Bahian warmth & charm. Rooms are big & bare & are housed in a series of huge blocky annexes. And the resort, whilst claiming to offer everything all-inclusive, charges extra for the various activities & services, making it pricey. $$$$$

🏠 **Pousada Caminho do Mar** (13 rooms) Caminho do Mar s/n, Imbassaí; ☎ 3677 1177; www.pousadacaminhodomar.com.br. A choice of dbl, trpl & quadruple terracotta-roofed beachside bungalows decorated with driftwood arts & crafts & sitting on a large lawn next to a pool. Generous b/fasts included. Very good value for groups happy to share a sgl bungalow. $$–$$$

🏠 **Pousada Imbassaí** (40 rooms) Rua da Igreja s/n, Imbassaí; ☎ 3677 1313; www.pousadaimbassai.com.br.

Simple but comfortable AC chalets & apts in large annexes, & a nice pool with surrounding deck. Popular with families. $$–$$$

🏠 **Pousada Lagoa da Pedra** (19 rooms) Rua da Igreja s/n, Imbassaí; ☎ 3677 1300; www.lagoadapedra.com.br. Lovely mock-colonial chalets set in lush tropical palm-shaded gardens around a lake 200m from the beach. Friendly & welcoming staff & a reasonable b/fast. Particularly good value – especially for groups of up to 4. $$

✗ **WHERE TO EAT** Hotels on the Costa do Sauípe have their own international restaurants and full board is usually included in the price. Food can be bland and there is little further choice in the village. For something different and more authentically Bahian head south to Imbassaí.

✗ **Sombra da Mangueira** BA-99 km68 & then 8km towards the beach; ☎ 9133 4860. This little restaurant under the shade of a huge mango tree serves some of the best Bahian cooking on the Linha Verde with good, fresh seafood, *moquecas* & great *petisco* starters – *casquinha de siri* & *bolinho de peixe*. $$

OTHER PRACTICALITIES There are no banks in Imbassaí. There are international ATMs in the village on the Costa do Sauípe. It is only possible to change currency for a 3% commission plus a transaction fee of US$20.

CONDE AND BEYOND *Telephone code: 75*

Conde is sufficiently far from Salvador to be relatively tourism-free. The town remains sleepy, provincial and very Bahian. Its centre preserves a tiny, squat 17th-century colonial church in a cobbled square surrounded by modest 19th- and early 20th- century civic buildings. The fishing village of Sítio do Conde sits on the coast 6km from Conde town. It's dominated by pousadas and beach homes but most are simple and low-scale and the village has yet to attract predatory development.

The beaches are not very good but it's an ideal base to explore other beaches at Barra do Itariri, 12km south, at the mouth of a river, which has fine sunsets. The road passes unspoilt beaches; the best are Corre Nu and Jacaré. You can also go to Seribinha, 13km north of Sítio do Conde. The road goes along the beach through coconut groves and mangroves; at Seribinha beach huts serve cool drinks or food.

GETTING THERE AND AROUND
By bus Hourly Linha Verde buses run from Salvador's rodoviária along the BA-099 and will drop visitors at the crossroads for Conde. There are nine buses daily from Salvador to Conde. Two buses a day run north from Conde and Sítio do Conde to Siribinha. Three buses a day run south from Sítio do Conde to Barra do Itariri.

By minivans and taxi Minivans (*combis*) and taxis run between the villages of Conde and Sítio do Conde costing R$1.50–20.

🏠 WHERE TO STAY AND EAT
🏠 **Hotel Praia do Conde** (30 rooms) Travessa Arsênio Mendes s/n, Sítio do Conde; ☎ 3429 1129; www.hotelpraiadoconde.com.br. A family resort with a pool & cloisters of terracotta-tile-roofed rooms overlooking a large lawn shaded by palms. $$$

🏠 **Praiamar** (10 rooms) Avenida Beira Mar s/n; ☎ 3449 1150; www.praiamarpousada.com.br. Plain whitewash & hardwood rooms with windows overlooking the beach. All have shady terraces hung with lacy hammocks & come with AC & fans. $$

Pousada Oásis (8 rooms) Av Beira Mar 30; ✆3449 1105. Very simple, plain AC & fan-cooled rooms run by a friendly local family who serve a decent b/fast. $

Pousada Siribinha (5 rooms) Praia Siribinha; ✆ 3449 9013. Plain rooms in a tiny beachfront hotel. Deserted during the week & very tranquil. $

OTHER PRACTICALITIES There are no banks or money-changing facilities in Conde or Sítio do Conde.

WHAT TO SEE AND DO

Beaches There are beautiful beaches close to Sítio do Conde village, some of them backed by long *sambaquis* – pre-Columbian rubbish dumps of shells and bone which attest to the large indigenous population that lived here for thousands of years before finally falling to Mem de Sá and the Portuguese slave trade. **Praia dos Artistas** and **Praia Corre Nu** are within walking distance of town. More beaches extend north on a dirt road from Sítio do Conde to **Praia das Poças** (where there is a tiny unspoilt fishing village and little else) and then **Siribinha**, 11km from Sítio do Conde, where the road ends and where there is another tiny hamlet where fishermen offer trips up the Rio Itapicuru for a few reais. Beyond Siribinha there is only beach all the way through **Barra do Itapicuru** (some 5km from Siribinha and where there is snorkelling on the offshore reef) and to **Costa Azul** (6km from Barra do Itapicuru, with dunes, a little village and a handful of very simple pousadas), where another dirt road leads inland to the BA-099.

South of Sítio do Conde there are long, straight beaches all the way to **Barra do Itariri** (16km along a dirt road), which is connected to the BA-099. A fishing village here has a few simple rooms which fill up at weekends with young Baianos, and there is swimming off a broad sandy beach with divides the sea from the River Itariri.

MANGUE SECO Telephone code: 75

Bahia finishes at this little village sandwiched between towering dunes and the broad mangrove-lined Rio Real. Until the turn of the millennium, few tourists made it here, but the broad beaches and laid-back way of life have slowly been drawing increasing numbers of more intrepid travellers looking for the mythical backpacker beach along the Brazilian coastal trail between the Amazon and Rio. They climb the dunes for sunset and mingle with the blue-collar weekenders from Sergipe state and Salvador in the proliferation of untidy *barracas* on the vast beach which seems to stretch south for an infinity of kilometres. Mangue Seco was immortalised in a television soap based on Jorge Amado's steamy novel *Tieta do Agreste*. Agencies throughout the town offer dune beach-buggy tours. The cars have

---

BEACH BUGGIES AND DEAD TURTLES

It is a federal crime in Brazil to drive vehicles on beaches where turtles nest. They nest on most Bahian beaches. Yet buggy tours operate with impunity. Environmental organisations suggest asking for walking tours of dunes and beaches in Bahia, or hiring bicycles. They also suggest asking for wildlife-watching tours as the forests of the Bahian coast are more biodiverse than the Serengeti plains of east Africa and preserve literally scores of critically endangered birds, primates and large mammals like jaguar and tapir. This is a development model that has worked well in parts of Central America. Not only does it increase demand for environmental preservation, it increases its value, ensures that locals gain a livelihood and that turtles are protected. For more information contact **Projeto Tamar** (*http://www.tamar.org.br*), **BirdLife International** (*www.birdlife.org*) or **IBAMA** (*www.ibama.gov.br*).

From the beginning of the slave trade until it ended in the final years of the 19th century, Africans offered strong resistance to the Portuguese. Modern Brazil and the forests of the Guianas are full of villages descended from communities of fugitive Africans who successfully escaped from and evaded capture. These are known as *quilombos*. And in these villages lost in the still unknown lands of the vast South American interior, the ragged remnants of myriad African nations attempted to recreate the lives they had lost in Africa.

The largest and most important of these *quilombos* was Palmares – a settlement which grew to become a network of villages and then a tiny nation within early Brazil, in a remote region of Alagoas state a few hundred kilometres north of Bahia. There is scant and unreliable information about Palmares in the historical record. It is mentioned in Portuguese chronicles – but only in passing or in triumphant self-satisfaction after the community was sacked. We know that it was formed in 1597 by 40 fugitive slaves from Pernambuco, became a Mecca for fugitives of all colour from all over the northeast and grew to be powerful enough to withstand repeated attacks from the Portuguese and the Dutch for almost a century. We also know that its last leader was called Zumbi. He has achieved iconic status in Brazil.

Information about Zumbi is equally meagre and mixed with myth. One story goes as follows. An invasion of Palmares by *bandeirantes* in the community's first years had seen scores of men, women and children massacred. A newborn boy survivor was taken by the *bandeirantes* to Recife, where he was probably raised by a priest, Father Antônio Melo. He was baptised Francisco, taught to read and write Portuguese and Latin and by the age of 12 had become an altar boy. The local community protested – that a white father had adopted a black boy as his own son, and that he should dare to allow him to serve in a church attended by whites. As his understanding of his position in the world deepened, Francisco resolved to flee and search for his place of birth. He eventually did so at the age of 15. He arrived in Palmares at the village of Serra da Barriga where as was customary in the *quilombos* he changed his name to Zumbi. With his superior education he soon became invaluable. By the age of 17 he was in charge of military tactics. At that time Palmares was governed by King Ganga Zumba who had made peace with the Portuguese and in the face of capitulation to their demands, Zumbi assumed power in 1678, reneged on Ganga Zumba's accord and took up arms. He was successful for some 14 years until a *bandeirante* expedition led by Domingos Jorge Velho laid waste to Palmares. Zumbi and a small band of survivors escaped but were captured on 20 November 1695, tortured

begun to do serious damage to the covered dunes and such trips, and where they ascend the dunes with vegetation, should be avoided (see box on page 229).

GETTING THERE   The village is most easily reached through Sergipe.

By bus   Any Aracaju-bound bus will drop visitors at the town of Estancia – just across the border – from where there are two southbound buses a day to Pontal (a port comprising little more than a jetty, sitting opposite Mangue Seco) or more frequent **Toyotas** (leaving when full) from in front of the Estancia hospital.

By boat   A private launch will cost R$30, but it is usually possible to find someone to share the ride and cost for the ten-minute crossing.

⌂ WHERE TO STAY

⌂ **Asa Branca** (21 rooms) ☎ 3445 9054. Simple but well-kept rooms in 2 storeys of terraces overlooking a pool & the river. The restaurant serves good seafood including excellent grilled fish. $$–$$$
⌂ **Fantasias do Agreste** (18 rooms) ☎ 3445 9011; www.pousadafantasiasdoagreste.com. One of the

and killed personally by Jorge Velho who carried Zumbi's head around Recife before leaving it on display in front of the Carmelite church in the city centre, where it remained for years until it had completely decomposed.

Zumbi has become the most powerful symbolic figure in the black resistance movement in Brazil. And the date of his death, 20 November, is commemorated widely in Bahia as it is nationwide, as a National Day of Black Consciousness.

The Paulistano poet Sandro Colibri captures contemporary feelings about Zumbi in his poem, 'Poesia, Palmares … Zumbi':

Sempre negro, (Always black,)
filho do preconceito, sim! (the son of prejudice, yes!)
Mas exijo respeito enfim. (But in the end I demand respect.)
Quero dignidade, (I want my dignity,)
que meus filhos se orgulhem de mim. (and that my children should be proud of me.)
Nas lembranças, (My memories,)
misturam-se dor e esperança, (are a mix of pain and hope,)
fé na crença (I have faith in a belief)
sem grilhões e correntes, (that without shackles and manacles,)
e o povo negro que dança. (it is black people that dance.)
Liberdade pro negro enfim; (Freedom for black people at last;)
Poesia; Palmares … Zumbi. (Poetry; Palmares … Zumbi.)
O negro sonhou. (The black dream.)
O negro lutou. (The black fight.)
Liberdade … Liberdade. (Freedom … Freedom.)
Mas que homem é este? (But what kind of man is it?)
Que diz que o negro é tão diferente. (Who says black men are different.)
Que diz, este negro não pode ser gente. (Who says black men are not people.)
Por que minha cor, te ofende assim? (Why does my colour offend you so?)
Sou negro sim! (Yes, I am black!)
Tenho orgulho sim! (And yes I am proud!)
Sou o grito forte de liberdade, (I am the loud cry for freedom,)
Sou Palmares. (I am Palmares.)
Sou Zumbi. (I am Zumbi.)

largest & most comfortable pousadas in town with brightly painted rooms with terracotta-tile floors & solid wooden furniture overlooking a garden with a little pool. Lively in high season with many couples & families. $$–$$$

⌂ **Village Mangue Seco** (18 rooms), ☎ 3224 2965; www.villagemangueseco.com.br. One of the more comfortable pousadas in town offering mock-adobe concrete chalets in a large palm-shaded lawn around a pool. Most have AC but there are cheaper fan-cooled options. $$

⌂ **O Forte** (12 rooms) ☎ 3445 9039; www.pousadaoforte.com. Simple but cosy little rooms

by the riverside, the best of which are brightly painted in deep orange or light blue & come with AC as well as fans. The owners can organise a range of activities including kayaking, hiking & boat trips in a saveiro yacht. $–$$

⌂ **Cantinho da Lua Clara** (7 rooms) ☎ 079 9935 7105. The cheapest guesthouse in town with tiny but clean boxy rooms (some with AC) & barely room for a bed, miniscule table (with a TV) & fridge. $

⌂ **Grão de Areia** (35 rooms) ☎ 075 9985 4865. Long hammock-slung corridors of ugly & hot motel-like rooms occupied by a bed & simple MDF furniture. $

OTHER PRACTICALITIES There are no banks or money-changing facilities in Mangue Seco. The website www.praiademangueseco.com.br has information on pousadas, restaurants and many photos.

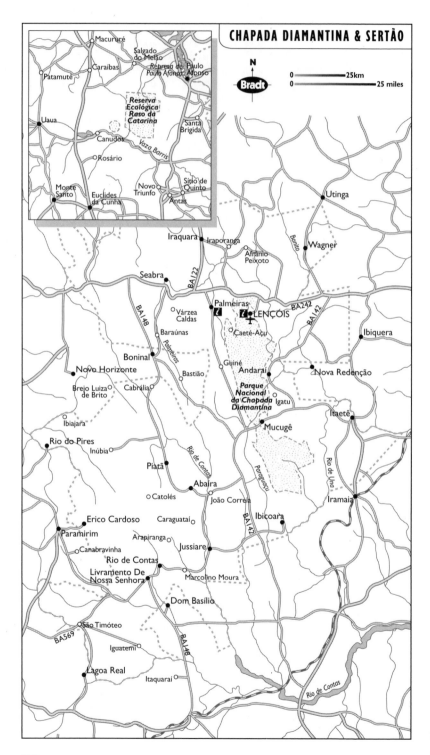

CHAPADA DIAMANTINA & SERTÃO

9

Chapada Diamantina and the Sertão

Telephone code: 75

A fairyland it was – the most wonderful that the imagination of man could conceive. The thick vegetation met overhead, interlacing into a natural pergola, and through this tunnel of verdure in a golden twilight flowed the green, pellucid river, beautiful in itself, but marvellous from the strange tints thrown by the vivid light from above filtered and tempered in its fall.

Arthur Conan Doyle, *The Lost World*

But for a series of upland oases, central Brazil is as arid and ancient as the Australian outback. And, but for a spine of worn and crumbling table-top mountains, it is almost as flat. This mountain ridge stretches from the rainforests of Bolivia in the far south, through the Pantanal swamps and the mines of neighbouring state Minas Gerais, and into the upper reaches of the Amazon on the Venezuelan border. In Bahia these mountains form the Chapada Diamantina – or the 'diamond hills' – rugged chocolate-brown escarpments, surrounded by dry sertão semi-desert, yet high enough to trap rain sweeping in from the Atlantic. As a result the Chapada is washed by rivers that fall over its cliffs to form a series of dramatic waterfalls, irrigating the surrounding plains. The Chapada Diamantina National Park is an oasis – with a pot pourri of Brazilian biomes that form a green patchwork in the sertão desert – of tropical rainforest, woody, richly flowered cerrado and even *pantano* swamp land. The scenery is magnificent. And it's easily accessible, either on an organised jeep tour or on a guided trek.

The Chapada protects some of the tallest waterfalls in Latin America. The Cachoeira da Fumaça (the 'smoky falls') drop 340m into a deep, clear plunge pool; the Coca-Cola-coloured Roncador (or 'snoring falls') rush over brilliantly coloured jasper; whilst others plunge through the Chapada as underground rivers that form glassy blue pools in caves like Poço Encantado. Most visitors arrive at the falls and the other sights, like the Pai Inácio lookout, on a jeep tour. But to really get a sense of the Chapada it's best to hike. Numerous trails traverse the national park; offering walks of a few hours to a few days. Tour operators in the pretty colonial town of Lençóis offer a range of options.

HISTORY

The Chapada belonged solely to Brazilian indigenous peoples – whose presence is marked by paintings and petroglyphs found daubed and carved into the escarpment walls – up until the 18th century when gold prospectors began to trickle in from the coast. The precious metal had been discovered in similar terrain in neighbouring Minas Gerais as early as the 17th century, but the then governor of the captaincy of Bahia, Dom Rodrigo da Costa, feared a rush would de-populate the coast, which at that time was in the incipient stages of sugar production, sparsely populated and thinly defended, and therefore still vulnerable to invasion and colonisation by rival European powers eager to gain a foothold in South America.

However, many intrepid Portuguese were intent on finding their fortune in the interior and carried on exploring nonetheless. Clandestine expeditions found gold nuggets in the Chapada's streams in the early 18th century, which brought a succession of small-scale miners – or *garimpeiros* – to the region. Finally, on 5 August 1720 the state government was forced to capitulate, authorising the establishment of a permanent gold-mining settlement at the mining camp of Jacobina in the northeast of the current national park.

In 1732 diamonds were found. However, previous discoveries to the south, in the Serro Frio of Minas Gerais, had been so large that they'd forced a 75% reduction in world prices, so the Portuguese suppressed the discovery and prohibited exploration. The secret was secure for almost 100 years until German naturalists Spix and Martius visited the region in the 1820s and recorded the presence of diamonds, stimulating *garimpeiros* to visit. By the 1840s, and despite prohibition, a *garimpeiro* called Pedro Ferreiro and his companions had made large strikes on the Rio das Contas near Mucugê which brought in thousands of treasure seekers. Diamonds were then discovered near Lençóis, which derives its name from the fields of white tents – like sheets or *lençóis* – that littered the Serra do Sincorá and the adjacent river valley.

Initially many of the *garimpeiros* were poor adventurers from coastal Bahia and adjacent Minas Gerais, but as the gold rush set in, increasing numbers of wealthier miners poured in from the Recôncavo and then from São Paulo far to the south. In their wake came cattle herders from the Rio São Francisco. By the 1860s, Lençóis had become a town with a representative in the state Senate and streets of handsome buildings.

But the new-found wealth brought not prosperity, but civil unrest. Lençóis and the Chapada were divided between warring bandit factions – the Serranos under the control of Coronel Felisberto Augusto de Sá from Tijuco in Minas Gerais, and the Baianos under Coronel Antônio Gomes Calmon from the Recôncavo. When political power shifted from appointment to election under the republic, both groups paid lip service to political respectability by aligning themselves respectively with the Liberal and Conservative parties. Under a practice known as *coronelismo* – which continues to this day in parts of backland Brazil – the coronels owned the lives of thousands of less-privileged town members, a system akin to medieval debt peonage. Potential voters were intimidated into supporting one or the other faction, often under pain of death.

By the 20th century, violence in the Chapada had reached critical levels. It culminated in an all-out war between families which saw Coronel Horácio de Mattos take control of the Chapada and subsequently the whole of the Bahian sertão. In 1927 de Mattos and his ally, Franklin de Albuquerque, employed their private armies of *jagunço* bandits and state police to quell the communist long-march led by Luís Carlos Prestes. The Prestes column – a Marxist crusader pilgrimage of thousands of peasants and disaffected army officers – had traversed some 25,000km through the Brazilian interior gathering support as it moved along. Its triumphant march into Rio had been seen as inevitable by many Brazilians. But when the column reached Bahia they made the mistake of killing two members of de Mattos's family. In response de Mattos formed the Batalhão Patriótico Lavras Diamantinas (the Patriotic Battalion of Lavras Diamantinas), attacked the column and forced them out of Brazil and into Bolivia. De Mattos was hailed as a hero. Yet ironically his battle paved the way for his downfall. The suppression of Prestes allowed Getúlio Vargas's fascist new state to sweep into power in 1930. All dissent was crushed; de Mattos was disarmed, imprisoned and then assassinated two days after his release in 1931.

With the quelling of the coronels and the depletion of the diamonds, Lençóis and the other towns fell into poverty. The forests of the Chapada – cleared for wood for the mines, housing and cattle grazing – began to regrow. Puma, jaguar and white-tailed deer returned and the Chapada became a forgotten backland. Then in the 1980s adventurous Brazilian journalists began to brave the long dusty drive in from Salvador and pictures showing the area's beauty began to draw increasing numbers of tourists to Lençóis. This led to a national park being established in 1985 and today the Chapada is finding prosperity once again – through ecotourism.

GEOGRAPHY

The Chapada Diamantina National Park covers some 1,520km^2. Rugged table-top mountains, between 400m and 1,200m high and made from 1.8 billion-year-old sedimentary rocks, run through the centre of the park, split by broad valleys filled with cerrado, caatinga scrub forest or savanna grasslands. These are at their most dramatic in the Vale do Paty in the south of the park and the Vale do Capão valley which runs north from the town of Capão to the Morro do Pai Inácio hill (and lookout point) just beyond the park's boundaries to the north. The best of the waterfalls dot the hills around the valleys including Fumaça, Sossego and Primavera. Various rivers cut through the Chapada, including the Rio Lençóis, the Rio Serrano and the Rio Paraguaçu, which eventually drains into the Baía de Todos os Santos. The principal point of access to the park is Lençóis, just off the Salvador to Brasília highway (BR-242) in the north of the national park.

NATURAL HISTORY

FLORA The Chapada forms a transition zone between three distinctive kinds of Neotropical vegetation: *terra firme* tropical moist forest in the east, *campos gerais* in the central areas and *caatinga* in the arid parts of the park, mostly in the west.

The tropical moist forest preserves similar broadleaf evergreen species to the Mata Atlântica (Atlantic coast forest), which runs across the coastal spine of Brazil from Paraíba all the way to Iguaçu.

The campos gerais are dominated by patchy cerrado and savanna grasslands and dotted with *pantano* swampland. Soils are very poor here: acidic and sandy and either sodden or bone dry depending on the time of year. Campos gerais are characterised by hardy, drought- and fire-resistant sedges and spectacular flowering plants and trees like the medicinal Velame branco (*Macrosiphonia velame*) and Ipe – trumpet flowers – (*Tabebuia* sp). Cerrado is Brazil's most threatened biome and the cerrado forests of central Brazil are one of Conservation International's designated biodiversity hotpots.

Caatinga is a uniquely Brazilian biome and is made up of drought-resistant shrubland and thorn forest of xeric desert-adapted plants and fire-adapted grassland savannas.

At higher altitudes there are also montane forests and campos rupestre, which biologist Roy Funch has termed 'rocky fields'. Campos rupestre are particularly high in endemic begonia, cactus and bromeliad species adapted to poor soil and dramatic fluctuations in rainfall and temperature. There are also gallery forests along the rivers. Some have more than 100 tree species (which rivals almost the whole of Europe) and all are dotted with epiphytic orchids, cacti and bromeliads. In the east of the park, alongside the tropical moist forest, there is an extensive pantano swampland area dominated by gallery forests, varzea and reeds.

FAUNA Despite problems with subsistence hunting, Chapada's diverse range of habitats supports a number of animal species. Mammals include elusive apex predators like puma and jaguar, smaller cats like margay and ocelot, tayra and racoons, coatis and two species of fox. There are four primates, including the rare masked titi monkey and numerous red brocket, white-tailed (also known as the pampas) deer. Reptiles include broad-snouted caiman and green anacondas.

Birds The Chapada is also rich in birdlife (though low in endemics), and boasts a bird list of over 250 species. The list is reproduced in its entirety in Roy Funch's *A Visitor's Guide to the Chapada Diamantina Mountains* (see *Further Information* page 257), which is available throughout Lençóis. The national park is considered a key area for the conservation of a number of rare and vulnerable species, including many caatinga species limited to arid northeastern Brazil.

Two species which *are* endemic to the Chapada and the adjacent Serra do Espinhaço in Minas Gerais are the grey-backed tachuriand the pale-throated serra-finch. The hooded visorbearer hummingbird is also unique to the park.

Other notable spectaculars include crowned eagle, white-necked hawk, white-browed guan, vinaceous amazon, golden-capped parakeet, blue-throated conure, blue-winged macaw, sharp-tailed streamcreeper, great xenops, narrow-billed antwren, red-ruffed fruitcrow, yellow-faced siskin and pectoral antwren.

Besides preserving these rare regional species, the Chapada is an important stopover for 33 species of migratory bird. More information on avifauna can be found through the birding guides listed in *Appendix 4*, page 258.

GETTING THERE AND AWAY

There is no public transport to the park, which is best visited with a tour company. Lençóis town – the nearest access point for the Chapada – lies 427km from Salvador and 297km from the transport hub of Feira de Santana, on the BR-242 highway. It can be reached by air and by bus. Brasília is 1,133km west along the same road.

BY AIR Lençóis airport (**↖** *3625 8100*) lies on the main BR-242 Salvador–Brasília road at km209, 20km from Lençóis town. There are weekly flights between Lençóis and Salvador with Trip (*www.voetrip.com.br*). They get booked up well in advance.

BY BUS Real Expresso (*www.realexpresso.com.br*) operate three direct buses daily between Lençóis and Salvador for R$40, leaving morning and afternoon from the bus station on the riverbank – where there is a booth selling tickets. The best bus to take is the early morning bus - as this arrives in Salvador before dark. Buses go via Feira de Santana. If travelling to or from other locations in Bahia change here; you do not need to travel via Salvador. There are also buses to Recife and other destinations in the northeast and connections to Goiás and Brasília via the town of Seabra west of Lençóis.

BY CAR There are no car hire companies in Lençóis. Salvador is a long, bumpy six-hour drive, but cars can be hired there.

WHAT TO TAKE

If you are going to be trail walking it's advisable to bring hiking boots or sturdy shoes. Mosquitoes are prevalent all year round so bring a DEET-based spray, and in the 'winter' months it can be cold, so a fleece, sleeping bag and rainwear will be needed. Sometimes, guides can arrange these. A tent is useful but optional, although many camps are beside reasonably hospitable caves. Torches (flashlights), a water bottle, a spare pair of laces and thick socks (to avoid blisters) are essentials. So is money: many of the sights have an entrance fee.

GETTING AROUND

The national park is traversed by dirt roads and trails running between the various settlements and the main attractions. Many of the routes have been used for centuries by locals, but finding your own way is difficult, so it is essential to use a guide or travel with a tour group when hiking in the park. There are many options, from long camping trips and treks, to jeep-based half-day or day tours (see pages 237–9 for a list of operators and guides). Entrance fees for the caves and attractions are not always included in the tour price – check with the company before booking. For detailed trekking information consult Roy Funch's book (see page 257), visit www.infochapada.com, or the **Sectur** tourist booth inside the market in Lençóis on the southern bank of the river.

Trail walking in the park can involve scrambling, so a moderate level of fitness is required.

TOURIST INFORMATION

The official IBAMA park headquarters are at Palmeiras (*Rua Barão do Rio Branco 25, 50km from Lençóis;* 3332 2420). It is not necessary to visit here. Lençóis offers far more facilities and more information than you will get from IBAMA. The bulk of the tour agencies and trekking companies operate from here.

See also www.guiachapadadiamantina.com.br, the most comprehensive source of up-to-the-minute information on the pousadas, hotels, restaurants and tour operators. In Portuguese, English, French and German.

TOUR OPERATORS

Chapada Adventure Av 7 de Seetembro 7; 3334 2037; www.chapadaadventure.com.br. A small operator offering economical jeep-based tours, canoeing in the Rio Marimbus pantano & rivers, & light hikes throughout the Chapada, concentrating mostly on the key sights.

Destino Chapada 3334 1484; www.destinochapada.com.br. Car-based trips, light adventure & light walks to all of the major highlights.

Expedições H2O Pousada dos Duendes, Rua do Pires s/n, Lençóis; 3334 1229; www.pousadadosduendes.com. Backpacker tours aimed at non-Brazilians travelling on a budget. Offer a range of cheap-&-cheerful trail walks, kayak trips & bus-bound highlight sightseeing stopovers.

Extreme Av 7 de Setembro 15; 334 1727; www.extremeecoadventure.com.br. One of the few companies to devote themselves seriously to hiking in the Chapada, with a good range of 2–6-day walks, canoeing trips & light adventure activities like rappelling & bungee jumping.

Fora da Trilha Rua das Pedras 202; www.foradatrilha.com.br. Offer longer treks, including the extensive Travessia Diamantina hike (give advance notice for this) & adventure activities including canyoning & rapelling.

Gaya Praça Horácio Matos s/n; 3334 1167; m 9992 2820; e rafa.gaya@yahoo.com.br. Offers budget backpacker trips in & around the Chapada in a battered Toyota. Around US $180 for 300km round trips for up to 10 people with visits to out-of-the-way & little-visited sights like the Cachoeira do Mosquito. Book ahead.

Nativos da Chapada Rua Miguel Calmon 29, Lençóis; 3334 1314. Perhaps the most adventure-orientated operator in Lençóis. Trips with this bunch are not quiet, contemplative affairs. Expect sound, fury & adrenalin on the cliff-top bungee jumps, waterfall rappels & zip-line descents. Bespoke activities available on request.

Venturas e Aventuras Praça Horácio de Matos 20; 3334 1304. One of the better trekking companies, offering longer camping & guesthouse-based trips, including 6-day hikes & the Travessia Diamantina trail.

TOUR GUIDES

Many of the guesthouses in town use bespoke guides. These are some of the best-known ones.

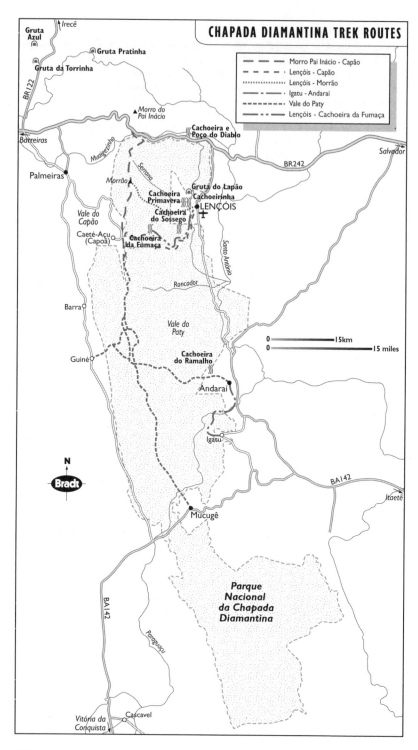

CHAPADA DIAMANTINA TREK ROUTES

— — — Morro Pai Inácio - Capão
— — · Lençóis - Capão
· · · · · · Lençóis - Morrão
— · — · Igatu - Andaraí
— — — — Vale do Paty
— · · — · · Lençóis - Cachoeira da Fumaça

Gruta
Azul

Irecê

Gruta Pratinha

Gruta da Torrinha

BR 122

Morro do
Pai Inácio

Cachoeira e
Poço do Diablo

Barreiras

Muquginho

Serrano

BR242

Salvador

Palmeiras

Morrão

Gruta do Lapão
Cachoeirinha

Cachoeira
Primavera

LENÇÓIS

Cachoeira
do Sossego

Vale do
Capão

Caeté-Açu
(Capão)

Cachoeira
da Fumaça

Santo Antônio

Roncador

Barra

Vale do
Paty

0 ————— 15km
0 ————— 15 miles

Guiné

Cachoeira
do Ramalho

Andaraí

N

Bradt

Igatu

BA142

Itaetê

Mucugê

Parque
Nacional
da Chapada
Diamantina

BA142

Paraguaçu

Vitória da
Conquista

Cascavel

238

Edmilson (aka Mil) Rua Domingos B Souza 70; ☎ 3334 1319. One of the best local guides, with excellent knowledge of the trails & beauty spots around the Chapada.
Luiz Krug Contact via Vila Serrano (see page 243); ☎ 3334 1102. The best guide for caves & geological explorations. Speaks good English.
Roy Funch ☎ 3334 1305; e funchroy@yahoo.com; www.fcd.org.br. The ex-director of Chapada Diamantina National Park & author of the best guidebook to the region (see page 257). Roy offers walking & wildlife trips, especially out of Lençóis, & is very knowledgeable on all aspects of the park from history & geology to fauna & flora.
Trajano Contact via Vila Serrano or Casa da Hélia (see pages 243 & 244); ☎ 3334 1143. A friendly & amenable English- & Hebrew-speaking guide with good prices who covers all the park highlights.
Zé Carlos Contact through Casa da Geleia or Vila Serrano (see pages 000 & 000; ☎ 3334 1151. The only guide in the area that we know of who has a thorough knowledge of the birdlife.

WHAT TO SEE AND DO

THE WATERFALLS The Chapada is replete with waterfalls, from thunderous cataracts that are among the tallest in the Americas, to gentle cascades that fall in series through perfectly moulded jasper pools. With a little walking, you can visit most on day tours. Some are only accessible on longer guided treks.

Cachoeira do Buracão The Buracão ('Big Hole') falls are the largest – according to water volume – in the Chapada. They are also one of the most beautiful and are especially photogenic. Dropping from a 120m-high vertical precipice they roar into a narrow fluted canyon that looks like Western Australia's famous Karijini gorges. A trail runs from the summit of the falls to the canyon and then to the base where it's possible to swim in the icy, windy plunge pool.

Getting there Buracão is remote. It's tucked away in its own municipal protected area outside the park boundaries in the far southeast of the Chapada, and as a result is not usually included on Lençóis tour programmes. Access is possible only with an accredited guide – hired either in Lençóis or by asking around in Mucugê or Igatu. These are the nearest towns to the falls and an hour away by dirt road. Expect to pay at least R$30 for the trip, including the park entrance fee and allow a couple of days to see the falls including a stopover in Mucugê or Igatu.

Cachoeira do Diabo and the Rio Mucugezinho A rocky trail descends from the BR-242 main highway for some 2km, cutting through scrubby caatinga before reaching the brown Rio Mucugezinho. It flows down the rockiest portion of the escarpment to form the dramatic Cachoeira do Diabo (or 'Devil's Falls'), which flow over a series of rocky steps before tumbling into a deep, 200m-wide plunge pool and spilling from there into a narrow gorge surrounded by verdant cerrado forest. Swimming here is heavenly. The falls are included on many of the day trips.

Cachoeira do Capivari This gentle falls runs through a series of plunge pools set in multi-coloured canyons off the Rio Capivari just south of Lençóis. The falls receive few tourists as they lie off the beaten track because they can only be accessed either along an obscure rocky trail or by wading and rock-hopping up an affluent of the Capivari River. Guides are essential.

Cachoeira da Fumaça The Chapada's most spectacular and most photographed falls, the Cachoeira da Fumaça ('Smoky Falls') lies in the north of the park near the village of Capão. It cascades 340m from an escarpment into a deep plunge pool and the backdraft from the fall, coupled with a constant easterly wind, blows the water vapour back up the mountain shrouding the landscape in a curtain of fine mist that looks like smoke. The falls are the second highest in Brazil after the Cachoeira do Aracá in Amazonas state and can be visited on a day tour – via the town of Palmeiras – or as part of a longer hike.

The falls are administered by a local NGO, which asks for a donation of R$3 from visitors. Jeep tours pull up near the base of the old cattle trail that climbs to the waterfalls' summit. The walk takes about two hours for the moderately fit. The path is rocky and when it's cloudy it can be slippery. It begins with a steep ascent, then cuts across former cattle pasture to a viewpoint at the head of a long canyon. Looking over the edge of the falls is hypnotically vertiginous. There are better views from the base, which is reachable via a steep and perilous trail from the summit or an easier path only reachable on walking tours of one–two days from Lençóis.

Cachoeira Roncador and the Rio Roncador

Cachoeira Roncador and the Rio Roncador The River Roncador cuts through rocky hills shrouded in scrubby forest before reaching a stepped escarpment looking out over the cerrado forests and wetlands of Marimbus in the eastern Chapada. Here the tea-coloured water flows into deep pools, wells up in gurgles and roars and falls again and again over a series of marble-smooth terraces of polished pink rock. Chapada Adventure (see page 237) include Roncador as part of their Chapada Marimbus wetlands tour.

Cachoeira do Sossego As the Rio Riberão tumbles out of the high Chapada it cuts through the hills in a series of steep canyons, the last of which forms one of the Chapada's most visited cascades: the boulder-strewn Cachoeira do Sossego (or 'Tranquil Falls'). Its cluster of deep, cool pools with natural smooth-rock slides are a great spot to cool off after the sweaty 5km walk.

Getting there Sossego is one of the few falls that can be reached directly from Lençóis town on a path that begins at Lumiar camping area near the Igreja de Nossa Senhora do Rosário. It is a three hour walk along the river, with occasional wading and much scrambling and is best done with a local guide.

THE MOUNTAINS AND VALLEYS

Morro do Pai Inácio The Chapada's emblematic shot – gracing every other brochure and tour agency pamphlet – is a sunset view over a broad forest-filled valley shadowed by a series of towering table-top hills. It's taken from the summit of the Morro do Pai Inácio ('Father Ignatius' Hill'), a table-top mountain in the far north of the Chapada, right next to the BR-242 highway. The summit is pocked with little pools, some lined with moss or ferns, others with dripping bromeliads or epiphytic cacti. In the late afternoon, vultures, hawks and eagles can often be seen riding the thermals in the valley below.

Access is easy. Tour coaches park in the dirt area at the hill's base and from here it's a 20-minute walk and light scramble to the flat summit. Unfortunately, most day tours visit Pai Inácio in the middle of the morning – the very worst time for photographs. Try and be here at daybreak or the late afternoon.

According to one local legend, Pai Inácio is named after an escaped slave who fell in love with the daughter (or some say wife) of one of the local coronels. When the coronel discovered the affair, he ordered his *jagunço* thugs to kill the man. For days Inácio evaded capture, but was eventually found on the summit of the mountain. Finding himself cornered, Inácio opened an umbrella given to him by his lover and jumped off the edge. His body was never recovered and the coronel's daughter disappeared. It's said she and Inácio fled to neighbouring Minas Gerais and lived happily ever after. If the story is true, Inácio's escape may not have been miraculous:

the summit of Pai Inácio is not as vertical as it first appears: a series of ledges jutt out just below the *meseta*'s rim and some guides claim that Inácio jumped onto these, hid until the *jagunços* left and later stole away with the coronel's daughter.

The Morro do Pai Inácio to Capão walking trail is a 25km day-hike that leads from the summit of the Pai Inácio escarpment around other table-top mountains, through cerrado, caatinga and arable areas to the Capão valley.

The Marimbus wetland The southwestern states of Mato Grosso and Mato Grosso do Sul boast the pantanal: the world's largest wetland, which is home to an enormous array of large mammals, reptiles and birds. The Chapada offers the Marimbus wetland: a similar – albeit significantly smaller – habitat, formed by the confluence of the Santo Antônio and Utinga rivers and located at the eastern edge of the national park.

To the untutored eye the wetland appears to be an untamed wilderness. In reality it isn't even natural. Marimbus was formed in the 19th and 20th centuries as a result of diamond and gold mining; tons of sediment washed down from the hills stilted the once rapid flow of the two rivers, eventually causing them to permanently flood and create large tracts of swampland.

Marimbus is dominated by gallery forest and thick pirí and taboá bullrushes, both of which provide nesting sites for the region's numerous wading and waterbirds, especially herons (including white-necked, striated and rufescent tiger), gallinules and jacanas. Sadly, widespread hunting has almost completely wiped out capybara and short-nosed caiman populations, both of which should be abundant in such an environment.

Getting there The wetland is included on many Lençóis tour-operator itineraries. The best trips take a day, involve at least three–four hours in the swamp, and include a walk to the Roncador Falls.

THE CAVES The Chapada is cut with numerous caves, many of them coursed by underground rivers or filled with glassy clear lakes. Among the best are the following.

Poço Encantado (⏰ *09.00–17.00 daily; R$10)* The 'Enchanted Pool' is a clear, cool-blue, fathom-deep cave pool, lit by a single shaft of brilliant light and another of the Chapada's brochure views. The light shines only between April and August and is at its best in June and July between 11.00 and 12.00. During these peak periods (and weekends), queues to take pictures and pose on the rocky platform overlooking the pool can be long and the atmosphere far from tranquil. The cave was closed as this book went to press.

The Gruta Pratinha and Gruta Azul (⏰ *09.00–17.00 daily; R$10)* The 'Silver and Blue Grottoes' are a series of pretty caverns and lily-covered pools, linked by an underground river full of wan cave fish. Large numbers of weekend visitors snorkel, swim or float through the caves on rubber tubes and, as a result, they're starting to show signs of wear and tear. If you look closely you'll see that the surface of the water is covered in a light scum of dust and suntan lotion. Such combinations have been responsible for the destruction of similar habitats in the Yucatan, so – even though there are no signs advising visitors to respect the caves – visitors should swim without suncream and be careful not to disturb the sediment. There is a gift shop.

The Gruta Azul lies just behind the expansive parking lot. It's quieter, but no swimming is permitted.

Caverna Lapa Doce (🕐 *09.00–17.00 daily; R$10*) This extensive cave system, some 20km northwest of the Pai Inácio hill, is the third largest in Brazil and stretches for over 23km underneath the Chapada. Only a small section of the system is open to the public, but it's a spectacular run of 15–20m-high rooms filled with stalactites, stalagmites and flow stones. They are reached through a quarry-like dip in the ground inhabited by hundreds of rock cavies, a rabbit-sized rodent endemic to arid eastern Brazil.

TREKS IN THE VALE DO CAPÃO AND THE VALE DO PATY These two mountain-lined valleys run through the north and south ends of the park. The Vale do Paty is steep and deep and inhabited by a few farmers who eke a subsistence life between the shadows cast by the adjacent mountains. The Vale do Capão is broader and wilder. Access can only be gained by foot.

Both offer good walking possibilities and, combined, they form the heart of the Chapada's longest trek: the 112km Travessia Diamantina ('Diamond Crossing)', which runs from Capão village in the north right across the park via the deep and narrow Vale do Paty, to the Cachoeira do Buracão in the far south. Accommodation is in a combination of tents and rustic pousadas and there are side-trips off to the Cachoeira da Fumaça (near Capão), Igatu, Poço Encatado, and the Marimbus pantanal area and Roncador falls. The shorter Vale do Paty hike is a four- to six-day walk running through the heart of the Serra along a valley surrounded by imposing table-top mountains; several scenic viewpoints, caves, swimming holes and waterfalls can be found along the way. The route also departs from Capão in the north and finishes at the village of Guiné, just west of Andaraí town.

Other walks A trail runs from **Igatu** village (see page 245) to **Andaraí** leaving from the central square of the former town past the cemetery and following the **Xique-Xique** River. The walk takes four hours and offers wonderful views of the mountain landscape. There are plenty of river-bank stops for a cooling swim. There are longer treks too, details of which can be found in Roy Funch's excellent book (see page 257) on the Chapada Diamantina, available in shops throughout Lençóis.

LENÇÓIS

The Chapada's principal town – and the only one with any real tourist infrastructure or transport links – lies nestled in a green valley astride a rushing mountain stream. Most of the town lies south of the river, clambering up the hill in streets of narrow cobbled stone, which are lined with small tidy stone cottages. In response to the boom in ecotourism, many of these houses have been converted into guesthouses, knick-knack shops, bakeries and restaurants, serving everything from Brazilian *feijoada* to backpacker-friendly apple pie and carrot cake. At the time of writing, the majority of backpackers are Brazilian, but Lençóis and the Chapada are becoming increasingly popular with foreign tourists and many of the local businesses speak better-than-average English and even a little Hebrew or Spanish. Lençóis has no real attractions of its own – Chapada owns those – but it's a pleasant place to hang out for a few days and it always attracts a mixed travel crowd.

HISTORY The town was founded as a mining camp in the 18th century and is named after the white tents which lay along the course of the river before the rough stone houses were built. From a distance they looked like white sheets (or Lençóis in Portuguese) spread over the surrounding scrubland.

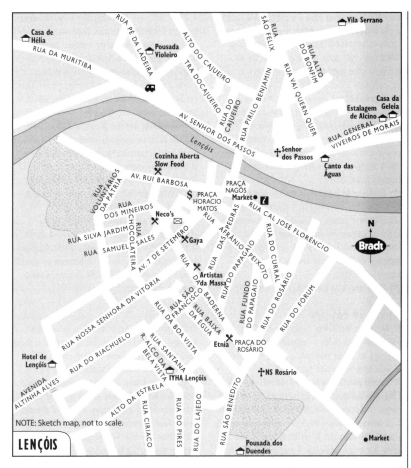

LENÇÓIS

NOTE: Sketch map, not to scale.

GETTING THERE AND AROUND (see page 236). Lençóis is so small you could walk across the entire town in less than ten minutes. It is best negotiated on foot.

TOURIST INFORMATION There is a booth (⊕ *sporadically 10.00–16.00 Mon–Fri*) in the market next to Praça Nagos.

🏠 WHERE TO STAY

🏠 **Canto das Águas** (100 rooms) Av Senhor dos Passos; ☎ 3334 1154; www.lencois.com.br. Lençóis' grandest hotel offers a range of spacious rooms. Some are a little musty & in need of attention, others are better appointed & in a new wing & all overlooking the river just opposite the rodoviária. $$$$

🏠 **Hotel de Lençóis** (71 rooms) Rua Altinha Alves 747; ☎ 3334 1102; www.hoteldelencois.com.br. This stately 19th-century townhouse, set in a little garden on the edge of the national park, houses a series of plain but comfortable white-tile & hardwood rooms & is disturbed by little but the sound of crickets & tree

frogs. B/fast is generous & there's a pool & restaurant. $$$$

🏠 **Vila Serrano** (13 rooms)Rua Alto do Bonfim 8; ☎ 3334 1486; www.vilaserrano.com.br. One of the best options in Lençóis – with a string of mock-colonial, but modern & well-appointed bungalow rooms set around a pretty fountain in a garden lush with orchids & bromeliads. The owners are warm & welcoming, knowledgeable about the area & they organise tours. $$$

🏠 **Casa da Geleia** (10 rooms) Rua Gen Viveiros 187; ☎ 3334 1151; www.casadageleia.com.br. A series of plain & simple cabana chalets set in a lawned garden at the entrance to town. B/fast is excellent — with bakery-warm bread & a range of homemade jams (which lend their name to the pousada). The owner, Zé Carlos, offers birdwatching trips & is very knowledgeable about the Chapada. $$

🏠 **Casa de Hélia** (8 rooms) Rua da Muritiba; 📞 3334 1143; www.casadehelia.com.br. An upmarket backpacker-friendly guesthouse perched on the side of a hill with a range of colourful rooms gathered around a little pool & overlooking the town on one side & the forest on another. Friendly & serves an excellent b/fast. $$

🏠 **Estalagem de Alcino** (8 rooms) Rua Gen Vivieros de Morais 139; 📞 3334 1171. A pretty 19th-century house set in a garden with a dozen or so rooms all furnished with period antiques. Most have shared bathrooms. B/fast is generous & served in the little hummingbird-filled garden next to the owner's pottery studio. $$

🏠 **IYHA Lençóis** (4 rooms) Rua Boa Vista 121;

📞 3334 1497; www.hostelchapada.com.br. A modern, spacious & friendly backpacker hostel based in a large period townhouse in the southern part of town. Much the best of the backpacker options, with a range of sgls, en-suite dbls & sgl-sex 4–6-room dorms, a kitchen & big hammock-filled garden. Tours can be arranged; though it's good to shop around in town before committing. $–$$

🏠 **Pousada dos Duendes** (8 rooms) Rua do Pires; 📞 3334 1229; www.pousadadosduendes.com. The town's most popular backpacker hostel offers a run of simple, boxy rooms & dorms. Operates an Australian-style all-inclusive policy — encouraging guests to eat (modest) b/fast & dinner in-house & tour with the pousada. Shop around before committing to a trip. $–$$

🏠 **Pousada Violeiro** (9 rooms) Rua Prof Assis 70; 📞 3534 1259; www.pousadavioleiro.com.br. A clean (very simple) quiet, Christian-run Brazilian guesthouse behind the rodoviária. Offers the cheapest, plainest rooms in town. B/fast is optional. $–$$

✖ WHERE TO EAT

✖ **Artistas da Massa** Rua Miguel Calmon. Offers respectable pasta dishes — although they'd be classed as stodgy by Italian standards — & a generous menu of wood-fired oven-baked pizzas. $$$

✖ **Cozinha Aberta Slow Food** Rui Barbosa 42; 📞 3334 1309; www.cozinhaaberta.com.br. Cozinha is the chicest restaurant in town. It's housed in a pretty Art Deco house overlooking the river between the main praça & the Canto das Aguas hotel. Food is slow to arrive, but organic, delicious & prepared by São Paulo chef, Deborah Doitschinoff. $$$

✖ **Etnia** Rua da Baderna 111; 📞 3334 1066. Cosy affair with only 5 candlelit tables. They serve Thai & Indian food, including a delicious Brazilian variant of

tom ka gai (chicken in coconut sauce served with jasmine — not sticky — rice). The Indian food is spiced down for the very sensitive Brazilian palate. $$$

✖ **Neco's** Praça Maestro Clarindo Pachêco 15; 📞 3334 1179. A meal here is an essential Chapada experience. Neco & his wife offer a set meal of local dishes inspired by the campfire cooking of diamond miners. Food is wholesome & ultra-fresh. Try the saffron-stewed mutton with prickly pear cactus & plantain banana. $$$

✖ **Gaya** Praça Horáçio Matos s/n; 📞 3334 1167; 🕐 lunchtimes only. A backpacker travel agency-cum-organic wholefood café offering big salads, tropical fruit juices & sandwiches. $–$$

ENTERTAINMENT AND NIGHTLIFE Lençóis celebrates both Carnaval (February/ March) and the Festas Juninhas (throughout June) with lively parades.

Nightclubs

☆ **Clube Sete** Rua das Pedras; opens from around 22.00 Fri & Sat. A lively little dance club playing Brazilian music.

☆ **Doce Barbaros** Rua das Pedras, 21; 🕐 from around 22.00. Named in honour of the tropicálistas & often playing their music. Offers different themed evenings every night of the week

SHOPPING Crystals, clothing and knick-knacks can be bought in many of the shops congregated around Praças Nagos and Horácio Matos, and in the adjacent market. Shops in Lençóis open when the proprietor arrives; there are no set opening times.

Zambumbeira Rua das Pedras at Tamandare; 📞 3334 1207. Upmarket bric-a-brac & household ware,

including some exquisite ceramics by renowned artisans like Zé Caboclo.

Instrumentos Rua das Pedras 78; ☎ 3334 1334. Unusual handmade variations on Brazilian & African musical instruments by expat Argentinian Jorge Fernando.

OTHER PRACTICALITIES
$ **Bradesco bank** Praça Horácio Matos s/n; ⏰ 09.00–16.00 Mon–Fri. With a Visa ATM.

Massage and treatments The Chapada has long attracted alternative medical practitioners and healers. The following are excellent and can be booked through hotels for in-room visits.

Anita Marti ☎ 9989 8328. Healing & therapeutic massage & treatments.
Dieter Herzberg ☎ 9984 2720; e dieterherzberg@yahoo.com.br. All manner of therapeutic & healing massage.

Jaques Gagnon ☎ 3334 1281; www.janeladaalma.com. Neuro-structural therapy & healing massage.

BEYOND LENÇÓIS

Infrastructure and services are poor outside Lençóis, but if you have the time there are a few other towns worth visiting in the Chapada. The further south you travel, the older the mining towns become because the Chapada was settled in stages by miners who ascended the Rio Paraguaçu - which runs all the way to the Baía de Todos os Santos.

MUCUGÊ Located in the far south of the national park, just off the BA-142 state highway, Mucugê is the oldest of the mining settlements. The original mining camp was founded when a wanderer called Cazuzinho do Prado stopped for a rest next to the Cumbuca River on his way to buy produce from farms in the south. He was a former *garimpeiro* from Minas Gerais and after sifting through the river gravel he decided that it would probably be rich in diamonds. So he returned with 14 men and panning equipment and subsequently discovered 108 carats of fine stone. Mucugê was initially known as São João do Paraguaçu, but was rechristened after a local sweet, apple-sized fruit that was once abundant along the riverside.

Although tourism is beginning to take off, Mucugê remains a sleepy, parochial town of a few thousand inhabitants. There are a few things to see: streets of pastel-coloured 18th- and 19th-century houses and a haunting brilliant-white cemetery nestled under a dark stone mountain just outside of town, which is beautifully illuminated at night. And about 2km west of Mucugê, the Paraguaçu River pours into the deep Mar de Espanha pool before rushing through the impressive, steep Siberia canyon. The water looks inviting, but is probably not clean enough for swimming.

Getting there Mucugê can be visited on a tour from Lençóis. A least three buses a day run between the towns, taking around 90 minutes. Return tickets cost R$5.

 Where to stay

🏠 **Pousada Mucugê** (30 rooms) Rua Dr Rodrigues Lima 30, Mucugê; tel: 3338 2210; www.pousadamucuge.com.br. Rooms are simple with ceiling fans, hot water & a small swimming pool. Advice on local guides, tour operators & walks available. $$

IGATÚ This crumbling mining-supply village is the most interesting of the Chapada settlements after Lençóis. It's a dying village fringed with the ghostly shell of a once prosperous mining town. Many of the thick-walled stone houses are now eerie ruins – lined up in ranks on streets being reclaimed by nature, with mango trees growing from what once were front rooms and vines clawing at the shells of empty window panes. Others are derelict shelters built into or on top of giant boulders, around weather-worn rock formations or into the rock face of towering mountains. A few hundred souls cling on in the village centre, eking out a living collecting flowers to dry in the hot sun and sell for floral displays in Brazil's urban capitals. However, in the last few years tourism has begun to provide some sustenance. There are now a handful of little guesthouses in the quirky old buildings, a few restaurants and even some freelance local guides – making Igatú an alternative base from which to explore the Chapada. Trails from the town lead to a series of waterfalls; the closest, Cachoeira das Pombos (or 'Dove falls'), is only a 15-minute walk away. A trail continues from here all the way across the southern portion of the park to Mucugê.

Getting there Igatú is accessible by car from Lençóis – lying on the rough road that runs south from the BR-242 to the BA-42 and Mucugê. There are sporadic buses from Lençóis and Mucugê (see page 245).

Where to stay Apart from the two options listed below, there are a handful of other simple accommodation options in the town centre. They are rarely full outside weekends.

⌂ **Pousada Pedras de Igatú** (15 rooms) Rua São Sebastião s/n, Vila de Igatú; ☎ 3335 2281; www.igatu.com.br. Simple, fan-cooled rooms overlooking a garden & a spring-water swimming pool on the edge of town. Good views & a decent b/fast included. The owners can advise on walks & guides, although they speak little English. MasterCard & Diners Club accepted. $$

⌂ **Estalagem Gota D'Agua** Igatú; ☎ 3335 2036; e jcosta@libero.it. A very simple little guesthouse in a pretty terracotta-tiled town cottage in the heart of Igatú. A very good b/fast is included in the price & advice on local attractions, guides & walks is also available. $

THE SERTÃO

Most of Bahia is made up of bone-dry scrub desert which looks like the Australian outback, where dirt-poor villages eke an existence from the poor soil. It's a landscape few tourists see, but which is etched deep into the Brazilian psyche. Those looking for something far from the beaten trail will find it worthwhile taking a side trip from Salvador – into the arid sertão interior at **Canudos**. This sombre one-street village was the site of one of Latin America's most astonishing and tragic rebellions; where in the 19th-century, a raggle-taggle band of brigands and bandits led by a messianic preacher clad in porphyry nearly brought the country's army to its knees … before being ruthlessly massacred. Their story is told in one of the masterpieces of early Brazilian literature, *Os Sertões* by Euclides da Cunha, and has recently been retold by Mario Vargas Llosa in his gripping epic novel, *The War of the End of the World* – which is surely one of the best books to read on bus journeys through Bahia. And in the area around Canudos there are a series of parks and reserves that preserve wild stretches of the sertão and some of the rarest plants and animals in South America.

CANUDOS Many of the country's epic historical figures come from the sertão: bandits like Lampião – a kind of rough-necked Robin Hood; the great writer João Guimarães Rosa; and Antônio Conselheiro – an extraordinary messianic figure who seemed to appear from nowhere in the early days of the Brazilian republic, and

The abolition of slavery in 1888 may have stopped the torture of Afro-Brazilians but it did nothing to raise their status in society. Moreover they lost their homes in the *senzalas* and many were literally kicked out into the Brazilian backlands. Some struggled as smallholders, others became Indians in lifestyle if not philosophy and still more became bandits or *cangaçeiros*, roaming the sertão and the lonely highways in search of easy money. In the late 1880s and 1890s Antônio Maciel, a small-time businessman turned penitent, became their prophet.

After his wife had run off with a soldier in the early 1870s, Antônio had abandoned his home and gone to wander the Bahian desert, dressed in religious robes and preaching a form of evangelical millenarianism. Bahia was in the end times, he said, Christ was on the point of return. By 1877 he had gathered such a following – of brigands, rapists, rural poor and the sick – that he decided to establish a religious community on an abandoned cattle ranch in one of the loneliest stretches of the Bahian sertão. They called him the Counsellor – Antônio Conselheiro – and he called their town Canudos and assigned plots of land and work to his disciples. Life was structured, self-sufficient and hierarchical, and it contrasted with the mix of state brutality (from the Imperial and subsequently the Republican-run national guard), disorder and disarray that followed the final years of monarchy, abolitionism and the instalment of the republic.

By the late 1880s Canudos had grown large enough to attract attention from the state authorities. By 1895, seven years after abolition, it had grown enormously and was the biggest town in Bahia after Salvador, with a population of around 25,000–35,000. The federal authorities became alarmed. They feared that Antônio Conselheiro's stubborn independence and anti-republicanism might provoke insurrection in the sertão, which could spread through the entire Brazilian underclass. And the new republicans responded just as the Portuguese had to rebellious Tupinambá; just as they had to rebellious African slaves; and just as successive Brazilian authorities have since when faced with an obstreperous poor: they sent in the cavalry.

But Canudos would not accept defeat. Conselheiro and is ragged brigand forces routed two armies. Then in 1896 the government dispatched a force of 6,000 soldiers led by Coronel Moreira Cesar – an old war dog who had earned the nickname 'the scourge of Desterro' for his ruthless quelling of the separatist rebellion in Santa Catarina and Rio Grande do Sul in 1894. He too was defeated and his army forced to flee for their lives. So the federal government sent a fourth expedition made up of 8,000 soldiers (whose numbers were made up in large part by former slaves), dragoons and heavy artillery, cannons purchased from Germany. The Brazilian minister of war personally planned the campaign. Canudos was finally pounded into submission. As the town's 5,200 homes were burnt to the ground the town's male survivors had their throats slit – in front of their families who were forced to watch. The body of Antônio Conselheiro, who had died of dysentery some days before the end of the battle, was exhumed and his head – stuck on a pike – was paraded around Bahia's major towns and cities.

The Republican army meanwhile disbanded. Its thousands of soldiers were sent packing. With nowhere to go they congregated in the hills around Rio, building shelter as they had done on the hills around Canudos. These were Brazil's first slums, called favelas by the soldiers after the wild plant that strews the hills around Canudos.

whose evangelical tirades against the advance of secularist materialism earned him a brigand following, a town and an army who nearly brought Brazil to its knees (see box above). The town was Canudos – deep in the northern Bahian sertão and whilst the original settlement has been submerged under the Vaza-Barris reservoir many of the original battlefields have been preserved, together with a wild and atmospheric stretch of caatinga forest as the Parque Estadual de Canudos. It's possible to use modern Canudos as a base. This too is a haunting place – little more than a line of low pastel-paint houses facing a tiny church on a shimmering torrid plain. By day the perpetually blue sky seems impossibly vast and at night becomes an infinitely deep swirling sea of stars.

Getting there At least four buses daily leave Salvador's rodoviária for the city of Euclides da Cunha. From here there are regular connections to Canudos. Taxis in Canudos town can be hired for a full day for R$50–100. Canudos town is so small that it doesn't have any proper street addresses.

Tourist information and local tour operators There are no banks, tour operators or tourist offices in Canudos. The website www.canudosnet.com.br offers some information in Portuguese.

 Where to stay and eat

⌂ **Pousada Por do Sol** Av Juscelino Kubitschek s/n; ☎ 3494 2128. Very simple concrete & tile rooms with AC & en suites & a little restaurant serving delicious sertão home cooking. $$

What to see and do

Parque Estadual de Canudos Canudos State Park was created to preserve the historical remnants of the Canudos war, including Fazenda Velha (where Coronel Moreira César died) and battlefields around the now-flooded town – like Alto do Mário and Alto da Favela. The latter is named after a caatinga plant – favela; and is thought to have given its name to the favela slum towns which ring many of Brazil's cities today. The first of these were founded by deconscripted soldiers from the Canudos War.

Estação Biológica de Canudos The 1,500ha Estação Biológica de Canudos lies a few kilometres from the state park. It was founded in 1989 by the Fundação Biodiversitas (*www.biodiversitas.org.br*) to protect the only remaining nesting sites of the critically endangered giant blue Lear's macaw. Fewer than 100 birds live on a large sun-baked terracotta cliff within the reserve. Brazil is the only country in the world to have giant blue macaws. These include the largest parrot in the world, the hyacinth macaw. It has already lost several species, including the glaucous macaw and Spix's macaw, both originally native to Bahia and the latter of which became extinct in the wild at the turn of the millennium. The state park can only be visited with a hire car, or a taxi from Canudos town. The Estação Biológica de Canudos can be visited on a birding tour with guides like Ciro Albano (see page 20).

Fazenda Morrinhos (*www.rppnmorrinhos.arq.br*) This small reserve preserves an area of virgin, wilderness caatinga in the district of Cel. Borges (also known as Riacho da Onça) in Queimadas, some 300km northeast of Salvador, is home to a rich array of fauna, including moco cavies, pampas deer, peccaries and many caatinga birds.

Getting there Buses run once a day from Salvador to Serrinha (6 hours; R$20) from where there are onward connections to Queimadas (2 hours; R$10) or the reserve can be visited on a birding tour with Ciro Albano.

Appendix I

LANGUAGE

Portuguese is a Latin language which sounds very different to either Spanish or Italian, and to how it is written on the page.

LETTER	PORTUGUESE	MEANING	PRONUNCIATION	ENGLISH
a	**a**bacaxi	pineapple	sounds like [a]	w**a**ter
	maracan**ã**	famous football stadium	nasal sound	
b	**s**ala	sitting room	sounds like [b]	**b**all
c	**c**asa	house	**ca/co/cu** sounds like [k]	**k**eep
	cebola	onion	**ce/ci** sounds like [s]	**c**ivil
ç	lou**ç**a	dish	**ça/ço/çu** sounds like [s]	**c**ivil
ch	**ch**oque	shock	sounds like [sh]	**sh**ip
d	**d**ama	lady	sounds like [d]	**d**og
e	voc**ê**	you	sounds like [e]	th**e**n
	deit**ar**	to lie down	sounds like [ee] at the end, if unstressed	br**ee**ze
	f**e**rro	iron	sounds like [e]	l**e**d
f	**f**arofa	flour	sounds like [f]	**f**ork
g	**g**ota	drop	**ga/go/gu** sounds like [g]	**g**ang
	gente	people	**ge/gi** sounds like [g]	ca**g**e
gu	**gu**arda	guard	**gua/guo** sounds like [gw]	Nicara**gua**
	fre**gu**ês	client	**gue/gui** sounds like [g]	**g**ang
	bilin**gu**e	bilingual	**gue/gui** sounds like [gw]	Nicara**gua**
h	**h**ora	hour	silent	
i	men**i**na	girl	sounds like [ea]	s**ea**l
j	**j**ogo	game	sounds like [g]	a**g**e
l	**l**obo	wolf	**la/le/li/lo/lu** sounds like [l]	**l**ip
	barri**l**	barrel	**al/el/il/ol/ul** sounds like [w]	cre**w**
lh	mo**lh**ado	wet	sounds like [ll]	gri**ll**ed
m	**m**esa	table	sounds like [m]	**m**ap
	bo**m**	good	sounds between **m** and **n**, similar to the French word *bon*	
n	**n**ata	cream	sounds like [n]	**n**ame
	lo**n**tra	otter	sounds like [n]	ba**n**k
nh	ma**nh**ã	morning	sounds like [ng], the French word *sauvignon*	

249

LETTER	PORTUGUESE	MEANING	PRONUNCIATION	ENGLISH
o	menino, avô	boy, grandfather	sounds like [o]	go
	banco	bank	sounds like a [w] at the end of a word	snow
	loja, bota	Shop, boot	sounds like [aw]	saw
p	**pr**ato	plate	sounds like [p]	**p**ipe
q	**qu**anto	How much	**qua/quo** sounds like [kw]	**qu**ite
	ca**qui**	persimmon	**que/qui** sounds like [k]	**k**eep
	fre**qu**encia	frequency	**que/qui** sounds like [kw]	**qu**ite
r	**r**ecordar	remember	similar to [h] sound	**h**op
	co**rr**er	run	similar to [h] sound, if preceded by **n**	**h**op
	cu**r**to	short	sounds like soft [r]	sto**r**m
	cla**r**o	clear	similar to [r] sound	fai**r**
rr	bu**rr**o	donkey	similar to [h] sound	**h**ole
s	**s**apo	toad	sounds like [s]	**s**ail
	in**s**ano	insane	like [s]	**s**ail
	trê**s**	three	after vowels sounds like [s]	gra**ss**
	cami**s**a	shirt	sounds like [z]	**z**ebra
sc	pi**sc**ina	swimming pool	**sce/sci** sounds like [s]	**s**ail
ss	pa**ss**ado	past	sounds like [s]	**s**ail
t	**chicle**te	chewing gum	sounds like [ch]	**ch**ip
u	**u**ma	one	sounds like [w]	b**oo**m
v	**v**oz	voice	sounds like [v]	**v**iper
x	a**x**é	joy	sounds like [sh]	**sh**ape
	bai**x**a	lower	after **ai/ei** sounds like [sh]	**sh**ape
	tá**x**i	taxi	sounds like [ks]	ta**x**i
	ma**x**imo	biggest	sounds like [s]	**s**ymbol
	e**xc**elente	excellent	**exce/exci** sounds like [s]	**s**ymbol
	e**x**ato	exact	**exa/exe/exi/exo/exu** sounds like [z]	**z**ebra
z	**z**ebra	zebra	before a vowel sounds like [z]	**z**ebra
	ve**z**	turn	after a vowel sounds like [s]	**s**ail

GENERAL WORDS AND PHRASES

Good morning	*Bom dia*
Good afternoon	*Boa tarde*
Good evening/night	*Boa noite*
Goodbye	*Tchau*
Excuse me	*Com licença*
Hello, pleased to meet you.	*Olá, prazer em conhecê-lo(a)*
here	*aqui*
How?	*Como?*

How are you?	*Tudo bom?*
I don't speak Portuguese.	*Não falo português*
Do you speak English?	*Fala inglês?*
I don't understand.	*Não compreendo.*
I'm on holiday	*Estou de férias.*
I'm sorry	*Desculpe*
good	*bom*
bad	*mau*
big	*grande*
Could you help me, please?	*Pode me ajudar, por favor?*
closed	*eechado*
enough	*suficiente*
later	*Mais tarde*
May I/Can I?	*Posso?*
My name is ...	*Meu nome é…*
Yes	*Sim*
No	*Não*
now	*agora*
open	*aberto*
Please	*Por favor*
See you later	*Até logo*
small	*pequeno*
Thank you	*Obrigado(a)*
there	*ali*
When	*Quando*
Where	*Onde*
Who	*Quem*
Why	*Porquê*

NUMBERS

1	*um*	16	*dezasseis*
2	*dois*	17	*dezassete*
3	*três*	18	*dezoito*
4	*quatro*	19	*dezanove*
5	*cinco*	20	*vinte*
6	*seis*	21	*vinte e um*
7	*sete*	30	*trinta*
8	*oito*	40	*quarenta*
9	*nove*	50	*cinquenta*
10	*dez*	60	*sessenta*
11	*onze*	70	*setenta*
12	*doze*	80	*oitenta*
13	*treze*	90	*noventa*
14	*catorze*	100	*cem*
15	*quinze*	1000	*mil*

TIME AND DATE

Monday	*Segunda-feira*	Friday	*Sexta-feira*
Tuesday	*Terça-feira*	Saturday	*Sábado*
Wednesday	*Quarta-feira*	Sunday	*Domingo*
Thursday	*Quinta-feira*		

A1

January	*janeiro*	July	*julho*
February	*fevereiro*	August	*agosto*
March	*março*	September	*setembro*
April	*abril*	October	*outubro*
May	*maio*	November	*novembro*
June	*junho*	December	*dezembro*
spring	*primavera*	autumn	*outono*
summer	*verão*	winter	*inverno*
Easter	*Páscoa*	today	*hoje*
Christmas	*Natal*	yesterday	*ontem*
morning	*manhã*	tomorrow	*amanhã*
afternoon	*tarde*	day	*dia*
evening	*fim da tarde*	month	*mês*
night	*noite*	year	*ano*

FOOD AND DRINK

avocado	*abacate*	lunch	*almoço*
bacon	*bacon/ toucinho*	mango	*manga*
bass	*robalo*	meat	*carne*
beans	*feijão*	milk	*leite*
beer	*cerveja*	mineral water	*agua mineral*
breakfast	*café da manhã*	olives	*azeitona*
black pepper	*pimenta do reino*	orange	*laranja*
bread	*pão*	papaya	*mamão papaya*
butter	*manteiga*	passion-fruit	*maracujá*
carrot	*cenoura*	pineapple	*abacaxí*
cheese	*queijo*	potato	*batata*
chicken	*frango*	rice	*arroz*
chilli	*pimenta*	salad	*salada*
cod	*bacalhau*	salt	*sal*
coffee	*café*	sandwich	*sanduíche*
courgette	*abobrinha*	sea food	*frutos do mar*
crab	*caranguejo/siri*	shrimp/prawn	*camarão*
cucumber	*pepino*	snack	*lanche*
dinner	*jantar*	soup	*sopa*
drink	*bebida*	spoon	*colher*
fish	*peixe*	squid	*lula*
fork	*garfo*	steak	*bife*
fruit juice	*suco*	sugar	*açúcar*
ham	*presunto*	tea	*chá*
ice	*gelo*	tomato	*tomate*
knife	*faca*	tuna	*atum*
lettuce	*alface*	turkey	*peru*
lime	*limão*	wine	*vinho*

BUYING AND SELLING

bakery	*padaria*	clothes	*roupa*
bookshop	*livraria*	Do you accept credit cards?	*Aceitam cartões de crédito?*
change	*troco*		
cheap/er	*barato/mais barato*	Do you have a bag for this?	*Tem um sacola para isto?*
chemist	*farmácia*		

expensive	*caro*	I'm just looking,	*Só estou olhando,*
How much is this?	*Quanto custa?*	thank you.	*obrigado(a)*
I'd like ... grams	*Queria ... gramas,*	market	*mercado*
please	*por favor*	money	*dinheiro*
I'd like a kilo of ...	*Queria um quilo de ...*	supermarket	*supermercado*
I'm looking for ...	*Preciso de ...*	this one	*este(a)*

HEALTH AND DIFFICULTIES

accident	*acidente*	I have been	*Fui assaltado*
Can you call	*Pode chamar*	robbed	
a doctor?	*um medico?*	I've got a fever	*Tenho febre.*
dangerous	*perigoso*	help	*socorro*
diarrhoea	*diarréia*	medicine	*remédio*
emergency	*emergência*	police	*polícia*
I don't feel well	*Não me sinto bem*	Where is the	*Onde é o hospital*
		nearest hospital?	*mais proximo?*

ACCOMMODATION

bathroom/toilet	*banheiro/toalete*	May I see the room?	*Posso ver o quarto?*
Do you have a room?	*Tem um quarto?*	Please can I pay	*Posso pagar a conta?*
Do you serve	*Servem jantar?*	my bill?	
evening meals?		single room	*quarto individual*
double room	*quarto de casal*	swimming pool	*piscina*
guesthouse	*pousada*	twin room	*quarto duplo*
hostel	*Albergue*	with bath/shower	*com banheira/choveiro*
Is the room	*O quarto tem ar?*	When do you	*Quando servem o*
air-conditioned?		serve breakfast?	*café da manhã?*
How much	*Quanto é por noite?*		
each night?			

Appendix 2

GLOSSARY OF PORTUGUESE AND TECHNICAL TERMS

aimoré	Literally 'bad people' in Tupi but a word used by the Tupi speakers and later the Portuguese for the fierce Ge-speaking tribes who reclaimed their ancestral homes along the coast (taken by the Tupi) after the arrival of the Portuguese.
antropofagismo	The most significant artistic movement in 20th century Brazil where artists and writers like Tarsila do Amaral and Mario de Andrade attempted to found a unique Brazilian style which cannibalised and consumed foreign influences (as the Tupinambá cannibalised the Europeans) re-constituting them in a Brazilian form.
azulejos	glazed usually blue, painted ceramic tile associated with Portugal, Spain and their colonies
baiano/a	A native of Bahia
bandeirante	Raiding parties who opened up much of the Brazilian interior searching for slaves and gold from the 16th century. Many bandeirantes were *mamelucos* (see list).
barraca	A makeshift beach shelter often selling food or drink – except in Porto Seguro where they have mutated into gigantic beachside entertainment complexes.
caboclo	A rural person of mixed race; usually African and indigenous Brazilian.
Candomblé	An African-native Brazilian spirit religion similar to *Santeria* or Voodoo
capoeira	A martial art dance of native Brazilian and African origin created in Bahia and the neighbouring state of Alagoas.
carioca	Denizen of Rio de Janeiro
catedral	cathedral
coronel (eis)	Despotic patriarchal landowners who ruled much of rural Bahia with hired jagunço guns after the collapse of slavery. They still exist in remote parts of Bahia and are widespread in Para and the far northeast.
engenho	Sugar cane *fazenda* and factory.
fazenda	Hacienda/working manor house with an estate.
forró	Jig-like accordion-driven music from northeastern Brazil popular as a bare-foot beach dance throughout southern Bahia.
igreja	church
maculelê	A martial art stick dance often played with capoeira.
mameluco	Of Portuguese (European) and indigenous blood.
midden	archaeological term used to describe a mound or deposit that indicates human settlement

mulatto	Of Portuguese (European) and African blood.
museu	museum
orixá	A Candomblé/Umbanda deity
parada (de ônibus)	bus stop
Parque Nacional	National Park
praça	plaza (square)
praia	beach
petisco	tapas/bar snack
quilombo	A free community set up by escaped African slaves.
restinga	A threatened coastal ecosystem of wetlands, grasslands and low forest. Unique to Brazil.
rodoviária	bus terminal
samba de roda	The uniquely Bahian roots samba from which carnaval samba was born in Rio at the turn of the 20th century.
santidade	A messianic cult born of African and indigenous beliefs in the late 16th century and at one time administered by a Jesuit-trained pope called Antônio who claimed to have survived the biblical flood in the heart of a palm tree. The cult survived for almost 100 years.
saveiro	A triangular-rigged small sailing wooden skiff used throughout Bahia and based on a similar boat used for sardine fishing at Leixoes in Porto and on the Tagus falua river boats, which in turn had their origins in the Arab felucca.
senzala	Slave quarters on an *engenho* or *fazenda*.
soteropoletano/a	A native of Salvador city
Tropicália/Tropicalismo	An artistic movement fusing the tenets of antropofagismo with psychedelia, *avant garde* and nouvelle vague and invented in Salvador in the 1970s by a group of artists which included Caetano Veloso, Gilberto Gil, Tom Zé and Glauber Rocha.
Tupinambá	The largest Tupi speaking tribe at the time of conquest.
Tupiniquin	A large Tupi speaking group once native to most of southern Bahia.

Appendix 3

GLOSSARY OF BAHIAN/BRAZILIAN FOOD AND DRINK

acarajé	mashed beans molded into balls fried in dendê oil and served with mild chilli
bacalhau	dried salted cod
badejo	whiting (sometimes used for bream)
batida	mildly alcoholic fresh fruit and crushed ice drink
bobo de camarão	prawn stew
bolinho de peixe camarão/ siri	fish/prawn/crab cake (but ball-shaped)
cachaça	sugar cane rum. The best comes from Minas
caipirinha	cachaça, sugar and lime crushed with ice
casquinha de siri	crab cooked in its shell
dendê	palm oil
farinha	manioc flour
farofa	manioc flour fried with oil, bacon and onion
feijão/feijões	brazilian (rosecoco) beans used as a staple throughout the country and the main ingredient in *feijoada*
feijoada	beans, offcuts and offal thrown in a pot and cooked for hours. The national dish.
frito/a la milanesa	dipped in batter/bread, deep-fried
mero	grouper - variou
moqueca	prawn/fish or crab broth cooked in dendê and coconut and served with rice
vatapa	bread, shrimp, coconut milk and palm oil mashed into a creamy paste.

Appendix 4

FURTHER INFORMATION

BOOKS
History
Da Cunha, Euclides *Backlands: The Canudos Campaign* Penguin, 2010. An account of the tragic Canudos war by a journalist who travelled to Canudos with the Brazilian army.

Hemming, John *Red Gold* Macmillan,1987. This clearly written and thoroughly researched history of the Brazilian Indians under the Portuguese is the Prescott (the classic and well-known historical account of the conquest of the Incas)of the 20th century. A marvellous, gripping, shocking read and a must for anyone with an interest in the history of Bahia or Brazil in general.

Brazilian people and culture
Bellos, Alex *Futebol: The Brazilian Way of Life* Bloomsbury, 2003. A retrospective of the Brazilian game from its early days to its greatest triumphs as told by the former Guardian Brazil correspondent.

Bourne, Richard *Lula of Brazil: The Story So Far* ZED Books, 2008. An account of Lula's rise to political power from poverty in rural Pernambuco to the politics of the left wing militant unions during the dictatorship and presidential office in the new millennium.

Harvey, Robert *Liberators* Constable and Robinson, 2002. A delightfully written bawdy ride through the colourful history of the liberation of South America from Spain and Portugal, concentrating on the exuberant heroes and villains who made it all happen.

McGowan, Chris & Pessanha, Ricardo *Brazilian Sound: Samba, Bossa Nova and the Popular Music of Brazil* Temple University, 1998. A comprehensive survey of the history and variety of Brazilian popular music including substantial information about Bahian sounds.

Page, Joseph, *The Brazilians* Da Capo Press, 1996. The best overall introduction to the idiosyncracies and intricacies of Brazil available in the English language. Written by a former US diplomat.

Robb, Peter *A Death in Brazil* Bloomsbury, 2004. Part travelogue, part exploration of the political and poetical mores of Brazil – as undertaken on a trip through from Rio to backlands of the sertão.

Wearne, Phillip *The Return of the Indian* LAB, 1996. A very readable account of the rise in profile of indigenous peoples throughout the Americas, with a list of contacts for support groups. Essential background reading for those interested in contemporary indigenous issues; if a little out of date.

Guidebooks
Funch, Roy *A Visitor's Guide to the Chapada Diamantina Mountains*, 2002. By far the best guidebook to the park.

Reines, Tuca *Living in Bahia* (Taschen's Lifestyle), 2008. Taschen Bahia as lived by a tiny, tiny percentage of the super-rich. But the photographs of the beaches, chic-shack mansion houses and tropical idylls are fabulous.

Natural history

Kricher, J C *A Neotropical Companion* Princeton University Press, 1989. The best available introduction to the Neotropical forests, their ecology and their plants and animals.

Mammals

Emmons, L H *Neotropical Rainforest Mammals* Chicago University Press, 1990. Invaluable field guide to most mammalian Neotropical rainforest species with excellent illustrations. Does not include caatinga and cerrado species.

Birds At the time of going to press, there are no first-class, comprehensive field guides to Brazilian birds. The Brazilian publisher **Avis Brasilis** (*www.avisbrasilis.com.br*) publish a poorly illustrated guidebook and a better DVD of photographs and bird calls. The **Neotropical bird club** (*www.neotropicalbirdclub.org*) publish two excellent magazines and have a website with invaluable links and information. *Where to watch birds in South America* (1994) by Nigel Wheatley and *Birding Brazil* (1993) by Bruce C Forrester have systematic lists and maps to sites throughout Brazil, including a handful in Bahia. However, both these publications should be used together with recent trip reports since they are almost twenty years old. *Important Bird Areas in Brazil* published by Birdlife International comprehensively describes what it says it does in the title.

Sick, Helmut *Birds in Brazil* Princeton University Press, 1985. This magnum opus lists 1,635 species with detailed accounts for most of them, including the taxonomic and behavioural characteristics of each bird family and excellent information on the country's range of habitats and their conservation state. Illustrations, however, are extremely poor and few and far between.

Souza, Deodato *All the Birds of Brazil: An Identification Guide* SubButeo Natural History Books, 2006. With concise species accounts organised by family and distribution maps but poor illustrations.

Van Perlo, Ber *A Field Guide to the Birds of Brazil* Oxford University Press, 2009. Covers every species and many subspecies found in each region and special attention given to the 218 Brazilian endemics, but the illustrations are poor.

Wheatley, Nigel *Where to Watch Birds in South America* Princeton University Press, 1994. An account of the principal birding areas in Brazil and the rest of the continent as researched in the early 1990s.

Zimmer, Kevin *Birds of Brazil* University of Princeton Press, due 2011.

Fiction Beyond the novels of Jorge Amado there are few novels written by Bahians or set in Bahia which have been translated into English.

Amado, Jorge *Gabriela, Clove and Cinnamon* Bloomsbury, 2005 (first publoished 1958). One of the few decent translations of a Jorge Amado novel. Most are unreadable. A picturesque, picaresque, bawdy romp set in 1920s Ilhéus with Amado's stock set of licentious characters.

Vargas Llosa, Mario *The War of the End of the World* Faber, 1984. A gripping, epic fictionalised account of the Canudos war inspired by Euclides da Cunha's *Backlands*.

Health

Wilson-Howarth, Dr Jane, and Ellis, Dr Matthew *Your Child Abroad: A Travel Health Guide* Bradt Travel Guides, 2005

Wilson-Howarth, Dr Jane, *Bugs, Bites & Bowels* Cadogan, 2006

WEBSITES
Birds

www.arthurgrosset.com Arthur Grosset's website has excellent photographs of many Brazilian species.

www.travellingbirder.com List Bahian trip reports.
www.birdtours.co.uk Have Bahian trip reports.
www.birdlife.org BirdLife International provides up-to-the-minute conservation information and news of new discoveries (Addresses to the different IBAMA offices are found at: www.ibama.gov.br).

Health

www.bloodcare.org.uk An NGO that will dispatch certified non-infected blood of the right type to the hospital/clinic where you are being treated.
www.cdc.gov Communicable Disease Control. A useful US site with good advice, tips and up-to-date disease maps.
www.doh.gov.uk/traveladvice Department of Health Travel Advice. Very useful with general information and vaccine requirements and advice for Brazil.
www.medicalalert.co.uk Produce bracelets and necklaces for those with medical problems.
www.netdoctor.co.uk A general health-advice site with a useful section on travel and an 'ask the expert' interactive chat forum.
www.who.int World Health Organization (WHO). List the latest outbreaks and vaccination recommendations.

Culture and daily life

http://redebma.ning.com Rede BM&A provides the best overview of Brazilian music on the internet, with thousands of downloads, artist profiles and a forum where you can discuss new discoveries and old favourites with thousands of other music lovers.
www.brazilmax.com BrazilMax is the best overall guide to the country on the web, with thousands of articles, features, reviews and lots of tips and what to see and where to see it.
www.carnaval.salvador.ba.gov.br Comprehensive information on Carnaval in Bahia, where to go and how to do it.

Wildlife and nature

www.biodiversityhotspots.org Conservation International's biodiversity hotspots site offers substantial species and habitat information on the cerrado and Mata Atlântica.
www.avisbrasilis.com.br Information on Brazilian birds.
www.arthurgrosset.com Photographs of many Brazilian bird species with some site and scientific information.
www.birdlife.org Comprehensive species information and details of bird conservation projects in Brazil.

Index

Page numbers in **bold** refer to major entries: those in *italics* indicate maps

Bradt Travel Guides

www.bradtguides.com

Africa

Access Africa: Safaris for People with Limited Mobility	£16.99
Africa Overland	£16.99
Algeria	£15.99
Angola	£17.99
Botswana	£16.99
Cameroon	£15.99
Cape Verde Islands	£14.99
Congo	£15.99
Eritrea	£15.99
Ethiopia	£16.99
Gambia, The	£13.99
Ghana	£15.99
Johannesburg	£6.99
Madagascar	£15.99
Malawi	£15.99
Mali	£14.99
Mauritius, Rodrigues & Réunion	£15.99
Mozambique	£13.99
Namibia	£15.99
Niger	£14.99
Nigeria	£17.99
North Africa: Roman Coast	£15.99
Rwanda	£14.99
São Tomé & Principe	£14.99
Seychelles	£14.99
Sierra Leone	£16.99
Sudan	£15.99
Tanzania, Northern	£14.99
Tanzania	£17.99
Uganda	£16.99
Zambia	£17.99
Zanzibar	£14.99
Zimbabwe	£15.99

Britain

Britain from the Rails	£14.99
Go Slow: Devon & Exmoor	£14.99
Go Slow: Norfolk & Suffolk	£14.99
Go Slow: North Yorkshire: Moors, Dales & more	£14.99

Europe

Abruzzo	£14.99
Albania	£15.99
Armenia	£14.99
Azores	£14.99
Baltic Cities	£14.99
Belarus	£14.99
Bosnia & Herzegovina	£14.99
Bratislava	£9.99
Budapest	£9.99
Bulgaria	£13.99
Cork	£6.99
Croatia	£13.99

Cyprus see North Cyprus	
Czech Republic	£13.99
Dresden	£7.99
Dubrovnik	£6.99
Estonia	£14.99
Faroe Islands	£15.99
Georgia	£14.99
Greece: The Peloponnese	£14.99
Helsinki	£7.99
Hungary	£15.99
Iceland	£14.99
Kosovo	£15.99
Lapland	£13.99
Latvia	£13.99
Lille	£9.99
Lithuania	£14.99
Ljubljana	£7.99
Luxembourg	£13.99
Macedonia	£15.99
Malta	£12.99
Montenegro	£14.99
North Cyprus	£12.99
Riga	£6.99
Serbia	£15.99
Slovakia	£14.99
Slovenia	£13.99
Spitsbergen	£16.99
Switzerland Without a Car	£14.99
Tallinn	£6.99
Transylvania	£14.99
Ukraine	£15.99
Vilnius	£6.99
Zagreb	£6.99

Middle East, Asia and Australasia

Bangladesh	£15.99
Borneo	£17.99
China: Yunnan Province	£13.99
Great Wall of China	£13.99
Iran	£15.99
Iraq: Then & Now	£15.99
Israel	£15.99
Kazakhstan	£15.99
Kyrgyzstan	£15.99
Lake Baikal	£15.99
Maldives	£15.99
Mongolia	£16.99
North Korea	£14.99
Oman	£13.99
Shangri-La: A Travel Guide to the Himalayan Dream	£14.99
Sri Lanka	£15.99
Syria	£15.99
Tibet	£13.99
Yemen	£14.99

The Americas and the Caribbean

Amazon, The	£14.99
Argentina	£15.99
Bolivia	£14.99
Cayman Islands	£14.99
Chile	£16.95
Colombia	£16.99
Costa Rica	£13.99
Dominica	£14.99
Grenada, Carriacou & Petite Martinique	£14.99
Guyana	£14.99
Nova Scotia	£14.99
Panama	£14.99
Paraguay	£15.99
St Helena	£14.99
Turks & Caicos Islands	£14.99
Uruguay	£15.99
USA by Rail	£14.99
Yukon	£14.99

Wildlife

100 Animals to See Before They Die	£16.99
Antarctica: Guide to the Wildlife	£15.99
Arctic: Guide to the Wildlife	£15.99
Central & Eastern European Wildlife	£15.99
Chinese Wildlife	£16.99
East African Wildlife	£19.99
Galápagos Wildlife	£15.99
Madagascar Wildlife	£16.99
New Zealand Wildlife	£14.99
North Atlantic Wildlife	£16.99
Pantanal Wildlife	£16.99
Peruvian Wildlife	£15.99
Southern African Wildlife	£18.95
Sri Lankan Wildlife	£15.99
Wildlife and Conservation Volunteering: The Complete Guide	£13.99

Eccentric Guides

Eccentric Australia	£12.99
Eccentric Britain	£13.99
Eccentric Cambridge	£6.99
Eccentric London	£13.99

Others

Something Different for the Weekend	£9.99
Weird World	£14.99
Your Child Abroad: A Travel Health Guide	£10.95